PARANOID MODERNISM

Paranoid Modernism

*Literary Experiment, Psychosis,
and the Professionalization
of English Society*

DAVID TROTTER

OXFORD
UNIVERSITY PRESS

OXFORD

UNIVERSITY PRESS

Great Clarendon Street, Oxford OX2 6DP

Oxford University Press is a department of the University of Oxford.
It furthers the University's objective of excellence in research, scholarship,
and education by publishing worldwide in

Oxford New York

Athens Auckland Bangkok Bogotá Buenos Aires Cape Town
Chennai Dar es Salaam Delhi Florence Hong Kong Istanbul Karachi
Kolkata Kuala Lumpur Madrid Melbourne Mexico City Mumbai Nairobi
Paris São Paulo Shanghai Singapore Taipei Tokyo Toronto Warsaw
and associated companies in Berlin Ibadan

Oxford is a registered trade mark of Oxford University Press
in the UK and in certain other countries

Published in the United States
by Oxford University Press Inc., New York

The moral rights of the author have been asserted
Database right Oxford University Press (maker)

First published 2001

British Library Cataloguing in Publication Data

Data available

Library of Congress Cataloging in Publication Data

Trotter, David, 1951–
Paranoid modernism: literary experiment, psychosis, and the professionalization of
English society/David Trotter.
p. cm.
Includes bibliographical references and index.
1. English fiction—20th century—History and criticism. 2. Modernism
(Literature)—Great Britain. 3. Lawrence, D.H. (David Herbert),
1885–1930—Knowledge—Psychology. 4. Ford, Ford Madox,
1873–1939—Knowledge—Psychology. 5. Lewis, Wyndham,
1882–1957—Knowledge—Psychology. 6. Psychological fiction, English—History and
criticism. 7. Experimental fiction, English—History and criticism. 8.
Professions—England—History—20th century. 9. Psychoses in literature. 10. Paranoia in
literature. I. Title.
PR888.M63 T76 2001   823'.9109112—dc21   2001032869
ISBN 0–19–818755–6

3 5 7 9 10 8 6 4 2

Typeset in Bembo by
Cambrian Typesetters, Frimley, Surrey
Printed in Great Britain
on acid-free paper by
Antony Rowe Ltd
Chippenham, Wiltshire

Contents

Introduction   1

1. A BRIEF HISTORY OF PARANOIA   15

2. PARANOIA, PSYCHOANALYSIS, AND
   CULTURAL THEORY   49

3. CAREER DEVELOPMENT: WILLIAM GODWIN,
   WILKIE COLLINS, AND THE PSYCHOPATHIES
   OF EXPERTISE   81

4. TOWARDS AN EPIDEMIOLOGY OF PARANOID
   NARRATIVE   127

5. ONE OF WHOM? *LORD JIM* AND 'ABILITY
   IN THE ABSTRACT'   159

6. FORD'S IMPRESSIONISM   187

7. THE WILL-TO-ABSTRACTION: HULME,
   LEWIS, LAWRENCE   220

8. D. H. LAWRENCE: WOMEN IN LOVE, MEN IN
   MADNESS   250

9. WYNDHAM LEWIS'S PROFESSIONS   284

10. BEYOND MODERNISM, BEYOND PARANOIA   326

Index   355

Introduction

THIS BOOK GREW out of, or got left over from, a previous study of the idea of mess in nineteenth-century art and fiction.[1] The main emphasis of that study is on the relation between mess and chance: messes tend to happen by accident, and the representation of mess in art and fiction can be a way to think about chance, about the part chance plays in our lives. Mess is contingency's signature; mess is what contingency's signature would look like, if contingency *had* a signature. Contingency, the dictionaries tell us, can be regarded either as a freedom or as a vulnerability. It is the condition of pure escape, of the absence of predetermining necessity; and it is the condition of being subject to chance and change, at the mercy of accident. Either way, it leaves little room for the meaning and value our habits of mind (religious, philosophical, ideological, literary) have often led us to expect from the world.

My aim in that previous study was to establish the scope and intensity of the interest taken in such matters by writers and painters who came to prominence during the second half of the nineteenth century. The evidence I assembled there would suggest that it was in the 1860s and 1870s, in European art and fiction above all, that mess became a definitive as well as a merely forceful preoccupation. The scope and intensity of that preoccupation had something to do with the gradual fading, amid a great deal of reassertion, of doctrines of determinism, whether natural, theological, or natural-theological; and something to do with democracy, which would be hard to imagine without the concept of litter. It is in the art and fiction of the 1860s and 1870s, I argued, that one finds, perhaps for the first time in the history of Western culture, a primary interest in mess as such. To put it another way, one of the tasks the idea of mess has been required to perform is an apprehension of the modernity of modern life: a task it

[1] *Cooking with Mud: The Idea of Mess in Nineteenth-Century Art and Fiction* (Oxford: OUP, 2000).

performed, for a while at least, under the auspices of, and without in any way disabling, a variety of representational strategies. There are messes of many kinds in nineteenth-century art and fiction, and they all have something to tell us about what D. H. Lawrence was to term the 'friability of actual life'.[2] The writers and painters of the period acknowledged by the interest they took in mess that a realism which did not want to know about the operations of chance would be no realism at all.

I had at first meant to carry these investigations forward into the Modernist period: the years during which Lawrence really got down to life's friability. For Lawrence was by no means the only one to do so. There is no shortage of friability in Modernist fiction, and it did not take me long to assemble a small archive of appropriate litterings and spillages. I also asked myself what a Modernist mess might *look* like. But there seemed to me to be something awkward, or gloomily self-conscious, about the way in which these early twentieth-century writers and painters had gone about imagining mess. Their hearts were not wholly in it.

An odd passage in *The Waste Land* suggests as much. One would think that rubbish counted as an altogether bad (and there-fore potent) thing in Eliot's view of the world. In 'The Fire Sermon', however, the complaint is that the Thames in autumn does *not* contain—and Eliot dutifully lists the absent items—empty bottles, sandwich papers, silk handkerchiefs, cardboard boxes, cigarette ends, or other testimony to the activities of summer nights.[3] So what is the problem? Eliot clearly needs his litter. But its purpose does not seem to be, as it would have been for a nine-teenth-century writer, an apprehension of 'the pressure of that hard unaccommodating Actual', in George Eliot's words, 'which has never consulted our taste and is entirely unselect'.[4] In nine-teenth-century fiction, the Actual litters, and its litter has the *fris-son* of an abrupt evacuation of the efforts we habitually make to impose meaning and value upon it. Eliot, by contrast, finds in his (virtual) rubbish an outline of elements of metre, the prole-gomenon to a way of *measuring* the Actual: the broken bottles and

    [2] *The First 'Women in Love'*, ed. John Worthen and Lindeth Vasey (Cambridge: CUP, 1998), 27.
    [3] *Complete Poems and Plays* (London: Faber & Faber, 1969), 67.
    [4] *Daniel Deronda*, ed. Terence Cave (Harmondsworth: Penguin Books, 1995), 380.

sandwich papers set up a trochaic murmur, and then—a new line, a marginal intensification—we come upon the silk handkerchiefs. An iambic pentameter, finally, itself as much a piece of literary flotsam as a controlling rhythm or point of view, rounds off the survey: 'Or other testimony of summer nights . . .'. Then a voice compelled by allusion ('But at my back . . . I hear . . .') hustles us on to properly Gothic unpleasantnesses like the rattle of bones and a chuckle spread from ear to ear. In 'The Fire Sermon', apprehensions of friability are subordinate to the poetic business in hand. They never convince; for reasons of genre, perhaps, or more likely for reasons of aesthetic agenda, of a new form and formality, of Modernism.

Think of the attempt T. E. Hulme made, in January 1914, to develop a 'philosophy' of modern art which would accord with the 'tendency to abstraction' Wilhelm Worringer had noted in the art of 'more primitive people'. 'The changing is translated into something fixed and necessary. This leads to rigid lines and dead crystalline forms, for pure geometrical regularity gives a certain pleasure to men troubled by the obscurity of outside appearance. The geometrical line is something absolutely distinct from the messiness, the confusion, and the accidental details of existing things.' That is one way to deal with contingency. By denying mess through dead crystalline forms, the primitive people had also delivered themselves from a certain entanglement in, or helpless subjection to, the world's changes and chances. And they had thereby also found a reason, Hulme cheerfully reported, not to develop naturalism in art. Defining the renewal of 'sensibility' in progress in January 1914, Hulme spoke of a violent revulsion, on the part of the adventurous in spirit, against both mess and mimesis. 'Expressed generally, there seems to be a desire for austerity and bareness, a striving towards structure and away from the messiness and confusion of nature and natural things.'[5] To get oneself into order was to stop imitating, and vice versa. It is the *obstinacy* of Hulme's abstractionism, its animus, which seems to me, as it did to Wyndham Lewis, at the time his ally and rival, its characteristic feature.[6] The Nietzschean spirit of the period during which Hulme and Lewis strove towards structure might even encourage one to speak of a 'will-to-abstraction'.

[5] 'Modern Art and its Philosophy', in *Collected Writings*, ed. Karen Csengeri (Oxford: Clarendon Press, 1994), 268–85, pp. 274, 278.
[6] *Blasting and Bombardiering* (London: Calder & Boyars, 1967), 100.

Was there a certain madness in this obstinacy? In *Memoirs of my Nervous Illness* (1903), as powerful a testimony to the effects of psychosis as any we have, Daniel Paul Schreber described his inability to shake off the conviction that there is no such thing as accident. By the end of 1895, Schreber wrote, after five years of torture, the 'miracles' inflicted on him by a persecutory God had for the first time begun to assume a relatively 'harmless' character. An end to his suffering was in sight. Life, however, did not return to normal. 'As example I will only mention my cigar ash being thrown about on the table or on the piano, my mouth and my hands being soiled with food during meals, etc.' Being raped by cosmic rays was as nothing in comparison to these new persecutions. When Schreber's mother and sister came to visit him, the cocoa he was drinking threw itself out of the mug. When he ate at the Director's table, plates broke in two of their own accord, without anyone having to drop them. Whenever he wanted to go to the lavatory, someone else always got there first.[7] To Schreber, these mishaps were not mishaps at all, but a vengeful assault on his hard-won serenity. There was a malevolent intention behind each shimmy of a mug of cocoa, each slamming of a cubicle door. Schreber never did get the world back, because he had forgotten what chance was.

Schreber we would now most likely regard as a paranoid schizophrenic, but it is the paranoia in his madness which could be said to have condemned him to meaning and value, to a universe devoid of accident. Paranoia was at the turn of the century one of the names given to a type of psychosis in which the patient develops an internally consistent delusional system of beliefs centred around the certainty that he or she is a person of great importance, and on that account subject to hostility and persecution. They hate me because I am special; I am special because they hate me. The paranoiac's delusions are from the very beginning 'systematized', as Richard von Krafft-Ebing put it, and thus constitute a formal 'structure'. The consistency of that system or structure depends on its ability to eliminate randomness: to convert the material trace an event leaves in the world into a sign which only ever has one

    [7] *Memoirs of my Nervous Illness*, ed. and tr. Ida Macalpine and Richard A. Hunter (London: William Dawson, 1955), 156.

meaning, one value. Once delusion has taken shape, it absorbs acci-dent into itself.[8] For the paranoiac, there is no event which does not already possess a meaning and a value. Paranoia, one might say, is anti-mimetic: it puts meaning and value *in place of* the world.

It is from Schreber and Hulme, from the obstinacy in their striv-ing towards structure, in their will to abstraction, that I start. The early psychiatric literature is not short of examples of anti-mimesis, and of the antipathy to mess which goes with it. Schreber remains our favourite psychotic, but there were others, since neglected, whose delusions can be shown to possess a comparable intensity of structure. Hulme, for his part, was perhaps the *most* obstinate of abstractionists (he did not live long enough to think better of it). But there was plenty of obstinacy around, among those English writers plotting insurrection in London in the years before the First World War. Lewis, of course, made a point, and a career, of being obstinate; while Lawrence's enduring concern for the 'friability of actual life' did not preclude a renunciation of the naturalism of his own early work (the phrase itself is missing from the published version of *Women in Love*). Lewis and Lawrence are not often read in tandem, which is one reason to do so here. But they inhabited the same literary milieu. Ford Madox Ford launched both of them in the *English Review*, and Ford himself was by no means immune to obstinacy. We might well ask where *The Good Soldier*'s striving towards structure came from. These three writers, together with a cohort of the seriously deluded, will be the focus of my inquiries into the will to abstraction.[9] It is not just that their books include penetrating accounts of serious delusion, but that in some sense they deluded themselves into modernity.

Did the writers read what the psychiatrists wrote? Obviously not. But one might argue that in their preoccupation with a particular kind of behaviour both the novels and the case-histories were addressing (or formulating) a problem endemic in Western societies. For literature and psychiatry converged in their belief that paranoia was a disease to which the professional classes were peculiarly

[8] *Textbook of Insanity*, tr. Charles Gilbert Chaddock (Philadelphia: F. A. Davis, 1904), 368–9, 381–2.

[9] To that extent, I am proposing to revisit and rework Michael Levenson's exem-plary description of the period: *A Genealogy of Modernism: A Study of English Literary Doctrine 1908–1922* (Cambridge: CUP, 1984).

prone. Literary and cultural historians have only just begun to take account of the transformation wrought by what Harold Perkin terms the 'rise of professional society'. Perkin has been able to show that the methods and the principles of the 'professional social ideal' had achieved something close to dominance in English society by around 1880.[10] This is a fact of which my chosen writers, like many of their contemporaries, were not unaware. Nor were they unaware of the aspirations and resentments often entailed by passionate adherence to that ideal.

Perkin's emphasis on the transforming effect of the emergence of a professional class has two advantages for the literary or cultural historian. In the first place, it enables us to envisage social conflict within as well as between classes: a difference of outlook which distinguishes not only the doctor from the mill-owner, but the shop-steward from the panel-beater. In the second place, it draws attention to the very specific problem of identity which afflicts those whose capital is symbolic through and through: those who only have their own integrity and an esoteric knowledge guaranteed by certificate to sell, rather than muscle, or the possession of land, or existing wealth.

Historians of the professional social ideal have always emphasized its precariousness. As Magali Sarfatti Larson puts it, the upwardly mobile professional classes had somehow to create a protected market within the free-for-all of a triumphant capitalism. They sought backing and guarantees for their expertise from the state. The state identified a knowledge 'inseparable from the expert' as a special kind of property. 'This special kind of market asset could yield income and social authority only insofar as the public accepted, by choice or sufferance, the professional definition of both its needs and the means to satisfy them.' The public had to accept, first, that the expert possessed a certain expertise, and, secondly, that he or she was willing and able to use it to good purpose. A credential had thus to be understood by all parties as the 'sign' of an 'internalized process of cognition'.[11] These are not straightforward negotiations.

---

[10] *The Rise of Professional Society: England since 1880* (London: Routledge, 1989).
[11] 'The Production of Expertise and the Constitution of Expert Power', in Thomas L. Haskell (ed.), *The Authority of Experts: Studies in History and Theory* (Bloomington, Ind.: Indiana University Press, 1984), 28–80, pp. 34, 46.

What is at issue in them is the assertion of authority through symbolism. 'For a symbolic exchange to function', Pierre Bourdieu argues, 'the two parties must have identical categories of perception and appreciation.' This has to be the case wherever and whenever the act of symbolic domination is exerted 'with the objective complicity of the dominated'.

Symbolic capital is an ordinary property (physical strength, wealth, warlike valour, etc.) which, perceived by social agents endowed with the categories of perception and appreciation permitting them to perceive, know and recognize it, becomes symbolically efficient, like a veritable *magical power*: a property which, because it responds to socially constituted 'collective expectations' and beliefs, exercises a sort of action from a distance, without physical contact.

For symbolic capital to exercise its power, there must have been formidable work done to produce among those who submit to its sway the necessary predisposition. Whoever can rely on that work having been well done earns the profit not only of power exercised, but of ease and elegance in the exercise, of apparent lack of effort.[12]

During the nineteenth century, the status the upwardly mobile professional classes sought for their expertise was the status of a 'magical power': a status previously or otherwise afforded to qualities such as wealth or warlike valour. They did not always find it. Sometimes, when they did not find it, they made it up. Paranoia is a delusion of magical power. One of the curious side-effects of the professionalization which transformed psychiatric theory and practice during the concluding decades of the nineteenth century was a systematic analysis of the ways in which professional people go mad. Paranoia, the psychiatrists maintained, was the professional person's madness of choice.

The writers who will concern me wrote about professional identities under extreme pressure. They were themselves, as professional writers confronted by a rapidly developing literary marketplace, under extreme pressure.[13] So they wrote about madness, and

---

[12] 'The Economy of Symbolic Goods', in *Practical Reason: On the Theory of Action* (Cambridge: Polity, 1998), 92–123, pp. 100, 102–3.
[13] For the professionalization of literature, see Peter Keating, *The Haunted Study: A Social History of the English Novel 1875–1914* (London: Secker & Warburg, 1989), chs.

they went a little mad themselves. I want to suggest that the literary experimentation by means of which they hoped to achieve a degree of magical power can be understood as a psychopathy of expertise.[14]

An approach to Modernism via the psychopathies of expertise cuts across the tendencies currently dominant in the study of the period at two points in particular: gender, and the politics of culture. I have suggested that paranoia's objection to mess was also an objection to mimesis. For the 'Men of 1914', as Peter Nicholls has pointed out, mimesis was a political issue. 'The polemical thrust given here to an anti-mimetic art was directed against the imitative tendencies associated with the mass politics of a democratic age in which, as Lewis put it, "the life of the crowd" forces man to "live only through others, outside himself".'[15] One can trace this anxiety back in British political thought at least as far as John Stuart Mill, who worried that the supposedly all-inclusive social order in prospect in Britain from the 1850s onwards would extinguish 'variety of situations'.[16] In the 1920s, Lewis was to speak, in very much the same spirit, of mass democracy's fundamental drive towards the 'suppressing of *differences*'.[17]

According to commentators like Mill and Lewis, the main

1 and 7. Thomas Strychacz has discussed (American) Modernist literature in these terms in *Modernism, Mass Culture, and Professionalism* (Cambridge: CUP, 1993). Strychacz discerns an affinity with the professional social ideal in Modernism's 'predilection for esoteric writing'. However, as Perkin points out in a critique of Bourdieu and others, specialized training does not of itself yield a differential return without control of the market: *Rise of Professional Society*, 7. The Modernist writers achieved only one of these objectives. They were specialists, but their specialism proved a dubious asset. We cannot therefore use the idea of professionalism to distinguish Modernist writing from its alternatives. My aim here is to characterize that writing as a specific *relation* to the professional social ideal. Recent studies have shown the lengths to which Modernist writers had to go in order to convert their training in the esoteric into property: Lawrence Rainey, *Institutions of Modernism: Literary Elites and Public Culture* (New Haven, Conn.: Yale University Press, 1999); Ian Willison, Warwick Gould, and Warren Chernaik (eds.), *Modernist Writers and the Marketplace* (Basingstoke: Macmillan, 1996).

[14] In this book, I use the terms 'psychosis' and 'psychopathy' interchangeably. The *OED* defines the former as a derangement which 'cannot be ascribed to organic lesion or neurosis', and the latter as a 'mental disease or disorder'. Both terms were in circulation by the 1840s.

[15] *Modernisms: A Literary Guide* (London: Macmillan, 1995), 251.

[16] *On Liberty and Other Essays*, ed. John Gray (Oxford: OUP, 1991), 81.

[17] *The Art of Being Ruled*, ed. Reed Way Dasenbrock (Santa Rosa, Calif.: Black Sparrow Press, 1989), 29. Lewis's emphasis. The book was first publ. in 1926.

instrument of that suppression was social mimesis, and its attendant psychology of imitative desire. René Girard has argued influentially that writers like Balzac took as their topic the mediation of desire in modern bourgeois societies. In such societies, desire for an object is always modelled on the desire of another, whose function as model becomes more important than the object itself.[18] Revising Erich Auerbach's propositions about literature's mimetic entanglements in the light of Girard's work, Gunter Gebauer and Christoph Wulf claim that in modern bourgeois culture mimesis is always already a social practice, from which literature has attempted with varying degrees of success to disentangle itself.[19] It would certainly be true to say that the distinction the 'Men of 1914' and their contemporaries made between the work of creative intelligence and the proliferating forms of social desire was absolute. According to Nicholls, the Modernist self is a self saved from modernity's passive imitations by an active imitation of the cultural past.[20]

There is, of course, as has long been recognized, a politics to the Modernist's social and literary will-to-abstraction. Emerging from within liberalism, as a visceral distaste for the spectacle of social mobility liberalism itself was staging, this politics took shape in opposition to bourgeois democracy. Across Europe, after the war, men of 1914 fell into step with the dictators. No longer liberal, not yet anything else, they followed where their instincts—their aesthetic principles, some would say—led. I call this susceptibility 'postliberalism'. During the period in question, postliberalism framed itself as an appeal to—which does not mean an unequivocal endorsement of—the interests of the professional 'class' in every class. It is at root a politics of expertise; or, more strictly, of an expertise freed from the institutionalized imitativeness of bureaucratic rationalism. Sometimes, the politics of expertise became an allegiance to fascism.

[18] *Deceit, Desire, and the Novel: Self and Other in Literary Structure*, tr. Yvonne Freccero (Baltimore: Johns Hopkins University Press, 1988).

[19] *Mimesis: Culture—Art—Society*, tr. Don Reneau (Berkeley, Calif.: University of California Press, 1995), 218–19. The other major influence on their revisionist account of mimesis is the sociology of Pierre Bourdieu. See Erich Auerbach, *Mimesis: The Representation of Reality in Western Literature*, tr. Willard R. Trask (Princeton: Princeton University Press, 1953).

[20] *Modernisms*, 253, 187. Nicholls relies as heavily as Gebauer and Wulf, and with equal justification, on Girard's thesis about 19th-cent. fiction (14, 184).

In this context, of course, one speaks advisedly of the '*men* of 1914'. The men of 1914 tended to characterize the mess and the mimesis their will-to-abstraction had pitted itself against as feminine. To avoid or to overcome entanglement in the world was to confirm oneself as at once fully masculine and fully Modernist. When Tarr, in Lewis's portrait of the artist as a young man, attacks the 'jellyish diffuseness' of the socially mimetic, it is not only women he has in mind; but women's spillages and litterings none the less serve as his preferred example of what the artist and young man with expertise to develop should disentangle himself from.[21] Peter Nicholls shrewdly observes that, while Lewis's work can with ease be convicted of misogyny, there is also much in it to show 'that he was trying to uncover a process of social identification which went beyond the categories of gender'.[22] The problem for Tarr, for the 'Man of 1914', was not that he might succumb to the feminine, in himself or in the world,[23] but that the agreed standard of manhood, the norm established by and operative in social mimesis, might fail to produce the degree of authority (the 'magical power') his chosen career would require. Tarr's objection to jellyish diffuseness is a career-move. The hypothesis I shall advance here is that some Modernist writers regarded masculinity above all as a form of symbolic capital.

In an illuminating essay on Robert Louis Stevenson's *The Strange Case of Dr Jekyll and Mr Hyde* (1886), Stephen Heath has argued that the story's virtual exclusion of women leaves male sexuality as something 'taken for granted and repressed in the one operation, simply "this poor wish to have a woman"'. The taking for granted depends to a dangerous extent on the exclusion. 'In

[21] *Tarr: The 1918 Version*, ed. Paul O'Keeffe (Santa Rosa, Calif.: Black Sparrow Press, 1990), 314. The consequences of Lewis's distaste for 'messy femininity' have been explored by Bonnie Kime Scott: *Refiguring Modernism*, 2 vols. (Bloomington, Ind.: Indiana University Press, 1995), i. 100, 104–5. Suzanne Clark has offered a comparable critique of the Modernist assumption that women writers were 'entangled' in sensibility. Her interest lies in the ways in which women writers of the period confronted and worked through the Modernist 'turn' against the sentimental: *Sentimental Modernism: Women Writers and the Revolution of the Word* (Bloomington, Ind.: Indiana University Press, 1991).

[22] *Modernisms*, 187.

[23] Historians of gender have on the whole found in the 'feminized male' the focus and emblem of turn-of-the-century anxieties: Rita Felski, *The Gender of Modernity* (Cambridge, Mass.: Harvard University Press, 1995), 91–3.

the overall system of sexuality that is tightened to perfection in the nineteenth century, male sexuality is repetition, unquestioned; female sexuality is query, riddle, enigma.' All the difficulty is with the woman, while the man's desire figures as the truly unspeakable 'at the same time as it represents itself—covers itself—in the continual refurbishment of those terms and assumptions of "man" and "woman" '. My aim here is to relate that process of continual refurbishment, of self-covering or self-supplementation, to the psychopathies of everyday professional life. The expert, who must everywhere assert his uniqueness, who cannot fall back on an imitative manhood, invests in hypermasculinity. But hypermasculinity is a dangerous game. 'Stevenson's story', Heath observes, 'can only come out like a case, mixed up with doctors and labelled strange since its question—about man, not woman—has no representation available from them.'[24] The stories I shall examine in this book are also strange cases mixed up with doctors. By 1914, however, the doctors had found a word for some aspects of masculinity's continual refurbishment: paranoia.

I have restricted myself in the main to a particular group of writers, for three reasons. In the first place, I wanted to follow the 'development' of each of these writers during the Modernist period—from around 1910 to around 1930—in considerable (and sometimes biographical) detail. That effort takes up Chapters 6 to 10. In the second place, I could not but be conscious that the descriptive psychopathology of the major mental illnesses has received far less attention from literary and cultural historians than the psychodynamic psychopathology of 'neuroses' such as hysteria. I knew that I would have to leave room for a fairly lengthy (albeit incomplete) exposition of contemporary ideas about psychosis. Chapter 1 thus constitutes a brief history of paranoia; and Chapter 2 an account of Freud's brilliant analysis of, and partial identification with, Daniel Paul Schreber. In the third place, I was determined to acknowledge the affinities, at once political and literary, between the work of my chosen Modernists and that of other nineteenth- and early twentieth-century writers. Chapter 3 describes a significant change of emphasis, during the course of the

---

[24] 'Psychopathia Sexualis: Stevenson's *Strange Case*', in Colin MacCabe (ed.), *Futures for English* (Manchester: MUP, 1988), 93–108, pp. 98, 102, 104–5.

nineteenth century, in the cultural deployment of paranoid fantasy: what had once been of use as an explanation of the forces impelling the upwardly mobile could now also serve to identify the threat posed by mass culture, by widespread social mimesis. Paradoxically, that deployment took place not only *outside* mass culture, as a resistance to it, but *inside* it as well, as its self-validating intensification. Chapter 4 proposes an investment in paranoid fantasy as the factor which distinguishes both the popular romances of the period and a certain kind of avant-garde writing from the domestic realism of mainstream Edwardian fiction. In Chapter 5, I find in Joseph Conrad's *Lord Jim* (1900) what others have found before me: a way to consider the relation between the fantasies motivating popular romance and the professional needs of an emergent avant-garde.

It is not my intention to suggest either that the writers I discuss were the only properly 'paranoid' Modernists, or that 'paranoid Modernism' was the only proper way to be modern. By no means all the writers I would associate with paranoid Modernism were English, or male, or novelists; and I readily concede that there are many Modernist writers to whose work the terms I shall develop here need not be thought to apply. Paranoid Modernism was markedly—though by no means without exception—English, male, and novelistic. But it was only ever one Modernism among several. I have on occasion sought to extend the terms of my argument by discerning 'schizophrenia', as that would have been understood during the early years of the twentieth century, in the behaviour represented by my chosen writers, or even in their literary methods. But an adequate historical understanding of schizophrenia's variegated cultural deployment in the modern era would require another book.[25] This one stops well short of a general

---

[25] It is, perhaps, one that should be written, because casual references to the 'schizophrenia' of modern and/or postmodern life abound in a particular kind of cultural theory. Frederic Jameson describes pastiche and schizophrenia as the two crucial features of the 'postmodernism' which expresses the 'inner truth' of the 'newly emergent social order of late capitalism': 'Postmodernism and Consumer Society', in *The Cultural Turn: Selected Writings on the Postmodern 1983–1998* (London: Verso, 1998), 1–20, p. 3. Jameson's essay, first publ. in 1983, has proved hugely influential in debates about postmodernism. His emphasis on schizophrenia derives from Gilles Deleuze and Félix Guattari, *Anti-Oedipus: Capitalism and Schizophrenia*, tr. Robert Hurley, Mark Seem, and Helen R. Lane (London: Athlone Press, 1984).

theory either of literary Modernism or of modern madness. To conclude its beginning, I will make brief mention of a writer whose work exceeds the scope of my argument, not least by its preoccupation with schizophrenia, but who provocatively formulated an idea I shall want to put to considerable use.

The writer is Robert Musil, and the idea that formulated by the title of his best-known novel, *The Man without Qualities*, whose first two parts were published in 1930 and 1934. Unlike the English writers whose work I shall discuss in the chapters which follow, Musil really was familiar with the psychiatric literature. In 1908, he successfully completed a doctoral thesis on the theories of the physicist and psychologist Ernst Mach. Shortly afterwards, he was offered a post as assistant to Alexius von Meinong, founder of the first Austrian laboratory of experimental psychology at the University of Graz. The offer forced him to choose between science and literature. The success of *Young Törless* (1906) inclined him to literature, but thirty years later he was still wondering whether he had made the right decision. Musil continued to read widely in psychology and psychiatry, and to visit asylums.[26]

There is a psychotic in *The Man without Qualities*: Christian Moosbrugger, a 34-year-old carpenter and vagrant who has been convicted of the brutal murder of a prostitute.[27] Moosbrugger is a constant focus for the protagonist's efforts to strip himself of those 'qualities' which, although they are widely regarded as admirable,

---

[26] In Sept. 1910, the wife of Musil's childhood friend Gustav Donat began to show signs of mental disturbance, and was admitted to Emil Kraepelin's clinic in Munich. Musil's notebooks contain a careful description of the progress of her disease: *Diaries 1899–1941*, ed. Mark Mirsky, tr. Philip Payne (New York: Basic Books, 1998), 123–6. In Oct. 1913, Musil visited an asylum in Rome where he saw and spoke to patients suffering from various kinds of psychosis, including paranoia and dementia praecox: ibid. 158–61. On his familiarity with the psychiatric literature, see David S. Luft, *Robert Musil and the Crisis of European Culture 1880–1942* (Berkeley, Calif.: University of California Press, 1980), 186; and Hannah Hickman, *Robert Musil and the Culture of Vienna* (London: Croom Helm, 1984), 55.

[27] Moosbrugger, we learn, 'had as often been confined in mental institutions as he had been let go, and had been variously diagnosed as a paralytic, paranoiac, epileptic, and manic-depressive psychotic, until at his recent trial two particularly conscientious forensic psychiatrists had restored his sanity to him': *Der Mann ohne Eigenschaften: Neu-Edition*, ed. Adolf Frisé (Reinbeck bei Hamburg: Rowohlt, 1978), 243; *The Man without Qualities*, 2 vols., tr. Sophie Wilkins and Burton Pike (London: Picador, 1995), 262. (The 2 vols. of the translation are numbered continuously, and references to it are therefore by page number only.)

or *because* they are widely regarded as admirable, mask his uniqueness. Ulrich has trained both mind and body to the pitch of nerveless perfection by diligently performing *die Arbeit der Starken* (the work of the strong). 'What this power would enable him to accomplish was an open question; he could do everything with it or nothing, become a saviour of mankind or a criminal.' The anxiety, for someone who has from the beginning trained himself to dispense with mere qualities, must be that his unique qualitylessness will never achieve the recognition it deserves. The man without qualities stands always on the brink of paranoia. Ulrich alone realizes that the sickness which has set Moosbrugger humiliatingly apart, which has put him endlessly on trial, is also the source of 'a stronger and higher sense of his own self'.[28] It takes one to know one.

It is appropriate that the Modernist man without qualities should object strenuously to mess. In chapter 54, Ulrich and his friends Clarisse and Walter go for a walk in early spring, with snow still on the ground. They solemnly discuss the temper of the age. Walter, whose modest but unmistakable qualities have earned him comfort and recognition, keeps faith with the doctrine of progress. Ulrich prefers stoical indifference (though Clarisse's efforts to interest him in Moosbrugger prepare the ground for a new and more radical perception of affinity). When they arrive home, the debate continues. 'Steaming snow rose from their shoes; Clarisse enjoyed the mess they were making on the floor.' Clarisse's enjoyment is shared by Walter, who observes 'with satisfaction' that some soil has clung to his shoes. Ulrich, by contrast, remains oddly free both of dirt and of the pleasure one might take in dirtiness.[29] It is a habit of mind we shall encounter again, in the chapters which follow, in English Modernism's men without qualities, and in the will-to-abstraction which conceived them.

[28] Ibid. 45–6/42–3, 71/71.
[29] Ibid. 214/230, 217/233.

CHAPTER 1

A Brief History of Paranoia

IF ANY TEXT can claim biblical status in the collective self-understanding of a profession, it is the current (fourth) edition of the American Psychiatric Association's *Diagnostic and Statistical Manual* (1994). According to this text, the 'essential feature' of 'Delusional Disorder', or paranoia, is the presence of one or more 'non-bizarre' delusions which persist for at least a month. These delusions are 'non-bizarre' in that they are comprehensible, and arise from circumstances which could conceivably occur in real life (being stalked, or betrayed, or conspired against, or loved at a distance). 'Apart from the direct impact of the delusions,' the *Manual* continues, 'psychosocial functioning is not markedly impaired, and behaviour is neither obviously odd nor bizarre.'[1] Despite important revisions of terminology and emphasis, the basic understanding of what constitutes 'Delusional Disorder' has not changed all that much over the last 200 years or so. Paranoia has been with us for a long time, and in more or less the same shape: a shape made palpable in textbooks, case-histories, newspaper articles, and, I shall suggest, literary fiction.

The *Manual* lists several subtypes of delusional disorder. In erotomania, the individual believes that another person has fallen in love with him or her (a belief framed more often in terms of romantic love or spiritual union than in terms of sexual magnetism). Furthermore, the person about whom this conviction is held is 'usually of higher status (e.g., a famous person or a superior at work)'. Status matters, too, in the 'grandiose' type of delusion, which involves the belief that one possesses some great but sadly unrecognized talent, or that one has made a significant discovery, again without reward. 'Less commonly', the *Manual* continues, the

---

[1] *Diagnostic and Statistical Manual of Mental Disorders*, 4th edn. (Washington, DC: American Psychiatric Association, 1994), 296–7. Henceforth *DSM-IV*.

individual may suffer from 'the delusion of having a special relationship with a prominent person (in which case the actual person may be regarded as an impostor)'. Such delusions sometimes have a religious content (God being the impostor). In jealous mania, the individual believes that he or she has been betrayed by a spouse or lover, and obsessively collects 'evidence' to that effect. In persecutory mania, the individual, convinced that he or she is the victim of conspiracy, may seek redress through legal action or even through violence. Somatic mania, finally, takes bodily function or sensation as its theme.[2] The delusion at the centre of each form of mania is perfectly comprehensible; its substance is the substance of ordinary life, distorted. The spotlight it trains on the sufferer illuminates only a part (a central core, perhaps) of his or her personality; beyond its reach, behaviour remains unaffected, and there is no widespread disturbance of thought and language. 'But does a form of mania really exist', asked the great French alienist J. E. D. Esquirol (1772–1840), 'in which those who are affected by it preserve the integrity of their reason, whilst they abandon themselves to the commission of acts the most reprehensible?'[3]

The trouble with paranoia is that we all think we know what it is. When we use the term 'paranoid' in conversation, in biographical inquiry, or in debates about modernity and postmodernity, we understand that we are talking about a mental illness, but we do not usually feel any need to make reference to the sort of psychiatric description I have just set out in summary form; as we might, perhaps, if our argument happened to depend on the terms 'schizophrenic' or 'manic-depressive'. These, too, of course, are partially naturalized terms. We (mostly) think we know (more or less) what they mean. But as far as the world at large is concerned, paranoia counts as psychiatry's degree zero. It is transparent to common sense. And there are reasons for this. After all, the disease gives rise to a relatively restricted symptomatology: a paranoiac is a person with a delusion. Furthermore, the degree of consensus about its definition has been such that a manual published in 1994 could perfectly well have taken one or

---

[2] *DSM-IV* 297–8.
[3] *Mental Maladies: A Treatise on Insanity*, facsimile edn., with an introduction by Raymond de Saussure (New York: Hafner, 1965), 362. Henceforth *MM*. First publ. in 1838, and tr. into English in 1845.

two of its terms, and a great deal of its emphasis, from a manual published in 1838. So why worry?

We *should* worry, I think, and precisely because the widespread naturalization of the term 'paranoia' has so reduced its proper opacity. There is something mildly shocking about its use in a biography, say, to describe the innermost state of mind of a person born 150 years ago; as though our ready grasp of what the term now means would give us automatic access, as historical knowledge would not, to experience in history, to thoughts and feelings. And the use of the term to define a historical moment or condition is scarcely less dubious. Historians have recently begun to investigate the cultural specificity of diagnoses of mental illness, and paranoia's relative permanence as a category should not necessarily exempt it from investigations of this kind.[4] Paranoia, too, has a history.[5] It, too, has always been a diagnosis made in (or *from*) a variety of institutional and discursive contexts.[6] To denaturalize it is to begin to understand its meanings, then and now.

An inquiry of the kind I shall mount here, into the literary will-to-experiment, cannot hope to make more than a limited contribution either to the history of institutional and discursive context (of descriptive psychopathology, of psychoanalysis), or to the history (as yet almost entirely unwritten) of the wider social and

[4] I have particularly in mind Ian Hacking's fascinating study of the rise and fall of so-called 'dissociative fugue', *Mad Travellers: Reflections on the Reality of Transient Mental Illnesses* (Charlottesville, Va.: University of Virginia Press, 1998). Hacking demonstrates that dissociative fugue in effect only became a disease in 1887 with the publication of Philippe Tissié's *Les Aliénés voyageurs*. The diagnosis flourished for a little over twenty years.

[5] On the term itself, see Aubrey Lewis, 'Paranoia and Paranoid: A Historical Perspective', *Psychological Medicine*, 1 (1970), 2–12. In Greek literature (Aeschylus, Euripides, Aristophanes, Plato, Aristotle), to be paranoid was to be no more and no less than 'out' of one's mind. Hippocrates applied the term to the delirium of high fever. It was revived for nosological purposes in the 18th cent., by Boissier de Sauvages, and subsequently entered 19th-cent. German psychiatry, in J. C. A. Heinroth's *Lehrbuch der Störungen des Seelenlebens* (1818), as the name for that class of mental disorder which predominantly affects the understanding.

[6] On the history of the nosology of psychotic disorders, see, in particular, German Berrios, 'Descriptive Psychopathology: Conceptual and Historical Aspects', *Psychological Medicine*, 14 (1984), 303–13; and 'Historical Aspects of Psychoses: Nineteenth-Century Issues', *British Medical Bulletin*, 43 (1987), 484–98. Equally valuable, where the history of particular disorders is concerned, are the relevant chapters in Berrios and Roy Porter (eds.), *A History of Clinical Psychiatry: The Origin and History of Psychiatric Disorders* (London: Athlone Press, 1995).

cultural use of psychopathological descriptions. In describing the literary will-to-experiment, I shall make frequent reference to psychiatric 'discourse', and I shall provide evidence of the extent to which the categories formulated within it had become a topic of debate in early twentieth-century Britain. But I shall start from what my chosen writers might conceivably have known about mental illness, by study or by intuition, and work towards the conclusions drawn in print and the cases made public by the most eminent psychiatrists of the day, rather than the other way round. On the whole, there is little to suggest that those writers had more than a passing familiarity with the psychiatric literature. I make no claims for extensive scrutiny, on their part, of Krafft-Ebing and Kraepelin. My aim, rather, is to demonstrate that what they wrote about mental illness has sufficient imaginative density to merit, indeed to demand, comparison with what the psychiatrists had to say.

There are three ways in which writers afflicted by a will-to-experiment can be said to have known what they were talking about when it came to madness in general. In the first place, they were familiar with, and made systematic use of, the term 'mono-mania': the common term for what we now call paranoia or delu-sional disorder in English culture until well into the twentieth century. In the second place, they had little difficulty in discern-ing the rough outlines of paranoid personality: characters in novels, that is, behave in very much the same way, on occasion, as the patients described in textbooks or case-histories. In the third place, through a process of convergence, through the profession-alization of English society, one might say, they began to think like psychiatrists, adapting the conceptual and narrative structure of the case-history to their own purposes (the influence was no doubt mutual). The use of the term 'monomania' is as consistent in early twentieth-century as it is in late nineteenth-century fiction. There were, however, significant developments from the turn of the century onwards in the clarity with which writers learnt to represent the outlines of paranoid personality, and in their willingness to incorporate and to reflect on psychiatric technique. We might call those differences, which are my subject, 'paranoid Modernism'.

In the next section of this chapter, I describe two independent but parallel lines of investigation in nineteenth-century descriptive psychopathology: the classification of varieties of 'monomania' which began with Esquirol's *Mental Maladies: A Treatise on Insanity*, and took root not only in France, but also in Britain, especially in the work of the physician and ethnologist James Cowles Prichard (1786–1848); and the development of the 'paranoia question' in Germany, which gained its momentum from Karl Kahlbaum's (1828–99) methodological boldness, and found full expression in Richard von Krafft-Ebing's (1840–1902) *Textbook of Insanity* (1873). Later in the chapter, I discuss the emergence in the 1890s, in the work of Emil Kraepelin (1856–1926), of the new and all-powerful diagnostic category of 'dementia praecox', or 'schizophrenia', as it subsequently became known. This development changed the terms in which paranoia was understood, by writers as well as by psychiatrists. For the delusions of grandeur and persecution which characterize paranoia also occur in schizophrenia, where they form part of a clinical picture which includes hallucinations, emotional withdrawal, and autism. Since Kraepelin, diagnosis of paranoia has been to some degree differential: today, one of the criteria applied is the failure of the patient's behaviour to meet the main criterion for schizophrenia.[7] In the third and final section, I examine the strange case of the schoolteacher and mass-murderer Ernst Wagner. Wagner, unlike Daniel Paul Schreber, whom I shall discuss at length in Chapter 2, has not yet attracted any attention from cultural historians. His case is extraordinarily revealing of the social motives and consequences of behaviour diagnosed at the time as unequivocally paranoid. It also reveals, I shall suggest, a certain amount about the professional certainties and uncertainties of those who investigated it.

MONOMANIAS

The logical starting-point for a history of modern ideas of delusional disorder is the concept of 'monomania' developed by J. E. D. Esquirol.[8] Esquirol's *Mental Maladies* includes a graphic and

---

[7] *DSM-IV* 301.

[8] Jan Goldstein provides a lucid account of Esquirol's work, and of its social and professional context, in *Console and Classify: The French Psychiatric Profession in the Nineteenth Century* (Cambridge: CUP, 1987), ch. 5.

highly influential section on 'monomania' and 'lypemania' (melancholy with delirium): monomania had often been confused with melancholy, he points out, because in both cases the delirium is 'fixed and partial'. Esquirol recognized monomanias of the intellect, emotions, and will. In his account of the first and most notable of these afflictions one can already hear the accent of *DSM-IV*. In intellectual monomania, he observes, disorder is confined to a single object, or set of objects: 'The patients seize upon a false principle, which they pursue without deviating from logical reasonings, and from which they deduce legitimate consequences, which modify their affections, and the acts of their will. Aside from this partial delirium, they think, reason and act, like other men.' Esquirol put considerable emphasis on the burgeoning delusions of grandeur which had turned so many of his patients aside into what one might think of as a parallel universe, a virtual reality. 'Some monomaniacs', he wrote, 'consider themselves kings, princes and lords; wish to command the world, and give, with dignity and condescension, their commands to those around them.'[9] What these patients crave above all is the kind of always already constituted authority, available only to kings, princes, and lords, which guarantees acknowledgement. In the lives they live, every claim to success is contested, every scrap of recognition has to be fought for. So they create a virtual reality in which they can gather up the reflection of their own radiance undimmed.

Those lives were lived in France, during and in the aftermath of revolution, and it is perhaps not surprising, therefore, that the nature and conditions of authority should be so palpably at issue in the fantasies to which they gave rise. The case-histories incorporated in *Mental Maladies* are scenes from a drama of social recognition. The first concerns M., a 36-year-old man with a history of hypochondria. In 1815, when M. lost a considerable fortune, his character changed, and he became suspicious and quarrelsome. He thought that people were trying to kill him, and made accusations against his wife and father-in-law. On 30 December 1817, he was committed to Esquirol's care, and soon began to make good progress, although he could not altogether divest himself of suspicion. Three days before his release, he persuaded himself that

9   MM 320–2.

someone had come into his room during the night and spread ashes around it. After his release, his condition deteriorated. In a coffee house, he read an article about the pretended dauphin: 'he at once conceives the idea that he is himself the son of Louis XVI; presents himself at the Tuileries, and penetrates even to the apartments of the king, in order to claim his rights'. This was the turning-point in M.'s illness, the moment when his belief in his own unique meaning and value became unshakeable (the moment of 'paranoid illumination'). Recommitted on 20 February 1818, he continued to maintain that the King was an impostor whose throne he meant to have. 'He issues proclamations to the French people, is in constant activity, endeavours to escape, and reviles the minister of police, who prevents him from fulfilling his high destiny.' M. was conscientious and highly intelligent. Between proclamations, he devoted himself to poetry and painting.[10]

In M.'s case, the delusion of grandeur appears to have eclipsed the delusion of persecution which it arose from, and which only became manifest again in the actions taken by the King's agents to thwart his claim to the throne. In other cases, however, the persecutory delusion predominates. A second M., this one a 30-year-old man, strong, lively, and cheerful, 'is very sensitive to any want of attention which may be his due in society, and has an ambition to pass for a very important personage'. Ambitious though he undoubtedly was, however, the second M. did not think to present himself at the Tuileries. His delusions of grandeur took a more oblique form. He supposed that attempts were to be made on his life. People had been issued with guns and knives to use in assaults on his person. 'Does he walk in the gardens, he immediately returns; saying that a ball has just whistled by his ears.' What made these persecutions all the more aggravating was that people refused to take them seriously. They would call out 'Madman! Madman!' as he went by. Confronted by hostility and disbelief, M. learnt to be always on guard. One morning, the barber stooped down to pick something up; without hesitation, he took a shot at the unfortunate man, and broke his arm. For the most part, though, he was benevolent and unassuming. 'When his mind is divested of his fears,' Esquirol reported, 'he converses with propriety, is amiable,

---

[10] *MM* 324–6.

plays at different games, and no disturbance of his reason is apparent.'[11]

Although the delusion of persecution predominated, in this case, its purpose was none the less to secure indirectly a delusion of grandeur. 'As it respects genius, he professes to be the first man in the world; and attempts are made to take his life, through fear that he will control the world.'[12] The person who believes that he or she possesses special qualities can only understand the world's indifference to those qualities as a form of persecution. Indeed, it is possible to go a step further, and understand the persecution as a form of tribute: the only tribute a corrupt world can bring itself to pay to a genius which has transcended it. 'They hate me because I'm special' becomes 'I'm special because they hate me'. In some cases, it would seem, paranoia operates like a homeostatic system, adjusting the degree of fantasized persecution to the degree of fantasized grandeur. The symmetry thus produced constitutes a parallel universe. In that parallel universe, the forms of social recognition (honours, awards, qualifications, flattery, and so forth) have been suspended. What obtains instead is a circumambient scrutiny. People have failed to notice that M. is a genius, but at least they take shots at him.

My hypothesis is that such symmetries became a necessity, for some, during the nineteenth century, in increasingly democratic societies in which identity could no longer be defined by the principles of rank and station. Those most in need of paranoid symmetry were those who had to make their way in the world by ability alone: that is, by the *exhibition* of ability. One of Esquirol's case-histories, which concerns the 32-year-old P., a healthy single man, provides some insight into the problems caused in a democratic society by a withholding of recognition. As a young student, P. had been remarkable for his intelligence, and for the 'variableness' of his disposition. He aspired to the 'chief places in society'. In the end, under circumstances which are not clear, he became a pharmacist. Needless to say, the profession did not offer advancement to the chief places in society, and he soon lost interest in it. 'Indifferent and disgusted with everything, he abandoned himself to idleness.' P. finally made enough of a nuisance of himself to get

[11] *MM* 326–7.   [12] *MM* 326.

himself sent to Esquirol's asylum at Charenton, where he began to develop delusions of grandeur: he was a prince, he was Christ, he could control the thunder, he could do without food. He made two attempts to hang himself, and routinely assaulted doctors and attendants, saying that they compelled him to it. He wrote voluminously, on the most elevated topics. He thought he was God, Napoleon, Robespierre all rolled into one: 'I am Robespierre, a monster, I must be slain.'[13] For P., the recognition afforded to a pharmacist was never going to be enough. He, too, would rather be a god, or an emperor. The really interesting identification, however, is with Robespierre. Robespierre had been the exponent of a revolution which sought to establish identity on some basis other than that of custom and ceremony; for him, recognition came only, and should only come, through the strenuous exercise of political talent and political will. Robespierre was the very embodiment of modern identity, of an identity made rather than given, and thus forever problematic, forever at issue. After revolution, the monsters rule, because monstrosity alone, in a world without rank, is what earns immediate and unequivocal recognition. In that world, the monster possesses by right a 'magical power' which the pharmacist has not known how to acquire, the power in which Bourdieu locates the efficacy of symbolic capital.[14]

James Cowles Prichard did much to advance the cause of psychiatric taxonomy in Britain. The main emphasis of his *Treatise on Insanity* (1835) was on what he termed 'moral insanity': 'a morbid perversion of the feelings, affections, and active powers, without any illusion or erroneous conviction impressed upon the understanding'. In his view, monomania was moral insanity with added erroneous conviction. 'The individual affected is rendered incapable of thinking correctly on subjects connected with the particular illusion, while in other respects he betrays no palpable disorder of mind.' Melancholia had traditionally been the term applied to this disease. But the derangements it gave rise to were not always of a 'gloomy character'; and

---

[13] *MM* 368–9.
[14] 'The Economy of Symbolic Goods', in *Practical Reason: On the Theory of Action* (Cambridge: Polity, 1998), 92–123, pp. 100, 102–3.

so monomania, a term proposed by Esquirol, 'has been universally adopted in its place'.[15]

Prichard was quite explicit about the social dimension of many monomanias. 'Such illusions turn always on some circumstance connected with the person of the lunatic, his treatment by his relatives or by society in this world, or his destiny thereafter.' The monomaniac, blinded by an 'excess of self-love', 'fancies himself a king, the pope, a favourite of heaven'. 'The illusion is always some notion as to the powers, property, dignity, or destination of the individual affected, which is engrafted upon his habitual state of desire or aversion, passion and feeling.'[16] Paranoid delusion's embeddedness in social fantasy is of course what makes it such a fertile resource for the historian.

A.B., a clergyman, of great warmth and simplicity of character, and strong powers of reasoning, had married a lady of high mental endowments who was well known in the literary world. He 'entertained the greatest jealousy lest the world should suppose that, in consequence of her talents, she exercised an undue influence over his judgement, or dictated his compositions'.[17] To prevent such a supposition, he made a point of not consulting her, and of never yielding to her influence. His madness thus began, we might note, in purely *professional* concerns, in a profound anxiety about the ownership of the symbolic capital to be derived from the products of genius.

As A.B.'s condition deteriorated, greatly to his wife's distress, he began to acquire 'strange peculiarities of habits'.

---

[15] *A Treatise on Insanity and Other Disorders Affecting the Mind* (London: Sherwood, Gilbert & Piper, 1835), 12, 26. Henceforth *TIOD*. Prichard subsequently made full use of Esquirol's definitions and case-studies as well as of his terminology: *On the Different Forms of Insanity in Relation to Jurisprudence* (London: Hippolyte Baillière, 1842), 74–6. Esquirol, it should be said, returned at least part of the compliment, incorporating some of Prichard's case-studies into *Mental Maladies*, while disagreeing with the diagnosis of moral insanity: *MM* 345–8.

[16] *TIOD* 31–4.

[17] *TIOD* 35. It is tempting to make connections between A.B. and another less-than-wholly-secure intellectual married to a woman of 'high mental endowments': Casaubon, in George Eliot's *Middlemarch* (1872). I discuss Casaubon's addiction to system in *Cooking with Mud: The Idea of Mess in Nineteenth-Century Art and Fiction* (Oxford: OUP, 2000), 3–4.

His love of order, or placing things in what he considered order or regularity, was remarkable. He was continually putting chairs, &c. in their places; and if articles of ladies' work or books were left upon a table, he would take an opportunity *unobserved* of putting them in order, generally spreading the work smooth, and putting the other articles in rows. He would steal into rooms belonging to other persons for the purpose of arranging the various articles.

According to Prichard, the development of these strange peculiarities was the point at which a case of moral insanity became a case of monomania. A.B.'s obsession with order appears to have had as its correlative an obsession with personal hygiene, or self-purging. 'He would run up and down the garden a certain number of times, rinsing his mouth with water, and spitting alternately on one side and then the other in regular succession. He employed a good deal of time in rolling up little pieces of writing-paper which he used for cleaning his nose.' Marriage to a brilliant and forceful woman would seem to have hardened A.B.'s resentment at a lack of professional recognition into a furious anxiety about his place in his own home. There is no evidence to suggest that A.B. disliked women. And yet a woman became the focus of his discontents. It was the ladies and their work he made a particular point of setting 'in order'. Furthermore, his habits—the rinsing, the preparations for nasal hygiene—took the form of some kind of restitution of the (male) body.[18] It was at the very edge of gender-difference— in separating himself vehemently from dirt, from his wife's influence—that he sought to accumulate the symbolic capital his sermons had apparently not yet accumulated.

The most significant change in the conceptualization of psychosis in Europe during the nineteenth century was the emergence of a predominantly 'anatomo-clinical' or 'neurological' orientation.[19] For much of the century, particularly in France, the psychoses were understood in the context of degeneration theory.[20] According to Krafft-Ebing, whose *Textbook of Insanity*

---

[18] *TIOD* 35.

[19] A development charted by Berrios in the essays cited in n. 6 above.

[20] I. Dowbiggin, 'Degeneration and Hereditarianism in French Mental Medicine 1840–1900', in W. F. Bynum, Roy Porter, and M. Shepherd (eds.), *The Anatomy of Madness: Essays in the History of Psychiatry*, i (London: Tavistock Publications, 1985), 188–232.

exemplifies the European understanding of paranoia in the period immediately before the arrival of dementia praecox, there was evidence of a hereditary 'taint' in 77 per cent of cases. Significant though it undoubtedly was, this change will not concern me here, except in so far as it further reduced psychiatry's interest in the social causes and implications of delusional disorder. For there remained a certain consistency in psychiatric descriptions of the disease. Krafft-Ebing, indeed, happily acknowledged that 'paranoia' was a synonym for Esquirol's 'monomanie intellectuelle'.[21]

For Krafft-Ebing, as for Esquirol and Prichard, the most notable aspect of paranoid fantasies is that they 'are, from the beginning, systematized, methodic, and combined by the process of judgement, constituting a formal delusional structure'. He paid more attention than they had done to the course of the disease, distinguishing carefully between passive and active stages. In the passive stage, 'correct perceptions' of the world are supplemented by 'impressions dependent upon the character of the patient and arising out of his unconscious mental life'. Unable to accept that the world really is as it seems, the patient goes looking for secrets, for concealed motives and intentions. He or she notices 'behind' the phenomena which attract his or her attention something which 'does not belong to them'. Even the most obviously accidental occurrences are incorporated into delusion, and thus made meaningful.[22] For the monomaniac, there is no such thing as accident.

In the active stage, unconscious suppositions develop into elaborate fantasy, 'until finally an astounding, though accidental, event changes in an instant the supposition to certainty'; so astounding is this event, and so emotive, that the delusions enter consciousness. Thereafter, judgement and reason are lost. Everything which happens 'has either a hostile or a favourable relation to the subject'. In Krafft-Ebing, the pairing of feelings of grandeur with feelings of persecution, already implicit in Esquirol, becomes explicit. Indeed,

---

[21] *Textbook of Insanity*, tr. Charles Gilbert Chaddock (Philadelphia: F. A. Davis, 1904), 371, 368. Henceforth *TI*. Krafft-Ebing looms large in a fascinating contemporary account of the development in Europe of a descriptive psychopathology: J. Séglas, 'Paranoia: Systematized Delusions and Mental Degenerations: An Historical and Critical Review', tr. W. Noyes, *Journal of Nervous and Mental Disease*, 13 (1888), 157–71, 225–8, 285–300, 366–73.

[22] *TI* 368–9, 373.

the attention he paid to the course taken by the disease as it passes from a passive to an active stage enabled him to conceive of paranoid symmetry as a dialectical process.

Where the delusion begins as an idea of persecution, not infrequently in the later course of the disease, ideas of grandeur become so powerful and numerous that they quite overcome the delusion of persecution. The persecuted person becomes a distinguished personality (transformation), and then both series of delusions are brought necessarily into relation; and, even though those secondarily developed are predominant, yet those that were primary, in the further course of the disease, still make their appearance now and then.[23]

In the specific disorder described here, the delusion of grandeur is a product of the delusion of persecution, which it does not so much supersede as raise to another level. The paranoid symmetry thus established seals the patient into a parallel universe.

Krafft-Ebing's emphasis on hereditary taint cannot altogether disguise the social content of the monomanias whose onset and progress he so painstakingly recorded. Thus, childhood delusions—he distinguished between 'original' paranoia, which begins at or before puberty, and 'late', or acquired paranoia—often stem from a sense of neglect or undervaluation. 'Feelings develop of being destined for something higher. In dreams and delirium come ideas of belonging to the higher class of society. These are carried over into waking life and become the starting-points of air-castles and high-flown ambition.' Children suffering from 'original' paranoia imagine that they have merely been adopted by the people who claim to be their parents. They notice 'the lack of resemblance with their family, and accidental resemblance to portraits of reigning princes or distinguished persons'. They believe that they are in fact the children of reigning princes or distinguished persons, and find elaborate ways to protect themselves against disillusionment.[24]

Krafft-Ebing showed rather more interest than his predecessors had done in what one might call the cognitive or epistemological dimension of paranoia. He was particularly good at describing the ways in which the paranoiac constructs a parallel universe by acts of (over)interpretation.

---

[23] *TI.* 373–5.   [24] *TI* 377–8.

He feels himself the object of annoying attention, and becomes himself attentive . . . He assumes that in his neglect of dress and in his secret vices, which his face reveals to others; and in former faults and crimes which have presumably become known, lie the cause of the change in those about him. Accidental, harmless remarks by others; frequently meeting the same person; accidental departure of those that were present when he enters a room; the passers-by that avoid him or stop; clearing the throat or coughing,—strengthen his suspicion.[25]

There are two concepts, above all, which the paranoiac cannot accept: chance, and causality. If someone leaves a room as you enter it, you could draw upon the balance of probabilities to explain their departure either as fortuitous (they just felt like leaving) or as the product of relations of cause and effect (bladder pressure, say, or an appointment elsewhere). Neither explanation is available to the paranoiac, who thinks only in terms of the meaning of an event in relation to him- or herself. Persons leaving a room as he or she enters it are invariably motivated by antipathy.

One of Krafft-Ebing's patients, E., a 42-year-old married man, a peasant, suffered from religious paranoia. In 1873, during a religious revival in his village, E. declares that he is destined for higher things, and allows his hair and beard to grow. In church, when some artificial petals drift down from a candle, he sticks them in his hair, claiming that they are a bridal gift from heaven. He is the bridegroom of the Virgin, and will shortly rule the world in place of the present incumbent. 'His wife and children were the only obstacles which prevented him from marrying the Virgin at once; but he would exterminate these useless people.' In 1874, his condition deteriorated further. Committed to an asylum, he began to develop a lordly manner. Further objects fell from heaven: flowers, a cane, a ring, an old umbrella. These, too, were bridal gifts. Seeing an old umbrella, one might idly wonder how it got there, or to whom it had once belonged. E. already knew. He always already knew the meaning of every event which took place in his vicinity.[26]

There was, then, considerable agreement among psychiatrists as to the nature of delusional disorder, though not necessarily as to its most appropriate name. British psychiatrists tended to regard

[25] *TI* 382-3.   [26] *TI* 406-8.

'paranoia' as a German invention which had unaccountably found favour in America. They preferred 'delusional insanity'.[27] T. S. Clouston proved particularly antagonistic to German psychiatry, finding in Krafft-Ebing's attribution of a sexual aetiology to some forms of paranoia a symptom of the disease itself. 'The whole subject of paranoia is allied to the "degeneracy" and the "hysteria" which Max Nordau so vividly describes as influencing our present-day literature and art.' Clouston's own descriptions of the disease tended to emphasize the social content of the delusions which characterize it. Thus, D.T.B., a clergyman, 'fancied that a conspiracy had been got up against him to put him out of every curacy he had held, and to prevent him getting a living, that the bishop had been concerned in this, and of course magistratres and authorities had refused him redress'. At the close of 1881, Clouston reported, there were 822 patients of all classes in the Edinburgh asylum, of whom eighty-seven suffered from delusional insanity. 'Out of 120 patients of the higher class socially, all with educated brains, and many of them of old families, there were 23 cases of monomania, or about one-fifth of the whole, while among the 554 pauper patients there were only 44 cases of this variety of mental disease, or only one-twelfth of the whole.' Interestingly, it was training rather than family, the acquisition of cultural rather than social capital, which seemed to Clouston the crucial predisposing factor. 'It seems, therefore, that delusional insanity is most apt to occur in brains of the highest education.'[28]

It is hard to know how far the news of this agreement about the nature of the disease, if not its name, had spread beyond the lecture-theatre and the specialist journal. But spread it certainly had. By the end of the century, and despite the hostility it aroused among British psychiatrists, the term 'paranoia' had gained at least a foothold in the public imagination. In July 1892, W. T. Stead's magazine *The Review of Reviews* published a short piece with the intriguing title 'Are you a Paranoiac? Or the Latest Nickname for Cranks'. Dr H. S. Williams, medical superintendent of the Randall's Island Hospitals, had apparently found a new word for

[27] P. Hack Tuke, *A Dictionary of Psychological Medicine*, 2 vols. (London: J. & A. Churchill, 1892), ii. 887–8. The case-histories Tuke cites are all American.
[28] *Clinical Lectures on Mental Diseases*, 6th edn. (London: J. & A. Churchill, 1904), 277, 265–7, 258, 270.

an old phenomenon. 'His new word is paranoia, paranoia being a modern form of insanity, and the name of the afflicted person is paranoiac.' Paranoia, the piece continued, 'bears fruit in delusions of persecution, or hallucinations, or delusions of grandeur'.[29]

Dr Williams, evidently a keen observer of 1890s faddishness, is quoted at length on the subject of the paranoiac's favoured activities.

Usually from time to time it suits his fancy to devote his energies to the cause of some reform league for revolutionising society or the government. If his native temperament be amiable he will be simply a fanatic, perhaps a socialist; if vicious, he will probably become an anarchist. He is usually nothing if not progressive, and a new fad, especially if it be an occult one, is meat and drink to him. Revivalism, spiritualism, faith cure, Christian science, theosophy are his pastimes. In short, everything that is vague, visionary, occult, finds a following . . . among the paranoiac ranks.

The paranoiac, Williams went on, does have a place in the 'social organism'. 'Differing in mental conformation from his fellows, he must needs move in different channels from the generality of mankind.' If his 'line of departure' proves useful to humanity, he will prosper, and be regarded as a prophet or a genius; if it does not, he and his methods will disappear, 'according to the law of the survival of the fittest'.[30] The concept of paranoia was evidently ripe for appropriation.

Three major emphases can be said to have emerged from this necessarily selective survey of the nineteenth-century psychiatric literature on paranoia. First, delusional insanity was reckoned 'most apt to occur in brains of the highest education', as Clouston put it: Esquirol's Robespierre-imitating pharmacist, Prichard's clergyman, Krafft-Ebing's infinitely resourceful hermeneuts. Secondly, paranoiacs condemn themselves to meaning; they lock themselves away inside interpretation, inside their own systems. For them, there is no such thing as accident, or mere causality (the ordinary operation of the laws of the universe). Thirdly, paranoia works like a homeostatic system, meticulously adjusting the degree of fantasized

---

[29] 'Are you a Paranoiac? Or the Latest Nickname for Cranks', *Review of Reviews*, 6 (1892), 56.
[30] Ibid.

persecution to the degree of fantasized grandeur: they hate me because I'm special, I'm special because they hate me. It was in one or more of these emphases, I shall try to show, that my chosen writers were able to discern the outlines of paranoid personality.

DEMENTIA PRAECOX

Schizophrenia is a different story. A 'disease' whose history is virtually synonymous with the history of modern psychiatry, it was from the beginning, and still remains, self-evidently problematic.[31] During the Modernist period, the tradition of descriptive psychopathology found a new conceptual and institutional focus in the work of three pioneering researchers: Emil Kraepelin, whom we have already encountered, professor of psychiatry at Dorpat (1886–91), Heidelberg (1891–1903), and Munich (1903–22), where he founded a world-famous Research Institute; Eugen Bleuler (1857–1939), medical director of the Burghölzli Hospital in Zurich; and Karl Jaspers (1883–1969), whose *General Psychopathology*, first published in 1913, gave immense authority to the view that psychiatric medicine is an art as well as a science.[32] To be sure, there were from the start significant psychoanalytic

---

[31] The literature on schizophrenia is enormous, and enormously varied in quality and emphasis. For instructive commentary on the history of the concept, see Sander Gilman, 'Constructing Schizophrenia as a Category of Mental Illness', in *Disease and Representation: Images of Illness from Madness to AIDS* (Ithaca, NY: Cornell University Press, 1988), 202–30; and Irving I. Gottesman, *Schizophrenia Genesis: The Origins of Madness* (New York: W. H. Freeman, 1991). Louis A. Sass has brought ideas about Modernist art and literature to bear on the understanding of schizophrenia: *Madness and Modernism: Insanity in the Light of Modern Art, Literature, and Thought* (Cambridge, Mass.: Harvard University Press, 1994).

[32] For a useful general account of the methodologies of Kraepelin, Bleuler, Jaspers, and Jaspers's follower Kurt Schneider (1887–1967), see J. Hoenig, 'The Concept of Schizophrenia: Kraepelin–Bleuler–Schneider', *British Journal of Psychiatry*, 142 (1983), 547–56. There is an intriguing contemporary description of Kraepelin's Munich asylum in C. K. Clarke, 'Notes on Some of the Psychiatric Clinics and Asylums of Germany', *American Journal of Insanity*, 65 (1908), 357–76, pp. 369–76. Clarke, a member of a Canadian government commission, thought the Institute 'the ideal to which we should aspire'. He was also intrigued by duvets, duelling, continental breakfasts, afternoon naps, and the Southern German predilection for beer and radishes. For a valuable account of Kraepelin's 'sociopolitical engagement' as director of the Institute, see Eric J. Engstrom, 'Emil Kraepelin: Psychiatric and Public Affairs in Wilhelmine Germany', *History of Psychiatry*, 2 (1991), 111–32.

contributions, by Freud, Jung, Abraham, Tausk, and others, to the understanding of psychosis. Jung and Abraham were colleagues at the Burghölzli, under Bleuler's direction, from 1904 to 1907; indeed, Jung's writings on psychosis, from *The Psychology of Dementia Praecox* (1907) to the articles and lectures of the 1950s, offer as good a view as any of developments in the field during that period.[33] Where schizophrenia is concerned, however, we must look primarily to the tradition of descriptive psychopathology.

The modern understanding of schizophrenia began in 1893, when Kraepelin introduced it into the fourth edition of his text-book of psychiatry as a diagnostic entity, under the name of dementia praecox. There it is described as one of three major 'psychic degeneration processes', the others being catatonia and dementia paranoides. The textbook's fifth (1896) edition estab-lishes dementia praecox as the overall term for a disease which might take catatonic or paranoid forms.[34] Sixth and seventh editions subsequently appeared, each considerably amplifying the discussion of dementia praecox, the seventh edition introducing an emphasis on the 'loss of inner unity' as the main cause of the disease. There was then a gap of several years before the eighth edition, a four-volume work of some 2,500 pages, appeared between 1909 and 1915. Its chapter on dementia praecox, which had assimilated the researches of Eugen Bleuler, was thought of sufficient interest to merit separate publication in English in 1919 as *Dementia Praecox and Paraphrenia.*[35]

Kraepelin distinguished between two main types of functional psychosis: manic depression and dementia praecox, the former phasic or 'circular', the latter a progressive disease which normally began in adolescence or early adult life, and thereafter followed an inexorable downward path, with little or no prospect of recovery. According to Kraepelin, the symptoms of dementia praecox can

[33] They have been assembled as vol. iii of the *Collected Works: The Psychogenesis of Mental Disease*, tr. R. F. C. Hull (London: Routledge & Kegan Paul, 1960).

[34] The original description in the 5th edn. of the *Psychiatry* has been translated as 'Dementia Praecox' in John Cutting and M. Shepherd (eds.), *The Clinical Roots of the Schizophrenia Concept* (Cambridge: CUP, 1987), 13–24.

[35] *Dementia Praecox and Paraphrenia*, ed. George M. Robertson, tr. R. Mary Barclay (New York: Robert E. Krieger Publishing Co., 1971). Facsimile of 1919 edn. Henceforth *DPP*.

be classified as catatonic ('frozen' posturing, mutism, loss of motor control), hebephrenic (inappropriate emotionality), or paranoid (delusions of grandeur). In all its forms, the disease involved a 'peculiar destruction' of the inner cohesiveness of the psychic personality whose effects were most evident in the 'emotional and volitional spheres of mental life'.[36] In Kraepelin's view, dementia praecox, unlike paranoia, was a totalizing disorder, a precocious form of senile dementia (de-mentia, loss of mind): neuro-physio-logical deficit or damage brought about an 'inevitable and progres-sive mental deterioration' during which the patient became 'completely incapable of comprehending and developing new ideas'.[37] Although objections were soon raised to his terminology, on the grounds that the disease need not be either precocious in its onset or irreversible in its outcome, Kraepelin's quantitative and clinically orientated account remained for many years the one to argue with. It put a new landmark on the map of mental illnesses: an affliction whose main characteristic was a profound disturbance of thought and language.

Eugen Bleuler's *Dementia Praecox, or the Group of Schizophrenias*, first published in 1911, introduced a different terminology, a more theoretical emphasis (Kraepelin had for the most part stuck to observation and statistical analysis), and a belief in therapy. Bleuler understood dementia praecox as the outcome of an as yet unknown toxin or cerebral disease process. *Dementia Praecox* describes in meticulous detail the various relations to the world, each an abrupt but comprehensible departure from what would be considered the norm, taken up by a wide range of schizophrenic patients.[38] It distinguishes between primary symptoms such as the dissociation of ideas, which are found in every case, and secondary symptoms such as delusion and hallucination, which derive from the random life experiences of the individual patient. To Kraepelin's disgust, Bleuler insisted that both primary and secondary symptoms could be understood as the expression of an

---

[36] *DPP* 3.   [37] 'Dementia Praecox', 14.

[38] Bleuler it was who, in Mar. 1919, diagnosed Vaslav Nijinsky as schizophrenic: Peter Ostwald, *Nijinsky: A Leap into Madness* (New York: Carol Publishing, 1991). Nijinsky's remarkable diary, a key document in Modernism's encounter with schizophrenia, has recently been republished in English in a new and unexpurgated edn.: *The Diary of Vaslav Nijinsky*, ed. Joan Acocella, tr. Kyril Fitzlyon (London: Allen Lane, 1999).

unconscious 'complex'. However, his reliance on Freud was no more than tentative.[39] Thus, stereotypy, which returns the patient again and again to the same idea, word, or sentence structure, is, he thought, a symptomatic act in the Freudian sense; and yet it also occurs in schizophrenia independently of any discernible complex.[40] Kraepelin was none the less routinely dismissive of Bleuler's 'metapsychiatry'.

The significance of Jaspers's *General Psychopathology* is that it put metapsychiatry on a more secure, or at least on a knowingly insecure, basis. Jaspers advocated a subjective or empathetic approach to mental illness, an approach which discovers in its own limits a powerful instrument of investigation. With schizophrenia, he wrote, we arrive at the limit of the empathy we are capable of feeling for another person much sooner than we would ordinarily; what the schizophrenic takes for granted is to us already incomprehensible. Schizophrenia is where will and conscience collapse into automatism or hallucination, overwhelmed by a reality on which they cannot get any kind of hold. Such utter catastrophe defies comprehension, and repels empathy. There is 'something queer, cold, inaccessible, rigid and petrified there, even when the patients are quite sensible'.[41] The gulf or abyss between minds represents at once the bar to understanding and the only place from which understanding, or rather explanation—some other kind of knowledge—can begin. When empathy and comprehension fail, the schizophrenic symptom or inner experience must be known *as* that very failure.

Jaspers's approach to schizophrenia can be understood as the outcome of a difference of emphasis within nineteenth-century psychiatry. According to the 'continuity' model of mental func-

---

[39] For Bleuler's attitude to psychoanalysis, see F. Alexander and S. T. Selesnick, 'Freud–Bleuler Correspondence', *Archives of General Psychiatry*, 12 (1965), 1–9. Freud's disciple Ernest Jones was at this time reiterating his faith in the 'psychogenesis' of dementia praecox, in a letter of 7 Feb. 1909, and distancing himself from Jung's preference for a toxin, produced by the dementia praecox complex itself, which damages the brain irreparably: *Complete Correspondence of Sigmund Freud and Ernest Jones 1908–1939*, ed. R. Andrew Paskauskas (Cambridge, Mass.: Harvard University Press, 1993), 16.

[40] *Dementia Praecox, or The Group of Schizophrenias*, tr. Joseph Zinkin (New York: International Universities Press, 1950), 454–6. Henceforth *DPGS*.

[41] *General Psychopathology*, tr. J. Hoenig and M. W. Hamilton (Chicago: University of Chicago Press, 1963), 581, 447.

tions, there was, as W. B. Carpenter put it in 1879, 'nothing in the psychical phenomena of insanity which distinguishes this condition from states that may be temporarily induced in minds otherwise healthy'. However, the gradual realization that insanity's more bizarre symptoms found no counterpart at all in normal behaviour led to the development of a 'discontinuity' model, of which Jaspers was perhaps the most sophisticated and influential early twentieth-century exponent.[42] Paranoia could be said to represent, by contrast with schizophrenia, the continuity model's best shot at psychosis: a condition whose 'psychical phenomena' are hard to distinguish from states which may temporarily be induced in minds which are otherwise healthy.

Schizophrenia was an invention of German-language psychiatry; but the power of the new diagnostic terminology soon made itself felt in other countries as well. Thus, the Royal Medico-Psychological Association held a symposium on dementia praecox in London in 1909, at which Kraepelin's terminology and clinical studies were subjected to intense and on the whole favourable scrutiny. One factor in the urgency of this debate was the dominance 'Kraepelinism' had already achieved in American psychiatry.[43] In France, too, the new diagnostic system swept all before it. In 1909, participants in the annual congress of French psychiatrists and neurologists at Nantes spoke of the episodes of vagabondage previously considered a symptom of dissociative fugue as a symptom of dementia praecox.[44]

Given the extent of Kraepelin's influence, it may have seemed as though paranoia was about to go the way of dissociative fugue. In his scheme, dementia paranoides, one of the three degenerative processes, is characterized by delusions of grandeur and persecution which might at first look like paranoia, but soon deteriorate further. In the event, however, schizophrenia's arrival on the scene *reinforced* the diagnostic validity of existing definitions of paranoia.

[42] Berrios, 'Descriptive Psychopathology', 306, 309. The quotation is from Carpenter's *Principles of Mental Physiology* (London: C. Kegan Paul, 1879).

[43] There is a full record of the debate in T. Johnstone, 'The Case for Dementia Praecox', *Journal of Mental Science*, 55 (1909), 64–91. Peter Barham summarizes it in *Schizophrenia and Human Value: Chronic Schizophrenia, Science and Society*, new edn. (London: Free Association Books, 1993), 36–42.

[44] Hacking, *Mad Travellers*, 72–4.

In 1904, in the seventh edition of his textbook, Kraepelin stated that paranoia is a 'chronic progressive psychosis' characterized by 'the gradual development of a stable progressive system of delusions, without marked mental deterioration, clouding of consciousness or involvement of the coherence of thought'.[45] In his *Lectures on Clinical Psychiatry*, he confirmed that the behaviour of paranoiacs is free from 'absurdity, automatic obedience, and negativism' (all symptoms of schizophrenia). Paranoia, he said, is a 'distinctive disease', 'in which delusions of being wronged and of over-self-esteem develop quite slowly, without independent disturbances of emotional life or of the will'.[46] Paranoid delusions, unlike those found in dementia praecox, are never 'incoherent' or 'nonsensical'. The eighth edition of his textbook announces that 'genuine' hallucinations, a hallmark of dementia praecox, do not occur in paranoia. The principle of differential diagnosis had been established. Dementia praecox was not just a new landmark on the map, a new object of study and reflection; it forced psychiatrists to conceive mental illnesses characterized by a profound disturbance of thought and language in one way, and those not thus characterized in another. The emergence of a discontinuity model of mental illness prompted redefinition, indeed reinforcement, of the continuity model. Kraepelin himself went on to suggest in his later work that paranoia is a psychogenic disorder, to be grouped with hysteria. It was perhaps because the concept had lured him away from the somatogenic premise of his own descriptive psychopathology that, as Lewis remarks, he never felt comfortable with it.[47]

Even so, the *Lectures on Clinical Psychiatry* contain a memorable case-history of paranoia or 'progressive systematized insanity'. 'The stately gentleman, aged sixty-two, who presents himself before us with a certain courtly dignity, with his carefully-tended moustaches, his eye-glasses, and his well-fitting if perhaps somewhat shabby attire, gives quite the impression of a man of the world.' As a young man, this patient had travelled extensively in

[45] *Clinical Psychiatry: A Text-Book for Students and Physicians* (London: Macmillan, 1902), 316. Adapted from the 6th German edn. of the *Lehrbuch der Psychiatrie* by A. Ross Defendorf.

[46] *Lectures on Clinical Psychiatry*, 2nd edn., ed. Thomas Johnstone (London: Baillière, Tindall & Cox, 1906), 147. Henceforth *LCP*.

[47] 'Paranoia and Paranoid', 5.

America, eventually settling in Quito, where he made a small fortune as a merchant. He returned to Germany, but in dissolving his business connections was done out of considerable sums. At first, he lived comfortably enough off his remaining capital. 'At the same time he occupied himself with all sorts of schemes from which he hoped for recognition and profit.' He submitted a plan whereby Germany might claim land in Africa and New Guinea, as well as the Galápagos Islands, to the Foreign Ministry. The plan was subsequently adopted, without 'due thanks' falling to the lot of the 'real originator'. His money began to run out. 'However, on the whole, he did not trouble himself much about it, for he was convinced that a man of his capability and knowledge, who spoke three foreign languages and had been all over the world, had merely to stretch out his hand to find a satisfactory post, according to his pretensions.' Bankrupted, he became a sponger and fantasist, and soon found himself in an asylum. 'That, he concluded with bitterness, was the thanks which the Fatherland bestowed upon him for his services.'[48]

These delusions of grandeur were closely connected to delusions of persecution. In the asylum a story emerges, little by little, 'that a woman whom he calls by the nickname of Bulldog, and who was the daughter of the English Consul at Quito, had persecuted him for twenty-three or twenty-four years with her plans of marriage, and sought in every way to cross his steps in order to reduce him to submission'. Everywhere he noticed the deceptions of the Bulldog and her accomplices. This 'half-crazy' American had 'insinuated herself into his neighbourhood', dressing herself as a man, approaching him under different names, and generally doing all she could to reduce him to dependence. He would by now be one of the richest men in California if she had not stood in his way. She was to blame for his commitment to the asylum. He was always running into her. 'He had discovered holes in his boots and stains on his clothes, which could not possibly have been caused except through the Bulldog.' The patient, Kraepelin concludes, has created for himself a 'delusionary view of the world', a parallel universe. In that parallel universe, the laws of cause and effect have been suspended, and their place taken by a

[48] *LCP* 142–3.

singular apprehension of meaning, value, and purpose. 'All small vexations, and, finally, his being brought to the asylum, are referred, not to the natural course of events, but to the deliberate dealings of a certain person and her accomplices.'[49] As with Prichard's clergyman, an anxiety about social and professional status finds its voice in violent and baseless accusations laid against a woman (there is no evidence to suggest that the Bulldog had ever set foot outside California). Again, the woman is associated with mess. The stains on the clothes are as disorderly as the bits and pieces lying around in the house, as invasive as the matter which must be expelled from mouth and nose. Again, the insistence on masculinity appears to derive from the failure of the schemes for recognition and profit. In conclusion, Kraepelin notes that his patient's outward bearing and behaviour 'are entirely unexceptionable and without remark, and are free from absurdity, automatic obedience, and negativism'. Whenever he acts 'senselessly', the sense of it is to be found in his delusions.[50]

Before developing my account of the category of paranoia any further, I want briefly to consider what it was about the category of schizophrenia which seemed so urgently to demand the acts (or gestures) of differential diagnosis I have drawn attention to. We have seen that paranoiacs cannot abide contingency; and we will see in the next section that their doctors felt very much the same way. One of the most remarkable things about the diagnostic category of schizophrenia, from the cultural historian's point of view, is the extent to which it became a meditation on contingency. What gets lost in schizophrenia, it was thought, is not the world but the principle of inner psychic unity: a drastic failure of will renders the patient fatally vulnerable to accident. The early literature on schizophrenic behaviour resembles an encyclopedia of mess. Schizophrenics, it would have us know, are (in) a mess. And in mimesis.

Dementia praecox, Kraepelin wrote, 'consists in the *loss of the inner unity* of the activities of intellect, emotion, and volition in themselves and among one another'. Schizophrenic behaviour has cut itself loose from meaning and value, from purposefulness. 'The work of the patients is not as in healthy people the expression of their view of life and temperament, it is not guided by the elaboration of perceptions, by deliberation and moods, but it is the incalculable result of chance external influences, and of impulses, cross impulses, and contrary impulses, arising similarly by chance internally.'[51] The neurotic, Jung said, can rely on the fact that his illness will never lose its 'systematic character', its 'unity and inner cohesion'; the schizophrenic, on the other hand, 'must always reckon with the possibility that his very foundations will give way somewhere', that his ideas and feelings will suddenly be stripped of any relation to each other or to the world. 'As a result, he feels threatened by an uncontrollable chaos of chance happenings.'[52]

Eugen Bleuler's exhaustive description of schizophrenia's fundamental symptoms is a litany of chance happenings. 'In this malady,' he begins, 'the associations lose their continuity.' Schizophrenic thinking is bizarre both in content and in form: 'two ideas, fortuitously encountered, are combined into one thought, the logical form being determined by incidental circumstances'. Under such circumstances conversation becomes a lottery. 'It is quite the usual thing to have the patients give us answers which merely seize haphazardly on any thought of the moment.' No less thoroughly penetrated by contingency are the secondary symptoms, such as delusions and hallucinations. Schizophrenic delusion, in short, unlike paranoid delusion, is an 'amorphous mass' of unrelated ideas.[53]

What is particularly interesting about these accounts, for the historian of literary Modernism, is the connection they make between the arbitrariness of schizophrenic behaviour and mimesis. Kraepelin believed that evidence of the loss of will in schizophrenia was to be found in the susceptibility of patients to 'echolalia' and 'echopraxis'. Schizophrenics mechanically repeat words spoken to them. For no particular reason, they imitate movements and gestures made within their view. Photographs in his textbook show schizophrenic patients maintaining postures they have been ordered to assume at random, oblivious to their own discomfort. The postures these patients fall into in response to random instruction express nothing at all except their vulnerability to accident:

---

[51] *DPP* 74–5.
[52] 'Schizophrenia' (1958), in *Psychogenesis*, 256–72, pp. 258–9.
[53] *DPGS* 14, 23, 125.

their disappearance, as it were, into a condition to which the observer can attach neither meaning nor value. According to Kraepelin, such 'waxy flexibility' was to be found 'in all stages of the disease, at the beginning as well as at the end, not infrequently also as the one noticeable remaining feature of the disease in otherwise apparently complete recovery'.[54] To imitate for imitation's sake, Kraepelin thought, was to abandon any notion of meaning and value, of purposefulness, of inner psychic unity. There could scarcely be a more graphic contrast than that between the waxily flexible sufferer from dementia praecox, rapt in arbitrary mimesis, and the paranoiac locked into interpretation, into system.

It was Bleuler who made explicit the connection between imitative behaviour of this kind and the habits of social mimesis against which, as I shall demonstrate in the chapters which follow, writers from John Stuart Mill to Wyndham Lewis were so violently to fulminate, thus constituting an anti-mimetic paranoid postliberalism. Bleuler compared the mannerisms which his patients could not help affecting to those out of which the social climber sought to create a new identity. The 'truly cultured' person, he maintained, demonstrates the 'greater independence of his fingers from each other' with every gesture of his hand. By contrast 'the person who wants to create an impression of more culture than he actually possesses will only notice how the other extends his little finger and will imitate this detail in an extreme manner at every opportunity'.[55] A certain fanatical attention to what other people happen to be doing, combined with a desire to do as they do, connects the schizophrenic to the social climber. Had English Modernist writers ever encountered the descriptive psychopathology of schizophrenia, as Robert Musil did, what they would have found in it is a way of thinking about their own objections to mimesis in life and literature.

PARANOIA AND THE NEW PSYCHIATRY

An 'understanding' psychiatry badly needed something to understand. The 'something queer, cold, inaccessible' in schizophrenic

---

[54] *DPP* 37–8.   [55] *DPGS* 453.

behaviour provided it with the sternest possible challenge, a challenge to which it rose, as we have seen, by developing new methods of diagnosis. Paranoia, by contrast, created opportunities for what one might almost call diagnostic collusion between doctor and patient. Paranoid fantasies make a kind of sense; schizophrenic automatisms and hallucinations do not. Furthermore, whereas paranoia could be said to constitute no more than a lapse, an aberration, schizophrenia is meltdown. Paranoia looked like a misfortune, while schizophrenia was the worst thing that could possibly happen to you. Understanding psychiatry certainly took to paranoia, as is evident from the work of Kraepelin's student Robert Gaupp (1870–1953), who became Professor of Psychiatry at Tübingen, where the foundations of the new psychiatry were laid, in 1906; and where he was eventually succeeded by *his* student, Ernst Kretschmer (1888–1964). Paranoia made both of them.

Robert Gaupp took as his subject the mass-murderer Ernst Wagner. Two of his many articles about Wagner, one published in 1914, the other in 1938, have recently been made available in English, and I base my account of the case on these.[56] Wagner was an educated man with literary aspirations, and much of the evidence for Gaupp's interpretation of his illness derives from his three-volume autobiography. Since the age of 18 he had masturbated assiduously, a habit which became the source of intense anguish and shame. In 1901, he was appointed assistant teacher at a school in the village of Mühlhausen-an-der-Enz. One night, on his way home from the local inn, he committed several acts of indecency with animals. There were no witnesses, but soon after he began to develop delusions of persecution. He thought that everyone in the village knew about the crime he had committed, and that they were laughing at him behind his back. 'If he went into the inn, he soon observed that obscene remarks with reference to him and to his sexual deviations were being made at the next table.' What infuriated him most was the thought that he, the

---

[56] 'The Scientific Significance of the Case of Ernst Wagner' (1914) and 'The Illness and Death of the Paranoid Mass-Murderer, Schoolmaster Wagner: A Case History' (1938), in S. R. Hirsch and M. Shepherd (eds.), *Themes and Variations in European Psychiatry: An Anthology* (Charlottesville, Va.: University of Virginia Press, 1974), 121–33 and 134–50. C. K. Clarke visited Gaupp's Tübingen asylum, and found particular praise for its well-stocked library: 'Notes', 366–7.

only educated man in the village, had become, or so he thought, an 'object of scorn and general entertainment' for peasant boys. He began a relationship with the innkeeper's daughter, made her pregnant, and married her. They moved to Radelstetten, a rough, lonely village in the hills. 'He took his grief and despair with him. His anxiety lest the men of Mühlhausen would again point the finger of scorn at him was coupled with self-loathing.' He wanted to kill himself, but could not find the courage.[57]

His wife bore him four children. He concluded that he would have to kill his family, as well as himself, since the children might carry within them the germ of his sexual 'anomalies'. He was sure that the men of Mühlhausen had not forgotten him. 'Whenever he went there he could tell by their bearing, gestures, and words that he was still an object of scorn and mockery.' In 1908 his delusions of reference expanded to cover Radelstetten and the neighbouring villages. He thought that he was despised there, too, 'his friends and colleagues making remarks which showed that they knew about his abnormal practices'. This increased his hatred of the men of Mühlhausen. By October 1909 he had a plan to destroy them. He got hold of pistols and a revolver. As the persecution in Radelstetten grew unbearable, he obtained a transfer to a city school at Degerloch, in the suburbs of Stuttgart. Outwardly, he was, as he had always been, the perfect family man, the consummate professional. Inwardly, though, he was still in torment. He came to believe that his bestial misdemeanours were common knowledge in Degerloch, 'attracting scorn and contempt'.[58] On the night of 3 September 1913, he at last put into action the plan he had hatched four years earlier. He cut the throats of his wife and children while they lay asleep in the family home in Degerloch, and then travelled by train and bicycle to Mühlhausen, where he set fire to several buildings and shot down the inhabitants as they fled, killing eight and wounding a further twelve.

When told that nobody in Mühlhausen, Radelstetten, or Degerloch had known anything at all about his sexual behaviour, and that nobody had consciously made fun of him on account of it, he was momentarily shaken. He had lived for twelve years 'under a delusion'. He had created for himself, out of his

---

[57] 'Scientific Significance', 127.   [58] Ibid. 128.

'delusionary view of the world', in Kraepelin's phrase, a parallel universe. And yet the insanity was partial. 'But does a form of mania really exist', Esquirol had asked, 'in which those who are affected by it preserve the integrity of their reason, whilst they abandon themselves to the commission of acts the most reprehensible?'[59] Wagner's case seemed to confirm that it did. Until the day of the murders, nobody had the slightest suspicion that the neat and obliging schoolmaster was a homicidal maniac.

Traditionally, Gaupp observed, paranoia had been understood as a 'disease process' which attacks a healthy brain, 'like general paresis or catatonia'. Against this, he went on, could be set the 'growing opinion' that paranoia represents a 'psychologically understandable development', a 'deviant state' which, 'under the influence of external events and personal experience, leads to a progressive alienation of the patient from his environment, a shift in his attitude to the world and the logical formation of a network of delusional systems'. Clearly, he concluded, this 'overvaluation of certain ideas and experiences' had nothing to do with 'mental defect'. Schoolteachers and governesses were particularly vulnerable to the disease because 'their profession provides a milieu in which their genuine mental superiority gives rise to suppressed mental arrogance'.[60] Gaupp acknowledges explicitly what had been implicit, as we have seen, in the nineteenth-century literature on paranoia: that recognition is a particular problem, sometimes leading to madness, for those who depend on their expertise, and on the symbolic capital it at once accumulates and relies upon for its furtherance, to make a living.

Gaupp's diagnosis did not meet with uniform acceptance. Some psychiatrists, including Bleuler, thought that Wagner suffered from a mild form of paranoid schizophrenia. To refute these claims, Gaupp conducted a two-hour conversation with his star patient at a meeting of German psychiatrists in Tübingen, in 1932. During this conversation, Wagner, fortunately, did not reveal the slightest sign of dementia. 'He defended his delusion against all argument, with ready wit and quick comprehension, even with sarcasm when this was called for, showing some emotion but still remaining polite.' In paranoia, Gaupp felt able to conclude, the 'residue'

---

[59] *MM* 362.   [60] 'Scientific Significance', 124, 130–1.

which remains 'beyond one's grasp and outside one's complete understanding' is 'less than in any other form of mental illness'.[61] We might imagine this two-hour conversation as the refinement of a further symmetry, between doctor and madman. Gaupp needs Wagner to be utterly coherent in delusion, if his diagnosis is to prevail, and thus win him the consent and approval of his peers; Wagner needs Gaupp to be utterly coherent in diagnosis, if he is to continue to think of himself as unique, and not just any old dement. There is paranoia in this symmetry: Gaupp betrays Wagner to the extent that he regards his delusion as a delusion; Wagner betrays Gaupp to the extent that he exhibits any symptom which the watching psychiatrists might interpret as evidence of paranoid schizophrenia. In Chapter 2, I examine a comparable paranoid symmetry of paranoias, between Sigmund Freud and Daniel Paul Schreber.

It would be hard to mistake the pride Robert Gaupp took in the mass-murderer Ernst Wagner. The man may have cut the throats of his wife and children and set light to a village, but there he is, twenty years later, on display at Tübingen, defending the delusion which caused him to commit those crimes with a ready wit. I do not mean to imply that Gaupp took mass-murder lightly. It is rather that he found in Wagner's subtle and lucid grasp of his own motives something not only admirable in itself, but a mirror-image of the analytic process which had brought him to the point where he could understand himself. 'From what he had heard and read, and above all from what he had *himself experienced*, Wagner gave a description of insanity which would be a credit to any textbook.' What Wagner had read included the textbook Gaupp had written about him, so it is scarcely surprising, perhaps, that the views of doctor and patient should coincide. 'But one thing is still certain: he was able to identify himself as closely as he did with the scientific theory of paranoid delusion *only because this theory corresponded to his own innermost experiences over a period of fifteen years.*'[62] If Wagner's professional identity was crucially at stake in the crimes he committed, then Gaupp's professional identity is crucially at stake, to the extent of a mild paranoia, in his long-drawn-out defence of his original diagnosis.

[61] 'Illness and Death', 149–50.   [62] Ibid. 142.

Gaupp's 1938 essay will also be of interest to literary and cultural historians because it has a lot to say about the political views Wagner developed in the asylum. Foremost among these was anti-Semitism. Like a number of the patients we have encountered in this chapter, Wagner wrote voluminously, and indeed set about developing a literary reputation. He began to believe that the poet Franz Werfel had plagiarized his work, and was basking in the acclaim due to him alone. Werfel was a Jew, and Wagner's hatred of him grew rapidly into 'a wild hatred of all Jewry, although previously he had, by his own account, not been at all anti-Semitic'. This 'literary delusion of persecution and grandeur' persisted until his last days. 'He rejoiced in the government's racial decrees and in the rejection of Jewish literature and art, and saw in the internal politics of the Third Reich a confirmation of his own theories of his own struggle against Jews in literature.' Indeed he claimed that he had been a National Socialist since 1930, the first in Winnenthal. Speaking about the murders he had committed, in March 1938, a few weeks before his death, he felt no remorse. '"A few hundred dead, what is that in comparison with my suffering." Then he went on: "People *speak* so much about racial hygiene—I *acted*, I put it into practice." '[63] Wagner thus found a retrospective political justification for a crime committed out of resentment at the indifference the world had shown to his unique abilities. Racial hygiene would do for Wagner what sexual hygiene had done for Prichard's clergyman, and Kraepelin's stately 62-year-old. It enacted the anti-mimesis—the withdrawal from entanglements, from mess, from contingency—necessary to the establishment of a system.

Ernst Kretschmer, with whom I shall conclude my rapid survey of descriptions of paranoia, published a famous book about the syndrome of Sensitive Delusion of Reference (SDR) in 1918.[64] Kretschmer wanted to show how a particular psychosis might arise from a particular type of 'character'. SDR is comparable in many respects to the disease Kraepelin and Gaupp understood as paranoia. It is characterized by persecutory, referential, and/or erotic delusions in individuals of a 'sensitive' type of personality: 'introverted people

[63] Ibid. 137, 146, 139.
[64] A partial translation of the 4th (1966) edn. into English is available in Hirsch and Shepherd (eds.), *Themes and Variations*, 153–95.

whose inner world of feeling is strongly ethically coloured, and who suffer from hidden and persistent emotional tension'.[65] The delusions suffered by such people are neither odd nor bizarre. Affect and volition remain unimpaired. In most cases, the outcome is favourable.

Like Gaupp, unlike Jaspers, Kretschmer was an adherent of the 'continuity' model in descriptive psychopathology. He saw SDR as the product of an abnormal personality subjected to a specific kind of stress. To be pathogenic, the stress must intervene at a moment of vulnerability, such as Wagner's drunken act of bestiality; its development thereafter is in psychological terms entirely understandable. In the case-history of his star patient, Helene Renner, Kretschmer insisted that the symptoms of SDR should not be mistaken for those of schizophrenia. During certain phases of her illness, he reports, Renner displayed symptoms which most psychiatrists would identify as those of 'full-blown schizophrenic disorder'. 'For her, everything appeared strange and altered, and she suffered sudden irrational whims, which for a time she attributed to a foreign hypnotic influence.' Previously, during the simple paranoid phase of the illness, her associations had been linked together by logic, by a concept of purpose: 'now, suddenly, the links were broken, things fell apart'. This is very much what Kraepelinian nosology would lead one to expect. Kretschmer, however, familiar though he was with the work of Kraepelin and Bleuler, resisted the diagnosis of dementia praecox. Renner's 'feelings of strangeness', he wrote, signified not the onset of dementia, but the last attempt of the 'still persisting central core of the personality' to find expression for the 'intangible twilight' which had fallen over it. So powerfully did Kretschmer feel that expression as a discovery from within that he began to wonder whether it did not exceed the genre to which it had been assigned.

Perhaps it should be called an autobiography rather than a case-history (in spite of all the wealth of complex psychotic material), so much do the pathological elements arise directly from the overall progression of her development, so intimately are they related to the groundswell of her emotional life, and so much have they been consciously experienced and suffered, fought over, and judged by the patient right through to their most painful consequences.

[65] 'Sensitive Delusion of Reference', 156.

The symmetry between doctor and patient converts case-history into autobiography: what appears to be told from the outside has in fact been told from the inside. Freud's case-history of Schreber had also been a reading of an autobiography. Certain psychoses, Kretschmer suggests, have a tale to tell. But the tale they tell is also, in a sense, the professional autobiography of the doctor to whom they speak. Kretschmer needed to believe in that indestructible central core of personality, because he had found in Renner, as Gaupp found in Wagner, a patient who could confirm from her own innermost experiences the truth of his theory. The patient, he reports, 'was in need of doctors, responded to soothing words, and after a thorough medical discussion could correct her ideas of reference almost completely'.[66] Here, at last, was something for an understanding psychiatry to understand.

Kretschmer understood Ernst Wagner, too. 'Some will object that this gruesome, blood-stained figure, whose illness culminated in one of the most brutal mass-murders of recent criminal history, can have nothing to do with the delicate, sentimental, refined people on whom we have based our portrayal of the sensitive character.' But Gaupp's analysis of Wagner had shown that brutality was by no means the dominant feature of his personality. Guilt, rather than rage, had been the feeling which nurtured his delusion. Kretschmer describes, in terms which will find an echo in what I have to say about Modernist writing, the transformation of a sensitive man into a psychopath. 'Suddenly, out of the brooding twilight of inward sensitivity, a man strode forth into the harsh light of day; with an embittered egoism and tenacious premeditation, infused with an heroic sense of honour and life, he exacted his right and his revenge from a whole world of enemies.' The man who set fire to a village was in some respects, Kretschmer concludes, a 'sublime' figure.[67]

---

[66] Ibid. 174, 173. Kretschmer, perhaps on account of his attentiveness to the self-expression hidden within case-histories, perhaps on account of his eloquence, was the psychiatric theorist whose work most powerfully appealed to Robert Musil: David S. Luft, *Robert Musil and the Crisis of European Culture 1880–1942* (Berkeley, Calif.: University of California Press, 1980), 186; Hannah Hickman, *Robert Musil and the Culture of Vienna* (London: Croom Helm, 1984), 55.

[67] 'Sensitive Delusion of Reference', 187. The best indication of what Kretschmer considered beyond the limits of even the most understanding of psychiatries is to be found in the account he gives of the 'schizoid temperament' in *Physique and Character*

Discussion of Ernst Wagner has taken me a long way from English Modernism, although in Chapter 6 I will make some reference to a comparable case, which both Conrad and Ford would most certainly have known about, and which aroused Ford's latent interest in psychopathy. Wagner none the less looms large over this study, as the embodiment and figure of Modernist paranoia: that is, of an old form of mania redefined in its sublimity against the new (or newly understood) form, against dementia praecox. We shall find equivalents of the men and women described in the nineteenth-century textbooks and case-histories in the novels of William Godwin, Wilkie Collins, Anthony Hope, and others. But it is Wagner, exacting his right and revenge from a whole world of enemies, who has most to tell us about certain episodes in the work of Conrad, Ford, Lawrence, and Lewis.

(1921), a book Musil certainly knew: 'we see a man who stands in our way like a question mark, we feel that we are in contact with something flavourless, boring, and yet with a certain problematic quality about it'. What is there, Kretschmer asks, behind this 'ever-silent facade'? Nothing, he concludes, but 'broken pieces, black rubbish heaps, yawning emotional emptiness': *Physique and Character: An Investigation of the Nature of Constitution and of the Theory of Temperament*, tr. W. J. H. Sprott, rev. edn. (London: Kegan Paul, Trench, Trübner, 1936), 150.

CHAPTER 2

Paranoia, Psychoanalysis, and Cultural Theory

IT COULD BE said of 'paranoia', though not of 'dementia praecox', that it was the point of intersection between developments in descriptive psychopathology and developments in the psycho-dynamic understanding of mental illness which had preceded Freud, but which he and his followers were to put into elaborate and authoritative order.[1] Kraepelin himself, as we have seen, argued in his later work that paranoia was a psychogenic disorder, like hysteria. Freud for the most part avoided discussion of the psychoses, which he thought inaccessible to his methods;[2] but he did regard the unmistakably paranoid (or paranoid-schizophrenic) Daniel Paul Schreber as a suitable case, if not for treatment, then at least for intensive analysis. Freud's psychodynamic understanding of the mind as a site of conflict produced a new slant on paranoia. It drew attention to features of paranoid personality which descriptive psychopathology had tended to ignore or downplay: notably, I shall argue, the nausea which in some cases either inaugurates delusion, or intervenes whenever its ability to make sense of the world comes under threat; and the end-of-the-world fantasies which figure the destructiveness of the mania disgust articulates.

Freud, of course, still looms very large indeed, both in cultural theory and in cultural history. From this point of view, from outside the history of psychiatry strictly understood, an inquiry

[1] For a cogent survey and useful bibliography, see Peter Gay, *Freud: A Life for Our Time* (London: J. M. Dent, 1988), 117–31, 754–5. The standard account is Henri F. Ellenberger's comprehensive *The Discovery of the Unconscious: The History and Evolution of Dynamic Psychiatry* (London: Allen Lane, 1970).

[2] 'Finally', he told the Hungarian psychoanalyst István Hollós in Apr. 1928, 'I confessed to myself that I do not like these sick people, that I am angry at them to feel them so far from me and all that is human.' Cited by Peter Gay, *Freud*, 537.

into what paranoia 'meant' in the early decades of the twentieth century would have the effect of a double displacement. First, it would divert attention from Freud's major preoccupation with the neuroses, upon which psychoanalysis was founded, to his minor preoccupation with the psychoses (or, significantly, with *a* psychosis); secondly, it would set that minor preoccupation against the wider background of a durable psychopathological tradition which had always taken psychotic illness as an object of study and, wherever possible, treatment. For the psychodynamic explanation of paranoia was deeply antipathetic to that put forward by descriptive psychopathology. It is one which, although virtually unknown to English Modernist writers, none the less illuminates their writing.

Indeed, it is tempting to regard this new and powerful emphasis on psychic conflict as a way in which we might distinguish Modernist experiment from the forms of domestic realism and sensational romance which dominated the literary market-place in the early decades of the twentieth century. Neither D. H. Lawrence nor Wyndham Lewis, after all, could be said to have baulked at the psychodynamic. There was, even in the period before the First World War when the Modernism which will concern me here came about, a certain traffic with psychoanalysis, on Lawrence's part, and on the part of other writers.[3] In the event, I shall suggest, both Lawrence and Lewis reproduced Freud's understanding of paranoia with eerie exactitude. At the same time, however, their representations of madness also have much in common with the account provided by descriptive psychopathology.

So did Freud's, for that matter. Freud put forward a theory of paranoia aggressively at odds with the theory advanced by Krafft-Ebing, or Kraepelin, or Gaupp; but the aggression conceals a complicity. For Freud put forward his theory at a time when he was struggling to establish the psychoanalytic movement on a

[3] See e.g. Suzanne Raitt's account of May Sinclair's extensive involvement in the work of the Medico-Psychological Clinic, the first clinic in Britain to offer psychoanalytic treatment, which was founded in 1913: *May Sinclair: A Modern Victorian* (Oxford: Clarendon Press, 2000), 135–44. Raitt observes that psychoanalytic concepts 'saturated' Sinclair's thinking 'to such an extent that she would eventually be described by Katherine Mansfield as an example of a writer whose work had suffered "the eclipse of psychoanalysis"' (p. 140).

professional footing, and the emphasis the theory expounds must be regarded as among other things a bid for symbolic capital. In that respect, the drama its exposition enacts is strictly comparable to the drama subsequently enacted during Gaupp's two-hour conversation with Ernst Wagner in Tübingen in 1932. There are, in short, parallels to be drawn between the respective configurations in psychoanalysis and in descriptive psychopathology of the subject of inquiry, who seeks status through control over method, and its object, whose no less methodical anguish is an anguish at the absence or loss of status. In this chapter, I begin with an account of the theory wars provoked in and by the clash between psychoanalysis and descriptive psychopathology. I then draw out of Freud's psychodynamic model what seem to me its distinctive emphases on nausea and on end-of-the-world fantasies, relating both to a work of popular fiction.

FREUD AND SCHREBER

Freud first expressed an interest in paranoia in the 1890s in correspondence with Wilhelm Fliess.[4] He began to develop a psychoanalytic explanation of the disease in 1908, in correspondence with Jung and Ferenczi: an explanation put fully to the test in a brilliant and seminal account of the *Memoirs* of Daniel Paul Schreber published in 1911. In the *Introductory Lectures* of 1915–17, Freud told his audience that the form of disease known as paranoia, or chronic systematic insanity, occupied an 'unsettled position' in attempts at psychiatric classification. Not much was to be expected, he went on, from psychiatry. His example of its lameness was the definition of paranoia given, as we saw in the last chapter, by descriptive psychopathologists from Esquirol to Kraepelin: 'it is suggested that the patient, who, owing to a primary disposition, believes that he is being persecuted, infers from his persecution that he must be someone of quite particular importance and so develops megalomania'. For Freud, paranoid symmetry simply would not do, as an explanation. In his contrary view, megalomania was

---

[4] *The Standard Edition of the Complete Psychological Works*, ed. James Strachey *et al.*, 24 vols. (London: Hogarth Press, 1953–74), i. 206–12, 226–8. Henceforth *SE*.

'the direct result of a magnification of the ego due to the drawing in of the libidinal object-cathexes—a secondary narcissism which is a return of the original early infantile one'. An upsurge of 'homosexual impulse' brought about regression.[5] Although Schreber was Freud's *pièce de résistance*, where paranoia was concerned, he did produce a number of other analyses, all of which he took to confirm his initial hypothesis.[6]

Daniel Paul Schreber, the most exhaustively documented and debated of all psychotics, was born in Leipzig on 25 July 1842, the third child of Daniel Gottlob Moritz and Pauline Schreber.[7] He began to study law in 1860, a year before his father's death, and eventually saw service in a variety of legal capacities, including the civil administration of Alsace-Lorraine during the Franco-Prussian war. He was a member of the federal commission charged to produce a new Civil Code for the Reich. Schreber married Sabine Behr in 1878, and was appointed administrative director of the District Court in Chemnitz. During the Reichstag elections of 1884, he ran as a candidate of the National Liberal Party. His defeat by the socialist candidate provoked his first nervous break-down, which led to six months in Leipzig University's Psychiatric Hospital under the observation of the director, Paul Emil Flechsig. His primary symptom was severe hypochondria. After his release, Schreber served as a district judge in Saxony, apparently in good health. However, after his nomination as presiding judge of the third chamber of the Supreme Court of Appeals, in June 1893, he began to develop new symptoms. He assumed his post in October

---

[5] *SE* xiv. 424.

[6] e.g. 'A Case of Paranoia Running Counter to the Psychoanalytic Theory of the Disease' (1915), *SE* xiv. 263–72; and the second part of 'Some Neurotic Mechanisms in Jealousy, Paranoia, and Homosexuality' (1922), *SE* xviii. 223–32.

[7] Eric Santner offers a lucid summary of the facts of the case, and a great deal else, in *My Own Private Germany: Daniel Paul Schreber's Secret History of Modernity* (Princeton: Princeton University Press, 1996), 3–6. The studies which provoked the current interest in Schreber are Morton Schatzman, *Soul Murder: Persecution in the Family* (London: Allen Lane, 1973), and Willam G. Niederland (ed.), *The Schreber Case: Psychoanalytic Profile of a Paranoid Personality* (New York: Quadrangle, 1974). The volume of commentary shows little sign of abating. See e.g. Zvi Lothane's monumental *In Defense of Schreber: Soul Murder and Psychiatry* (Hillsdale, NJ: Analytic Press, 1992); and the essays collected in David Allison, Prado de Oliveira, Mark Roberts, and Allen Weiss (eds.), *Psychosis and Sexual Identity: Toward a Post-Analytic View of the Schreber Case* (Albany, NY: SUNY Press, 1988).

1893. Thereafter anxieties plagued him. During a bad bout of insomnia, he experienced an 'extraordinary event': time and time again a 'crackling noise' in the bedroom wall awoke him just as he was falling asleep. He thought it might be a mouse. 'But having heard similar noises innumerable times since then, and still hearing them around me every day in daytime and at night, I have come to recognize them as undoubted divine miracles.'[8] The conspiracy against him had begun.

From that moment on, Schreber was never not suspicious. By 9 November, the day before the anniversary of his father's death, he was thinking of suicide. He consulted Flechsig again, and was readmitted to the University Clinic. A few months later, while his wife was visiting her father in Berlin, his condition deteriorated. 'Decisive for my mental collapse was one particular night; during that night I had a quite unusual number of pollutions (perhaps half a dozen).'[9] It was at this point that the structure of his delusion took definitive shape. Flechsig was installed as his chief persecutor. After a brief stay at a private clinic, Schreber was transferred, on 29 June 1894, to the Royal Public Asylum at Sonnenstein, where he remained under the observation of the director, Guido Weber, until 20 December 1902. In the mean time, he had officially been declared incompetent. To get the ruling reversed, he had to file his own writ of appeal to the Supreme Court. Among the documents submitted to the court was the text of the *Memoirs*, which he had more or less completed by 1900. Following his release, he published the *Memoirs*, and went to live with his wife in Dresden. His general good health was punctuated by fits of bellowing. He did not speak much about his illness, but the voices which had tormented him for years became a kind of white noise. Sabine Schreber suffered a stroke in November 1907. Within weeks, Schreber was hospitalized for the third and last time, at a new state asylum in the village of Dösen, outside Leipzig. He remained there until his death on 14 April 1911. Among the symptoms recorded in his chart are outbursts of laughter and screaming, periods of depressive stupor and insomnia, and fantasies of his own decomposition.

[8] *Memoirs of my Nervous Illness*, ed. and tr. Ida Macalpine and Richard A. Hunter (London: William Dawson, 1955), 64. Henceforth *Mem*. First publ. as *Denkwürdigkeiten eines Nervenkranken* in 1903.
[9] *Mem*. 68.

The drift of Freud's 'Psychoanalytic Notes on an Auto-biographical Account of a Case of Paranoia (Dementia Paranoides)' (1911) becomes clear in the first section, which establishes the facts of the case by reference both to the *Memoirs* and to material submitted to the Supreme Court of Saxony. The salient features of Schreber's delusional system are said to be the belief that he has been chosen by God to redeem the world from the chaos generated in large measure by his own nervous agitation, and the belief that God will transform him into a woman and inseminate him in order to create a new race. In Freud's view, the second of these beliefs, the fantasy of feminization or *Entmannung* ('unmanning'), came first. 'There can be no doubt, moreover, that originally he believed that the transformation was to be effected for the purpose of sexual abuse and not so as to serve higher designs.' It was only later that he started to think of himself as the Redeemer, at which point God took Flechsig's place in the annals of persecution. The delusion of grandeur thus supplements the delusion of persecution, retroactively endowing the abjectness that had entailed with sublimity. Freud's version of paranoid symmetry insists, as his commitment to libido theory required, on the primacy of sexual motive. Its major claim is that paranoia is brought on by a return of repressed homosexuality, and its most gripping insights have to do with the mechanism of projection whereby the paranoiac expels feelings or wishes which he or she finds too shameful to acknowledge. What is expelled in fantasies of persecution, Freud observes, is inadmissible homoerotic desire: '*I* (a man) *love him* (a man)' becomes 'I do not *love* him—I *hate* him', which in turn becomes, by projection, 'I do not *love* him, I *hate* him, because he persecutes me'.[10] By this account, the paranoiac attributes the hatred he has unconsciously made of his love to someone else.

It has become customary to read Freud's account of Schreber allegorically, as a reflection on his highly charged friendship with Wilhelm Fliess (1858–1928), which he was at that time bringing to an end. 'To study Schreber was to remember Fliess,' Peter Gay remarks, 'but to remember Fliess was also to understand Schreber.'[11] Fliess, indeed, served as a kind of proto-Schreber. In February 1908, when he was formulating his ideas about the relation between

---

[10] *SE* xii. 18, 63.   [11] *Freud*, 279.

paranoia and homosexuality, Freud told Jung that Fliess had 'developed a dreadful case of paranoia after throwing off his affection for me, which was undoubtedly considerable. I owe this idea to him, i.e. to his behaviour.'[12] The paranoid symmetry we have already observed in Gaupp's relation to Ernst Wagner, and Kretschmer's to Helene Renner, here obtains, even more troublingly, between one colleague and another. On 6 October 1910, Freud told Sándor Ferenczi, who had been with him in Italy the previous summer when he was working on the Schreber material, that this work had enabled him to sublimate his own homosexual inclinations. 'A piece of homosexual charge has been withdrawn and utilized for the enlargement of my own ego. I have succeeded where the paranoiac fails.'[13] Fliess was soon to be reincarnated in two particularly troublesome members of Freud's Vienna circle, Alfred Adler (1870–1937) and Wilhelm Stekel (1868–1940). In December 1910, Freud told Ferenczi that he had now 'overcome' Fliess. But he added immediately that 'Adler is a little Fliess redivivus, just as paranoid. Stekel, as appendix to him, is at least named Wilhelm.'[14] In the same month he told Jung that Adler awakened in him the memory of Fliess. 'The same paranoia.'[15] Hard at work on Schreber, Freud was also hard at work on the future of psychoanalysis itself. Could it be that the future depended on the proliferation rather than the overcoming of paranoia?

The problem with Freud's emphasis on Schreber's delusions of persecution, in which he has been followed by the majority of commentators, is that it relegates the equally prominent delusions of grandeur to the status of an epiphenomenon. Eric Santner has recently offered a valuable corrective to this emphasis. Santner draws attention to the surprising vehemence with which, towards the end of his essay, Freud insists on the originality of the views he has advanced, defending it against the claims not only of other theorists, but of Schreber himself.

---

[12] *The Freud/Jung Letters*, ed. William McGuire, tr. Ralph Manheim and R. F. C. Hull (London: Hogarth Press, 1974), 121. Henceforth *Freud/Jung*.

[13] Cited by Gay, *Freud*, 275. According to Eve Sedgwick, the value of Freud's conclusion that paranoia in men results from repressed homosexual desire lies in its exposure of 'intense male homosocial desire' as at once the most compulsory and most dangerous of social bonds in 19th-cent. bourgeois society: *Epistemology of the Closet* (Berkeley, Calif.: University of California Press, 1990), 186–7.

[14] Gay, *Freud*, 274.   [15] *Freud/Jung*, 376.

Schreber's 'rays of God', which are made up of a condensation of the sun's rays, of nerve-fibres, and of spermatozoa, are in reality nothing else than a concrete representation and projection outwards of libidinal cathexes; and they thus lend his delusions a striking conformity with our theory. His belief that the world must come to an end because his ego was attracting all the rays to itself, his anxious concern at a later period, during the process of reconstruction, lest God should sever his ray-connection with him,—these and many other details of Schreber's delusional structure sound almost like endopsychic perceptions of the processes whose existence I have assumed in these pages as the basis of our explanation of paranoia. I can nevertheless call a friend and fellow-specialist to witness that I had developed my theory of paranoia before I became acquainted with the contents of Schreber's book. It remains for the future to decide whether there is more delusion in my theory than I should like to admit, or whether there is more truth in Schreber's delusion than other people are as yet prepared to believe.[16]

The friend and fellow-specialist was Ferenczi, who is here implored to deny not only Schreber's claim to priority, but his own.[17] Santner points out that Freud reproduces in this passage Schreber's intense anxiety about the originality of his own thoughts. 'If there is indeed a transferential dimension to Freud's passionate involvement with the Schreber material,' he concludes, 'then it concerns not only matters of same-sex passion but also questions of originality and influence, questions pertaining to the transfer of knowledge and authority in the very domain that Freud was staking out as his own.' Santner draws on Bourdieu's analysis of symbolic capital to suggest that what was at issue in Freud's claim to priority was the 'performative magic' necessary to re-establish his status and prestige in a movement under threat both from within and from without. Freud's crisis, in 1910, like Schreber's in 1884 and 1893, was a crisis of symbolic investiture: a ceremony which, as Bourdieu puts it, sanctions and sanctifies a difference, by making it known and recognized as such.[18] Freud,

---

[16] *SE* xii. 79.

[17] Pamela Thurschwell has described the priority dispute between Freud and Ferenczi in an illuminating essay about relations between the two men: 'Ferenczi's Dangerous Proximities: Telepathy, Psychosis and the Real Event', *differences*, 11 (1999), 150–78. I am grateful to her for her comments on a draft of this chapter.

[18] *My Own Private Germany*, 20–1, 23–6. The reference is to Bourdieu, *Language and Symbolic Power*, tr. Gino Raymond and Matthew Adamson (Cambridge, Mass.:

in effect, *performed* libidinal theory, in his reflections on Schreber, in order to establish it as the embodiment and emblem of psychoanalytic legitimacy. To fail to acknowledge it, as Adler and Stekel did, and Jung after them, was to earn expulsion from the movement.

Santner goes on to explore in illuminating detail various aspects of Schreber's 'private Germany' (the array of anxieties, irreducible to homosexual panic, which viscerally impeded his progress towards symbolic investiture). But I think that his account of Freud's investment in the Schreber material requires two minor qualifications. The first concerns Freud's affinity for Schreber, for paranoia. What exactly was the status of the 'truth' in Schreber's delusion which other people were so reluctant to admit? Santner summarizes the crisis of investiture Freud brought on in himself through his study of Schreber as an anxiety that he, a 'scientist', might be thought to have 'plagiarized a dement'.[19] Accurate though this is as an indication of Freud's state of mind, it unnecessarily closes off the possibility that Freud did not regard Schreber as a 'dement'. As we have seen, the differential diagnosis of paranoia as a disease which did not exhibit the symptoms of schizophrenia had already been instituted by the time Freud wrote his essay. Although its title hesitates between 'paranoia' and 'dementia paranoides', and although it draws heavily on Karl Abraham's paper on 'The Psycho-Sexual Differences between Hysteria and Dementia Praecox',[20] the essay insists, as vehemently as Gaupp and Kretschmer were to do, that paranoia 'should be maintained as an independent clinical type, however frequently the picture it offers may be complicated by the presence of schizophrenic features'.[21] The basis of Freud's identification with and fear of Schreber lies in the degree to which Schreber was *not* a dement. To put it another way, paranoia resembled the science Freud was seeking to establish to the extent that there was method in both madnesses.

Harvard University Press, 1991), 119. Santner observes that in the notion of transference psychoanalysis 'has, in essence, formally inscribed the dependence on performativity into its very foundations' (p. 25).

[19] *My Own Private Germany*, 21.

[20] *Selected Papers*, tr. Douglas Bryan and Alix Strachey, with an introductory memoir by Ernest Jones (London: Maresfield Reprints, 1979), 64–79. Abraham, of course, like Jung, was heavily involved in Bleuler's efforts to redefine dementia praecox.

[21] *SE* xii. 76.

Unable to accept that the world really is as it seems, Krafft-Ebing had concluded, the paranoiac goes looking for secrets, for concealed motives and intentions. He or she notices 'behind' the phenomena something which does not 'belong' to them.[22] The something Freud had noticed 'behind' phenomena was of course the insistence of sexuality, and the system he had developed to account for it was libido theory, a theory which could be said to have found astounding confirmation in Schreber's *Memoirs*. Freud's method was suspicion.[23] 'One day I was to examine a young man, whom I did not know, at his mother's house', Freud had written in *The Psychopathology of Everyday Life* (1901): 'As he came towards me I was struck by a large stain on his trousers—made by albumen, as I could tell from its peculiar stiff edges.' The young man apologized for the mess, explaining that he had just taken a raw egg to ease a sore throat; as soon as his mother left the room, Freud, 'without further ado', raised the topic of masturbation.[24] For Freud, the stain was an overdetermined symptom rather than an underdetermined event (a chance event, an event whose causality is not worth pursuing). 'The task', as he was to put it in the *Introductory Lectures*, 'is then simply to discover, in respect to a senseless idea and a pointless action, the past situation in which the idea was justified and the action served a purpose.'[25] Psychoanalytic theory constructs a parallel universe in which an intense desire to make meaning has displaced a tolerance of or complicity with cause and effect.

[22] *Textbook of Insanity*, tr. Charles Gilbert Chaddock (Philadelphia: F. A. Davis, 1904), 368–9, 373–4.

[23] In a classic study, Paul Ricœur places Freud with Marx and Nietzsche in a 'school of suspicion'. 'Beginning with them', Ricœur argues, 'understanding is hermeneutics: henceforward, to seek meaning is no longer to spell out the consciousness of meaning, but to *decipher its expressions.*' Suspicion confronts, not an implicit meaning which must be made explicit, but a systematic attempt to conceal or to distort meaning. The 'man of suspicion', he adds, in a formulation which has considerable resonance for my argument, 'carries out in reverse the work of falsification of the man of guile'. Guile will be met by double guile. See *Freud and Philosophy: An Essay on Interpretation*, tr. Denis Savage (New Haven, Conn.: Yale University Press, 1970), 32–4. Ricœur does not develop this suggestion of a certain paranoia at work within the hermeneutic project.

[24] *SE* vi. 199–200. Freud's psychopathology of everyday life develops a 'scientific reading of apparently causeless and inexplicable events', as Peter Gay puts it, in order to reveal 'the hidden order governing the human mind': *Freud*, 125. Freud himself spoke of the danger, in interpreting parapraxes, of a 'combinatory paranoia' which makes too much out of 'small indications': *SE* xv. 66.

[25] *SE* xvi. 270.

The *Psychopathology* offers a wonderfully lucid account of the denial of contingency in paranoia to which Krafft-Ebing had drawn attention. Paranoiacs, Freud observed, 'attach the greatest significance to the minor details of other people's behaviour which we ordinarily neglect, interpret them and make them the basis of far-reaching conclusions'. One patient noticed the way people flourish their walking-sticks, another a hand-movement made simultaneously by the passengers on a train. 'The category of what is accidental and requires no motivation, in which the normal person includes a part of his own psychical performances and para-praxes, is thus rejected by the paranoiac as far as the psychical manifestations of other people are concerned.' Freud found reason to admire such curiosity, such attentiveness. The paranoiac, he concluded, 'sees more clearly than someone of normal intellectual capacity'; but the 'displacement on to other people' of the state of affairs he alone can recognize 'renders his knowledge worthless'.[26] He was to make the same point in 'Some Neurotic Mechanisms', where he suggests that paranoiacs 'let themselves be guided by their knowledge of the unconscious, and displace to the uncon-scious minds of others the attention which they have withdrawn from their own'. Much the same might be said, surely, about the analyst's relation to his or her patient. Like paranoia, psychoanaly-sis involves 'the hypercathexis of the interpretations of someone else's unconscious'.[27]

In the Schreber essay, Freud placed considerable emphasis on the constructiveness of paranoid delusion. The paranoiac rebuilds the world which has been destroyed around him (which he has had to destroy because it remains stubbornly indifferent to him). 'He builds it up by the work of his delusions. *The delusional forma-tion, which we take to be the pathological product, is in reality an attempt at recovery, a process of reconstruction.*' Freud marvels at the autonomy of the world reconstructed in and by delusion. In paranoia, the process of repression which detaches libido from people and things previously loved happens in silence, as it were. What forces itself 'noisily' on our attention, by contrast, is the process of recovery which brings libido back again on to the people and things it had previously abandoned. 'In paranoia this process is carried out by

[26] *SE* vi. 254–6.   [27] *SE* xviii. 226, 228.

the method of projection. It was incorrect to say that the perception which was suppressed internally is projected outwards; the truth is rather, as we now see, that what was abolished internally returns from without.' It is as though the methods of psychoanalysis reach, in this self-correction, some kind of limit.[28] In 'The Neuro-Psychoses of Defence' (1894), Freud had suggested that there are mechanisms 'much more energetic and successful' than the repression found in neurosis. In psychosis, the ego 'rejects (*verwirft*)' the incompatible idea together with its affect, and in general behaves as though the whole ghastly experience had never happened at all.[29] The violence with which that idea 'returns from without' in persecutory mania is thus a product of the violence with which it had once been expelled from within.[30]

Freud, I think, grasped the violence at work (or at play) in psychosis far more effectively than the descriptive psychologists. He did so, one might note, not through analysis or self-analysis, but through a critical reading of an 'autobiographical account' of severe illness. The affinity Freud felt for Schreber, an affinity he could not have admitted in his feelings for one of his own patients, had a great deal to do with his determination to take part in, and indeed to control, nosological debate. He had to become Schreber, a better Schreber than Fliess, or Adler, or Stekel could ever be, in order to

---

[28] *SE* xii. 70–1: emphasis in original. The passage was a key text and Schreber a key figure for Jacques Lacan, who took over from Freud the task of defining a defence mechanism specific to psychosis. Building on hints in the case-history of the 'Wolf Man' (*SE* xvii. 1–122), Lacan identified *Verwerfung*, which he translates as *forclusion*, as the defence mechanism specific to psychosis. If repression confines the incompatible idea within the unconscious, foreclosure expels it. According to Lacan, what is foreclosed in psychosis is the Name-of-the-Father, the 'paternal metaphor', the symbol of an authority whose intervention in psychic life makes symbolism possible. And what has been foreclosed—i.e. 'refused' in the symbolic order—inevitably 'returns in the real': *The Psychoses: The Seminar of Jacques Lacan*, ed. Jacques-Alain Miller, tr. Russell Grigg (London: Routledge, 1993), 12–13. Lacan published his doctoral dissertation on paranoia in 1932, and sent a copy to Freud: *De la psychose paranoïaque dans ses rapports avec la personnalité* (Paris: Éditions du Seuil, 1975).

[29] *SE* iii. 58.

[30] Peter Gay dramatizes the violence inherent in Freud's psychodynamic model of the mind by comparing the unconscious to 'a maximum-security prison holding antisocial inmates languishing for years or recently arrived, inmates harshly treated and heavily guarded, but barely kept under control and forever attempting to escape': *Freud*, 128. By that standard, whatever comes back from the outside in psychosis must be reckoned to do so with the force of an invading army. This was after all an era of arms race and invasion scare.

defeat, as Schreber had in a sense defeated, official psychiatry. It may be no coincidence that the first statement in the essay of the need to distinguish between paranoia and dementia praecox—an implicit refutation of the dominance of the latter concept in official psychiatry—immediately precedes the astonishing *tour de force* of its exposition of the 'grammar' of persecutory delusion.[31] This is the text's moment of 'paranoid illumination', one might say, and it arises out of an anxiety about status, about symbolic investiture.

My second qualification of Santner's argument therefore concerns his exclusive emphasis, in itself extremely valuable, on relations within the group of psychoanalytic pioneers. Santner argues that the key to Freud's symbolic investiture as the group's leader depended on his claim to originality. However, as Perkin points out in his critique of Bourdieu, the conversion of symbolic into material property depends not on specialized training as such, including the development of original ideas, but on control of the market.[32] At the time when he was studying Schreber, a time when 'official science' consistently boycotted physicians who sought to apply psychoanalysis in their practice, Freud had begun to think about the establishment of institutes which would turn psychoanalysis itself into an official science by guaranteeing the competence of its practitioners. It was this aim, and nothing else, he later wrote in his 'History of the Psychoanalytic Movement', which prompted him to found the International Psychoanalytic Association: the main accomplishment of the Nürnberg Congress of 30–1 March 1910.[33] 'With the Nürnberg *Reichstag*', Freud told Ferenczi triumphantly on 3 April, 'the childhood of our movement has ended.'[34] We need also to consider relations *beyond* the group of pioneers. The language of violent *Verwerfung* which Freud used about rivals outside the group was a product of the nosological

---

[31] *SE* xii. 62–3. Freud identifies a similar disposition to narcissism in paranoia and in 'patients suffering from Kraepelin's dementia praecox or (as Bleuler has named it) *schizophrenia*'. His aim is to trace back differences between the two disorders to differences of 'dispositional fixation'.

[32] *Rise of Professional Society*, 7.

[33] *SE* xiv. 42–4.

[34] Cited by Gay, *Freud*, 218. The Schreber analysis might be considered the mature product of the movement's adulthood. In a letter of 17 Oct. 1911, Ernest Jones commented on the 'enormous clarification' it had brought about. 'Was there ever a new science that progressed at such a pace?' (*Complete Correspondence*, 117).

debate required by competition for status in the market-place, and itself reproduced, as we shall see, the terms of that debate.

Freud's earliest adherents in the Vienna Psychoanalytic Society found Jung's appointment as the Association's president hard to swallow, and held a private meeting to discuss the outrage and its consequences. Freud, who had not been invited, put in an appearance. According to Fritz Wittels, who was present, he informed the assembled physicians, most of whom were Jewish, that as Jews they were not competent to 'win friends' for the new teaching. 'It is absolutely essential', he went on, 'that I should form ties in the world of general science. I am getting on in years, and am weary of being perpetually attacked. We are all in danger.' The Swiss, in the shape of Jung, who was not only a gentile but a colleague of the celebrated Eugen Bleuler at the celebrated Burghölzli Mental Hospital, would undoubtedly save them all.[35] Freud was then not quite 54, but he knew that in order to lead the movement effectively he had to forge alliances—and pick fights—beyond it. Feelings of persecution suited at least one of those purposes admirably. The help he sought in establishing the movement's credentials, and thus gaining control of the market in mental therapies, was not only that of the world of general science. When, in February 1910, Jung was invited to join a new International Order for Ethics and Culture, Freud for a moment thought there might be something in it. The programme's 'aggressive and protective aspect' seemed to him a way in which psychoanalysis might arm itself against its 'future adversaries' with 'methods other than those of scientific work'.[36] Freud seems here to have created a parallel universe in which persecutions yet to come justify the immediate implementation of methods supplementary to a specific expertise which will establish its superiority in advance.

Freud's correspondence with Jung, his closest ally during this period, and his link to the world of general science, provides considerable insight into the ways in which psychoanalysis was arming itself against future adversaries with a variety of weapons, scientific and otherwise. The enemies within the movement were of course troublesome, but Freud could at least discern in their behaviour a reflection of his own. To characterize Adler as a para-

---

[35] Quoted by Gay, *Freud*, 218.   [36] *Freud/Jung*, 295.

noiac was after all to confer upon him the status of 'the wonderful Schreber', who, as Freud told Jung on 22 April 1910, 'ought to have been made a professor of psychiatry and director of a mental hospital'.[37] In his 1914 essay 'On Narcissism', Freud was to examine in detail the link between paranoia and the construction of speculative systems. There he maintains that the paranoiac is an interpreter of an especially ambitious and systematic kind, who displaces the love he has withdrawn from the world into hermeneutic activity.[38]

The movement's adversaries, or those who hovered uncertainly around its periphery, found themselves on the receiving end of an altogether different terminology. Jung had undertaken to establish the Association's Zurich group, and to secure Bleuler as its first president. Bleuler, alas, got away. But Jung was not to worry, Freud said, since Bleuler's tendency to confuse the progress of science with social amelioration—he was a strong advocate of abstinence societies—rendered him unfit for such a role. 'We can't very well inscribe such things as providing freezing schoolchildren with warm clothing on our banners side by side with the furtherance of [psychoanalysis]', he thundered. The movement's single-mindedness gave it the advantage: 'when a man stands firm as a rock, all the tottering, wavering souls end by clinging to him for support'.[39] The paranoia in this response to the failure of a promising alliance finds expression as machismo.

Consider also the fate of the unfortunate Adolf Albrecht Friedländer (1870–1949), psychiatrist at the Hohe Mark Sanatorium, near Frankfurt am Main, who began to make a nuisance of himself in the autumn of 1909 by publishing a series of attacks on psychoanalysis. At first, Freud advocated turning the other cheek. What Friedländer wanted, he told Jung on 17 October, was rehabilitation through the movement's hostility. 'Now he is inconsolable because we have shown by our silence that we regarded him as unfit to duel with, so to speak.'[40] The self-conscious turn of phrase foreshadows the terms in which the engagement was to be conducted. On 17 April 1910, Jung reported that Friedländer had been 'puking' again, in an attack on

---

[37] Ibid. 311.   [38] *SE* xiv. 67–102.
[39] *Freud/Jung*, 314.   [40] Ibid. 253.

Ernest Jones's interpretation of *Hamlet*. To the man standing firm as a rock, such criticism must seem like a mess to be sluiced away. In the same letter, Jung records his powerful sense that psychoanalytic inquiry had created for him a kind of parallel universe. 'I often feel I am wandering alone through a strange country, seeing wonderful things that no-one has seen before and no-one needs to see.'[41]

On 28 May 1910, someone calling himself Hofrat Schottländer phoned Freud to ask whether he could come and see him. It turned out to be Friedländer, who had thought Freud might not admit him under his own name, and who on gaining access immediately began to abuse Freud's disciples. What interests me about Freud's report of the incident is the pleasure he takes in recalling his own brutality. Friedländer 'whined and whimpered', he told Jung, 'but he was helpless against my [psycho]analytic frankness'. Freud's final judgement on his visitor was that he was a 'braggart and faker', and, unfortunately, a man of considerable influence. This capacity for influence earned the braggart a violent *Verwerfung* both from Freud's study and from polite consideration. If Friedländer had not remained wholly unaware of himself, Freud concluded savagely, he would 'drown in filth'.[42] Friedländer, Jung joyously concurred, was a 'slimy bastard' whose 'filth' could be read in his face; his own inclination under those circumstances would have been to administer a 'sound Swiss thrashing'.[43] On his return from Rome, where he had been working with Ferenczi on the Schreber material, Freud took the opportunity to deride another article by the 'fleetingly improvised Professor and Hofrat Schottländer'. 'Fleeting-improvised-men' was Schreber's term for 'human shapes set down for a short time by divine miracles only to be dissolved again'.[44] Freud could imagine how Friedländer might appear from Schreber's point of view, but he could not imagine Friedländer *as* Schreber; that would have been to do the slimy bastard too much honour. Psychoanalysis was too good for such people, Jung responded: Freud should adopt his own 'kicking-out technique'.[45] That is exactly what he *had* done, Freud bristled in return, before going on to reiterate his view that paranoia stems

[41] *Freud/Jung*, 308.   [42] Ibid. 322–4.   [43] Ibid. 325.
[44] Ibid. 354. For the 'fleeting-improvised-men', see Schreber, *Mem.* 43.
[45] *Freud/Jung*, 356.

from a 're-cathexis' of 'homosexual leaning', and to worry that people might think he had lifted his theory from the *Memoirs*.[46] The methods Freud and Jung deployed against the contemptible but influential (and therefore persecutory) Friedländer were those of disgust (one does not argue with messes, one wipes them up) and of disavowal (the kicking-out technique). Their behaviour towards him must be reckoned mildly psychotic.

Freud had one language for his rivals within the movement, and another for his rivals without. In a letter written on 25 November 1910, he spoke of Adler's paranoia, and expressed his delight that Friedländer had once been caught cheating at cards.[47] Jung soon outdid him in bloodcurdling threats against the 'hogs' whose hoggishness gave them every reason to oppose the movement.[48] Of course, rivals within might turn into rivals without. At that moment, their madness ceased to be an honourable madness, a paranoia. Writing to Jung on 5 July 1910, Freud complained that the behaviour of the 'Zürich people' had become 'extraordinarily schizophrenic'.[49] They, presumably, unlike Schreber, really *were* dements. Freud's comment reproduces the nosological distinction between paranoia and dementia praecox as a distinction between 'us' and 'them', as an expression of disgust and disavowal. The worst thing that could ever happen to you, after all, was not that you might find yourself trapped in a delusionary system, but that your delusions might be entirely without system. Freud's aversion to schizophrenia had something to do with his failure to understand it, and something to do with descriptive psychopathology's apparent success.

PARANOID NAUSEA

I have noted the metaphors Freud and Jung thought fit to apply to the fleetingly improvised Friedländer. While the pioneers remain rock-hard and implacable, their detractor-in-chief whines, wriggles, and squirms. He is soft, slimy. He spreads his filth. He vomits his calumnies. What was even worse, perhaps, was the thought

---

[46] Ibid. 357.   [47] Ibid. 373.   [48] Ibid. 375.
[49] Ibid. 339.

that Friedländer had tricked his way into their homes. He had spread his stench inside psychoanalysis. He had polluted its hearth, and wallowed like a hog on its best carpet. Like foreign matter, he must be expelled, spat out—projected, one might say.

The feeling of disgust has played a minor but by no means insignificant part in descriptions of paranoid fantasy from Esquirol through Kraepelin and Freud to *DSM-IV*. While the presence of hallucinations has generally been thought to distinguish schizophrenia from paranoia, a note in *DSM-IV* stipulates that 'tactile and olfactory hallucinations' may occur in paranoia if they are connected to the delusional theme.[50] Touch and smell are the faculties of contamination. To touch something repellent is to feel polluted; to inhale a bad smell is to have the bad smell inside you before you know it is there. The only possible response is nausea: to void oneself, to wipe oneself clean. We have already seen, in Prichard's clergyman, a person whose peculiarity of habit was to rinse his mouth with water and spit it out in accordance with a pattern of projections.[51] Paranoia's commitment to system has as its obverse a commitment to nausea.

It is possible that the new diagnosis of dementia praecox, and the need to preserve the diagnosis of paranoia against it, helped to bring these commitments into sharper focus. For the schizophrenic, as the literature on schizophrenia had made abundantly clear, knows neither orderliness nor nausea. 'Let us suppose ourselves', Karl Abraham wrote in the paper upon which Freud drew in his analysis of Schreber,

in a mental hospital. We see before us a patient suffering from a severe form of the illness and in an advanced stage of it . . . He speaks to nobody and avoids everyone. He has no desire to occupy himself, neglects his appearance, eats noisily, is dirty, smears himself with excrement and masturbates openly without shame. It is as though his surroundings did not exist for him.[52]

It is utterly inconceivable that Schreber, or Ernst Wagner, or

---

[50] *Diagnostic and Statistical Manual of Mental Disorders*, 4th edn. (Washington, DC: American Psychiatric Association, 1994), 301. Henceforth *DSM-IV*.

[51] *A Treatise on Insanity and Other Disorders Affecting the Mind* (London: Sherwood, Gilbert & Piper, 1835), 51.

[52] 'Psycho-Sexual Differences' (see n. 20 above), 68.

Prichard's clergyman, would ever have behaved in such a fashion. And the mess which does not seem to bother Abraham's patient is as much in the mind as on the body. It is constituted by the 'amorphous mass' of delusional ideas which Bleuler found in schizophrenia, but not in paranoia.[53]

I have already written at some length elsewhere about the disgust which mess provokes, and I do not want to repeat myself here.[54] But I think that it is important for my current purposes to say something about the narrative and rhetorical uses to which feelings of disgust have been put in the descriptions or self-descriptions of patients diagnosed as paranoid or paranoid schizophrenic. For it would seem that paranoia mobilizes disgust at moments of crisis, moments when the 'still persisting central core of the personality', in Kretschmer's phrase, is felt to be under threat. By contrast, the early psychiatric literature often defined those kinds of schizophrenia which did not involve paranoid delusion in terms of the absence of feelings of disgust.[55]

A characteristic delusion in paranoid schizophrenia concerns the so-called 'influencing machine' which has somehow taken control of the patient's thoughts and feelings. In 1919, the Freudian Victor Tausk, who understood psychotic self-disturbance as a 'loss of ego boundaries', described how a patient of his, Natalija A., had fallen under the influence of an 'electrical machine' made in Berlin.[56] The machine took the form of a human body, indeed of her own body, though its head remained invisible. Natalija felt that she was incapable of purposeful action; her own experiences were mere epiphenomena, automatic responses to the obscene promptings of a machine whose exact location could only be said to be 'elsewhere'. 'Those who handle the machine produce a slimy

[53] *Dementia Praecox, or The Group of Schizophrenias*, tr. Joseph Zinkin (New York: International Universities Press, 1950), 125. Henceforth *DPGS*.

[54] *Cooking with Mud* (Oxford: OUP, 2000), ch. 5. There are extremely useful facts and observations to be found in William Ian Miller's recent *The Anatomy of Disgust* (Cambridge, Mass.: Harvard University Press, 1997).

[55] Abraham, 'Psycho-Sexual Differences', 73; Kraepelin, *Dementia Praecox and Paraphrenia*, ed. George M. Robertson, tr. R. Mary Barclay (New York: Robert E. Krieger Publishing Co., 1971), 34. According to Bleuler, schizophrenic hallucinations do include disgusting tastes and smells, but not with any special emphasis: *DPGS*, 105.

[56] 'On the Origin of the "Influencing Machine" in Schizophrenia', *Psychoanalytical Quarterly*, 2 (1933), 519–36.

substance in her nose, disgusting smells, dreams, thoughts, feelings.'[57] It seems odd that a persecutory system equipped with all the most up-to-date technology, as this one was, should have its way by the manufacture of snot and bad smells. In Tausk's terms, the disgust these products aroused in Natalija were a despairing protest at the loss of ego boundaries. When something bad is already inside us, we can only protect ourselves by a gesture of expulsion: by spitting it out, by vomiting. Nausea restores the violated boundary between inside and outside, self and world. Natalija's disgust was perhaps the only feeling she could still call her own.

To put it another way, nausea may be, in its vehement restoration of boundaries, the final act of that genius for system-building on which the essential dignity of paranoia depends. The slime the machine produces must seem, in its repellent viscosity, in the overpowering organicism of its trace, a threat to the very principle of system. Disgust is somehow paranoia's most rational act.

The first extended case-history of a paranoid schizophrenic is John Haslam's *Illustrations of Madness* (1810).[58] Haslam, apothecary (or resident medical officer) at Bethlem Hospital, wrote the book in order to justify the confinement of one James Tilly Matthews, whose family were petitioning vigorously for his release. Matthews was committed to Bethlem in January 1797, and remained there until 1809, when his relatives petitioned for his release, on the grounds that he was sane, and that conditions in the hospital were destroying his health. In my next chapter, I shall discuss the relation between Matthews's career-ambitions, the political developments which he hoped would further those ambitions, and the content of his paranoid fantasies. Here, I want simply to draw attention to the Schreberian uses to which he put his feelings of disgust.

[57] Ibid. 530. In his excellent commentary on Tausk's paper, Tim Armstrong concentrates on the visual dimension of Natalija A.'s hallucinations: the 'influencing machine', which can create pictures as well as sensations, is itself an image of the patient's genitalia. Seen in this light, Armstrong comments, Modernism's insistence on the 'ontological priority' of the body is the opposite of materialism. 'Williams's Modernist slogan "No ideas but in things" (or no ideas but those located in the body) *is* at one level paranoia; a paranoia which attempts to defend the reality of body experience at the point where it is already penetrated by the desiring machines of modernity': *Modernism, Technology, and the Body* (Cambridge: Cambridge University Press, 1998), 105.

[58] *Illustrations of Madness*, ed. Roy Porter (London: Routledge, 1988). The biographical details which follow are taken from Porter's illuminating introduction.

According to Haslam, Matthews believed that a gang of spies and criminals skilled in pneumatic chemistry had taken up residence at London Wall in Moorfields, close to Bethlem, and had chosen to torment him by means of an 'Air Loom', a diabolical machine emitting rays. Interestingly enough, given the Air Loom's appearance of high technology, the preparations employed in it for the purposes of 'assailment' include a wide range of putrid effluvia and noxious gases. Vilest of all is the 'Egyptian snuff', a 'dusty vapour', and extremely nauseous. In a footnote, Haslam explains that the Egyptian snuff comes into effect when the 'pneumatic adepts' have placed Matthews, by their 'dream-workings', in the marshes near the mouth of the Nile, at that season when the heat is most oppressive, and the stagnant pools diffuse a 'putrid and suffocating stench': the eye being equally 'disgusted' by the landscape, 'which is made to assume a hateful tinge, resembling the dirty and cold blue of a scorbutic ulcer'. From this 'cheerless scene', the adepts awaken Matthews abruptly, 'when he finds his nostrils stuffed, his mouth furred, and himself nearly choaked by the poisonous effects of their Egyptian snuff'.[59] This, perhaps, is the kind of hallucination *DSM-IV* might allow in a diagnosis of delusional disorder. For the problem with the Egyptian snuff, as with Natalija A.'s slime, is that it is always already inside Matthews before he becomes aware of it. Nausea is his response, a temporary restoration of the integrity of the boundaries which define him.

Disgust appears in Schreber's *Memoirs of my Nervous Illness* at the moment when he is describing how God, in order to counteract his extraordinary powers of attraction, has sought to unman him. Schreber says that he regarded this as among the worst of his torments. 'I myself felt the danger of unmanning for a long time as a threatening ignominy, especially while there was the possibility of my body being sexually abused by other people.' He reacted to the diffusion throughout his body of 'female nerves, or nerves of voluptuousness', by exerting his 'sense of manly honour'. However, God's assault on him continued, in an increasingly desperate attempt to extinguish that still dangerously attractive manliness. 'Incessantly therefore, day after day and hour after hour, poison of corpses and other putrid matter which the rays carried was heaped upon my body, in the belief that it would be possible in this way to suffocate me eventually and in particular to rob me of my reason.'[60] In Schreber's case, the boundary violated by the influencing machine, a boundary which would only ever be put back into place by nausea, was the boundary between masculinity and femininity. Nausea was the only manliness he could still call his own.

It is interesting, from the point of view I am trying to develop, that Schreber should also associate these inflictions of nauseous matter with a particular use (or abuse) of language. There is, he thought, a kind of 'nerve-language', of which the healthy human being remains unaware; as, for example, when a child learns a poem by heart, or a priest a sermon. Nerve-language, we might say, is language mechanically reproduced. Schreber felt that it was inflicted on him by talking birds, inside which there were 'remnants' of the souls of human beings. To him, the 'senseless phrases' these birds reeled off mechanically were like the 'poison of corpses'.[61] His objection to the birds was an objection to the echolalia characteristic, according to the textbooks, of dementia praecox. The toxins secreted in the birdsong Schreber thought he heard were, as Santner puts it, 'bits of linguistic matter, phrases learned by rote and repeated mechanically *without concern for meaning*'.[62] Echolalia, like echopraxis, brings social mimesis back to haunt the asylum.

Paranoid disgust reinforces the systematic nature of the delusion in which the paranoiac is enclosed. It acts as a kind of direction-finder, enabling the subject of the delusion to locate and identify his or her persecutors: for the machines which heap one with putrid matter, or secrete slime and Egyptian snuff in one's nostrils, must be controlled by *someone*, in Moorfields, or Berlin, or wher-ever. The paranoiac's disgust is always a response to the machina-tions of an enemy. In so far as disgust makes it possible to locate and identify a diabolical persecutor, it becomes a source of mean-ing. There is no such thing as accidental disgust in paranoia, because in paranoia there is no such thing as accident. According to Krafft-Ebing, the vivid hallucinations experienced by patients whom he thought of as paranoid were invariably of a 'hostile and

---

[60] *Mem.* 120–1.   [61] *Mem.* 69, 167.   [62] *My Private Germany*, 34.

unpleasant' nature. Food tasted of arsenic, chloroform, or faeces; drink, of urine. There was a stench of decay. All these sensations would strengthen the patient in his conviction that an attempt was being made to destroy him.[63]

We need, I think, to understand how and why these commentaries on slime and snuff are tied into the production of paranoid meaning and value. One kind of theory disgust has invited is the kind which conceives of many varieties of conscious and unconscious behaviour as an attempt to impose order on experience. According to this view, even bodily paroxysm can be a way to confront and resolve urgent abstract dilemmas: you vomit because you have lost confidence in your ability to make sense of the world. Disgust is the product of conceptual trauma. The two classic statements, one anthropological in emphasis, the other psychoanalytic, both widely influential in cultural theory and cultural history, are Mary Douglas's *Purity and Danger* (1966) and Julia Kristeva's *Powers of Horror* (1980). Douglas argues that in a wide variety of cultures 'pollution behaviour' can best be understood as the reaction which condemns any object or idea likely to confuse or undermine established classifications. 'Where there is dirt there is system.' In a seminal analysis of the dietary rules laid down in Leviticus, Douglas points out that the creatures designated as abominable are abominable not so much in themselves as in their confounding of the classificatory scheme which orders the natural world. In their anxiety about diet, and about pollution by 'bodily issues' (blood, pus, excreta, semen), the Israelites were attempting to secure the social and political unity of a minority culture under persistent threat. 'The threatened boundaries of their body politic would be well mirrored in their care for the integrity, unity and purity of the physical body.' The mistake usually made in the analysis of reactions to impurity, Douglas concludes, 'is to treat bodily margins in isolation from all other margins'.[64]

If Douglas generalizes disgust, so that every gesture of revulsion from a swarming creature or an abscess is a statement about the body politic, then Kristeva renders it primordial. She incorporates

---

[63] *Textbook of Insanity*, 384.

[64] *Purity and Danger: An Analysis of the Concepts of Pollution and Taboo* (London: Routledge, 1966), 35, 41–57, 124, 121.

Douglas's fascination with boundaries which are at once physical and conceptual into an abiding interest in the status of the mother in psychic life. According to her, disgust and horror endlessly recapitulate a moment before the subject's entry into the symbolic (into language) when it first distinguishes itself from what it is not (from the maternal entity it is still a part of). This violence expels something which is no longer subject and not yet object: the 'abject', whose primary site is the maternal body, but which recurs in all those objects and ideas and events which make us sick. Feelings of horror and disgust, in short, derive from an original disturbance of the symbolic universe caused by separation from the mother. Skin on the surface of milk is abject, as is refuse, or a wound, or a corpse; or, indeed, anything at all which disturbs system and order: the in-between, the ambiguous, the composite. Skin on the surface of milk is abject, but so is 'immoral' or 'scheming' behaviour, so is 'a debtor who sells you up, a friend who stabs you'. Although she has just declared that abjection draws one towards 'the place where meaning collapses', Kristeva often finds in it or behind it a sinister intent: parents coax a child to drink up its milk, a debtor defaults, a friend betrays you. Her climactic example of the abject is a pile of children's shoes in the museum at Auschwitz.[65]

According to the Douglas–Kristeva hypothesis, disgust is tied into the production of meaning because it assumes a motive in events: someone, somewhere, is out to upset the symbolic universe. The bodily margin is always already meaningful. Disgust cannot be triggered by mere accident. There is something mildly paranoid, I would suggest, about this conviction that disgust and horror can only be understood as a response to conceptual trauma. Corruption in the body politic, Kristeva claims, is the 'socialized appearance of the abject'. This, surely, is cultural theory after Watergate.[66] As such, it has genuine explanatory force, and I shall make use of it to probe the feelings of disgust which shape and animate historically specific expressions and enactments of paranoia. My reservation about it, which need not apply to the use I

[65] *Powers of Horror: An Essay on Abjection*, tr. Leon S. Roudiez (New York: Columbia University Press, 1982), 2–4.
[66] Ibid. 16.

shall make of it here, is that its most enthusiastic exponents have not always taken full account of Douglas's remark that the 'pollution behaviour' which concerns her is only likely to arise in circumstances 'where the lines of structure, cosmic or social, are clearly defined'.[67] This is not something which happens anywhere at any time.

But it does happen. We remember Freud, at the time of the foundation of the International Psychoanalytic Association, telling the Viennese analysts that the movement itself was in desperate peril; and we remember him cleansing himself, his home, and his life's work from the slimy Friedländer. Freud's theory of paranoia took shape at a time when, as Santner puts it, the institution of psychoanalysis was in a 'state of emergency': both a state of *emergence*, of coming-about, and a state of *crisis*, of endangerment.[68] The 'pollution behaviour' which formed part of his response to that state of emergency might very well be understood, I think, as an attempt to clarify 'lines of structure'.

THE END OF THE WORLD

During the spring of 1894, while he was still a patient in Flechsig's clinic, Schreber endured a period of 'gruesome' suffering which was also 'the *holy* time' of his life. During this period, he came to believe that the end of the world was imminent, or had already come about. He thought that he was the 'last real human being

---

[67] *Purity and Danger*, 113. The Douglas–Kristeva hypothesis is of course by no means the only available account of the social and psychic functions of disgust, and not all of them tie the feeling to conceptual trauma. But it is worth noting that Jean-Paul Sartre's vivid phenomenological account, in many respects at variance with the Douglas–Kristeva hypothesis, is none the less not without its own whiff of paranoia. According to Sartre, 'nausea' is what the world is like when you stop having ideas about it: the very 'taste' of contingency itself. Roquentin, in *Nausea* (1938), is, as it were, a *nauséaste*: a man overcome by revulsion, permanently beyond himself, sick with sickness. In *Being and Nothingness* (1943), Sartre identified slime (*le visqueux*) as the ultimate glue, the nauseous essence of being. Slime, he wrote, appears to us not only as an object or substance, but as a relation, in which we are always already implicated, to the world. Sartre's paranoid thought is that to exist is to get stuck: *Being and Nothingness: An Essay on Phenomenological Ontology*, tr. Hazel E. Barnes (London: Routledge, 1969), pp. xli, 604–11. I discuss some of these issues further in *Cooking with Mud*, chs. 5 and 6, and in 'Fanon's Nausea', *Parallax*, 5 (1999), 32–50.

[68] *My Private Germany*, 24.

left', the few human shapes he saw around him being 'fleeting-improvised-men' put together for his benefit.[69] Schreber associ-ated this feeling of doom with political and religious conflict, and in particular with Protestant Germany's death-struggle against the forces (Catholic, Slav, Jewish) ranged against it.[70] In the next chapter of the *Memoirs*, he went into detail. To begin with, he located the causes of catastrophe in phenomena such as earthquake or the loss of the sun's heat. Then he changed his mind. The news that the wizard Flechsig had been able to spirit away and confine a person as eminent as himself must have 'spread terror and fear among the people, destroying the bases of religion and causing general nervousness and immorality'. In its train devastating epidemics had 'broken upon' mankind.[71] The paranoiac's ultimate vindication is the ending of the world which had for so long remained indifferent towards him, refusing to recognize his true worth. The best man (the only valuable man) has survived. And there is nobody left to persecute him.

Turn-of-the-century English writers took a vivid interest in global catastrophe. None more so than M. P. Shiel, who during the 1890s made a name for himself as the author of fantasies in the manner of Edgar Allan Poe, and was for a while a peripheral figure in the Wilde circle. Shiel is worth discussing at this juncture because he put his thoroughly Decadent prose style at the service of the most schematic and all-encompassing of fantasies about England's imperial destiny. His books hyperventilate, and the pathology of the writing aligns them rather more closely with the case-histories we have been examining than the products of the merely workmanlike fantasist: none more so than *The Purple Cloud* (1901).

The Purple Cloud takes the form of a notebook sent to the author by an old friend, Dr Arthur Lister Browne, who realizes that he is about to die. One of Browne's patients, Miss Mary

---

[69] *Mem.* 85. For a more recent view of the phenomenon, see Robert Jay Lifton, 'The "End-of-the-World" Vision and the Psychotic Experience', in Joseph H. Berke, Stella Pierides, Andrea Sabbadini, and Stanley Schneider (eds.), *Even Paranoids Have Enemies: New Perspectives on Paranoia and Persecution* (London: Routledge, 1998), 59–74.

[70] Santner ably addresses Schreber's delusions concerning Catholics and Jews in *My Private Germany*, ch. 3.

[71] *Mem.* 97.

Wilson, is a time-traveller, and dictates under hypnosis the contents of a journal kept, twenty-five years in the future, by another doctor, Adam Jeffson. An American multimillionaire and 'king of faddists', Charles P. Stickney, has bequeathed $175 million to the first person to reach the North Pole. A ship, the *Boreal*, is equipped for the purpose, and Jeffson's fiancée, the Countess Clodagh, a fan of Lucrezia Borgia, obtains for him the post of medical officer by poisoning the present incumbent. 'Be first—for Me', she murmurs. Getting into the spirit of things, Jeffson murders two further members of the expedition and steals a march on the rest. Arriving at the Pole, he discovers a pillar of ice surrounded by a lake which has 'the substance of a living creature'.[72] Returning, after many adventures, to the *Boreal*, he finds it a ghost-ship, the crew all dead or missing. He sails south, encountering trawlers, then a liner, each a graveyard. In fact, the whole world is a graveyard, having been enveloped for a few days by a cloud of poison. Jeffson travels the length and breadth of Britain in an unsuccessful search for survivors. He is a Robinson Crusoe cast away on a global desert island. After seventeen years, he at last finds, in the ruins of Constantinople, a mate: a young woman who was little more than a baby, and captive in an airtight cellar, when the poison-cloud passed over. After coyness on an epic scale, they marry, and embark on the arduous task of repopulating the world.

The novel's cumbersome framing devices—the fraternity of doctors, the hypnotism—integrate the protocols of Wellsian science fiction into the protocols of descriptive psychopathology. Shiel furnishes his protagonist with enough symptoms to populate an asylum. Jeffson has been tormented from an early age by 'voices' more consistent and more intimate than mere 'contradictory impulses'.[73] He has always felt that 'two Powers, which hated each other, must be continually after me, one wishing for some reason to kill me, and the other for some reason to keep me alive'. The result of this pursuit is a conviction that he is not 'a boy like

---

[72] *The Purple Cloud* (London: Chatto & Windus, 1901), 41, 70. Henceforth *PC*.

[73] By modern standards, a patient who reports hallucinations in which two or more voices converse with each other meets by that fact Criterion A for schizophrenia: *DSM-IV* 285. Dementia paranoides, rather than paranoia, might well have been the Kraepelinian diagnosis. What will concern me here is the content of the patient's paranoid delusions.

other boys, but a creature separate, special, marked for—something'. Adulthood merely reinforces the conviction. Outwardly an 'ordinary youth' of his time, dawdling in clubs and cramming for exams, Jeffson is inwardly a monster, a Robespierre. When he returns to his ship to find his companions dead or missing, he experiences a moment of paranoid illumination in which he understands for the first time the full extent of his own uniqueness. The Unseen Powers, he records, 'who through the history of the world had been so very, very careful to conceal their Hand from the eyes of men, hardly any longer intended to be at the pains to conceal their Hand from *me*'.[74] As he sails south towards London, it becomes clear to him that he is indeed the only survivor, and that a world which did not sufficiently appreciate his uniqueness has been sacrificed to it. The two 'voices' now reveal themselves as megalomania and persecutory delusion.

The world in which Jeffson alone survives is however by no means empty. What it is full of is mess. Everywhere the dead fester, and Shiel emphasizes again and again the visceral disgust and terror caused by contact with or immersion in this encumbering putrescence. Landing at a small town in Norway, Jeffson wanders into a courtyard and climbs the stairs to a darkened room. 'At the same time I had made another step forward, and trodden upon a soft abdomen.' Another charnel-house awaits him at Dover. At this point, as he stands once again on the threshold of England and Englishness, the conceptual trauma Douglas and Kristeva have taught us to discern in nausea becomes apparent. The poison-cloud had rolled over the world from East to West, with people of all nations and races fleeing before it.

I wandered and wandered, till I was tired of spahi and bashi-bazouk, of Greek and Catalan, of Russian 'pope' and Coptic abuna, of dragoman and Calmuck, of Egyptian maulawi and Afghan mullah, Neopolitan and sheik, and the nightmare of wild poses, colours, stuffs and garbs, the yellow-green kefie of the Bedouin, shawl-turbans of Baghdad, the voluminous rose-silk tob of women, and face-veils, and stark distorted nakedness, and sashes of figured muslin, and the workman's cords, and the red tarboosh.[75]

The exhaustion felt here, as the sheer matter of ethnic difference accumulates, is a pathology of style, staunchly English writing sickened by an overload of imported terms, driven almost mad:

---

[74] *PC* 22–3, 89–90.   [75] *PC* 121, 142.

that the white cliffs should have to absorb such colours, such colouredness.

Paranoia cannot abide mess. Jeffson proceeds to Harbour Station, where, amid an orgy of good English technical description, he prepares a locomotive for the journey to London. Paddington Station, alas, is choked with corpses. To walk is to wade: 'for flesh was everywhere, on the roofs of trains, cramming the interval between them, on the platforms, splashing the pillars like spray, piled on trucks and lorries, a carnal quagmire'. In Printing House Square, where Jeffson has gone to catch up on back-issues of the *Times*, mixture strikes again: 'even there, the ground was strewn with calpac and pugaree, black abaych and fringed praying-shawl, hob-nail and sandal, figured lungi and striped silk, all very muddled and mauled'.[76] A litter at once physical and metaphysical figures the contingency he will have to construct his system against, or over. We need to note both the emphasis on muddle and mixture, and the emphasis on carnal quagmire, on a residue of worldliness (of the world as it once was) which must be experienced as sensation, as the impact of body on body. The contamination is at once of body and of race, and the paranoid nausea it arouses in Adam Jeffson—a nausea produced by a disturbance of the symbolic universe, but felt in the flesh—is at this point the only sense he has of himself. Obscurely persecuted by the detritus which obstructs and sickens him, he knows vividly that he is still alive.

It is on the basis of obscure persecution that Jeffson constructs a fantasy of grandeur. Having left London in search of survivors, and found none, he returns—rather oddly, one might have thought, given the scenes of desolation he has witnessed—with his head held high, his step 'royal', and his eye 'cold and calm'. A 'burdened, cowering wight' when he sets out on his tour of the regions, he feels every inch the 'Sultan' at the end of it.

For there were many men to the eye: but there was One only, really: and I was he. And always I knew it:—some faintest secret whisper which whispered me: '*You* are the Arch-one, the *motif* of the world, Adam, and the rest of the men not much.' And they are gone—all! all!—as no doubt they deserved: and I, as was meet, remain . . . I will be restless and turbulent in my territories: I will say to my soul: 'Be Full'.[77]

---

[76] *PC* 142–3, 164, 167.   [77] *PC* 214.

As, no doubt, they deserved. The world's miserable population has finally acknowledged the Arch-one as the Arch-one by ceasing to exist.

Freud would surely have seen in Jeffson's megalomania a secondary narcissism: a regression, framed in phylogenetic rather than ontogenetic terms, to a stage before the emergence of any distinction between self and world. Mastered by 'primitive' attitudes, Jeffson overcomes his fear of finding other human beings alive by developing an 'arrogance of royalty' taken to the point of 'wantonness': 'good or no, the arrangement of One planet, One inhabitant, already seems to me, not merely a natural and proper, but the *only* natural and proper, condition'. The symbolic capital Jeffson accumulates, in this realized parallel universe where the only recognition available is self-recognition, is that of masculinity, or hypermasculinity. Encountering in his old home a portrait of himself as he once was— unremarkable in appearance, but possessing a 'King's brow' to which the painter has unaccountably failed to do justice—he resolves upon improvement. The improvement is a regression. 'But I seem to have gone right back to the very beginnings, and resemblance with man in his first, simple, gaudy conditions.' An immense paragraph describes the surplus of garish clothing and oiled and scented beard in which he encases himself. This is a masculinity so hyper that it can happily incorporate, by way of vindication of its own excess, what might ordinarily be regarded as signifiers of femininity. 'My ankles— my ten fingers—my wrists—are heavy with gold and silver ornaments; and in my ears, which, with considerable pain, I bored three days since, are two needle-splinters, to prepare the holes for rings.' The king's brow has been converted, and not without the necessary authentication by due suffering, into performance, into symbolic capital. 'O Liberty! I am free', he exclaims.[78]

Jeffson's problem is that he can never be sure that the world really has come to an end, that he has what remains of it entirely to himself. Previously, he had found in the fact that the hands of all the clocks in London were stuck at ten past three something 'hideously solemn, yet mock-solemn, personal, and as it were addressed to *me*'. Megalomania has not expunged the traces of the persecution out of which it was born. No sooner does Jeffson free

[78]   *PC* 221–3.

himself through Orientalism than he becomes convinced that someone is following him. 'Hideously frequent is this nonsense now become with me—in streets of towns—in deep nooks of the country: the invincible assurance that, if I but turn the head, and glance *there*—at a certain fixed spot—I shall surely see—I *must* see—a man.' Terrified though he is, he still feels a 'monarch indignation' against the 'intruder', and his neck 'stands stiff as sovereignty itself'. Paranoid symmetry requires that the degree of fantasized grandeur should match as closely as possible the degree of fantasized persecution. Symmetry's eventual outcome is destructive mania: 'the rage to burn and raven and riot, was upon me like a dog-madness, and all the mood of Nero, and Nebuchadnezzar'. Planting explosives across London, he retires cackling to a tower in Hampstead to watch the city explode.[79]

There are aspects of Shiel's portrayal of Adam Jeffson—his narcissism, on the one hand, and on the other his fear of contamination, his rage to burn and raven and riot—which anticipate Freud's analysis of Daniel Paul Schreber. Jeffson, like Schreber, is a personality in conflict, and the psychodynamic 'model' to which both Shiel and Freud adhered made possible an account of the aetiology of 'dog-madness', of the moods of Nero and Nebuchadnezzar, which the domestic realism dominating the nineteenth-century novel and the nineteenth-century case-study alike would have found it hard to conceive. It was the emergence of a psychodynamic model, against the background of the rapid evolution of descriptive psychopathology, which constituted psychiatry's Modernism. In drawing the part of this book which deals directly with the psychiatric literature to a conclusion, however, I would like to emphasize once again the parallels between psychoanalysis and descriptive psychopathology. Some of the positions taken by exponents of both methods were the product of an anxiety about professional status. The methodological paranoias developed by Freud and Gaupp in the masterful accounts they gave of paranoia were also a kind of Modernism: the product of a will-to-abstraction whose purpose was, in part at least, to master anxieties about professional status. I shall resume the story of the Modernist will-to-abstraction in Chapter 7.

[79] PC 216–17, 223, 234, 249–51.

First, I need to establish a relation between the accounts of the psychopathies of expertise provided in nineteenth-century descriptive psychopathology and in English fiction before Modernism. However psychodynamic their inquiries, however conscious they might be of literary experiment as a reserve of symbolic capital, the Modernist writers did not disavow a social and political consciousness initially framed by nineteenth-century aversions to social mimesis. In order to understand where those aversions came from, we must first identify the moment of their emergence within the history of paranoid narrative since Rousseau.

CHAPTER 3

Career Development: William Godwin, Wilkie Collins, and the Psychopathies of Expertise

THE SUBJECT OF my first two chapters was the discovery or fabrication, during the nineteenth century, of an 'ecological niche', in Ian Hacking's phrase, within which the disease entity we now call paranoia might take shape, and within which it has survived, more or less intact, despite significant changes of emphasis, to this day.[1] Early psychiatry's symptomatologies and case-histories constituted a way to think about and to represent a certain kind of behaviour, a certain attitude: a kind of behaviour and an attitude, familiar enough in society at large, the extreme version of which the asylums were built to contain (and perhaps in some sense to preserve). In the chapters which follow, I shall explore a sample of nineteenth- and twentieth-century English fiction: a different way to define, and significantly redefine, the same kind of behaviour, the same attitude.

I shall argue that, in the fiction as well as in the symptomatologies and the case-histories, the idea of paranoia made it possible to express concern about the consequences of a profound and far-reaching transformation of English society: the inexorable spread, at all levels, and in all activities, of professional methods and ideals.

---

[1] According to Hacking, the ecological niche in which a mental disease can thrive requires four 'vectors': it should fit into a larger framework of diagnosis, a taxonomy of illness; it should be situated between two 'elements' of contemporary culture, one romantic and virtuous, the other vicious and tending to crime; it should be 'visible' as disorder and suffering, as something to escape; and it should also provide some 'release' not available elsewhere in the culture. *Mad Travellers: Reflections on the Reality of Transient Mental Illnesses* (Charlottesville, Va.: University of Virginia Press, 1998), 1–2. Paranoia fits that model. What will concern me in particular in this and subsequent chapters is the 'release'—the moral, social, political, and imaginative scope—it may have provided.

Paranoia is meritocracy's illness, a psychopathy of expertise. The process I shall examine, as it is represented in English fiction from late eighteenth-century Gothic to early twentieth-century Modernism, is that of *becoming-paranoid*. The protagonist of these stories is invariably a man of rare gifts, with aspirations to match, which the world does not seem disposed either to acknowledge or to reward. Unwilling or unable to settle for indifference, he reimagines indifference as implacable persecution; with all eyes on him at last, with every man's hand against him, he can no longer doubt his own uniqueness. Paranoid symmetry adjusts the degree of fantasized grandeur to the degree of fantasized persecution. Thus far, the fictional protagonist has much in common with the subject of the psychiatric case-history. We recall Freud's summary, in the *Introductory Lectures*, of the definition of paranoia provided by descriptive psychopathology: 'it is suggested that the patient, who, owing to a primary disposition, believes that he is being persecuted, infers from his persecution that he must be someone of quite particular importance and so develops megalomania'.

The difference is that in fiction narrative does the protagonist's reimagining for him. Narrative enmeshes him in 'actual' conspiracy. Narrative externalizes paranoid symmetry as the mutual pursuit of hero and villain, whose ultimate cornering of each other gives both a reason to live, a certain (doubled) uniqueness.[2] The protagonist was not mad, after all, we think, because people really did laugh at him behind his back, and spread rumours about him, and try to assassinate him; and their attentions, however unwelcome, must have meant that he possessed some value for them, that in some sense they could not do without him.

This process of becoming-paranoid has been consistently and inventively imagined by English writers since at least the time of the French Revolution: the formal and irreversible institution in France, in theory if not in practice, of bourgeois democracy.[3] No

---

[2] It is at this point that my use of the term 'paranoid symmetry' coincides with that to which Eve Kosofsky Sedgwick has put it in *Between Men: English Literature and Male Homosocial Desire* (New York: Columbia University Press, 1985).

[3] I am by no means the first literary or cultural historian to want to trace the psychopathies of everyday modern life back to the institution of bourgeois democracy. See e.g. Peter Brooks's *The Melodramatic Imagination: Balzac, Henry James, Melodrama and the Mode of Excess* (New Haven, Conn.: Yale University Press, 1976), and

doubt 'paranoia' existed before the Revolution. But the creation of a stable ecological niche for the disease does seem to date from that period. I have already noted one rather suggestive calibration of madness by political change, in Esquirol's patient, who thought he was God, Napoleon, and Robespierre all rolled into one. It was the identification with Robespierre, above all, a leader who had perpetually to improvise authority, which led this patient to doubt his own sanity, to regard himself as a deviation from nature. 'I am Robespierre, a monster, I must be slain.'[4] The demise of the *ancien régime* could be conceived, and not just by mad people, as the demise of a system which underwrote the attribution of social identity. Gods and emperors radiate well-being because they know who they are; without ever becoming one of them, we absorb that radiance, which we have after all created through our variously attentive acts of worship. But who, or what, was Robespierre? And how could he ever be sure that the world saw him as he saw himself?

The context I want to propose for the generality of this new unease is the emergence and gradual self-definition during the nineteenth century of a professional or non-capitalist middle class. You did not have to be a doctor or a lawyer or a clergyman to suffer from paranoid delusion, but it certainly helped. Medicine, the law, and the church constituted the original professions. 'All "true" professions stem from these three', Harold Perkin argues, 'and are characterized by expert, esoteric service demanding integrity in the purveyor and trust in the client and the community, and by non-competitive reward in the form of a fixed salary or standard and unquestioned fee.' According to Perkin, the Industrial Revolution 'emancipated' not only the entrepreneur and the wage-earner, but the 'professional man' as well, releasing

---

Sedgwick, *Between Men*. T. J. Clark begins his account of Modernism as a 'distinctive patterning of mental and technical possibilities' with David's *Death of Marat* (1793): *Farewell to an Idea: Episodes from a History of Modernism* (New Haven, Conn.: Yale University Press, 1999).

4 Historians have not found it hard to discern the 'paranoia' in Robespierre's own behaviour. Thus Simon Schama describes the speech Robespierre made in the Assembly on 29 Sept. 1791, in which he decried attempts to emasculate the political clubs, as the 'climax' of his career to date, and as 'patriotic paranoia at its most creative': *Citizens: A Chronicle of the French Revolution* (Harmondsworth: Penguin Books, 1989), 577, 580.

him (and eventually her) from dependence on a handful of wealthy patrons. As the professional 'class' expanded rapidly during the course of the nineteenth century, its methods and ideals began to diffuse themselves throughout society. Unlike land and capital, those methods and ideals do not belong to the few. Based on expertise, on human 'capital', professionalism potentially extends as far as there are men and women willing and able to invest human capital in the acquisition of expertise.[5]

Perkin's emphasis on the transforming effect of the emergence of a professional class has two advantages for the cultural historian. In the first place, it enables us to envisage social conflict within as well as between classes: a difference of outlook which distinguishes not only the doctor from the mill-owner, but the shop-steward from the panel-beater. In the second place, it draws attention to the very specific problem of identity which afflicts those whose capital is symbolic through and through: those who only have their own integrity to sell, rather than muscle, or the contents of a bank account (not for nothing was a clergyman's income known as a 'living'). Perkin dates the dominance of the professional ideal in English society from 1880. But he also points out that the most significant development during the first half of the nineteenth century was the rise in the status of the intelligentsia. Not only did literature become a profession; writers were responsible for framing the methods and ideals by which the three major classes contending for supremacy—aristocracy, bourgeoisie, and proletariat—sought to conduct themselves.[6] The transformation of English society by expertise was a topic which could not but be of pressing concern to those who meant to earn a living (or 'living') by the exercise of their pens.

In the chapters which follow this one, I shall discuss representations of professional 'identity' and of the process of becoming-paranoid in early twentieth-century fiction: Conrad, first, and then the High Modernist triumvirate of Ford, Lawrence, and Lewis.

[5] *The Origins of Modern English Society 1780–1880* (London: Routledge & Kegan Paul, 1969), 252–70. Perkin's account was completed by *The Rise of Professional Society: England since 1880* (London: Routledge, 1989).

[6] For an acute and detailed account of the ways in which literature became a profession at this time, see John Sutherland, *The Life of Walter Scott* (Oxford: Blackwell, 1995).

Here, I want to explore the vicissitudes of the professional life, bordering at times on madness, as it is represented in three very remarkable novels: Godwin's *Caleb Williams* (1794), Dickens's *David Copperfield* (1849–50), and Collins's *The Woman in White* (1860). I do not have in mind a history, however brief, of the monomania in and of nineteenth-century fiction, English or otherwise. My primary subject is Modernism, and it would be unwise of me to try the reader's patience by circumspect excavations of an earlier period. But I will maintain (it is scarcely an original idea) that English Modernism was to some extent the outcome of long-term developments in English culture and society which had arrived at a particular complexity or involution by 1914. What interests me about the three novels I shall discuss is that they are all—in the case of *Caleb Williams*, despite appearances—success-stories. Meritocracy triumphs, ambiguously or unambiguously; the delusion into which it plunges the hero brings about a social ascent which would otherwise have been barely imaginable. Under Freud's influence, we tend to suppose that paranoia encodes a certain helplessness, above all, a condition of panic. These novels remind us that before Freud paranoia was as often conceived as a way to think about and to represent aspiration. In order to define the 'discourse' of aspiration to which they belong, in its late eighteenth-century context, I turn first to a classic modern autobiography, the *Confessions* of Jean-Jacques Rousseau, posthumously published in two parts in 1782 and 1789.

ROUSSEAU'S SECRETARIAL FANTASY

In the early years of the twentieth century, the German philosopher and historian Wilhelm Dilthey (1833–1911) sought to reconstitute the 'human sciences' by incorporating them into an ambitious 'critique of historical reason' which would do for the foundations of an understanding of culture and society what Kant had done for the foundations of the natural sciences. Biography and autobiography were central to this project. One of the ways in which 'experience' becomes intelligible, Dilthey thought, is through the essentially (auto)biographical concept of the 'life-course' or the 'life-as-lived': an emergent frame or pattern by means of which part can be related to whole. Thus life interprets itself. Autobiography is a literary variant of a self-reflection inherent in experience. 'In autobiography', Dilthey wrote, 'we encounter the highest and most instructive form of the understanding of life.'[7]

In his 'Drafts for a Critique of Historical Reason' (1910), Dilthey argued that Rousseau's *Confessions* develop a 'new conception' of the ways in which a human being might make sense of his or her life by relating part to whole.

Here, too, the outer events of a life have been interpreted by seeking connections which are not merely those of cause and effect. To name these we can only find such words as value, purpose, significance and meaning. When we look more closely we see that interpretation only takes place through a special combination of these categories. Rousseau wanted, above all, to justify his individual existence.[8]

The emergent frame or pattern to which Rousseau self-justifyingly 'confesses' is the product not of causality, but of an apprehension of an essential meaning and value whose performance can be discerned in its consistent relation to 'outer event'.

Dilthey had little doubt as to what urged Rousseau to autobiography:

All France swarmed with rumours about his marriage, and his past. Misanthropic to the point of persecution mania and in dreadful loneliness he contemplated the incessant intrigues of his enemies against him. When he looked back in memory he saw himself driven from his Calvinistically strict home, struggling upwards from an obscure life of adventure towards a confirmation of his greatness, soiled on the way by the dirt of the streets, forced to put up with bad food of all descriptions and impotent in the face of the domination of the elegant world and the leading intellectuals around him.[9]

The sense which Rousseau made of his life, in short, was paranoia's sense: persecution, a pattern only too visible, he thought, in

---

[7] 'Drafts for a Critique of Historical Reason', in *Selected Writings*, ed. and tr. H. P. Rickman (Cambridge: CUP, 1976), 207–31, p. 214. Dilthey is a key figure in Laura Marcus's compelling *Auto/biographical Discourses: Theory, Criticism, Practice* (Manchester: MUP, 1994), which in some respects runs in parallel to my own account of developments in English literary fiction.

[8] *Selected Writings*, 214.   [9] Ibid. 213–14.

outer event, confirmed his greatness. Dilthey rightly draws attention to the sense of physical defilement—by bad food, by the dirt of the streets—which so often inaugurates the paranoid construction of system. For paranoia is above all abstraction: the abrupt displacement of events by signs, of matter by meaning. Its motto is: where contingency was, system shall be.

Part i of the *Confessions* (books 1–6) was composed during the first half of the 1760s, at a time when Rousseau's work had begun to meet steadily mounting hostility. Rousseau began a fair copy of what he had written so far before seeking refuge from his persecutors in England in December 1765, and continued it at Wootton Hall, the mansion on the borders of Staffordshire and Derbyshire lent to him by Richard Davenport, an elderly gentleman of means. However, he did not last long in England. His inherent suspiciousness led to a violent quarrel with David Hume, who had hitherto supported him to the very considerable extent of securing him a pension from King George III. Rousseau began to believe that public opinion had turned against him, and that he was no longer welcome at Wootton. He feared that slanders spread by his enemies, old and new, would soon contaminate his idyllic seclusion beyond repair. Fearing for his life, he resolved to leave England; he even went so far as to request a bodyguard to conduct him to Dover. According to Hume, his behaviour at this time was 'absolutely lunatic'.

In June 1767, Rousseau settled at the château de Trye in Normandy, as a guest of the prince de Conti. There he suffered a further recurrence of his fears of persecution. He thought there were spies everywhere, and interpreted the slightest occurrence as proof of conspiracy. In August 1767, he became embroiled in yet another controversy, over a false claim for reimbursement. 'He was undoubtedly suffering from paranoia', his biographer concludes, 'but in this instance, as in some of the others, he had some cause to feel that he was being persecuted.'[10] By the end of 1767, he had drafted all of part i, much of book 7, and probably passages from later books. In November 1769, after a gap of two years, he began writing again. Most of part ii was written within

---

[10] Maurice Cranston, *The Solitary Self: Jean-Jacques Rousseau in Exile and Adversity* (London: Allen Lane, 1997), 175.

three or four months, and the work as a whole was virtually complete by April 1770. On 24 June 1770, Rousseau returned to Paris, where he wrote the final pages of the *Confessions*, which he read in salons in presentations lasting from fifteen to seventeen hours at a stretch. In such bold fashion would he confront his enemies, and obtain justice in the eyes of the world. With doubtful success, it would seem. 'Thus I concluded my reading', part ii concludes, 'and everyone was silent.' The only response came from a Madame d'Egmont, who trembled slightly. 'Such was the advantage I derived', Rousseau muses, 'from my reading and my declaration.'[11]

Book 7, written at the height of Rousseau's absorption in conspiracy theory, fully inhabits a parallel universe from which causality has long since been banished. 'The ceiling under which I live has eyes, the walls that enclose me (*m'entourent*) have ears. Uneasy and distracted, surrounded (*environné*) by spies and by vigilant and malevolent watchers, I hurriedly put on paper a few disjointed sentences that I have hardly time to re-read, let alone to correct.'[12] Those who have placed these barriers around him are terrified that the truth will none the less escape through some crack or fissure. In the parallel universe, there is nowhere to hide from meaning and value; mere conspiracy will never extinguish confession. By book 7, then, the pattern or frame through which Rousseau was to envision his life-course had taken shape. Rousseau now knows himself, and would have us know him, by virtue of an emergent paranoid symmetry which faultlessly matches grandeur to persecution. He *is* that chiasmus. What book 7 does is to investigate the circumstances under which this pattern or frame originally arose.

Book 7 describes Rousseau's attempts to furnish himself with a career. Arriving in Paris in the autumn of 1741, he had at first sought to make a living as a composer. He hoped that by expounding and promoting a new system of musical notation he would attain the kind of celebrity which, 'dans les beaux-arts', is usually accompanied by a fortune. For the aspiring professional, however, the difficulty is always accreditation. The certificate

[11] *Les Confessions*, ed. Jacques Voisine (Paris: Éditions Garnier, 1980), 781; *The Confessions*, tr. J. M. Cohen (Harmondsworth: Penguin Books, 1953), 606. Henceforth *Con.* Reference will continue to be to both texts.
[12] Ibid. 324/263.

Rousseau received for his system from the Academy of Sciences was full of fine compliments, but a profound scepticism could be read easily enough between its elegant lines.[13]

Opera was another possibility. One evening, on his way to the opera house, Rousseau felt so overwhelmed ('maîtrisé') by his ideas for a heroic ballet that he went straight home and wrote the first act. The act concerned the hopeless passion entertained by the Italian poet Torquato Tasso (1544–95) for Leonora, wife of his patron, Alphonso II of Este. Tasso spent many years at the court of Ferrara. His fear of persecution, and the conduct it gave rise to, resulted in his confinement as insane between 1579 and 1586. It is no longer thought that the duke put him away on Leonora's account, but the myth had a wide circulation in seventeenth- and eighteenth-century Europe. As we shall see, the belief that the consort of a public figure has fallen in love with you, and that steps have accordingly been taken to stop a relationship developing, is a classic symptom of paranoia. In his compositional frenzy, Rousseau identified thoroughly with the unfortunate Italian poet. 'I may say that my love for the Princess of Ferrara—for I was the Tasso at that moment—and my proud and noble feelings when confronting her unjust brothers made my night a hundred times more delicious than if I had spent it in the arms of the princess herself.' It did not trouble him too much that the next morning only a small part of what he had written remained in his head. New to Paris, unable to obtain official acknowledgement of his abilities, and suffering routine social humiliation because of his poverty, yet entirely sure of those as yet unacknowledged abilities, and indeed subject to triumphal delusion, Rousseau can be said to have become intimate with the psychopathies of expertise.[14]

Rousseau was deflected from his heroic ballet by the offer of a job as secretary to the new French ambassador to Venice, the count de Montaigu. Despite his lack of experience, he adapted quickly to the demands of his new post, and was soon wielding the authority which went with it. The honesty and zeal with which he performed his duties won him the regard, he says, if not of his employer, then of all the other diplomats with whom he had dealings. There can be no doubt that the talent he had discovered for

[13] Ibid. 331–2/268–9.   [14] Ibid. 343–4/277, 336/272.

diplomacy gave him real pleasure, and an incentive to train himself for the profession. The reward for eagerness and integrity would of course be symbolic capital of a kind he could convert into career prospects. 'It seemed quite fair to me that if I gave good services I should look for the normal acknowledgement, which is the esteem of those in a position to judge such services.'[15]

There is always, however, a potential excess in acquired expertise, an over-reaching. Rousseau's diplomatic feats earned him the distrust and dislike of his bungling employer, and the hostility of his employer's extensive retinue. Montaigu's hangers-on turned him against his omnicompetent secretary, who felt he had no option but to resign. Returning to Paris, Rousseau found that 'dans les bureaux et dans le public tout le monde était scandalisé des folies de l'ambassadeur'. But despite the public outcry both in Venice and in Paris, and the irrefutable proofs he was able to produce of his shameful treatment at Montaigu's hands, he did not obtain justice. The laws of society ('le bon ordre') decreed it. The fruitlessness of Rousseau's complaints, despite their evident validity, left in him a 'seed of indignation' against the 'absurd civil institutions' ('sottes institutions civiles') whereby 'the welfare of the public and true justice are always sacrificed to some kind of apparent order, which is in reality detrimental to all order'.[16] This seed of resentment and complaint, sown in the fertile ground prepared for it by the difficulties inherent in the accumulation of symbolic capital through expertise alone, was later to develop into a politics which contributed to the overthrow of the *ancien régime*. One might note that those difficulties, with their accompanying freight of social humiliation, continued to haunt Rousseau long after he had begun to transform them into political theory. Cranston points out that when Voltaire, an erstwhile ally, wanted to cause trouble for him, he did so by maintaining that Rousseau had not been the ambassador's secretary, at Venice, but his valet.[17]

It is important to recognize that the *Confessions*, a book shrouded in gloom, and worse than gloom, is a book about ambition *fulfilled*. Madame d'Egmont's friends may not even have

---

[15] Ibid. 351/280, 355/283, 360/287, 362/288.
[16] Ibid. 365–6/290–1, 383/304–5, 385/306.
[17] *The Solitary Self*, 122.

condescended to tremble, but some of them, at least, must have thought it remarkable, if odious, that the person thus recapitulating his life and career for their benefit was a watch-maker's son from Geneva. How otherwise than through the persecutions he had suffered could such a man ever hope to hold the attention of such an audience? There is a politics, as well as a sociology, in this obdurate and vehemently hopeful address to unmoved listeners. Rousseau, as Greg Dart puts it,

represented the autobiographical subject as an anticipation, in individual form, of the transparency and virtue which would be the defining feature of the ideal political community of the future, inviting his readers [and before them his listeners] to break down the aristocratic obstacle to liberty and equality and enter the realm of transparency by engaging in a sympathetic reading of his work.[18]

Before the politics, or with the politics, there was at last the outline of a career. The intricate, long-drawn-out revelation of becoming-paranoid which constitutes Rousseau's autobiography—at once transparency's source and its product—was itself a triumph of professional expertise. When all eyes are finally on *that*, indifference dissolves. Any response will do, for the time being. The meaning and value the *Confessions* render transparent is the meaning and value of meritocracy.

It was Rousseau's utter incorrigibility, Dart observes, which made him so attractive to William Hazlitt, writing forty years after the storming of the Bastille, and in an atmosphere of profound political reaction. In the sixteenth of his *Conversations with Northcote* (1830), Hazlitt selected an episode from book 3 of the *Confessions* to exemplify the ways in which the book's author had 'stamped his own character and the image of his self-love on the public mind'.

When Rousseau stood behind the chair of the master of the house of —, and smiled to hear the company dispute about the meaning of the motto of the arms of the family, which he alone knew, and stumbled as he handed the glass of wine to his young mistress, and fancied she coloured at being waited upon by so learned a young footman—then was first kindled that spark which can never be quenched, then was formed the germ of that strong conviction of the disparity between the badge on

[18] *Rousseau, Robespierre, and English Romanticism* (Cambridge: CUP, 1999), 9. I am grateful to Greg Dart for some illuminating comments on a draft of this chapter.

his shoulder and the aspirations of his soul—the determination, in short, that external situation and advantages are but the mask, and that the mind is the man—armed with which, impenetrable, incorrigible, he went forth conquering and to conquer, and overthrew the monarchy of France and the hierarchies of the earth.[19]

Paranoia is never not a success-story.

GODWIN'S SECRETARIAL FANTASY

I begin with the novel formerly known as *Things as they are, or The Adventures of Caleb Williams* (1794), but now more often referred to as *Caleb Williams*, for two reasons. In the first place, unlike most of the novels I shall discuss in this book, it is already regarded as the expression, if not the product, of paranoia. Literary historians have taken to describing it, along with Charles Robert Maturin's *Melmoth the Wanderer* (1820) and James Hogg's *Confessions of a Justified Sinner* (1824), as an example of 'paranoid Gothic'.[20] Such novels terrify and amaze, it is said, by drawing the reader further and further into the experiences of a protagonist who may or may not be utterly deluded. In the second place, *Caleb Williams* is political through and through. Set in the present day, during a period of escalating international crisis, it tells a story of grandeur and persecution which could easily be read, and was read, as a protest against the violence directed at the exponents of liberal reform by

[19] Ibid. 209–10. The quotation is from Hazlitt's *Complete Works*, ed. P. P. Howe, 21 vols. (London: Dent, 1932), xi. 278.

[20] David Punter, *The Literature of Terror: A History of Gothic Fictions from 1765 to the Present Day*, 2 vols. (London: Longman, 1996), i. 114–39. The inaugurator of this line of inquiry was Eve Kosofsky Sedgwick. Sedgwick's association of the paranoia in paranoid Gothic and its successors with the institutionalized homophobia of modern Western societies has produced a distinctive and influential corpus: *Between Men* (above, n. 2); *The Coherence of Gothic Conventions*, rev. edn. (London: Methuen, 1986); *Epistemology of the Closet* (Berkeley, Calif.: University of California Press, 1990). Sedgwick uses the (Freudian) concept of paranoia historically, to investigate the 'homosexual panic' instilled in men by a specific disciplinary regime; she does not historicize the concept itself. If we ask what the men subjected to this regime might actually have understood by paranoia (or monomania), we discover that to them the concept articulated a fantasy of grandeur as well as a fantasy of persecution. In general, the mistake made by those analyses of paranoid Gothic which concentrate exclusively on its rendering of persecution is to have consulted Freud, but not Rousseau.

an increasingly repressive state. *Caleb Williams* and the *Enquiry Concerning Political Justice* (1793) were Godwin's contribution to a native English republicanism which took shape during the early 1790s, in response to events in France, but which faded once war broke out. What follows will fall some way short of a comprehensive account either of *Caleb Williams* or of its author. But a discussion of episodes from the novel should help to define some of the tasks paranoid narrative has been required to perform in the modern era.

One of the things everyone knows about *Caleb Williams* is that the novel was plotted backwards. Godwin first conceived the mutual dependence in fear and loathing of the book's protagonists, Caleb Williams and Ferdinando Falkland, and the former's pursuit by the latter's implacable agent, Gines; and then found a pretext for it, in events in Falkland's earlier life (he has committed a murder, and stood by while two innocent men were hanged for it). By volume iii, in which Caleb is hunted from one side of the country to the other by the false character Falkland has given him, and finally resolves to confront his tormentor in public, paranoia's parallel universe is fully in place. A system of meanings and values has been superimposed on contingency: on the sane person's habitual belief that the world is a place in which many events occur for reasons it is not worth inquiring into. Caleb has escaped from gaol, and, like many fugitives in nineteenth- and twentieth-century fiction, he feels that the whole world is against him. He realizes that he has begun to suffer from delusions of reference. 'Every new incident that had occurred to me tended to impress upon my mind the extreme danger to which I was exposed. I could almost have imagined that I was the sole subject of general attention, and that the whole world was in arms to exterminate me.'[21] There is nothing, in the parallel universe his fears have created, which does not refer to him, and him alone. Nobody else is worth attending to; by the same token, nobody else more richly deserves extermination. 'I am Robespierre, a monster', he might almost say to himself, 'I must be slain.' Slaughter would be a belated tribute to monstrosity: the only uniqueness attainable in a world which remains indifferent to merit.

---

[21] *Things as they are, or The Adventures of Caleb Williams*, ed. Maurice Hindle (Harmondsworth: Penguin Books, 1988), 247. Henceforth *CW*.

The parallel universe constructed in paranoid Gothic is *bipolar*. Bipolarity stabilizes this system of meanings and values around the irreducible antipathy between protagonist and antagonist, and ·endows it with a transparency the real world lacks, an uncanny evenness of illumination. To evade Falkland's pursuit Caleb would have to step outside the very system which is his only hope of advancement. He would have to 'leave the country', as he twice tries to do, only to be thwarted as much by his own ambition, one might think, as by Gines's pertinacity. The parallel universe has no 'outside', and no shadows within. 'Did his power reach through all space', Caleb wonders of Falkland, 'and his eye penetrate every concealment?'[22] The transparency brought about by the revelation of secrets, and the hatred which continually deepens and extends it, is in important ways mutual. Freud, we remember, defined paranoia as the 'hypercathexis of the interpretations of someone else's unconscious'. 'The vigilance even of a public and systematical despotism is poor', as Caleb puts it, 'compared with a vigilance which is thus goaded by the most anxious passions of the soul.'[23] In Gothic fiction, hypercathexis works both ways, as hero and villain seek each other out in a place even darker, in some respects, than sexuality or conscience: the intricate psychopathies of expertise.

What Gothic does very well is to seal off the parallel universe. It is not just that Caleb cannot leave the country, but that he cannot leave meaning and value. Mutual transparency dissolves chance, so that nothing at all will ever happen except by intent. It was by chance, of course, by sheer bad luck, that Caleb first got himself into Falkland's mess. But without him knowing it, chance, alas, had already been abolished. To find your employer rummaging in a

---

[22] *CW* 249.

[23] *CW* 144. It is passages such as this which encourage the supposition that the hostility between the two men is a love which dare not speak its name, or does not know its name. For Sedgwick, *Caleb Williams* belongs to a subgroup of Gothic novels 'whose subplots might be mapped almost point for point onto the case of Dr Schreber: most saliently, each is about one or more males who not only is persecuted by, but considers himself transparent to, and often under the compulsion of, another male' (*Between Men*, 91). Panic, I shall argue, homosexual or otherwise, is not what *Caleb Williams* is 'most saliently' about. For a fine essay on the politics of Caleb's 'romantic attachment', see Alex Gold, 'It's Only Love: The Politics of Passion in Godwin's *Caleb Williams*', *Texas Studies in Literature and Language*, 19 (1977), 135–60.

chest might ordinarily be thought cause for embarrassment, perhaps, but no more. In this case, however, the employer, a man burdened by his own criminality, has stopped believing in chance. Entering through his own curiosity and expertise the employer's parallel universe, Caleb will soon have to learn to do without it as well. To be sure, accidents—productive randomness like the untidy desk in which he finds a crucial piece of evidence—continue to exacerbate his curiosity and confirm his expertise.[24] But their very productiveness ensures their extinction. Caleb presides over the demise of his own faith in contingency. This loss of faith, as dramatic in its way as the more blatant effects of Falkland's tyrannical malevolence, takes place in the seemingly uneventful gaps between confrontations.

When Caleb tries to cross the Severn, *en route* for London and its saving anonymity, and by 'some strange inadvertence' loses his way, nightfall finds him wholly out of his road on an uninhabited heath. Cold, hungry, soaked to the skin, he feels, with some reason, 'full of loathing and abhorrence of life'. He stumbles painfully against unseen obstacles. By the law of averages anyone wandering across heathland in the middle of the night is likely to fall over a lot. The difference in Caleb's case is that he can no longer bring himself to believe in mishap as mishap. 'There was', he observes, 'no strict connection between these casual inconveniences and the persecution under which I laboured. But my distempered thoughts confounded them together.'[25] Caleb knows that his distemper has excluded him from the world he was once familiar with, a world in which things happen for reasons not worth inquiring into.

The only occasion on which Caleb appears likely to escape Falkland's vigilance is during his sojourn in an 'obscure' market town in Wales. Here he finds both employment and hospitality. However, just as he is congratulating himself on his restoration to the 'immunities of a human being'—that is, to an existence for the most part unburdened by meaning and value—the arrival in the market town of a gang of labourers brings about a subtle change of atmosphere. His students leave him. Nobody talks to him any more. Since all evils appear trivial to him by comparison with his 'parent misfortune', he tries to reassure himself that his ostracism,

---

[24] *CW* 9–10, 119.   [25] *CW* 260.

like his tumbles on the darkened heathland, is not Falkland's fault.[26] Fat chance. To the paranoiac, all misfortunes always have a single parent. And Falkland is indeed behind the ostracism.

That Gothic seals off its parallel universes to such effect, allowing neither hero nor villain a way out, should not prevent inquiry into their conditions of possibility. Indeed, the purpose of *Caleb Williams* would seem to be to provoke such an inquiry. The novel's first reviewers took it for granted that Godwin was indulging in political allegory, and the assumption persists. According to Gary Kelly, for example, 'Godwin was presenting a fictionalized case of that central aspect of the Enlightenment debate on political theory, the right of the state to punish, and to enforce its "contract" by the sanction of the law.'[27] The novel has to do with hierarchy, Marilyn Butler observes; it is a vivid contribution to the debate about the merits and defects of the *ancien régime* which Burke and his republican opponents had been conducting since 1790. Butler argues that the relationship between Caleb and his employer is profoundly 'political'; its destructiveness, she says, is the consequence of the inequality built into it. Furthermore, the novel's third volume directly conveys the 'mood' of the 'beleaguered intellectual minority' in which Godwin found himself in the mid-1790s. *Caleb Williams*, Butler concludes, is a 'psychological' novel set in revolutionary times, and thus a precursor of works by Stendhal, Dostoevsky, and Conrad.[28] According to Kelly and Butler, then, it is the inequality built into the relationship between Caleb and Falkland which drives Caleb mad, or almost mad.

More recently, Greg Dart has suggested that, although the novel does indeed mount a powerful critique of the *ancien régime*, and in particular of Falkland's hypocritical sponsorship of Burkean doctrines of chivalry, it also challenges the faith which English radicals like Tom Paine had put in the value of legislative reform. According to Dart, it is the novel's resistance both to the ancient fiction of chivalry *and* to the modern fiction of law which identifies it as a 'Jacobin' text. The virtue of his analysis is that it exposes a degree of (Gothic) complicity between protagonist and antagonist.

[26] *CW* 299, 306–7.
[27] *The English Jacobin Novel 1780–1805* (Oxford: Clarendon Press, 1976), 181.
[28] 'Godwin, Burke, and *Caleb Williams*', *Essays in Criticism*, 32 (1982), 237–57, pp. 251–2, 256.

'Locked in an implacable enmity, Falkland and Caleb are also bound together by the recognition that true justice transcends the formal categories of jurisprudence.' Caleb's aim is thus not that Falkland should be punished for committing a crime, but that his own innocence (and indeed his own magnanimity) should achieve due recognition, from Falkland above all. The two men, separated by a gulf in status, and perhaps in temperament, none the less share a notion of the superiority of private judgement to the judgements delivered by institutional law. Hence their pact of silence.[29] The pact confirms politically, by the contempt it displays for society's institutions, the extent to which protagonist and antagonist have become transparent to each other. This mutual transparency is the bipolar structure of paranoia's parallel universe.

With Godwin, however, as with Rousseau, it is important not to detach the politics developed in the context of debates about republicanism from the preoccupations of the emergent class to which both men belonged, the non-capitalist bourgeoisie. Godwin had hopes, as well as fears, for the 'beleaguered intellectual minority'. *Caleb Williams* is both a political and a social allegory. It is revolutionary to the extent that it champions expertise. One of the objections to aristocracy that Godwin most strenuously advanced in *Political Justice* was that aristocracy had restricted social recognition to the accident of birth. Privilege 'kills all liberal ambition in the rest of mankind, by opposing to it an apparently insurmountable bar'.[30]

Caleb Williams is liberally supplied with liberal ambition. He was born of 'humble parents', he tells us, whose occupations were such as usually fall to the lot of peasants. Self-taught, and of 'inquisitive mind', the 'improvement' he had achieved in himself was greater than his 'condition in life' might have led one to expect. After the death of his parents, Falkland offers him the position of secretary, an offer he eagerly accepts. 'I formed golden visions of the station I was about to occupy.' Caleb's fantasy, like Rousseau's, is secretarial. At first, the station fulfils him, as a similar station had fulfilled Rousseau. However, the very qualities of industry and inquisitiveness which ought to have converted the golden visions into real gold in the event prove his undoing. 'I was excited by every motive of interest and novelty to study my master's character.'[31] It is necessary to the expertise Caleb wishes to acquire and to be rewarded for that he should study his master's character. There is, as he soon discovers, a fatal instability in expertise. Needing to know more, he learns too much.

It is the eruption of that excess, an eruption from within the professional ideal, which marks the turning-point of Caleb's life and career. The house catches fire. Since both Falkland and his steward are away at the time, Caleb takes charge, a responsibility 'to which indeed my station in the family seemed to entitle me, and for which I was judged qualified by my understanding and mental resources'. The fire is an opportunity any ambitious professional would welcome. But the zeal the opportunity engenders in Caleb proves a dangerous supplement. His mind already raised to the 'utmost pitch' by the assumption of responsibility, he enters the room containing the chest in which Falkland's secrets have been deposited, and proceeds to break it open. Falkland finds him at it, and the antagonism which has hitherto simmered between the two men comes nicely to the boil. Reflecting on the impulse which drove him to commit this 'monstrous' act—an act worthy, one might say, of a Robespierre—Caleb identifies within professional etiquette itself a certain madness, an 'instant insanity'. A hundred years later, Conrad's Lord Jim was to find himself in exactly the same 'general situation', on the bridge of a steamer which seems likely to sink. For Caleb, as for Lord Jim, the giving way proves decisive. Falkland now knows that Caleb is on the threshold of his secret, and will have to be dealt with. 'This epoch was the crisis of my fate, dividing what may be called the offensive part from the defensive, which has been the sole business of my remaining years.'[32]

Paranoia, as Freud observed, is not breakdown, but reconstruction after breakdown. For Caleb, as for Schreber, reconstruction begins in nausea. Falkland's demand that Caleb present himself in order to explain his conduct during the emergency rouses him from a trance. 'In recovering, I felt those sickening and loathsome sensations which a man may be supposed at first to endure who should return from the sleep of death.' Sickness is the way Caleb knows that he is still alive, and that health of mind and body remains, in theory at least, a possibility. Separating life from death, it also separates sensibility from trance. 'Gradually I recovered the power of arranging my ideas and directing my steps.' What Falkland has to announce, once the steps have been directed, is Caleb's (re)birth into the parallel universe their agreement to conceal his crime will create. 'I had made myself a prisoner, in the most intolerable sense of that term, for years—perhaps for the rest of my life.'[33] We should not let Caleb's palpable despair blind us to the fact that, as Freud knew, imprisonment in meaning and value is never not productive. Thereafter, like Schreber, he will find what disgusts him not in himself, but in the persecutions to which other people subject him: including, in his case, commitment to prison.

It is worth noting that the reconstruction involves various attempts at professions other than that of secretary. One reason Caleb settles in London, after his escape from gaol, is to earn a living as an author. His 'qualifications' seem slender, but it is not long before he has put himself on an 'established footing' as an essayist and translator. Indeed, this professionalism generates a secondary doubling, a secondary paranoia. Gines, Falkland's agent, gets decisively on Caleb's trail through the loose talk of the printer who has typeset some of his stories. Their subsequent antagonism derives from a curious mirroring of aspirations. Once a thief, Gines has now become 'peculiarly expert' in the 'profession' of thief-taker, and is currently exercising this 'art' in a 'very prosperous manner'.[34] Indeed, he exercises it in peculiarly expert fashion on Caleb, against whom he bears an ancient grudge. Both are men of humble origins who seek wealth, and perhaps fame, through expertise, through their unique qualities. The novel pits good professionalism against bad.

It is Falkland's recognition, not Gines's, which Caleb wants, and finally gets during his day in court. ' "Williams," he said, "you have conquered! I see too late the greatness and elevation of your mind".' It is, to be sure, a hollow victory, since Falkland survives

---

[33] *CW* 140, 144.   [34] *CW* 266, 268, 273, 269.

his own magnanimity by no more than three days.[35] The outcome of liberal ambition is tragedy. But not tragedy alone. For it is important to understand that Caleb has achieved, through the development of expertise—a secretary's, and an author's—an equality with Falkland which he would not under any other circumstances have been able to achieve. Caleb's professionalism, the product at once of expertise and of integrity, is the antidote both to the ancient fiction of institutionalized chivalry and to the modern fiction of institutionalized law. The tragedy is that it should take effect so circuitously, and at such an expense of madness. The tragedy is that, given the way things are, extraordinary talent can only ever earn acknowledgement in and through delusion. Patrick Brantlinger neatly defines the implicit triumphalism of the novel's conclusion when he remarks that the pen which Caleb wields, and which in effect causes Falkland's death, might be conceived not as a dagger (Caleb's term for it), but as a guillotine: it brings down the *ancien régime*.[36]

The pen in question is surely Godwin's, as well as Caleb's. Butler points out that in the early 1790s radicals like Godwin were able to 'image' for themselves an unprecedented power to think and act.[37] As government repression increased late in 1793 and early in 1794, Kelly observes, it became all the more important for Godwin to 'communicate to his readers some of his own sense of elevation and passion in the pursuit of truth'.[38] It was the first edition of his *Enquiry Concerning Political Justice*, published in February 1793, which made Godwin famous. *Political Justice* was at one and the same time, and not without contradiction, an assault on Lockean natural rights philosophy, which in Godwin's view had sacrificed considerations of duty to considerations of self-interest; and an assault, in the name of individual autonomy, on the power of institutions. Godwin thought that the 'active rights of man' were 'all of them superseded and rendered null by the superior claims of justice'; and yet 'it is necessary that every man should stand by himself, and rest upon his own understanding'. *Political*

---

[35] *CW* 335–6.
[36] *The Reading Lesson: The Threat of Mass Literacy in Nineteenth-Century British Fiction* (Bloomington, Ind.: Indiana University Press, 1998), 47–8.
[37] Butler, 'Godwin, Burke', 255.
[38] Kelly, *English Jacobin Novel*, 186.

Justice remains memorable above all for its insistence that no one who does not on every occasion 'consult his own reason' can hope to behave in an active, resolute, and generous fashion. It was Godwin's hope that the strenuous consultation of private judgement would eventually bring about the 'true euthanasia of government'.[39]

The appendix to book viii, chapter 8 of *Political Justice* offers a wonderfully provocative critique of all forms of co-operation in society, including marriage. 'It is a curious subject', Godwin mildly begins, 'to enquire into the due medium between individuality and concert.' On the one hand, human beings are 'formed for society', and nobody possessing the 'genuine marks of a man' can stand alone; on the other, individuality is the very essence of 'intellectual excellence'. 'He that resigns himself wholly to sympathy and imitation', Godwin declares, 'can possess little of mental strength or accuracy.' The medium he imagines between individuality and concert is a society in which all men have learnt to think for themselves, and thus need not agree with, or even understand, one another, since they will arrive by different routes at the same truth. What is needed, in short, is *dis*agreement. The local agreements between persons brought about by social, political, and legal coercion will give way to a universal agreement derived from infinitely variable processes of self-correction and self-improvement. 'The proper method for hastening the decline of error, and producing uniformity of judgement, is not by brute force, by laws, or by imitation; but, on the contrary, by exciting every man to think for himself.'[40] This antipathy to imitation is one which was to intensify markedly among the members of a 'beleaguered intellectual minority' during the course of the nineteenth century, as we shall see. In some cases, it overtook an antipathy to brute force or laws as the primary focus of radical thinking.

One might note Godwin's emphasis on *intellectual* strength. His commitment was already, in the 1790s, in the midst of the debate about republicanism, to the professional ideal which had begun to transform English society, and which promoted both the value of expertise and the need to devote it to the common good. Sidney and Beatrice Webb are not all that far away. Brute force, laws, and imitation have always been identified as the enemy of expertise (even of that expertise whose function is to disguise the first, put into practice the second, and justify the third). Paranoia, furthermore, professionalism's madness, could also be understood as a medium between individuality and concert. The paranoiac is never not in public, in full view of his persecutors; and yet the attention uniformly devoted to him only goes to prove his uniqueness, to confirm his own assessment of himself. The paranoiac feels that all eyes are on him all the time, that the whole world is acting in concert against him; in that excess of attention he finds his own triumphant excess of singularity. Paranoia, as Freud was to emphasize, is the solution, not the problem. It is the fantasy of the means to a place in the world.

Critics have tended to argue that *Caleb Williams* controverts the vision of a medium between individuality and concert put forward in *Political Justice*.[41] Caleb's probity is universally acknowledged, but the acknowledgement does him no good at all: it is not the making of him, as he had hoped. However, Greg Dart's insistence on the complicity between Caleb and Falkland allows one to identify a certain consistency between the novel and the philosophical tract. Dart points out that during the private trial which follows Falkland's accusation that Caleb has robbed him, in volume ii, chapter 10, Caleb remains silent about Tyrrel's murder, unwilling to confront Falkland in the context of a courtroom. Caleb does not want Falkland punished by the law; he wants his deed to be understood for what it is, a blameworthy but explicable action which should be judged on its own terms, rather than by legal precedent. Caleb is a good Godwinian by instinct.[42] Falkland, for his part, strongly resists the idea of putting Caleb on trial. He stoutly maintains that he will never lend his assistance to the reformation of mankind by 'axes and gibbets'.[43] Falkland, too, for all his Burkean attachment to chivalry, must be reckoned a good Godwinian by instinct. 'Locked in an implacable enmity,' Dart

---

[41] For a sophisticated argument along these lines, see Frances Ferguson, *Solitude and the Sublime: Romanticism and the Aesthetics of Individuation* (London: Routledge, 1992), 99–100. Ferguson argues that in *Caleb Williams* the relation between Caleb (man as individual) and Falkland (man as species) is figured as a monstrosity. The two men are Siamese twins so joined that dividing them would be disastrous, and yet unity remains intolerable: *CW* 313–14.

[42] *Rousseau, Robespierre*, 90.

[43] *CW* 181–2.

adds, 'Falkland and Caleb are also bound together by the recognition that true justice transcends the formal categories of jurisprudence.'[44] Paradoxically, there is in this implacable enmity, in this interlocking of paranoias, a medium between individuality and concert.

Again, however, although it seems convincing to me to define the complicity between Caleb and Falkland in political terms, as a Godwinian critique of institutional law, of axes and gibbets, we should also understand it, I think, as a fantasy of social recognition. Caleb is a Godwinian by instinct to the extent that he has noted Godwin's emphasis, in *Political Justice*, on due reward in accordance with talents and exertions. 'Of all the principles of justice, there is none so material to the moral rectitude of mankind as that no man can be distinguished but by his personal merit.'[45] It is this emphasis, I think, which may have persuaded Godwin to introduce into his novel Falkland's half-brother, Mr Forester, who presides over the private inquiry into Falkland's accusation that Caleb is a thief. Visiting Falkland, Forester had singled Caleb out as a companion: an acknowledgement doubly welcome in view of Falkland's increasing coldness towards him. 'It was his principle to do every thing that his thoughts suggested, without caring for the forms of the world. He saw no reason why a peasant, with certain advantages of education and opportunity, might not be as eligible a companion as a lord.' An admirable man, and potentially an alternative employer: what the undervalued professional has always done is to take his or her unique abilities and integrity elsewhere. Forester, alas, despite his indifference to the forms of the world, is in fact 'deeply impressed with the venerableness of old institutions'; and especially, it would seem, with the venerableness of the law.[46] It is Forester who, overruling Falkland's antipathy to the cold formality of statutes, has Caleb committed to prison to await trial. Forester is the last vestige of a world in which personal merit might conceivably be acknowledged without the intervention of madness. He represents that against which or within which paranoia constructs its parallel universe.

---

[44] *Rousseau, Robespierre*, 91.
[45] *Political Justice*, 472, 474.
[46] *CW* 147.

THE CAREERS OF JAMES TILLY MATTHEWS

In Chapter 1, I drew a comparison between the end-of-the-world fantasies detailed in Schreber's autobiographical memoir, of which Freud rightly made so much, and the end-of-the-world fantasy constituting M. P. Shiel's *The Purple Cloud*. Before leaving *Caleb Williams*, I want to draw attention to a contemporary case-history, that of James Tilly Matthews, confined in Bethlem from 1797 to 1814.[47] Matthews, too, was a victim of the law. His madness, which we would now regard as paranoid schizophrenia, was intimately connected to, and conceivably the product of, the political turmoil of the 1790s. It would be nice to think that he had read *Caleb Williams*, but the little we know about him does not tend to confirm the supposition. In Chapter 2, I discussed his nausea. My topic here, by no means unrelated, is his political and professional ambition.

Matthews's commitment to the asylum followed the interruption of a debate in the House of Commons on 30 December 1796. The House was debating the King's Message respecting the breakdown of negotiations with France. A shout of 'treason' from Matthews, who was present in the public gallery, halted proceedings. Matthews was arrested and taken to a secure workhouse in Tothill Fields, where he was held until his admission to Bethlem on 28 January 1797. He was transferred to the incurable establishment in January 1798. In 1809, his family, friends, and parish petitioned for his release on the grounds that he was no longer insane. When their petition was rejected by the Bethlem authorities, they took out a suit of habeas corpus at the King's Bench. Two London practitioners, George Birkbeck and Henry Clutterbuck, examined Matthews, and pronounced him sane. James Haslam, resident medical officer at Bethlem, thought otherwise. Like other expert witnesses, he maintained that Matthews's delusions on political subjects were such as to render him a danger to the royal family, the government, and the public at large. *Illustrations of Madness* is Haslam's vindication of his own conduct.

---

[47] P. K. Carpenter, 'Descriptions of Schizophrenia in the Psychiatry of Georgian Britain: John Haslam and James Tilly Matthews', *Comprehensive Psychiatry*, 30 (1989), 332–8.

According to Haslam, Matthews believed that a gang of spies and criminals skilled in pneumatic chemistry had taken up residence at London Wall in Moorfields, close to Bethlem, and had chosen to torment him by means of an 'Air Loom', a diabolical machine emitting rays. The unheard-of calamities induced by the rays included '*Lobster-cracking*', during which the circulation of the blood is prevented by the deployment of a magnetic field, '*Stomach-skinning*', which seems self-explanatory, and '*Apoplexy-working with the nutmeg grater*', or the introduction of fluids into the skull.[48] Although Falkland's agents cannot be said to go in for lobster-cracking or apoplexy-working with the nutmeg grater, it is of some interest that Godwin should have changed the name of the chief among them from 'Jones' to 'Gines' between the first and second editions of his novel. Gines is frequently referred to as an 'instrument' or 'engine'.

The purpose of the gang which so calamitously has it in for Matthews is espionage. Indeed, there are numerous gangs equipped with Air Looms positioned all over London. They employ auxiliary 'pneumatic practitioners' to premagnetize potential victims with 'volatile magnetic fluid' as they sit in coffee houses. Their primary targets, in addition to Matthews, are leading figures in the government. By directing rays at a minister, they can introduce thoughts into his mind, or discover what he is thinking about: William Pitt himself is apparently 'not half' susceptible to such measures. Whatever they learn they pass on to the French. Matthews held these 'expert' magnetists responsible for the British disasters at Walcheren and Buenos Aires, and for the Nore Mutiny, which broke out immediately after he himself had been rendered helpless by confinement to Bethlem.[49] There can be no question that his delusions had a political content.

This is not surprising, since he had enjoyed a brief and inglorious career as an intermediary between the French and English governments.[50] In the early 1790s, anxious about the likelihood of

---

[48] *Illustrations of Madness*, ed. Roy Porter (London: Routledge, 1988), 19–21, 30–41.
[49] Ibid. 53–4, 68, 55, 64.
[50] David Williams, 'The Missions of David Williams and James Tilly Matthews to England (1793)', *English Historical Review*, 53 (1938), 651–8; Robert Howard, 'James Tilly Matthews in London and Paris (1793): His First Peace Mission—In his Own Words', *History of Psychiatry*, 2 (1991), 53–69.

war, Matthews travelled to France in the company of the radical intellectual David Williams, who was friendly with Girondin leaders like Brissot and Le Brun. When Williams's efforts at mediation failed, Matthews took over the task. Astonishingly, given the bizarreness of the statements he was in the habit of making, he gained, for a while, the trust of the French government. Then, on 2 June 1793, the Gironde fell. When the Jacobins achieved power, Matthews came under suspicion, partly because of his Girondin sympathies, and partly because he was thought to be a double agent. He was arrested, and held until 1796, when the authorities concluded that he was a lunatic and let him go. Returning to London in March 1796, he wrote on two occasions to Lord Liverpool, accusing the Home Secretary of treason, and complaining about conspiracies against his life.

Matthews, like David Williams, of whom Brissot had a high opinion, was a moderate republican. It could be argued that Godwin's novel dramatizes the moral and political dilemma faced by such men. Indeed, Gary Kelly has drawn an explicit comparison between Caleb's vicissitudes and those of reformers of the 'Brissotin connection' who, pursuing political justice, found themselves in turn pursued.[51] Again, though, we need to take account of the preoccupations out of which moderate republicanism arose. What connects Matthews's delusion to Caleb's is that both are the product of a fantasy of social recognition. Matthews was a tea-broker, trading from 84 Leadenhall Street, and living at Biggin House, Mitcham, Surrey. Commerce clearly afforded him little satisfaction. His ambition was to succeed in public affairs. It is 'more than probable' that David Williams was Matthews's tutor in political theory, a capacity in which he had already acted for several other prosperous businessmen with aspirations to public service.[52] By offering himself as a mediator, on the basis of tutorials in which mention must surely have been made of the works of William Godwin, Matthews applied to join the non-capitalist bourgeoisie. It may have been the failure of his attempts to establish himself as someone to be reckoned with professionally which led to his breakdown. The gang of pneumatic chemists performs the same function

---

[51] *English Jacobin Novel*, 194–5.
[52] Williams, 'Missions', 661.

in his delusionary system as Gines does in *Caleb Williams*: to act out a darkly mocking burlesque of professional expertise.

Expertise, indeed, remained Matthews's object and obsession. In Bethlem, he taught himself calligraphy and technical drawing. The governors thought so well of the 46-page dossier of architectural designs for a new asylum building he had submitted in public competition that they made him an *ex gratia* payment of £30. Not one to rest on his laurels, Matthews subsequently made himself useful as an 'advising manager' on the treatment of inmates.[53] The recognition he so desperately sought was as much social as political.

The paranoiac finds in the institutions and machines which surround him the object of disgust he no longer finds in himself. Thrown into gaol on suspicion of theft, Caleb's first reaction is nausea. 'I have seen dirty faces in dirty apartments, which have nevertheless borne the impression of health, and spoke carelessness and levity rather than distress. But the dirt of a prison speaks sadness to the heart, and appears to be already in a state of putridity and infection.'[54] Now it is the prison and its inhabitants which play the part of the corpse. As long as the sight sickens him, Caleb knows that he is still alive. On the basis of this inaugural or resurrectionary distinction between self and other, he will gradually recover once again the power of arranging his ideas and directing his steps. As we have already seen, Matthews, like Schreber, seems to have attributed putridity and infection to the machine by means of which his persecutors harass him.[55] In its emphasis on nausea, Matthews's awakening from the 'Egyptian snuff' recapitulates Caleb's awakening in gaol. System, so pure on the inside, and transparent in all directions, discovers its outside in the spectacle of impurity, in the smell and feel of opaque effluvia. Its only acknowledgement of a world to which meaning and value cannot be attributed is disavowal.[56]

---

[53] Porter, Introduction to *Illustrations*, p. xxxviii.   [54] *CW* 184.

[55] *Illustrations*, 28–9.

[56] The term 'system', like the terms 'method' and 'theory', was an important one in the political debates of the 1790s. As David Simpson has demonstrated, (conservative) advocates of sound British 'common sense' took particular exception to the abstract reasoning which in their view permeated both French and English 'Jacobinism'. Simpson argues that the belief in method and system—i.e. in the 'progressive application of mental techniques to practical-political ends'—came itself

DICKENS AND CLASS HATRED

David Copperfield includes Dickens's most heartfelt tribute to the essential benevolence of eighteenth-century fiction. The narrator remembers the solace he found, after his mother's second marriage, in the books housed in an upstairs room. 'From that blessed little room, Roderick Random, Peregrine Pickle, Humphrey Clinker, Tom Jones, The Vicar of Wakefield, Don Quixote, Gil Blas, and Robinson Crusoe, came out, a glorious host, to keep me company.'[57] The glorious host, it would seem, did not include Caleb Williams. There is, however, no reason to doubt that Dickens was familiar with Godwin's novel, or, indeed, that his familiarity with it added a little extra darkness to some of his own 'dark' novels.[58] One might wonder, in fact, whether the novel once known as *Things as they are, or The Adventures of Caleb Williams* is not in some respects a precursor of the novel once known as *The Copperfield Survey of the World as it Rolled, Being the Personal History, Adventures, Experience, and Observation of Mr David Copperfield the Younger, of Blunderstone Rookery.*[59] In each case, a predominant emphasis on the history of the person surveying does not rule out a subordinate emphasis on the history of the world surveyed.

David Copperfield, famously, is the novel in which Dickens, without ever writing autobiography, both drew upon and in some measure exorcised unbearably painful memories of his own early life. The memories drawn upon in particular were those of the period of his father's imprisonment for debt in the Marshalsea, from February to May 1824, when he laboured mortifyingly in Warren's blacking-warehouse. As reimagined in

to be regarded, in Britain, as 'a wild and visionary delusion—a delusion of "theory"'. The *philosophes* themselves were of course quite capable of recognizing system's tendency toward delusion. While avoiding a 'mania for systems', Condillac maintained, we should seek by a proper use of the inductive method to produce a set of principles—in effect, a system. *Romanticism, Nationalism, and the Revolt against Theory* (Chicago: University of Chicago Press, 1993), 8, 73.

[57] *David Copperfield*, ed. Nina Burgis (Oxford: OUP, 1983), 44. Henceforth *DC*.
[58] William J. Palmer has recently noted similarities between *Caleb Williams* and *Little Dorrit*: *Dickens and New Historicism* (New York: St Martin's Press, 1997), 40–8.
[59] Nina Burgis includes some of the titles proposed for *David Copperfield* as appendix B in the World's Classics edn.: *DC* 719–21.

the novel, this mortification had a lot to do with the thwarting or still-birth of a prospective professional identity. Looking back at that period of life, the narrator simply cannot understand how a 10-year-old boy still in mourning for his mother could have been 'so easily thrown away at such an age'. 'A child of excellent abilities, and with strong powers of observation, quick, eager, delicate, and soon hurt bodily or mentally, it seems wonderful to me that nobody should have made any sign in my behalf.'[60] Nobody, in short, had made the sign which Falkland makes on behalf of Caleb Williams, another child of excellent abilities with strong powers of observation.

In Murdstone and Grinby's warehouse, amid 'dirt and rottenness' reminiscent of Caleb's putrefying prison-cell, David inspects and cleans bottles in the company of the children of watermen. 'No words can express the secret agony of my soul as I sunk into this companionship.' He realizes that he no longer has any hope of 'growing up to be a learned and distinguished man'. Rarely can the loss of social capital, and of the identity it makes possible, have been more plangently mourned. As it happens, of course, David not only regains his lost capital, but vastly increases it, with help from his aunt, Betsey Trotwood. She it is who sends him to a school where he acquires cultural capital by memorizing Greek verses and neglecting his boot-laces; and reacquires social capital by contact with the sons of gentlemen, and the fists of a young butcher, who by the same brutal manœuvre knocks the senses out of him and class difference into him. The point of the warehouse episode, or rather of its intensity, is that David should be seen to triumph despite rather than because of the efforts of the local Falklands.[61] He is no Caleb Williams.

There is, however, a Caleb Williams in the novel: Uriah Heep,

---

[60] *DC* 124–5.

[61] *DC* 126, 219. For an excellent account of the novel's desire to 'construct a professional who *knows* something, yet still, paradoxically, must undergo the labour of learning it', see Jennifer Ruth, 'Mental Capital, Industrial Time, and the Professional in *David Copperfield*', *Novel*, 32 (1999), 303–30, p. 324. For other, fruitful approaches to the issue of professionalism in Dickens's work, see Bruce Robbins, 'Telescopic Philanthropy: Professionalism and Responsibility in *Bleak House*', in Homi K. Bhabha (ed.), *Nation and Narration* (London: Routledge, 1990), 213–30; and Cathy Shuman, 'Invigilating *Our Mutual Friend*: Gender and the Professional Legitimation of Authority', *Novel*, 28 (1995), 154–72.

a man of conspicuously humble birth who after his parents' death is taken on as an articled clerk by Betsey Trotwood's Canterbury lawyer, Mr Wickfield, and eventually becomes a partner in the firm. Heep, of course, is a villain: he succeeds surreptitiously, by deceit and malpractice. Something has happened, between the 1790s and the 1840s, to the idea of Caleb Williams, to the story of a young man's achievement of social recognition through expertise. My topic here is the historical difference between Caleb Williams and Uriah Heep. For what is most remarkable about Uriah is the visceral hatred which Dickens, in the person of David Copperfield, directs at him. *David Copperfield* has long been understood as an exorcism. In it, Dickens got rid of some bitter resentments. By inventing Micawber, for example, he was able to come to terms with his father's profligacy: to see it as a human failing inextricable from a certain generosity of attitude, rather than a campaign directed at himself. Micawber's invention was the antidote to a lingering paranoia. But the novel none the less contains a full measure of fear and loathing, much of it attached, for reasons not wholly apparent, to Uriah Heep. Uriah is repellent first, and harmful second. His loathsomeness precedes anything he does, or might be thought to have done. What is it about him that provokes such violent antipathy?

Uriah's first appearance is as a 'cadaverous face' at a window of Mr Wickfield's house, where Betsey Trotwood and her nephew have gone to enquire after the best school in Canterbury. When the door opens, it is the face, rather than any person it might be thought to belong to, which emerges. 'It was quite as cadaverous as it had looked in the window, though in the grain of it there was that tinge of red which is sometimes to be observed in the skins of red-haired people.' Uriah is always already a revenant, a corpse tinged with red, an ambiguous resuscitation. The physicality of this description is extraordinary even by Dickens's standards. The eyes in the cadaverous face possess neither brows nor lashes; so 'unsheltered and unshaded' do they seem that David wonders how their occupant ever goes to sleep. The eyes are accompanied by a 'long, lank, skeleton hand' which rivets his attention. While Wickfield and Miss Trotwood set off to inspect a school and some boarding-houses, David remains in the office in Uriah's company. The unsheltered and unshaded eyes inspect him stealthily, like 'two red suns'. Whatever he does, he cannot escape their scrutiny.[62] There is in this surveil-lance the first stirring of paranoid antagonism.

As yet, the antagonism remains unstated, groundless, a physi-cal event. Returning from a walk at the end of his first day as a lodger in Wickfield's house, David goes into the office to shake Uriah's hand. 'But oh, what a clammy hand his was! as ghostly to the touch as to the sight! I rubbed mine afterwards, to warm it, *and to rub his off.*' Uriah is a contamination rather than a person. The grounds for David's feeling of revulsion gradually become apparent, justifying in retrospect its strange intensity. When David next encounters him, Uriah is engaged in improv-ing his legal knowledge. His 'lank forefinger' leaves 'clammy tracks' across the book he is reading. The contamination which is Uriah lies in, or has somehow become associated with, the development of cultural capital.

'I suppose you are quite a great lawyer?' I said, after looking at him for some time.

'Me, Master Copperfield?' said Uriah. 'Oh no! I'm a very umble person.'

It was no fancy of mine about his hands, I observed; for he frequently ground the palms against each other as if to squeeze them dry and warm, besides often wiping them, in a stealthy way, on his pocket-handkerchief.[63]

The issue Uriah raises is one which would have been of consuming interest to Caleb Williams: class background as a bar to entry into the professions. Uriah is a humble person with aspirations, and as such Dickens might well have been expected to approve of him, but very evidently does not. So what has gone wrong?

The problem is not that Uriah aspires, but that he aspires to the same things as David. He has a 'way of writhing' when he wants to express enthusiasm, which David finds distasteful for the simple reason that the enthusiasm expressed is enthusiasm for Wickfield's daughter, Agnes. Uriah knows something it will take David several hundred pages to find out: that he wants Agnes. He perceives David as a rival not only for Agnes, but for a partnership in Wickfield's firm. ' "Oh indeed!" exclaimed

[62] DC 178–80.   [63] DC 183, 190–1.

Uriah. "I should think *you* would come into the business at last, Master Copperfield!".[64] Heep's existence makes it possible for Dickens to distinguish, at the level of physical disgust, between a valid and an invalid version of the same success–story. Heep has to be marked in this way, by slime, because he is in other respects altogether too close to the hero. The antagonism between David and Uriah has none of the mutually clarifying and mutually consolidating usefulness of David's demolition by the butcher. Class hatred is here displaced into a rivalry between two young men who share the same aim: the acquisition through professional training of the symbolic capital required to obtain social and sexual status. Its displacement ensures that it can only be known as physical loathing.

What is wrong with Uriah is mimesis. He seeks to obscure the essential differences between David and himself by imitation. His aim is to resemble David, and then to take his place. This antagonism of imitation develops throughout the narrative, as an incidental but deeply felt subplot. When David, himself now an articled clerk with Spenlow and Jorkins, encounters Uriah at a dinner-party in London and invites him back to his rooms for coffee, Uriah promptly implicates himself with David, and David with himself, by announcing that it was David who first kindled the sparks of ambition in his breast: ambition for professional advancement, we conclude, and for Agnes. Again, the feeling is associated with a physical mannerism, and the nausea it arouses: 'he writhed and undulated all over, in his deferential servility'. This time, David cannot help noticing that his instinctive hatred of Uriah has a reason. He gets a sudden sense of being no match for him, 'and a perplexed suspicious anxiety as to what he might be going to say next, which I felt could not escape his observation'. David's hypercathexis of his own interpretations of Uriah's unconscious has finally begun in earnest. And with good cause, since the balance of power has changed decisively, as the drunken

---

[64] *DC* 192. It is significant, I think, that while Jennifer Ruth has much of interest to say about Agnes Wickfield as the 'endpoint' of David's 'professionalizing trajectory' ('Mental Capital', 324–7), she does not mention Uriah Heep, his companion and rival on that trajectory. Uriah is the focus for what the novel has to say about the psychopathies of expertise, and I would insist that in Dickens, as in the Modernist writers I shall discuss in subsequent chapters, no professionalizing trajectory would be complete without them.

Wickfield becomes increasingly dependent on his new partner. The problem, again, is the erasure of essential difference. It is not that Wickfield has lost his good looks, or 'his old bearing of a gentleman', for he has not: 'but the thing that struck me most, was, that with the evidences of his native superiority still upon him, he should submit himself to that crawling impersonation of meanness, Uriah Heep'.[65] In Dickens's eyes, Uriah is such a creature of imitation that even his meanness is a fake.

The sociology of this mutual antagonism and its political consequence are explored most fully in chapter 39, 'Wickfield and Heep'. On a visit to the Wickfields, David finds Uriah in possession of a new, plaster-smelling office built out into the garden. When he goes for another of his walks, along the Ramsgate road, Uriah follows him, putting imitation into practice, as it were. He announces that he regards David as a 'dangerous rival' for Agnes's affections, and explains his imitation of 'umbleness' as a strategy not only of self-advancement, but of class-revenge. ' "People like to be above you," says father. "Keep yourself down." I am very umble to the present moment, Master Copperfield, but I've got a little power!' Uriah's aim is to humble those before whom he has so conspicuously humbled himself. The sociology reveals a political motive. No wonder, then, that Uriah should be subjected to one of the explosive purgings Dickens was so fond of, when Micawber exposes him for what he is. And yet Dickens knew that imitation would not easily be purged from English society. Our final glimpse of Uriah is as a convict: a convict who clearly means to imitate his way, by conspicuous penitence, to an early release.[66]

The idea of a class hatred at once producing and produced by professional rivalry is one whose significance for Dickens's later fiction would merit further investigation: not least on account of the remarkable imaginative gains he derived from rehearsing it. The idea is as forceful in *Our Mutual Friend* (1864–5) as it is in *David Copperfield*. *Our Mutual Friend*, too, has its Caleb Williams: the 'highly certificated stipendiary schoolmaster' Bradley Headstone. Headstone has extricated himself from pauperdom by the laborious acquisition of cultural capital. 'From his early childhood up, his mind had been a place of mechanical stowage.'

---

[65] *DC* 309, 421.   [66] *DC* 467, 469, 609–21, 694–701.

Dickens spells out the psychic damage done to him by this long-drawn-out process of social and professional certification: 'the habit of questioning and being questioned had given him a suspicious manner, or a manner that would be better described as one of lying in wait'.[67] Headstone has achieved respectability, but at immense cost.

Dickens seems to be in two minds about the highly certificated schoolmaster. On one hand, he gives the advantage to Bradley's rival for the affections of Lizzie Hexam, Eugene Wrayburn, a lawyer whose main ambition is to practise as little law as possible. Headstone is Uriah Heep to Wrayburn's David Copperfield, a creature of imitation. His expertise is entirely mechanical. There is a 'want of adaptation' between himself and his thoroughly decent attire, 'recalling some mechanics in their holiday clothes'. Most damagingly of all, he is defined as a product of urban (or suburban) sprawl: 'school-buildings, school-teachers, and school-pupils, all according to pattern and all engendered in the light of the latest Gospel according to Monotony'.[68] It is hard to feel that Dickens does not share the brutal contempt Wrayburn directs at the monotonous schoolteacher, just as he shares David Copperfield's loathing for Uriah Heep.

And yet there is a singularity to Bradley Headstone, which Dickens acknowledges, somewhat against his own best (or worst) instincts, by allowing him to voice the fantasy of grandeur which inhabits his fantasy of persecution:

'Do you throw my obscurity in my teeth, Mr Wrayburn?'

'That can hardly be, for I know nothing concerning it, Schoolmaster, and seek to know nothing.'

'You reproach me with my origin,' said Bradley Headstone; 'you cast insinuations at my bringing-up. But I tell you, sir, I have worked my way onward, out of both and in spite of both, and have a right to be considered a better man than you, with better reasons for being proud.'

Headstone is, as Wrayburn puts it, a 'monomaniac'. Dickens saw in him, not just a creature of imitation, but a man tormented by the knowledge that his abilities will never receive the recognition they deserve. The product of that knowledge is a self-induced murder-

---

[67] *Our Mutual Friend*, ed. Stephen Gill (Harmondsworth: Penguin Books, 1971), 265–7.

[68] Ibid. 266–8.

ousness. 'Tied up all day with his disciplined show upon him, subdued to the performance of his routine of educational tricks, encircled by a gabbling crowd, he broke loose at night like an ill-tamed wild animal.' Headstone's murderousness is his work of art, the achievement for which he will become famous. 'He knew equally well that he fed his wrath and hatred, and that he accumulated provocation and self-justification, by being made the nightly sport of the reckless and insolent Eugene.' Still Gothic after all those years, despite his certificates, Headstone relishes a 'nightly sport' in which, as in Caleb Williams's pursuit of and by Falkland, it is hard to tell hunter from hunted.[69] His assault on the reckless and insolent Eugene is as brutal as the indifference Eugene had always displayed towards him, and the only answer to it. For the account Dickens gives of Bradley Headstone uncannily prefigures the story which was to emerge at the trial of Ernst Wagner, the schoolteacher who 'broke loose at night' to the extent of mass-murder.

Dickens may allow Headstone his singularity, to superb effect, but the novel as a whole remains, as *David Copperfield* had been in its antipathy to Uriah Heep, a polemic against the Gospel of Monotony. 'He that resigns himself wholly to sympathy and imitation', Godwin had staunchly declared in *Political Justice*, 'can possess little of mental strength or accuracy.' The way to produce uniformity of judgement, he went on, is not by brute force, by law, or by imitation, but by 'exciting every man to think for himself'.[70] What had changed between the 1790s and the 1860s was that social mimesis had become the main principle in the Gospel of Monotony. It was imitation, from which Bradley breaks free through monomania, which prevented independence of thought. Such, at any rate, was the burden of the third chapter of John Stuart Mill's *On Liberty* (1859), which magnificently reanimates Godwin's preoccupation with the relation between individuality and 'concert' (Mill's term is 'custom'). 'He who lets the world, or his own portion of it, choose his plan of life for him', Mill thundered, 'has no need of any other faculty than the ape-like one of imitation.' He worried that the all-inclusive social order in

---

[69] Ibid. 346–7, 608–9. It is this recall of the Gothic in *Our Mutual Friend* which persuades Sedgwick to find in it further evidence for a connection between the portrayal of paranoid delusion and homophobia: *Between Men*, 161–79.

[70] *Political Justice*, 757–8.

prospect from the 1850s onwards would extinguish 'variety of situations'. 'The circumstances which surround different classes and individuals, and shape their characters,' he wrote,

are daily becoming more assimilated. Formerly, different ranks, different neighbourhoods, different trades and professions, lived in what might be called different worlds; at present, to a great degree in the same. Comparatively speaking, they now read the same things, go to the same places, have their hopes and fears directed to the same objects, have the same rights and liberties, and the same means of asserting them.

'And the assimilation', Mill concluded glumly, 'is still proceeding.' Indeed, he seems to have had the thought which crossed Dickens's mind when he released Bradley Headstone from monotony into paranoid delusion. Under present circumstances, he says, those who insist on maintaining a sturdy independence of mind and conduct 'incur the risk of something worse than disparaging speeches—they are in peril of a commission *de lunatico*'; and he added a lengthy footnote to prove his point.[71]

In England in the 1860s, the thing the professional man or woman has to fear, the thing which he or she may go mad in resisting, is not brute force, or the law, but imitation. We are not all that far, now, from Modernism's all-out assault on literary and social mimesis alike. The note of Mill's chapter is the note of Wyndham Lewis's polemical writing of the 1920s, and the note of *The Apes of God* (1930), which associates ape-like imitation with Bloomsbury amateurism. That assault is the topic of the chapters which follow. Sue Bridehead, in Thomas Hardy's *Jude the Obscure* (1895), could be said to speak for literary experiment itself when she pays her respects to Mill's denunciation of social mimesis.

Phillotson writhed.
Sue continued: 'She, or he, "who lets the world, or his own portion of it, choose his plan for him, has no need of any other faculty than the ape-like one of imitation." J. S. Mill's words, those are. I have been reading it up. Why can't you act upon them? I wish to, always.'
'What do I care about J. S. Mill!' moaned he, 'I only want to lead a quiet life!'[72]

---

[71] *On Liberty*, ed. Edward Alexander (Peterborough, Ontario: Broadview Press, 1999), 104, 120, 115.
[72] *Jude the Obscure*, ed. Patricia Ingham (Oxford: OUP, 1985), 234.

What we now mean by Modernism, at least in the context of English literary fiction, is an attempt to put an end to quiet lives by an assault at once on the principles of social and of literary mimesis.

Catherine Gallagher has enabled us to recognize this attempt in political terms, as a rethinking of liberal theories of government. According to Gallagher, the doctrine of literary realism (of fidelity to the world as it is rather than as it ought to be) which informed George Eliot's early work corresponds to the theory of political representation developed in the 1820s by James Mill. For Eliot, facts were continuous with values: the way to get from one to the other was, in Gallagher's words, 'by the process of inclusion, equalization, and acceptance, by the slow-moving narrative method we now call metonymic realism'. The meaning and value of any principle which in due course emerged from the accumulation of facts would depend on its fidelity to the observable social world. It is this doctrine which Gallagher reframes in political terms. James Mill's best possible Parliament, she observes, like Eliot's best possible novel, would be a detailed proportional rendering of British society. In his view, the meaning and value of parliamentary representation depended on the closeness of the fit between a representative and the social world (the specific constituency) he represented.[73] Both the political and the literary doctrine assume an unbroken continuity between facts and general principles.

Gallagher goes on to argue, however, that the novels Eliot published in the 1860s 'manifest a deep skepticism about the principles of mere aggregation in literature as well as politics'. One source of this scepticism was the critique of liberal theories developed by John Stuart Mill, in 'On Representative Government' (1861). Mill sought to ensure the disproportionate representation of 'instructed minds' by giving plural votes to those who could demonstrate 'mental superiority'. 'His proposed Parliament would not correspond to any empirical social reality', Gallagher explains, 'but would, rather, directly express, by distorting what is, that which ought to be.' Parliament would thus represent value *to* the people.[74] Mill's theory of government, in short, rested on a radical

---

[73] *The Industrial Reformation of English Fiction: Social Discourse and Narrative Form 1832–1867* (Chicago: University of Chicago Press, 1985), 221–3.
[74] Ibid. 224–33.

discontinuity between facts and principles. Eliot, who followed his work closely, found in his revision of liberal doctrines of government a political role for the writer, and a reason to revise her own doctrine of literary realism. Gallagher compares Eliot's later work to the novels of Gustave Flaubert, Thomas Hardy, and Henry James in its readiness to separate fact from value. Like John Stuart Mill's ideal Parliament, these proto-Modernist works represent value (the value of art) *to* an audience enmired in personal and class interests.[75] In subsequent discussions of Conrad, Ford, Lawrence, and Lewis, I shall speak of the politics of this assault at once on social and on literary mimesis as a postliberalism. But I want now to make a final, and more direct, connection between nineteenth-century English fiction and contemporary psychiatric discourse.

WILKIE COLLINS: THE DRAWING-MASTER'S DREAM

I shall argue here that Wilkie Collins's *The Woman in White* can be taken to demonstrate the durability of the (paranoid) fantasy of social recognition through expertise which had animated Godwin's *Caleb Williams*. As far as we know, Collins had no special regard for Godwin.[76] That the sensation novel of the 1860s drew inspiration from 'paranoid Gothic' has, however, become a critical commonplace.[77] By the 1860s, of course, both the terminology of and the provision for mental disease had achieved an elaborateness not known in the 1790s; and novelists could expect in their readers a

[75] *Industrial Reformation of English Fiction*, 266.

[76] Godwin's biographers have made considerable claims, in passing, for their man's influence on Collins: Peter H. Marshall, *William Godwin* (New Haven, Conn.: Yale University Press, 1984), 391. Collins's biographers do not seem to want to commit themselves on the subject. It is however worth noting that his grandfather, a picture restorer and pamphleteer, had some connection with the English Jacobin culture of the 1790s: Catherine Peters, *The King of Inventors: A Life of Wilkie Collins* (London: Secker & Warburg, 1991), 10–12.

[77] David Punter explores the connection in *The Literature of Terror*, ch. 8. Patrick Brantlinger states it succinctly: 'In the sensation novel, the Gothic is brought up to date and so mixed with the conventions of realism as to make its events seem possible if not exactly probable' (*Reading Lesson*, 147). Jenny Bourne Taylor seems to me to be on secure ground when she finds echoes of *Caleb Williams* in Collins's earlier novel, *Basil* (1852): *In the Secret Theatre of Home: Wilkie Collins, Sensation Narrative, and Nineteenth-Century Psychology* (London: Routledge, 1988), 24.

degree of familiarity with such matters.[78] To acknowledge the fantasy of social recognition which animates *The Woman in White* is to acknowledge in it a wildness—a utopianism—to which even the most recent investigations of its 'hysteria' have not done justice.

Walter Hartright, the hero of *The Woman in White*, teaches drawing. His is one of those professions, like schoolmastering and governessing, which in Robert Gaupp's view engendered a susceptibility to paranoia. An artist by training, Hartright offers instruction in an important social skill to genteel young women whose accomplishments will help them to secure a wealthy husband. He is employed by Mr Frederick Fairlie, of Limmeridge House, in Cumberland, to 'superintend the instruction of two young ladies in the art of painting in water-colours'. He falls in love with Laura Fairlie, and she with him, an event which reminds him brutally of his ambiguous position as a gentleman who is also an employee.

> I had long since learnt to understand, composedly and as a matter of course, that my situation in life was considered a guarantee against any of my female pupils feeling more than the most ordinary interest in me, and that I was admitted among beautiful and captivating women, much as a harmless domestic animal is admitted among them.

His foreboding is well merited. Marian Halcombe, the other young lady, takes him to one side and tells him that Laura is engaged to be married, to Sir Percival Glyde; if he is to behave honourably he must leave Limmeridge House at once.[79]

Such is what one might call the kernel narrative of *The Woman in White*, and it bears some relation to a common paranoid fantasy: the glamorous consort of a very important person has fallen in love with you; the very important person's henchmen find out about the affair, and decide that it constitutes a threat to state security; so they take steps to dispose of you.[80] The fantasy is a fantasy of social recognition through and for expertise, a fantasy we have already

[78] Taylor explores this familiarity with great insight in *In the Secret Theatre of Home*. For a related discussion, see Sally Shuttleworth, *Charlotte Brontë and Victorian Psychology* (Cambridge: CUP, 1996).

[79] *The Woman in White*, ed. John Sutherland (Oxford: OUP, 1996), 15, 64, 68–76. Henceforth *WW*.

[80] I take this 'plot-summary', with slight modifications, from Ronald K. Siegel, *Whispers: The Voices of Paranoia* (New York: Crown Publishers, 1994), 6.

seen in action in Tasso's madness, and in Rousseau's fascination with Tasso's madness.

Like Tasso, and Rousseau, Hartright must reimagine indifference as persecution. It is only with all eyes on him, with every man's hand against him, that he will no longer be able to doubt his own uniqueness. Unlike either Tasso or Rousseau, Hartright inhabits a novel. He can expect narrative itself to do the work of reimagining for him, to enmesh him in 'actual' conspiracy. And it does. What happens to Hartright is that he becomes involved, at the very moment of his expulsion from Limmeridge House, in a campaign to defeat a conspiracy against Laura Fairlie which justifies him in his paranoia. He is right to feel persecuted, because Sir Percival Glyde and Count Fosco really are out to exploit and humiliate Laura; and he is right to feel a sense of grandeur, because Laura really does love him, and because, in defeating the conspiracy, he becomes not only her husband, but the father of the heir to Limmeridge (a drawing-master no more).

Paranoia, *The Woman in White* seems to say, as *Caleb Williams* had seemed to say, will equip a young man of humble origin but with considerable charm and talent for life in the modern world. The primary or kernel narrative is a paranoid fantasy which would have had little or no chance of realization, as Collins very well knew, in Britain in 1860; the secondary narrative he wove around it, in which an illegitimate baronet and a mice-toting Italian count conspire to rob and incarcerate a helpless young woman, enables the primary narrative to achieve a resolution it would not otherwise have been able to achieve.

The reason for thinking of Hartright's suspicions about Sir Percival Glyde in these terms is that they are the terms in which he himself begins immediately to think. As a result of his chilling exchange with Marian Halcombe, a dense web of connections begins to form in his mind, which implicates both Laura Fairlie and Anne Catherick, the woman in white encountered on Hampstead Heath. He admits that he has 'not the shadow of a reason' for connecting Sir Percival Glyde with the 'suspicious words of enquiry' spoken to him by Anne Catherick. 'And yet, I did connect him with them.' Is it because he has just heard of Sir Percival's engagement to Laura Fairlie, who herself bears an 'ominous' resemblance to Anne Catherick? 'Had the events of the morning so unnerved me already that I was at the mercy of any delusion which common chances and common coincidences might suggest to my imagination?' In paranoid narrative, as we have seen, common chances and coincidences are usually the first thing to go. Before long, Hartright, like Caleb Williams before him, will have to bribe his imagination to make believe that they exist. Although there are, of course, compensations. Marian Halcombe is soon telling him that he is the only person competent to advise her, as she too becomes increasingly concerned about Sir Percival's intentions. Hartright's progress towards paranoid symmetry has begun in earnest. 'It seemed almost like a monomania to be tracing back everything strange that happened, everything unexpected that was said, always to the same hidden source and the same sinister influence.'[81] Like Caleb Williams, he goes mad, or something very like mad, by tracing all common chances and coincidences back to the 'same hidden source'.

Helen Small has argued very persuasively that *The Woman in White* can best be understood as the last in a long line of stories about women who go mad when they lose their lovers. Anne Catherick and Laura Fairlie both belong in that category. Anne and Laura, like Dickens's Miss Havisham, in *Great Expectations* (1862), bear a clear resemblance to the madwomen of early nineteenth-century sentimental fiction; but the scrutiny their symptoms invite is a scrutiny framed by the unsentimental doctrines of mid-nineteenth-century psychological medicine. 'These women in white fit the outward signs of love-madness, but they no longer make sense to the world, or to themselves, as figures for benignly pitying contemplation.' Collins at once opposes the classificatory zeal of medical diagnosis, insisting with the right-hearted Hartright that a lover's eyes are more subtle than a physician's; and implicitly endorses it, by adapting forensic procedures to literary use, and by remaining as sceptical about romance as he was about medicine.[82] My aim here is to suggest that *The Woman in White* is a novel not only about love's madness, but about ambition's madness.[83] If hysteria was the name

---

[81] *WW* 76–7, 80.

[82] *Love's Madness: Medicine, the Novel, and Female Insanity 1800–1865* (Oxford: Clarendon Press, 1996), 194–207.

[83] One might even think of the sensation novel as a genre in these terms. In M. E. Braddon's *Lady Audley's Secret* (1863), the mysterious disappearance of his friend

often given to women suffering from love's madness, then paranoia is the name we might give to men like Caleb Williams and
Walter Hartright who suffer from ambition's madness.[84]

This is not to say that Collins understood ambition's madness in
terms of wealth and status alone. *The Woman in White* does seem
to regard that gendered form of symbolic capital known as
masculinity as one of the means by which social recognition is to
be achieved. But it 'produces' masculinity as an effect of narrative
procedure rather than of characterization.

What could be more sublimely masculine than the face which
crowns Marian Halcombe's beautifully feminine figure, with its
firm mouth and jaw, its swarthy complexion, and the dark down
on the upper lip?[85] So striking are these features, so awful in their
effect, that Collins feels obliged to withdraw them from view.
They are never mentioned again. Helen Small attributes this
erasure of Marian's physical identity to Collins's collusion with
medical diagnosis. In her view, Collins suppressed the firm jaw
and the moustache in order to implicate Marian with Laura Fairlie
and Anne Catherick in 'the condition and the spectacle of the
nervously ill woman'.[86] Marian herself, looking back over her
journal the night before Laura's wedding to Sir Percival Glyde,
fears that she may have caught the 'feverish excitement' of Laura's
spirits like an infection.[87]

However, evidence to which Small draws attention might also
suggest a rather different blurring of identities. Commenting on

George Talboys provokes in Robert Audley, another of 19th-cent. fiction's many
briefless barristers, an uneasiness bordering on insanity: 'am I to be tormented all my
life', he wonders, 'by vague doubts, and wretched suspicions, which may grow upon
me till I become a monomaniac?' Recalling the terror which seized him on the day
of George Talboys's disappearance, he asks himself whether he should account it a
'monition' or a 'monomania'. 'What if I am wrong after all? What if this chain of
evidence which I have constructed link by link is woven out of my own folly?' *Lady
Audley's Secret* (London: Virago, 1985), 125, 217–18.

[84] D. A. Miller refers to the state of mind of the main protagonists as at once hysterical and paranoid: '*Cage aux folles*: Sensation and Gender in Wilkie Collins's *The
Woman in White*', in Catherine Gallagher and Thomas Laqueur (eds.), *The Making of
the Modern Body: Sexuality and Society in the Nineteenth Century* (Berkeley, Calif.:
University of California Press, 1987), 107–36. By 1860, it would have been possible
to distinguish between these afflictions.

[85] *WW* 32.   [86] *Love's Madness*, 199–200.

[87] *WW* 194.

the first batch of proofs, Dickens remarked that the three narrators (Hartright, Marian Halcombe, and Mr Gilmore) share a 'dissective' habit which is essentially the author's, rather than their own.[88] Marian might be said to masculinize herself, to develop the dissective habit of medical psychology, when she assumes her duties as a narrator. Appropriately enough, one of her first topics is Walter Hartright's paranoia, his suspicion that he has been 'perpetually watched and followed by strange men'. And she soon succumbs to paranoia herself, an infection which outlasts any contact she might have had with Laura's feverish excitement. Reviewing what she has written so far, she realizes that a prejudice against Sir Percival Glyde has taken root in her mind. 'Is it Laura's reluctance to become his wife that has set me against him? Have Hartright's perfectly intelligible prejudices infected me without my suspecting their influence?'[89] Marian, I think, has caught her madness from Walter rather than from Laura. The infection masculinizes her. It makes her into a narrator the equal in aspiration and in suspiciousness to the drawing-master himself. The strange disappearance of Marian's swarthiness and moustache may have as much to do with Collins's interest in ambition's madness as with his interest in love's madness.

One might note in this respect an odd parallel between Hartright's arrival at Limmeridge House, early in the novel's first volume, and Marian's arrival at Blackwater Park, the home of Sir Percival Glyde, at the beginning of the second. Hartright's journey from London is interrupted when the engine breaks down between Lancaster and Carlisle, and he does not get to Limmeridge until midnight; Marian, held up in London by various calls and commissions, arrives at Blackwater Park after dusk. Both therefore awake the next morning and take in all at once the full and unshadowed appearance of landscapes which will to a considerable extent define their experience in the weeks and months to come. Collins's model, here, I believe, is photography, or the production of what Marian calls 'sun-pictures'.[90] Photography was at first known as 'heliography', because it required

[88] Letter of 7 Jan. 1860, to Wilkie Collins: *Letters*, 3 vols., ed. Walter Dexter (London: Nonesuch, 1938), iii. 215.

[89] *WW* 168, 188. [90] *WW* 29–30, 199, 201.

long exposures in bright sunlight.[91] Walter Hartright and Marian Halcombe are to be imagined as exposing themselves to a world replete with meaning and value. They are exposed as psychosis exposes, all at once. That Collins should so explicitly connect Marian to Walter in this and other ways suggests that her moustache has been sublimated into a narrative habit at once dissective and psychotic, into ambition's madness: at no time more so, perhaps, than when, in a 'trance' or 'daydream', Walter addresses her from another continent, indeed from another genre, promising to survive pestilence and poisoned arrows.[92] The distinction operative in *The Woman in White* is thus between 'masculine' narrators like Walter and Marian, whose psychosis alerts them to danger, and 'feminine' narrators like Mr Gilmore and Mrs Michelson, whose fatally reassuring lack of paranoia we ourselves must dispel if we are to keep track of the conspiracy against Laura Fairlie.

Ambition's madness is played out most luxuriously in the book's final 'epoch', during which Walter, reunited with Laura and Marian, establishes a base for his detective expeditions in the East End of London. Marian has by this time been re-subsumed into femininity (she even undertakes to do the housework). The narrative is now once again under Walter's more or less exclusive control. Like Caleb Williams, he values the anonymity London alone can offer; like Caleb, he finds work providing material for the press. The exercise of his skills in this fashion is a last resort, and yet also a reminder of those qualities in himself which had once earned Laura's love, and the prospect of a measure of social recognition, at Limmeridge. Laura is at least alive, 'with the poor drawing-master to fight her battle, and to win the way back for her to her place in the world of living beings'. Only in poverty and in hiding will such a woman be able to acknowledge, or be obliged to acknowledge, her dependence on the poor man's

[91] It might be that Collins had in mind the 'Calotype' process, invented by Fox Talbot in 1841, which reduced the necessary exposure to sunlight to three minutes. See Michel Frizot, 'Automated Drawing: The Truthfulness of the Calotype', in Frizot (ed.), *A New History of Photography* (Cologne: Könemann, 1998), 59–90. Whether or not he had photography in mind, Collins clearly uses such moments to put in place the 'structure of abrupt revelation', in Patrick Brantlinger's phrase, which distinguishes the sensation novel from domestic realism and makes of it a 'mass-cultural commodity' (*Reading Lesson*, 153, 163).

[92] *WW* 278–9.

talents and character. Indeed, Walter reconstitutes their original relationship by teaching Laura how to draw; she is now once again his pupil, or even his child. Paranoid symmetry thus adjusts the degree of fantasized persecution, by enemies who 'would leave no stone unturned, no sacrifice unattempted, no treachery untried, to discover the place in which their victim was concealed', to the degree of fantasized grandeur: the self-assurance generated by Walter's possession of 'the righteous purpose of redressing an infamous wrong'.[93]

For Walter Hartright, as for Caleb Williams, professional identity is at once that which he aspires to and that which he dangerously exceeds. Seeking professional help, he consults Mr Kyrle, a lawyer 'to the very marrow of his bones'. The story he has to tell tests Kyrle's 'professional composure' to the limit. He clearly believes that Walter is 'the victim of a delusion'. 'As a lawyer, and as a lawyer only, it is my duty to tell you, Mr Hartright, that you have not the shadow of a case.' Institutional law is that against which Walter, like Caleb, must test his faith in himself. This is the first time that the story of the conspiracy against Laura has been presented to him 'from a stranger's point of view', from a point of view outside the delusionary system. The stranger's point of view is the point of view of institutional justice. 'In short, Mr Hartright,' Kyrle reiterates, 'there is really no case.' Like Caleb, however, Walter asserts a law higher than the law of the land, the law of individual conscience. Fosco and Glyde will answer for their crime, he insists, 'to ME, though the justice that sits in tribunals is powerless to pursue them'. As if to underline that powerlessness, Fosco's agents are waiting for him outside Kyrle's office. The true (that is, paranoid) professional must always resist the expertise of mere institutions, mere tribunals, whatever the risks attached to that resistance. And yet Walter never detaches himself quite so radically from the law as Caleb had. Once supplied with concrete evidence, Kyrle has his uses.[94]

A final detail might serve at once to reinforce the tenuous connection between Walter Hartright and Caleb Williams, and to connect the attitude both protagonists strike to the critique of social mimesis mounted in the 1860s by John Stuart Mill and

---

[93] *WW* 420–1, 443–6, 440.   [94] *WW* 449–56, 631.

others. From its origins, paranoid narrative had incorporated a profound, visceral loathing for the idea of disguise. Caleb Williams, who has always possessed a 'considerable facility' in the 'art of imitation', disguises himself on occasion in order to evade his persecutors. Such, he declares, are the 'miserable expedients' which man, 'who never deserves the name of manhood but in proportion as he is erect and independent', may find it necessary to employ 'for the purpose of eluding the inexorable animosity and unfeeling tyranny of his fellow men!' He endures these miserable expedients with 'pining', 'abhorrence', 'aversion', and 'disgust', and eventually resolves to do without them altogether.[95] The paranoiac wishes above all, and at almost any cost, to be recognized for what he uniquely is, and the loss of identity which mimicry always entails is fatal to that project. Walter Hartright is of the same mind. He feels that if he were to adopt a disguise he would reduce himself to the level of the 'common herd of spies and informers'.[96] By associating disguise with commonness, as well as loss of manhood, Walter acknowledges the force of Mill's sombre lament at the diminishment of 'variety of situations' in the modern world. Ape-like imitation is not for him, either. Gothic enough in his delusion of grandeur, he none the less recognizes that in England in the 1860s it is social mimesis, rather than tyranny, which is at once paranoia's stimulus and its primary antagonist.

[95] *CW* 246–7, 263–5, 298, 315.   [96] *WW* 493.

CHAPTER 4

Towards an Epidemiology of Paranoid Narrative

By Harold Perkin's account, it was during the period between 1880 and the First World War that 'professional society' finally and unequivocally 'rose'. 'By 1911,' Perkin notes, 'if we add the lesser professionals and technicians to the higher ones, the professions were 4.1 per cent of the occupied population, not much short of the 4.6 per cent who were "employers" in the census of industrial status, and if we add "managers and administrators" the figure rises to 7.5 per cent, larger than the category of "employers and proprietors" (6.7 per cent).' As significant as the overall increase in numbers was the degree of organization now to be found within the majority of professions. To the seven qualifying associations extant in 1800—two Royal Colleges, four Inns of Court for barristers, and the Society of Apothecaries—twenty had been added by 1880. In the period between 1880 and the First World War, by contrast, no less than thirty-nine further associations were formed: for chartered accountants, estate agents, insurance brokers, and so on. Several non-qualifying associations, such as the National Union of Teachers, also came into being, as did an 'intellectual class' consisting of 'men of letters', 'men of science', and university teachers. Some members of the intellectual class began to seek professional status. The Society of Authors was founded in 1883, in defence of copyright. At the same time, the professionalization of science proceeded through the establishment of bodies such as the Physical Society (1876) and the Institute of Chemistry (1877) and of laboratories at Oxford (1872) and Cambridge (1874). By 1900, professional society had developed not only size, but muscle, a formidable presence.[1]

---

[1] H. Perkin, *The Rise of Professional Society: England since 1880* (London: Routledge,

The professionalization of English society and culture in the first decades of the twentieth century is the broad context for the account I shall give in the chapters following this one of a range of texts in which literary experiment would appear to proceed by means of an inquiry into representations of psychosis. If Perkin is right in arguing that by 1900 professionalization had transformed English society and culture from top to bottom, then an interest in professional identity, on the part of a writer, cannot in itself have been in any important way distinctive. In approaching literary Modernism, I need to be able to say what it was that distinguished the kind of interest taken in professional identity by writers we normally associate with literary experiment from the kind of interest taken in it by writers we do not normally associate with literary experiment. In this chapter, I shall attempt a preliminary sifting.

BEYOND EFFICIENCY: PROFESSIONALISM AND CHARISMA

'Between 1880 and 1914', Perkin argues, 'the professional social ideal took a further step, from *ad hoc* criticism of capitalist society to a series of organized assaults on the concept of absolute property.' The step was first taken, he maintains, by social philanthropists such as Octavia Hill and Arnold Toynbee, and by academics such as the Oxford philosopher T. H. Green and the Cambridge economist Alfred Marshall, in whose work the professional social ideal found expression as a critique of *laissez-faire* liberalism. Charles Masterman, Marshall's pupil, and a close friend of Ford Madox Ford, helped Lloyd George and Winston Churchill to prepare the People's Budget of 1909 and the National Insurance Act of 1911, as well as various other reforming measures. Many of the leading figures in the socialist movement of the time—from Sidney and Beatrice Webb through J. A. Hobson, Graham Wallas, and L. T. Hobhouse to Bernard Shaw and H. G. Wells—belonged to the professional middle class; the social order

1989), 84–6. The classic account of the emergence of an 'intellectual class' is Edward Shils, *The Intellectuals and the Powers* (Chicago: University of Chicago, 1972). For the professionalization of literature, see Peter Keating, *The Haunted Study: A Social History of the English Novel 1875–1914* (London: Secker & Warburg, 1989), chs. 1 and 7.

they sought to create was a social order run by an administrative and technocratic élite.[2] In *A Modern Utopia* (1905), Wells described in some detail the functions of the 'samurai' who, beginning as a 'revolutionary organisation', would eventually seize power in the Western democracies and establish a world state. He conceived his 'samurai' as an aristocracy of public service exempt from financial transactions, like Plato's Guardians or the Knights Templar.[3] The Fabians gave intellectual property a status equivalent to the property defined by land or capital; Graham Wallas even spoke of the three 'rents', of land, capital, and ability. Their emphasis on expertise gained an extra dimension through social imperialism and its campaigns for 'national efficiency'. The Webbs attempted to bring leading imperialists together with experts in the various departments of culture and society in a group called the 'Co-Efficients'. Wells, inevitably, became literature's representative. National Efficiency, Perkin points out, had the great merit from the samurai point of view of appealing to the self-interest of land, labour, and capital alike.[4]

By 1900, the professional social ideal was pervasive in English culture, recognizable not only in the utopian fantasies to which it gave rise, but also in the hostility it provoked. In the first volume of his autobiography, Leonard Woolf recalled the 'bitter lesson' he had learnt on the boat out to Ceylon (Sri Lanka), where he was to take up a post in the colonial civil service. The lesson had to do with the 'spontaneous malevolence' displayed toward the budding samurai on board by a group of Colombo businessmen led by the flamboyant Mr X. 'It gradually became clear to us that Mr X and his friends regarded us with *a priori* malignity because we were civil servants. It was my first experience of the class war and hatred between Europeans which in 1904 was a curious feature of British imperialism in the East.'[5] That '*a priori* malignity' has remained a feature of imperial and post-imperial Britain. It would, for example, be one way to define Thatcherism.

---

[2] Perkin, *Rise of Professional Society*, 123, 126–31.

[3] *A Modern Utopia*, ed. Mark R. Hillegas (Lincoln, Nebr.: University of Nebraska Press, 1967), 277–8. The samurai are for the most part engaged in 'administrative work', Wells notes, and have been 'forbidden to buy to sell on their own account or for any employer save the state' (pp. 278, 287).

[4] *Rise of Professional Society*, 132, 158–9.

[5] *Growing: An Autobiography of the Years 1904–1911* (London: Hogarth Press, 1967), 16.

The vertical division between the professional and commercial middle classes which Leonard Woolf had cause to regret on the boat out to Ceylon, and which Perkin finds everywhere in Edwardian social theory, is not hard to find in the kind of Edwardian social fiction we do not customarily regard as Modernist. The protagonist of Wells's *Tono-Bungay* (1908), for example, participates with a mixture of reluctance and glee in the commercial exploitation of a worthless patent medicine, but ends up, after the inevitable smash, designing and test-driving destroyers: an occupation Wells obviously regards as altogether more worthwhile.[6]

Expertise—Wallas's 'rent of ability'—could be conceived as a novel's topic, and as its method: as a source of the symbolic capital accruing to literature. In the opening paragraph of Galsworthy's *The Man of Property* (1906), the narrator observes that 'psychological analysis' is 'a talent without monetary value', and thus ignored by the Forsytes.[7] It is the 'saga' itself, of course, which for the next 900 pages will exercise that gift on behalf of a professional social ideal discerningly represented within it. In this respect, there is little difference to be observed between novels by Galsworthy and Wells, and novels by Lawrence and Joyce. *Women in Love* (1920) and *Ulysses* (1923) oppose a representative of the professional social ideal (Rupert Birkin, Stephen Dedalus) to a representative of industry or commerce (Gerald Crich, Leopold Bloom). To be sure, both Birkin and Dedalus defect from that ideal, deliberately, or by lapse. Such defections, however, as Birkin's case will amply demonstrate, do not amount to an erasure; both are professionals against professionalism. And one could conceivably argue that the novels in which they feature belong to them, or their 'point of view'.[8] Gerald Crich could not have written *Women in Love*. Leopold Bloom could not have written *Ulysses*. Modernism,

---

[6] *Tono-Bungay* (London: Pan Books, 1964), 324–30.

[7] *The Forsyte Saga* (Harmondsworth: Penguin Books, 1978), 11.

[8] Such, at any rate, was the burden of Wyndham Lewis's elaborate critique of *Ulysses* in *Time and Western Man* (London: Chatto & Windus, 1927), ch. 16. Lewis regarded *Ulysses* as an autobiographical text whose degree of literary specialization cannot conceal a certain indulgence towards its young protagonist's yearning for status. 'But the implicit theme of the whole piece, what moves Joyce to churn up the english tongue in a mock-elizabethan frenzy, is the burning question still of his shabby-genteel boyhood, namely To be a "toff", or not to be a "toff"' (p. 125).

in short, shares with the mainstream fiction of the period an interest in expertise and its discontents.

Furthermore, professionalism has long been regarded as an issue in the emergence towards the end of the nineteenth century of mass-market genre fiction. In the spy-thriller and the detective story, as Jerry Palmer has noted, the self-reliant expert is defined both against the agency bureaucrat, who only ever acts by the book, and against the clueless amateur: Lestrade's errors and Watson's bafflement are the true measure of Holmes's genius.[9] Nicholas Daly finds in 'team' novels such as Bram Stoker's *Dracula* (1897) a shift of emphasis away from self-reliance towards the kind of associative enterprise which was becoming an important part of professional life. Where previous critics have maintained that *Dracula* reflects one or more of a range of contemporary anxieties, Daly regards the text as a peformance whose aim is to reshape society in the image of an association among and between men. Van Helsing, the 'great specialist' who is also a doctor and a qualified lawyer, could be seen as the 'super-professional' leader of a band of professional men. Dracula himself is a 'back-formation' which the narrative requires not as an embodiment of degeneracy, but as the catalyst for the creation of a group of experts.[10] The vampire-hunters are in a sense samurai; and the narrative which demands that they be brought together is, for all its Gothic accessories, as close to science fiction as *A Modern Utopia*.

We need to complicate the picture a little, if we are to see how the rendering of professional identity might be held to indicate differences, rather than similarities, between one kind of writing and another. The first necessary complication is that there was no consensus, even among the professional middle classes, about the function and value of expertise. Wells might have thrilled in a bleak fashion to the designing of warships, but few other writers shared his appetite for expertise in the raw. There was simply too much professionalism around, in the Edwardian era, for it to serve as a *de facto* source of significant identity. By 1900, the pervasiveness of bureaucratic rationalism in Western societies was such that

---

[9] *Thrillers: Genesis and Structure of a Popular Genre* (London: Edward Arnold, 1978).
[10] *Modernism, Romance and the Fin de Siècle: Popular Fiction and British Culture 1880–1914* (Cambridge: CUP, 1999), 39, 46.

Max Weber was able to define 'charisma' as its antithesis. To adapt Weber's terms, we might say that expertise, as commonly understood, had lost the charisma which, under particular social and political circumstances, in English society at any rate, it had once possessed for men and women from humble backgrounds; and that the task accordingly undertaken by some members of the Edwardian intelligentsia was a renewal of expertise in the name not so much of 'efficiency' as of charisma. Weber, incidentally, would have been under no illusions as to the difficulty of that project. 'Charismatic authority', he wrote, 'is naturally unstable.'[11]

In *The New Machiavelli* (1911), a novel about the achievements and shortcomings of the New Liberalism which swept to power in the General Election of 1906, Wells satirized the 'Co-Efficients' as the 'Pentagram Circle'; the Fabian exponents of 'sham expert officialdom' were, he makes it clear, a bloodless lot. Remington, his protagonist, a Liberal MP who finds that he can no longer stomach his own party's pieties, goes over to the principle of aristocracy, and then to the party which in his view still just about embodies it. However, the task Remington sets himself—to produce a 'self-conscious, highly selective, open-minded, devoted aristocratic culture'—does not seem incompatible, apart from its lingering attachment to the world of chivalry, with Fabian ideas about professional public service.[12] Wells manages to obscure this basic compatibility by having Remington succumb to sexual impulse and thus leave politics before he is called upon to put samurai doctrine into practice. Like *A Modern Utopia*, *The New Machiavelli* has no more to offer politically than a souped-up version of expert officialdom.

Unlike Caleb Williams, Walter Hartright, or Bradley

---

[11] 'Charisma and its Transformation', *Economy and Society: An Outline of Interpretative Sociology*, 2 vols., ed. Guenther Roth and Claus Wittich (Berkeley, Calif.: University of California Press, 1978), ii. 1111–57. 'In radical contrast to bureaucratic organization, charisma knows no formal and regulated appointment or dismissal, no career, advancement or salary, no supervisory or appeals body, no local or purely technical jurisdiction, and no permanent institutions in the manner of bureaucratic agencies, which are independent of the incumbents and their personal charisma. Charisma is self-determined and sets its own limits. Its bearer seizes the task for which he is destined and demands that others obey and follow him by virtue of his mission' (ii. 1112).

[12] *The New Machiavelli*, ed. Norman Mackenzie (London: J. M. Dent, 1994), 238, 242.

Headstone, Remington does not go (even a little bit) mad. The monomania which had sometimes been thought to attend the production of symbolic capital through expertise somehow eludes him. There were others, as we have already seen, whom it did not elude. The schoolmaster Ernst Wagner, for example, found himself well and truly short of charisma in Mühlhausen-an-der-Enz. He might just as well have been buried alive. The men who go mad, in early twentieth-century fiction, are either already expert, like Adam Jeffson in *The Purple Cloud* and Rupert Birkin in *Women in Love*, or independently wealthy, and thus able to scorn mere officialdom. They do not go mad, as Caleb Williams and Walter Hartright had done, *in pursuit of professional status*.

Wells is an interesting case, in this respect. In the late 1880s, he taught in schools in Wales and London, while studying for a B.Sc. in zoology, and for diplomas in the history and theory of education. Trained as an educator, he gave up education for writing, but wrote, for the rest of his life, as an educator. Through his career, the charisma which in his view a well-run (a Wells-run) society ought to attach to the figure of the educator remained a central preoccupation. Shadowing this preoccupation was an uncomfortably vivid sense of the megalomania which often accompanies the will to educate. Wells's fiction is full of global potentates and luminaries with a Wagner-like propensity for murderousness. As Peter Kemp has pointed out, *The Holy Terror* (1939) might be seen as an attempt, at the very end of his career, to come to terms with precisely these 'triumphalist obsessions'. The protagonist, Rud Whitlow, is like Wells in a number of ways. He believes, as Wells did, in a World State; and, like Wells, only because no organization of lesser scope would ever do justice to his own powers of leadership. Whitlow's capacity for involvement with another person, deliberately suppressed early in life, returns as 'a vague, cloudy desire to be appreciated, admired, obeyed—loved by all the world'.[13] Kemp is able to show that Wells had abundant reason to recognize in himself the rampant megalomania he recognized in Whitlow.[14]

In paranoia, Freud observed, 'internal catastrophe' often finds

---

[13] His obsessions develop into full-blown paranoid delusion: *The Holy Terror* (London: Michael Joseph, 1939), 423–4.

[14] *H. G. Wells and the Culminating Ape: Biological Imperatives and Imaginative Obsessions*, new edn. (Basingstoke: Macmillan, 1996), ch. 5.

expression in fantasies of the end of the world. 'The patient has withdrawn from the people in his environment and from the external world generally the libidinal cathexis which he has hitherto directed on to them.'[15] Science fiction allowed Wells, as it was to allow M. P. Shiel, to imagine (and revel in) that ending of worlds which paranoia so often demands as tribute. Wells, too, had his Schreberian moments. John Carey has vividly described the inventiveness of Wells's books when it comes to getting rid of people.[16] Like Shiel, Wells relished the materiality of catastrophe. The description in *The War of the Worlds* (1898) of panic at Chalk Farm—'the engines of the trains that had loaded in the goods yard there *ploughed* through shrieking people'—was surely the inspiration for Shiel's account in *The Purple Cloud* of the 'carnal quagmire' through which Adam Jeffson wades in Paddington Station.[17] Wells also provides in the figure of the artilleryman the narrator encounters on Putney Hill—no 'ornamental soldier', this, but a true expert—a point of view from which the carnage inflicted by the Martians can be seen as eugenic. 'Life is real again', the artilleryman observes, 'and the useless and cumbersome and mischievous have to die. They ought to die.' The artilleryman's belief that life has become real again is a Schreberian belief that other people have become unreal, and can thus be disposed of at will. It is out of the rubble of the world demolished before his eyes that, as Freud might have put it, the paranoiac builds the delusion which should be understood not as the pathological product of illness, but as the first step towards recovery. Schreber persuaded himself that he would redeem the world by giving birth to a new race; the artilleryman persuades himself that he will redeem it by forming and leading a resistance movement, a band of 'able-bodied, clean-minded men'. Gratifyingly, he means to include the narrator, who thereupon warms to his 'grandiose plans', as the

---

[15] *The Standard Edition of the Complete Psychological Works*, ed. James Strachey *et al.*, 24 vols. (London: Hogarth Press, 1953–74), xii. 70–1.

[16] *The Intellectuals and the Masses: Pride and Prejudice among the Literary Intelligentsia* (London: Faber & Faber, 1992), ch. 6.

[17] Wells could be said to have returned the compliment in *The War in the Air* (1908), in which a German air-raid on New York provokes global war and the destruction of the world's major cities. The narrator eventually returns to England to find that a plague called the Purple Death has decimated the population. London is a ghost city. Advertisements for canned peaches loom over an almost medieval landscape.

movement's chief of education. 'We must make great safe places down deep, and get all the books we can; not novels and poetry swipes, but ideas, science books. That's where men like you come in.'[18] Science fiction could be said to have done for Wells what mass-murder did for Ernst Wagner. It got rid of people. In *A Modern Utopia*, as the vision of the future fades, its exponent reiterates his furious and abiding desire to '*smash* the world of everyday'.[19]

Many of Wells's novels are of course set in the present rather than the future. Far from smashing the world of everyday, these novels tend to uphold it in and through the intensity with which they describe its appearance. One sign of their compliance with mimetic convention is that they set a firm limit to the triumphs of any character whose megalomania expresses contempt for the art of the possible: Masterman, in *Kipps*, for example, a novel published in the same year as *A Modern Utopia*; or Teddy Ponderevo, in *Tono-Bungay*, disciple of Nietzsche and Napoleon. Fascinating though Wells found both men, he could not in the end allow them to reshape society in their own image. One has to recognize in that holding back, that withdrawal from science fiction, a moral and literary achievement. Indeed, Peter Kemp quite plausibly makes Wells's resistance to his own sense of himself as a world-saviour the criterion for his success as a writer. Detail 'scooped from life' constantly enriches the work of the period from 1895 to 1910, Kemp argues, acknowledging by its specificity a randomness in the world's arrangements which system will never subdue.[20] Roughly the same could also be said of the writers most often associated with Wells, Arnold Bennett and John Galsworthy.[21] Bennett and Galsworthy are not best known for their portrayal of megalomaniacs.

Perhaps the most striking example of domestic realism's delib-erate withholding from paranoia occurs in George Gissing's wonderfully sardonic account of the literary life, *New Grub Street*

<hr />

[18] *The War of the Worlds*, in *The Science Fiction*, i (London: Phoenix, 1995), 251, 300, 302–3.

[19] *A Modern Utopia*, 363.

[20] *Culminating Ape*, 213–14.

[21] It is because he resisted the delusions of grandeur common among the literary intelligentsia, and not unknown to the Wells who liked getting rid of people, that Bennett emerges as the 'hero' of Carey's anti-Modernist polemic in *The Intellectuals and the Masses*.

(1891). *New Grub Street* is a book about symbolic capital and the difficulties of acquiring it. Edwin Reardon, the novel's failed novelist, is also a failed man. He does not possess the masculinity which, we are given to believe, would generate status through success either in marriage or in homosocial collaboration. Paranoia becomes at once testimony and solution to his incapacity, a structured parallel universe. In his description of Reardon's decline, Gissing adheres to the formulae, if not the exact terminology, of contemporary psychiatry. 'Refuge from despair', we learn, 'is often found in the passion of self-pity and that spirit of obstinate resistance which it engenders.' In some cases, self-pity leads to self-scorn, and ultimately to self-destruction. There are, however, 'less fortunate beings' whose ability to endure is *strengthened* by the 'vehemence' of their revolt against fate. 'These latter are rather imaginative than passionate', Gissing claims: 'the stages of their woe impress them as the acts of a drama, which they cannot bring themselves to cut short, so various are the possibilities of its dark motive'. Such people do not kill themselves. 'He who survives under like conditions does so because misery magnifies him in his own estimate.' This is as perceptive an account of the state of mind of an Ernst Wagner as anything the psychiatrists managed. At first, it seems that Reardon will go the same way. 'An extraordinary arrogance now and then possessed him; he stood amid his poor surroundings with the sensations of an outraged exile, and laughed aloud in furious contempt of all who censured or pitied him.' In the event, he does not. And one of the reasons he does not is the benevolent presence of domestic realism itself, in the shape of his fellow-novelist Harold Biffen, author of *Mr Bailey, Grocer*.[22] Unlike Wagner, Reardon does not put his 'furious contempt' into practice.

Paranoia, as we have seen, is in its very essence anti-mimetic. One might therefore expect to find it explored up to or even beyond the limit of implicit sympathy in kinds of writing which do not make a point of mimesis. It is the stuff of sensational fiction, of romance, of stories which extravagantly engineer duels to the death in inhospitable wastelands beyond the boundaries of civil and domestic society. And it is the stuff, I shall propose in subsequent

---

[22] *New Grub Street*, ed. Bernard Bergonzi (Harmondsworth: Penguin Books, 1968), 375–6.

chapters, of a programmatically anti-mimetic variant of Modernism. Inquiry into the madness attendant upon the search for a professionalism which would not exclude charisma connects mass-market romance, a genre revived to spectacular effect in the 1880s by Robert Louis Stevenson and Rider Haggard, to Modernist literary experiment, and distinguishes both from the domestic realism of whose durability Wells, Bennett, and Galsworthy were the main beneficiaries. Here, I want to track outbreaks of paranoid narrative—of a narrative both informed by and performing paranoia—across different varieties of exotic and/or sensational romance. The purpose of this epidemiology is to establish just how widespread the preoccupation with charisma and its discontents had become by 1914.

BECOMING-PARANOID: GENRE FICTION AT THE TURN OF CENTURY

First glimpsed in *The Prisoner of Zenda* (1894), by Anthony Hope (Anthony Hope Hawkins), Ruritania remained a steady favourite with Edwardian readers. The young Winston Churchill, for example, saw enough promise in the fledgling genre to try his hand at it. The hero of *Savrola* (1900), a brilliant soldier with a reputation for philosophy, especially on the subject of polo, has formed a revolutionary party to restore Laurania, once a republic, but now languishing under the iron heel of a dictator, to its ancient liberties.[23] The philosopher is edged out, but eventually returns in triumph. The sign that all is well again is the dispatch of the Lancers' polo team to England to defeat the Amalgamated Millionaires in the final of the Open Cup: another triumph, this time on the sports field, of principled professionalism over mere money. The plot creaks, but Churchill evidently took considerable pride in the military details, of which there are many.

The glamorous consort of a very important person has fallen in love with you; the very important person's henchmen find out about the affair, and decide that it constitutes a threat to state security; so they take steps to dispose of you. I have already suggested

[23] *Savrola: A Tale of the Revolution in Laurania* (London: Longmans Green, 1900).

that this fantasy might serve as an outline of the primary or kernel narrative of *The Woman in White*. It would also describe *The Prisoner of Zenda*.

In the opening chapter, Rudolf Rassendyll finds himself under attack by his sister-in-law, who is under no illusion as to the 'uselessness' of the life he has hitherto led. His defence, addressed as much to the reader as to his fulminatory relative, consists of a catalogue of the skills he has acquired by generally knocking about in the world. He may not have chosen a career, but he can speak German like a native, and handle a sword. 'If you say that I ought to have spent my time in useful labour, I am out of Court and have nothing to say, save that my parents had no business to leave me two thousand pounds a year and a roving disposition.' Rassendyll tends to think that his potential uniqueness lies in his ability to combine this chivalric expertise with the cultural capital invested in the gene-pool. His long, sharp, straight nose and mass of dark red hair would seem to connect him with the Elphbergs, the ruling dynasty of Ruritania, a mythical Central European state. He likes nothing better than to discern this distinctive physiognomy in portraits of ancestors belonging, he feels sure, to the Royal House of Ruritania.[24] 'The idea of being the child of other people becomes more and more powerful', Krafft-Ebing noted of patients whose paranoia had taken hold before puberty. 'The patients notice the lack of resemblance with their family, and accidental resemblance to portraits of reigning princes or distinguished persons.' The result, Krafft-Ebing adds, is 'a formal romance of persecution and grandeur'.[25] One could not ask for a better description of *The Prisoner of Zenda* and its like.

Visiting Ruritania to witness the coronation of Prince Rudolf of Elphberg, Rassendyll finds himself caught up in deadly political intrigue. The prince has been kidnapped by 'Black' Michael, duke of Strelsau, and Rassendyll, to whom he bears a striking physical resemblance, must stand in for him until he can be found and released from captivity. At which point, the beautiful Princess Flavia, who thinks he *is* the prince, though somehow a lot sexier

[24] *The Prisoner of Zenda*, ed. Tony Watkins (Oxford: OUP, 1994), 7–8. Henceforth *PZ*.

[25] *Textbook of Insanity*, tr. Charles Gilbert Chaddock (Philadelphia: F. A. Davis, 1904), 378.

and far more considerate than the man she married, falls in love with him. Sensing dynastic trouble, the prince's agents use Rassendyll to defeat Black Michael, and then terminate the romance. This, too, is a fantasy of recognition.

Rassendyll's paranoid illumination occurs in a scene midway through the novel when he becomes aware of two all-important facts: first, that the princess loves him for himself, for the man he is rather than for the role he has undertaken to play; and, secondly, that this immensely gratifying acknowledgement of his uniqueness is not going to do him any good at all, because the prince's faithful retainers, Colonel Sapt and Fritz von Tarlenheim, will prevent him from revealing his true identity, and thus gaining a wife at the cost of a kingdom. Sapt and von Tarlenheim do not hesitate to remind him of these facts. They admit that he would make a better king than the prince, but point out that he is not a prince, and will thus never be a king. They persecute him, in short, *because* he is special. The scene concludes with Rassendyll's renunciation of Princess Flavia, a sacrifice rewarded by crowning evidence of his own uniqueness, and his dispensability.

I bowed my head to meet my hands, and crushed the rose between my fingers and my lips.

I felt his hand on my shoulder, and his voice sounded husky as he whispered low in my ear:

'Before God, you're the finest Elphberg of them all. But I have eaten of the king's bread, and I am the king's servant. Come, we will go to Zenda!'

And I looked up and caught him by the hand. And the eyes of both of us were wet.[26]

One might say that this passage represents the novel's own paranoid illumination: the first and last of the paragraphs quoted break out exuberantly into blank verse, the very medium of English genius, of William Shakespeare, of Milton and Wordsworth.

Ruritania is a time, not a place.[27] But *which* time? The past, it

[26] PZ 83.

[27] It has been argued that Ruritania is an intermediate zone between Europe and Asia, and that Ruritanian romance is thus a version of Orientalist fantasy: Vesna Goldsworthy, *Inventing Ruritania: The Imperialism of the Imagination* (New Haven, Conn.: Yale University Press, 1998). Having published three Ruritanian romances, Hope wrote *Sophy of Kravonia* (1906), the story of an English peasant girl who

has been said.[28] Ruritanian romance, by this account, nurtured an ideologically productive nostalgia. There is a difficulty here, however. The difficulty is that most of the Ruritanias I am familiar with are laboratories rather than museums. They are a way of imagining social and political change, indeed revolution, not stability. In *Savrola*, for example, the hero's agitations have the support of the British government; what interests Churchill, polo and parade-grounds apart, is the nature and consequences of upheaval. The only thing we learn about Strelsau, in *The Prisoner of Zenda*, is that it is partly old and partly new. 'Spacious modern boulevards and residential quarters surround and embrace the narrow, tortuous and picturesque streets of the original town.' Furthermore, this social division corresponds to a political division, the new town being for the king, the old for Black Michael.[29] Rassendyll may enjoy the rehearsal of chivalric codes, but his basic allegiance, like that of his creator, is to modernity. Ruritania, then, is not a place, but a time, a *condition*: the condition of becoming-modern.

I have said that Rassendyll's allegiance is to modernity. It might be more accurate to say that during his sojourn in Ruritania he *develops* an allegiance to modernity. Ruritania, the condition of becoming-modern, modernizes him. How? It all begins at the frontier. At the frontier, Rassendyll, a man without qualities who has 'knocked about' a good deal, but not left his mark anywhere, suddenly becomes, for the first time in his life, an object of attention. The officer presiding over the Custom House favours him with 'such a stare that I felt surer than before of my Elphberg physiognomy'. At the hotel in Zenda where he spends his first night in Ruritania, he is once again the recipient of glances he can only describe as 'intense, searching, almost fierce'. Eyes follow him wherever he goes. That these people are looking at him because

becomes the queen of an imaginary Balkan state. In the public imagination, it seems, Ruritania slid in a south-easterly direction across the map. The original Ruritania, however, is in Central Europe, its capital less than a day's journey from Dresden.

[28] Thus, Mark Girouard argues that 'Anthony Hope's inspired invention of Ruritania allowed him to move his English hero straight from modern clubland into a world of castles, kings, beautiful women, and feudal loyalties': *The Return to Camelot: Chivalry and the English Gentleman* (New Haven, Conn.: Yale University Press, 1981), 265.

[29] *PZ* 37.

he is unique, and because they resent his uniqueness, is shortly confirmed by an odd encounter. Taking a stroll in the forest before the arrival of the train for Strelsau, he falls asleep, and dreams that he has married the Princess Flavia, and is about to become the king of Ruritania. He wakes to find two men—Colonel Sapt and Fritz von Tarlenheim—staring at him.[30] These are the men who will before long insist both that Rassendyll take the prince's place and that he subsequently relinquish it, however painful the sacrifice. Ruritania modernizes Rassendyll by educating him in paranoia: paranoid, he is more than a match for the prince's enemies, and thus able to ensure the triumph of New Strelsau over Old Strelsau.

For Rudolf Rassendyll to become modern is to become paranoid. Before Ruritania, his life, while pleasant enough, had no purpose, no meaning, no passion: after Ruritania, he at least knows who he is. But since his regeneration is through paranoia, it can never be acknowledged fully, or made public: the banal world on whose miserable behalf it has been undertaken will for ever remain incapable of grasping its significance. When Rassendyll returns to London, he cannot quite bring himself to accept any of the jobs he has been offered. Why should someone who has tasted sovereignty want to turn diplomat? He has been a king, the queen loved him, and no one will ever know. The only proof is the single red rose Flavia sends him every year, with a note which reads 'Rudolf—Flavia—always'.[31] Ruritania keeps alive the dream shared by Rousseau, Godwin, and Collins, of a democratic modernity. But the arena of a democratization through expertise is now, and in some way has to be, self-consciously elsewhere. Furthermore, Rassendyll's background, unlike Caleb Williams's, or Walter Hartright's, can scarcely be counted humble, or even modest. His paranoia has to do less with a class-society's failure to acknowledge and reward talent than with the perceived mundaneness, in a society given over to professionalism, of mere expertise. However ambiguous his feelings about the diplomatic corps, Rousseau would not have turned down a job as an ambassador. These differences were to widen as paranoid narrative became disseminated across other genres.

I have used Ruritanian romance to illustrate a pattern which seems to me characteristic of turn-of-the-century mass-market fiction: regeneration through paranoia. John Buchan could be said to have given a shape to regenerative romance, and indeed a name, in *The Half-Hearted* (1900), whose hero—a supercilious, lethargic, 'over-cultured' young man—is persuaded to use his academic knowledge of the Indian frontier to help foil a Russian invasion. The Russians get him in the end. But he has saved India, and been regenerated in the process. He has mastered his disabling lethargy and understood the purpose of empire. This double awakening constitutes his adventure.[32] Rassendyll's regeneration, by contrast, is not so much physical and moral as psychodynamic. His adventure transforms him from a man without qualities into a man for whom the possession of mere qualities is neither here nor there. Neither marriage and a proper job nor a sacrificial death on the Indian frontier would have done for him what paranoid symmetry has done. What survives in the romance of regeneration through paranoia is the belief, evident in *Caleb Williams* and *The Woman in White*, that psychosis may under certain circumstances prove a progressive force. Spy fiction, another genre which flourished during the Edwardian era, found a way to exploit that belief to the full, though in the name of national rather than social renewal.

The years between 1900 and 1914 saw the establishment, not at all coincidentally, of the British spy novel and the British secret service.[33] Both invested heavily in fantasy. Indeed, they invested in the *same* fantasy, of an omnipotent German adversary. They invested in paranoia. Edwardian spy fiction found its hero in the amateur agent or accidental spy: sleepy young Englishmen whose complacency is shattered when they stumble across a German plot.

[32] *The Half-Hearted* (London: Isbister, 1900). I describe the Edwardian novel of half-heartedness in *The English Novel in History 1895–1920* (London: Routledge, 1993), ch. 9.

[33] Nicholas Hiley, 'The Failure of British Counter-Espionage against Germany, 1907–1914', *Historical Journal*, 28 (1985), 835–62, pp. 843–4. See also his 'The Failure of British Espionage against Germany, 1907–1914', *Historical Journal*, 26 (1983), 867–89, and 'Decoding German Spies: British Spy Fiction, 1908–1918', *Intelligence and National Security*, 5 (1990), 55–79. Equally useful are the relevant sections of Christopher Andrew's *Secret Service: The Making of the British Intelligence Community* (London: Heinemann, 1985) and Bernard Porter's *Plots and Paranoia: A History of Political Espionage in Britain 1790–1988* (London: Unwin Hyman, 1989); and David French, 'Spy Fever in Britain, 1900–1915', *Historical Journal*, 21 (1978), 355–70.

The spy novel's agenda had been set by invasion-scare stories which, from 1904 onwards at least, favoured 'the Hun' as invader.[34]

Thomas Richards has argued that such stories construct a 'corporate subject' whose job is to internalize the 'epistemological paranoia' rampant in an era of frantic rearmament: 'the hero of the invasion novel reads the visible world for evidence of an invisible but comprehensive design fraught with hostile intentions'.[35] This is not quite right. For the problem the invasion novel addresses is that created by an *insufficiency* of 'epistemological paranoia' in the national psyche, among the public at large. Its invading armies seem always to have established themselves firmly on British soil before anyone even knows they are there; resistance, however plucky, is always last-ditch, and often hopeless. What spy fiction did was to imagine a suspiciousness triggered early enough in the game to avert catastrophe. Its subject is the 'internalization' of paranoia by a young man who thereby renews both himself and a ruling élite which had hitherto been sunk in complacency. The young man's (belated) reading of the visible world for evidence of an invisible but comprehensive design endows him with charismatic professionalism, and belatedly earns recognition of his singular expertise.

In 'An Accidental Spy', the opening chapter of E. Phillips Oppenheim's *A Maker of History* (1905), Guy Stanton—'just a good-looking, clean-minded, high-spirited young fellow, full of beans, and needing the bit every now and then'—stumbles across a secret meeting between the Kaiser and the Tsar in a forest on the German border. A page of secret treaty, which floats out of a window and lands close to his hiding-place, reveals that they are co-ordinating an attack on Britain. Stanton, who speaks neither language, and is in any case too full of beans to be interested in politics, becomes a focus of deadly intrigue. The French get hold

---

[34] The only writer who could not keep a straight face was P. G. Wodehouse, who, in *The Swoop! Or, How Clarence Saved England* (London: Alston Rivers, 1909), had the Germans landing on the Essex coast, the Russians in Yarmouth, the Mad Mullah at Portsmouth, the Swiss navy at Lyme Regis, the Chinese at an unpronounceable Welsh bathing-resort, the Young Turks at Scarborough, and a small but determined band of warriors from the island of Bollygolla at Margate. The classic account of the genre is I. F. Clarke's *Voices Prophesying War, 1763–1984* (Oxford: OUP, 1966). For the relation between the spy novel and its immediate precursors, terrorist and invasion-scare stories, see my *English Novel in History, 170–5*.

[35] Thomas Richards, *The Imperial Archive* (London: Verso, 1993), 114–15.

of him before the Germans, and the elusive page persuades their government to ally itself with Britain rather than Russia, thus averting war. What connects the various protagonists is that they are all 'accidental spies' to begin with, and that they all become paranoid: they learn that, in a world where rulers meet in remote forests to plot global war, there is no such thing as accident. As one of them puts it triumphantly, 'We amateurs have justified our existence.'[36] In an important sense they are amateurs no longer. In becoming paranoid, they have acquired a certain expertise, an ability to read the visible world, an awareness that there is no such thing as accident. The symbolic capital invested in that expertise distinguishes them both from the public at large, which can just about be forgiven its amateurism concerning affairs of state, and from the political and administrative élite, which had thought itself thoroughly professional but turned out to be merely bureaucratic.[37] The belief in the imminence of a catastrophic European war which informs the variant of paranoid narrative known as spy fiction stands in stark contrast to the disbelief expressed by Remington, in Wells's *The New Machiavelli*.[38]

Richard Hannay, in Buchan's *The Thirty-Nine Steps* (1915), a wonderfully economical recapitulation of the form developed by Oppenheim and others, is the last of the accidental spies, the last amateur paranoiac. Finding in his flat the dead body of Franklin P. Scudder, who has uncovered a vast conspiracy, Hannay takes off for the lowlands of Scotland, with police and enemy agents hot on his heels. So singular is the knowledge he has accidentally obtained that every man's hand is against him. Hannay is a professional man, a mining engineer, but his knowledge makes him something more than that; it endows him with charisma. His moment of paranoid illumination, the moment when he knows that he really is special, occurs after he has returned to the south of England to brief Sir Walter Bullivant, Permanent Secretary at the Foreign Office.

---

[36] *A Maker of History* (London: Ward Lock, 1905), 40, 177.

[37] The most plausible and most gripping of these inductions into charismatic professionalism is described in Erskine Childers's *The Riddle of the Sands* (1903), where a bored civil servant combines with an amateur yachtsman and all-purpose 'civilian agitator' to thwart a German plan to launch an invasion of Britain from the area behind the East Frisian Islands: *The Riddle of the Sands*, ed. David Trotter (Oxford: OUP, 1998).

[38] *New Machiavelli*, 255.

Briefing Sir Walter, Hannay feeds his own hard-won knowledge into the bureaucracy, the political and administrative élite. But although the bureaucrats may now know as much as he does, they will never *be* him. They do not know by paranoia. Lunching in the Savoy grill, Hannay feels utterly convinced that no one can so much as glance at him without believing him to be a murderer. What confirms him in his uniqueness is thus the near-universality of the persecution he has suffered. 'I felt the sense of danger and impending calamity, and I had the curious feeling, too, that I alone could avert it, alone could grapple with it.'[39]

Edwardian spy fiction has on the whole been understood, with good reason, as an allegory of anxieties about class and nation. But the drama it performs is the drama of the internalization of an expertise which will enhance rather than extinguish charisma (and in the process save the world). Its structuring principle is paranoid symmetry. The person who ransacked Richard Hannay's writing-table and dumped a corpse on his best carpet did so with full and deliberate intent, and the mess he or she has left matters not in itself, but as evidence of that intent: as evidence in the visible world of an invisible but comprehensive design. The mess condemns Hannay to the kind of 'compulsive thinking' which so afflicted Daniel Paul Schreber that he felt he must investigate the nature and purpose of even the most self-evidently trivial occurrences. Workmen installed a stove in the next room, and he had to know why. A certain grandeur derives from this compulsive thinking. Schreber felt that his enquiries concerning stove-installation and the like had given him a 'deeper insight' into universal laws, into the 'essence' of human behaviour.[40] Hannay's enquiries bring about the defeat of an otherwise omnipotent adversary. Accidental spying—an espionage which disavows the very idea of accident, including that in which it itself began—takes place in the virtual asylum. Hannay's difference from the hero of *The Half-Hearted* is that he has gone mad, to the lasting benefit of a grateful nation.

[39] *The Thirty-Nine Steps*, ed. Christopher Harvie (Oxford: OUP, 1993), 85–6.
[40] *Memoirs of my Nervous Illness*, ed. and tr. Ida Macalpine and Richard A. Hunter (London: William Dawson, 1955), 179.

MODERNISM AND POPULAR FICTION

In this chapter, I have tried to demonstrate the connection between efforts to imagine a professional identity based on singularity, or charisma, and a type of fiction which did not bother too much about mimesis—which did not authenticate itself by investing in substantial quantities of descriptive detail 'scooped from life', in Peter Kemp's phrase. In the chapters to come, I shall suggest that some varieties of Modernist fiction—varieties customarily identified in part by their hostility to mimesis—also sought to re-establish the aura (and the psychopathies) of expertise.[41] I want now to review the terms in which one might relate Modernism to Edwardian popular fiction.

The Edwardian period would seem to have quite a lot going for it, as a period. It is short, well-defined (especially if we take it to end in 1914), and not lacking in political and socio-economic excitements: National Insurance, suffragettes, an armaments race, the strange death of liberal England. What more could one possibly want? And yet the feeling persists that as far as the evolution of British culture is concerned the Edwardian period was something of an interregnum, or pause for breath. Historiographically, a bypass connects the theme-park of *fin-de-siècle* decadence and renovation to the Modernist metropolis, and few commentators spare as much as a glance for the unprepossessing market town it carries them around. Books with titles like *Sexual Anarchy* or *A Widening Sphere* always turn out to deal with some other—more pivotal, more palpably crisis-ridden—time.[42] A 'turn of mind', in

---

[41] It is not my intention here to pursue any correlation between the idea of charisma which Weber opposed to bureaucratic rationalism and the idea of aura which Walter Benjamin opposed to mechanical reproduction. It is worth noting, however, that Benjamin regarded the diffusion of professional expertise as an important factor in the work of art's loss of uniqueness. 'Thus, the distinction between author and public is about to lose its basic character. The difference becomes merely functional; it may vary from case to case. At any moment the reader is ready to turn into a writer. As expert, which he had to become willy-nilly in an extremely specialized work process . . . the reader gains access to authorship': 'The Work of Art in the Age of Mechanical Reproduction', in *Illuminations*, ed. Hannah Arendt, tr. Harry Zohn (London: Fontana, 1973), 219–53, p. 234.

[42] Martha Vicinus, *A Widening Sphere* (Bloomington, Ind.: Indiana University Press, 1977); Elaine Showalter, *Sexual Anarchy: Gender and Culture at the* Fin de Siècle (London: Virago, 1992).

Samuel Hynes's phrase, is all the 1900s can be accused of propagating.[43] Writers on Edwardian literary culture in particular often give the impression of having bitten off rather less than they can chew.

In his recent and engagingly speculative study of Modernism's relation to nineteenth-century British culture, Nicholas Daly makes little effort to buck this trend. Daly's subtitle indicates that he means to examine developments in British culture in the period from 1880 to 1914; but he, too, has taken the Edwardian bypass. His aim, like that of many other commentators, is to connect Modernism back to cultural forces at work in Britain in the 1880s and 1890s: the difference being, and it is a productive difference, that the forces he has in mind are those of late Victorian romance rather than late Victorian aestheticism. Modernist writers, Daly claims, shared a 'broader culture of modernity' with the authors of works like *Treasure Island* and *King Solomon's Mines*. Modernism and popular romance are said to have been cast in the 'same historical mould', rooted in the 'same historical soil', cut from the 'same cultural cloth'.[44] The claim is a bold one, and I think Daly is right to make it. As his resort to metaphor might suggest, however, it needs some making.

Daly would like to rescue popular fiction from the condescension to which it has been subjected explicitly, by literary critics, and implicitly, by cultural historians for whom it is no more than an expression of the anxieties pervading a particular culture at a particular time. To do so, he adapts Louis Althusser's notion of a 'descriptive theory' which is capable of explaining almost all the observable facts in a given case, but itself remains metaphorical. Through the stories it told, Daly argues, popular fiction 'provided its readers with a *working* knowledge of Britain as a modernizing imperial society'.[45] His redefinition of popular fiction as a theory about or a working knowledge of social change, rather than an expression of the anxieties to which social change has given rise, enables him to understand it as an agent of modernization—and even of Modernism.

According to Daly, the proof of a 'family resemblance' between

[43] *The Edwardian Turn of Mind* (Princeton:Princeton University Press, 1968).
[44] *Modernism, Romance*, 9, 22, 150.
[45] Ibid. 25.

Modernism and late Victorian romance lies in the extent and intensity of the imaginative debt they both owe to empire. Modernism,
he says, depended on the 'same imperial imaginary' as late Victorian
romance. One of the virtues of his study is that it does justice to the
variety of ways in which the cultures and spaces constituting that
'imaginary' could be conceived. Thus he is able to show how
Stoker's *The Snake's Pass* (1890), where the culture and space at issue
is the West of Ireland, could be read either as a quest-story in the
exotic mode of *Treasure Island* and *King Solomon's Mines*, or as a
'response' to a crucial event in the history of Anglo-Irish relations,
the Land War of the 1880s. Daly's thesis is that the 'map of the
world' sketched by Haggard, Stevenson, Stoker, and other late
Victorian romancers was not so much 'discarded' as 'transvalued' by
Modernists like Hemingway and Lawrence.[46]

By his account, this transvaluation of the late Victorian map of
the world was the result of a critique of (or in some cases despair
at) the susceptibility of modern Western societies to commercial
process and habit. Commodification, the Modernists thought, had
remade those societies both from within and, through the medium
of empire, from without. Using the 'map' supplied by such as
Haggard, Stevenson, and Stoker, these writers managed to
convince themselves that they had found in the odd remaining
blank space a 'realm' beyond commodity fetishism—an as yet
uncorrupt 'margin' from which they could express their dissatisfaction with all aspects of modern metropolitan culture, including
the literary works of Haggard, Stevenson, and Stoker.[47] In
Hemingway's 'Big Two-Hearted River', for example, fisherman
and style guru Nick Adams presides over the cultural rebirth of
tinned spaghetti and pork and beans; in *The Sun Also Rises*, Jake
Barnes contrasts the authenticity he has conjured up during his
Spanish holiday with the 'imaginary amorous adventures' of
perfect English gentlemen in romances by A. E. W. Mason and
W. H. Hudson.[48]

In Daly's view, the commodity fetishism which prompted
Hemingway and others to a counter-investment in the marginal

---

[46] *Modernism, Romance*, 118.
[47] Ibid. 116, 118.
[48] *The Essential Hemingway* (London: Grafton Books, 1977), 346, 91.

found its descriptive theory in the 'mummy fiction' which had a considerable vogue in the 1880s and 1890s, and which could be said to culminate in Stoker's *The Jewel of Seven Stars* (1903). In this work an archaeologist called Abel Trelawny plans to use his knowledge of Egyptian mysteries to bring back to life one of the most notable adepts of ancient lore, Queen Tera, whose sarcophagus stands in his bedroom. His daughter Margaret—with whom the narrator, a young lawyer called Malcolm Ross, has fallen in love—soon shows signs of knowing rather more than she should about all things Egyptian: she is, it turns out, Queen Tera's double, and the medium and agent of the queen's carefully planned resurrection. Inspired by her familiarity with ancient protocol, Trelawny carries out his 'great experiment'. The result is a billowing cloud of acrid smoke, and the death of most of those concerned. Ross alone survives to tell his cautionary tale.[49]

The Egyptological heroes of *fin de siècle* mummy fiction have an alarming tendency to fall in love with reanimated Egyptian queens and princesses. Daly thinks that this susceptibility has to do with the subject's relation to the object world, and specifically with changes brought about in that relation by consumer capitalism. 'In these stories the relations of subjects and objects are problematized so that objects become subjects, and subjects come under the spell of objects that embody their desire.'[50] For Daly, mummy fiction

---

[49] When the book was republished in 1912, someone who may or may not have been Stoker himself supplied a happy ending, in which all the participants in the great experiment other than the unfortunate mummy survive, and Ross marries Margaret Trelawny. The alternative ending is reprinted in the Oxford Popular Classics edn., 212–14.

[50] *Modernism, Romance*, 111. The context Daly adduces for this lively interest on the part of popular novelists in commodification is that of a change of emphasis in the British economy during the second half of the 19th cent. 'If Britain had pushed its way to the front of world trade by developing its *productive* power, after mid century *consumption* assumed a new importance, as if the worship of the world was becoming the shop of the world' (p. 90). Such is the case made e.g. by W. Hamish Fraser, in *The Coming of the Mass Market 1850–1914* (Hamden, Conn.: Archon Press, 1981), and, to somewhat different effect, by Lawrence Birkin, in *Consuming Desire: Sexual Science and the Emergence of a Culture of Abundance 1871–1914* (Ithaca, NY: Cornell University Press, 1988). On the literary and cultural implications of this change of emphasis, see Rachel Bowlby, *Just Looking: Consumer Culture in Dreiser, Gissing, and Zola* (London: Methuen, 1985); Nancy Armstrong, 'The Occidental Alice', *differences*, 2 (1990), 2–39; and Thomas Richards, *The Commodity Culture of Victorian England* (Stanford, Calif.: Stanford University Press, 1990).

constitutes a narrative 'theory' of commodity fetishism. His main point is made rather nicely for him, early on in *The Jewel of Seven Stars*, by a dispute between the narrator and a Scotland Yard detective as to whether Trelawny's assailant was a person or a thing. And the novel could certainly be said to devote a fetishist's lavish and animating attention to the antiquities on display in Trelawny's London house: all of which then need to be transported to Cornwall, where the great experiment will be conducted, amid some lively collateral fetishization of packing-cases and 'strong tackle with multiplying blocks of the Smeaton order'.[51]

The problem with Daly's thesis about the relation between late Victorian romance and Modernism is that it leaves the power of transvaluation exactly where it has always been, on the side of the latter. It is at this point, I think, that his relative neglect of Edwardian romance tells against him. *The Jewel of Seven Stars* is the only Edwardian popular novel he examines, and that is treated as though it could have been written at any time from the 1880s to the 1900s. In order to understand the 'descriptive theory' it expounds, we need first to place it within the kind of context I have sought to establish in this chapter: an Edwardian context.

It is not empire which the Egyptian antiquities introduce into Trelawny's London home, but Ruritania. For Queen Tera's will-to-resurrection enables Ross to imagine, during an all-too-brief Ruritanian idyll in London and Cornwall, that he is loved by royalty. Ross is a lawyer, but, like Rudolf Rassendyll, like Robert Audley, he knows that a bureaucratic career is the wrong medium for a man of his unique abilities. For him, as for Rassendyll, the only proper acknowledgement of those abilities would be the love of a queen; or, in his case, of the double of a dead queen.

The opening chapters of *The Jewel of Seven Stars* are a study in professional rivalries, as relays of detectives and doctors attempt to outshine each other in resolving the mysteries of the crime and the victim's condition. Ross alone attends, at Margaret Trelawny's invitation, as something other than the member of a profession; his presence is an implicit tribute to qualities one would not necessarily expect a lawyer to possess. When the professionals have left the house, the two friends sit in silence. 'At last she raised her eyes and looked at me for a moment; after that I would not have exchanged places with a king.' No need to, since he may yet become a king by marriage. So significant does this inaugural dissociation from bureaucratic rationalism seem to Stoker that he makes amply sure we get the point. 'I am a Barrister', Ross tells the convalescent Trelawny. 'It is not, however, in that capacity I am here; but simply as a friend of your daughter.' When either Trelawny condescends to use his first name, he practically has to be helped from the room. As preparations for the great experiment advance, Ross allows himself the thought that Queen Tera might conceivably intend to begin life again as a 'humble individual': that is, as Margaret Trelawny, as Mrs Malcolm Ross. His moment of 'paranoid illumination' occurs during the great experiment itself, when Trelawny unwraps the mummy to reveal a body which has somehow been preserved in all its original freshness. 'It was not right that we should be there,' he reflects, 'gazing with irreverent eyes on such unclad beauty: it was indecent . . . And yet the white wonder of that beautiful form was something to dream of.'[52] The illumination lies in the indecency. For the beautiful form Ross gazes at is that both of Queen Tera and of the 'humble individual' in whose shape she may intend to return to life. It is his to possess. Something to dream of, indeed.

In Ruritania, however, winning the love of the queen is only half the battle, because those who surround her know that you yourself are not of royal blood, and that a liaison would therefore endanger the state. So they persecute you. The equivalents of Ruritanian Colonel Sapt and Fritz von Tarlenheim are the detective and the doctor, both self-evidently capable men, who first voice the suspicion that Margaret Trelawny is not all she appears to be. Suspecting a conspiracy, Ross resolves simply to listen and learn. 'When the time should come for the dissipation and obliteration of the theories, I should be quite willing to use all my militant ardour, and all the weapons at my command.' However, the suspicions recur, with gathering force, until he can no longer deny their appropriateness.[53] What these highly competent professionals are telling him, as Sapt and von Tarlenheim had told

52 Ibid. 22, 127, 181, 203.   53 Ibid. 57–8, 60–2, 57, 83, 126.

Rassendyll, with an entirely justifiable ruthlessness, is that Margaret Trelawny is not for him. In *The Jewel of Seven Stars*, as in *The Prisoner of Zenda*, paranoid fantasy requires both the belief that the subject is loved where he loves (grandeur) and the belief that outside forces will none the less intervene to thwart his entirely justifiable expectations (persecution). Both novels pack a powerful social 'imaginary'. Indeed, they pack the *same* social imaginary. The working knowledge they provide is a working knowledge of the paranoid articulation of charisma among middle-class professional men at the turn of the century.

One would not guess from Daly's description of *The Jewel of Seven Stars* that the novel is in fact utterly specific in its reference to historical event. Trelawny undertakes his expedition to Egypt in search of Queen Tera's tomb in November 1884. 'This was soon after Arabi Pasha, and Egypt was no safe place for travellers, especially if they were English.'[54] Arabi's revolt, an uprising of army officers infuriated by the subservience of the khedive's regime to the interests of European bondholders, occurred early in 1881. Before the end of 1882 a British fleet had bombarded Alexandria and a British army under Wolseley had broken the Egyptian forces at Tel-el-Kabir. That the upper Nile still counted as bandit country as late as November 1884 was due not to Arabi, but to the Mahdi's campaigns to purge the area of Western influence. An Egyptian army led by Hicks Pasha had been defeated at El Obeid in November 1883. Gordon was to die in Khartoum in January 1885. The local violence which accompanies Trelawny's removal of the mummy from its resting-place in November 1884 is an oblique but telling acknowledgement of the instabilities endemic in the imperial enterprise.

What makes Daly's silence concerning the history embedded in *The Jewel of Seven Stars* even more curious is that Arabi's revolt broke out at more or less the same time as the Irish Land Wars. Gladstone had to decide what to do about Egypt while arranging for the arrest of Charles Stewart Parnell and the suppression of the Land League. In the longer view, the interest of the decision he took lies in the difference of emphasis it reveals within the imperial 'imaginary'. If the state of Ireland was an acute political

54 *Modernism, Romance*, 106.

embarrassment, in the early 1880s, the state of Egypt was a threat to the very existence of empire. In one case, Gladstone chose negotiation and appeasement; in the other, he installed Evelyn Baring, later Lord Cromer, as resident and consul-general. Cromer governed Egypt, behind a façade of khedivial authority, until 1907. By that time, indirect rule had become a paradigm of engagement in empire. Indeed, Stoker recognizes as much, in *The Jewel of Seven Stars*, by sending Corbeck, Trelawny's assistant, back to Egypt in 1900, to collect some lamps which will be needed for the great experiment. 'The country', Corbeck explains, 'was now in a condition very different to that in which it had been sixteen years before; there was no need for troops or armed men.'[55] If the novel does hold some reassurance for the reader, despite its tragic denouement, that may well be because the political instability with which we cannot help but associate the mummy's removal from the tomb has been resolved.

Mummies, in short, were by no means the only Egyptian business likely to sell books during the Edwardian period. The nation's novelists were not slow to respond to the publication in 1908 of Cromer's two-volume study of *Modern Egypt*, which reviews in majestic fashion the achievements of indirect rule. The prolific Hall Caine, who had made his name by portraying the Isle of Man as a hotbed of superstition and vice, got in early with *The White Prophet* (1909), an ambitious and complicated romance which explores through the fluidities of personal allegiance the scope and justification of the British presence in Egypt. *The White Prophet* is notably liberal, by the standards of the time, in its willingness to criticize Cromer's regime. Its hero is a British army officer, Gordon Lord, whose sympathy for the spiritual basis of Arab nationalism runs so deep that he comes close to identifying himself with it. However, this relative indeterminacy at the level of 'culture'—a rule so indirect that it becomes an identification with the ruled—provokes a counter-insistence at the level of 'nature'. In a further gesture of partial identification, the white woman who had once been the hero's fiancée agrees to marry the leader of the nationalist campaign, in the hope that the campaign will have run out of steam before she is called upon to consummate the

---

[55] Ibid. 122.

marriage. When Ishmael Ameer presses his suit, however, Helena's response is a visceral disgust which re-establishes in an instant the antagonisms ideological sympathy might be thought laboriously to have undone. 'My skin was creeping', she reports, 'and I had a feeling which I had never known before—a feeling of repulsion—the feeling of the white woman about the black man.' The climax of the plot involves the juxtaposition of two scenes: in one, Lord finds himself, to his own dismay, doubly disguised (he pretends to be Ishmael Ameer pretending to be one Sheik Omar Benani, chief of the Ababdah); in the other, Ameer makes his far from spiritual intentions plain to Helena ('Let me go, I tell you! You shall! You must! Can't you see that you are hateful and odious to me—that you are a black man and I am a white woman?').[56] It is as if the humiliation and vivid self-loathing the white man suffers in disguise—that is, in the cultural production of identity through mimicry—have generated in the white woman a nausea which by its violence re-establishes the boundaries of race (that is, nature's boundaries).

It was by such reflections on the potential for and the risks attaching to indirectness that Edwardian romance reworked the imperial 'imaginary' of Stevenson, Haggard, Kipling, and the rest. Its descriptive theory was a descriptive theory of not quite sleeping with the enemy. By the 1920s, the theory had become doctrine. In *Seven Pillars of Wisdom* (1926), T. E. Lawrence distinguished between the John Bull type of imperialist and the more 'subtle and insinuating' type who somehow 'caught the characteristics of the people about him, their speech, their conventions of thought, almost their manner'. The latter 'directed men secretly, guiding them as he would. In such frictionless habit of influence his own nature lay hid, unnoticed.'[57] Lawrence himself was of the second type: his own nature hidden, he frictionlessly drew his Arab followers after him into revolt against Turkish rule. Thomas Richards describes him as a 'state nomad'. State nomads do not necessarily work for the state, but they are adept at developing lines of alliance and affiliation which transfer intelligence to it; they

---

[56] *The White Prophet*, 2 vols. (London: Heinemann, 1909), ii. 167, 205–7, 241.
[57] *Seven Pillars of Wisdom* (Harmondsworth: Penguin Books, 1962), 354–5.

do the state's business by infiltrating forces which would otherwise elude or oppose its activities.[58]

The descriptive theory of state nomadism in Edwardian romance is at its most radical in its discovery or invention of new territories: territories such as Egypt, where indirect British rule prevailed,[59] or such as Morocco, Tunisia, and Algeria, where no British rule prevailed at all. The appeal of Morocco can be gauged from a rather striking story by A. J. Dawson, 'The Richard Merlin Document', which was published in *African Nights' Entertainment* (1900), and is set in El Kasr el Kebeer, a remote inland town in Morocco. Dawson was a journalist-adventurer of the kind fervently admired by the late Victorian and Edwardian reading-public. In the mid-1890s, he spent some months in Morocco, where he lived, according to an interview in the *Bookman*, 'in native fashion, hob-nobbing a good deal with murder and sudden death'.[60] He went on to edit the *Imperialist*, and to publish, in 1907, an invasion-scare novel, *The Message*. Morocco did not become a factor in Great Power rivalries until 1903, when British support for French intervention paved the way for the *entente cordiale*. When Dawson lived there in the 1890s, it was from the British point of view extraterritorial.

'The Richard Merlin Document' rewrites, or transfers to politically neutral territory, one of Kipling's most vivid early stories, 'Beyond the Pale', which was reprinted in *Plain Tales from the Hills* (1890). 'Beyond the Pale' begins with the observation that 'A man should, whatever happens, keep to his own caste, race and breed'. It is the story of an English official, Trejago, deeply interested in 'native life', who discovers, behind a grated window at the end of a dark alleyway, a beautiful Indian woman, Bisesa, and becomes her lover. 'The Richard Merlin Document' begins with the observation that 'The man who ignores or seeks to override the laws of caste and race courts trouble, and wins it'. It is the story of Richard

[58] *The Imperial Archive: Knowledge and the Fantasy of Empire* (London: Verso, 1993), 135.

[59] Most strikingly, perhaps, in another novel published in 1909, Robert Hichens's *Bella Donna: A Novel*, whose heroine decides to 'let the ugly side of her nature run free with a loose rein' by falling for a physically and mentally 'compelling' Turco-Egyptian millionaire, who secretly hates the British and regards women from an 'Oriental' point of view.

[60] 'Chronicle and Comment', *Bookman*, 12 (1901), 435–7, p. 437.

Merlin, a man born in Tangiers of English parents who can 'pass anywhere for a Moor', and who discovers, behind a grated window at the end of a dark alleyway, a beautiful Moorish woman, Fatima, and becomes her lover.[61] Its interest lies in the tenacity, the sheer excess, with which it reworks Kipling's account of the risks attaching to direct rule into an account of the risks attaching to a rule so indirect as barely to qualify as rule. Kipling found it hard to imagine indirect rule: witness his failure to develop, in his early writing, either the figure of Strickland, the policeman expert in disguise with an immense knowledge of native life, or the figure of McIntosh Jellaludin, the drifter who has abandoned his Oxford education and status as a sahib for opium and a native wife. There is, of course, *Kim. Kim*, Richards says, is the 'first sustained narrative of state nomadology'.[62] This seems to me almost right: the point about *Kim* is that the narrative of state nomadology can only be sustained as long as its protagonist remains a boy, and his cultural indeterminacy is therefore unproblematic. Dawson's interest lay in an adult, and therefore problematic, indeterminacy.

Trejago's fascination with 'native life' is, until he meets Bisesa, largely academic: it compromises neither his appearance nor his conduct as an Englishman through and through. Merlin, by contrast, realizes that nomadism will necessarily involve the loss of his existing (Westernized) identity. 'It's a pity I ever adopted the habit of dressing Moorish fashion, with my djellab-hood well forward, when I took my walks abroad, looking about me, more or less seeking whom I might devour.' The devourer is duly devoured. In Kipling's story, Bisesa sits behind a barred window waiting for Trejago; in Dawson's, Fatima sits behind a window like a 'barred mouth', in a room which juts out like a chin over the alley from which Merlin first glimpes her. When Merlin cuts through the bars and climbs in, he finds himself a prisoner of Fatima's uncle, Kaid Hamet: he has been swallowed up.

There was a muttered oath from lips quite other than Fatima's, an instant's rending struggle, and with hardly a thought of resistance on my

---

[61] Kipling, 'Beyond the Pale', in *Plain Tales from the Hills*, ed. H. R. Woudhuysen (Harmondsworth: Penguin Books, 1987), 162–7, p. 162; Dawson, 'The Richard Merlin Document', in *African Nights' Entertainment* (London: William Heinemann, 1900), 79–98, pp. 80–1.

[62] *Imperial Archive*, 23.

part, I was stretched on my back in the little room which is a chin to Kaid Hamet's house, with the Kaid himself, an iron-wristed figure of vengeance, astride upon my chest. Never was vermin more simply and safely trapped.[63]

The metaphor of the vermin strikes an odd note. In narrative terms, it scarcely does justice to the struggle and the pinioning. What matters, I think, is that it should evoke a disgust which is also self-disgust. It marks, from within, nomadism's limit, the point at which a frictionless habit of influence becomes abjection.

Trejago's punishment for courting Bisesa is a wound in the groin which causes him to limp slightly. Socially and racially, he has lost nothing: he pays his calls regularly, and is reckoned a 'very decent sort of man'.[64] Merlin's punishment is to have his tongue torn out.

And then, by Allah's favour, I lost consciousness, choked to death, so it seemed to my vanishing understanding, by my own blood. I woke to find myself head down over a stool, M'Barak stepping back from me with a smoking iron in his hand, and, as it were, in every part of me, a taste of singed flesh, smoke, and blood.

The branding seems like a rape. It transforms Merlin into the vermin he had already imagined himself to be. Spat upon, tortured, and sold into slavery, he comes to loathe his own muteness. 'It occurred to me to shout; and again the inarticulate bestiality of the sound I made, fell upon me with a strong sense of repulsion.'[65]

Since Trejago's knowledge of 'native' culture is never more than academic, he can pick up his old life more or less where he left off. By contrast, the wreck of a man who enters the narrator's house at the end of 'The Richard Merlin Document' has become indistinguishable from the environment he now inhabits, a pariah among pariahs, 'pouring out meantime a horrid, broken torrent of inarticulate sounds, from a mouth matted over with shaggy, earth-stained hair'.[66] His resemblance to another revenant from extraterritoriality, the wreck of a man who enters the narrator's office at the end of Kipling's 'The Man who would be King', is clear. Like Kipling's Afghanistan, Dawson's Morocco is a place where the

---

[63] 'Richard Merlin Document', 82, 85, 88.
[64] 'Beyond the Pale', 167.
[65] 'Richard Merlin Document', 91–2, 97.
[66] Ibid. 97.

abandonment of 'English' identity which nomadism would seem to require exacts its terrible toll. Kipling could not imagine that happening in the British Raj, or at least not to a fully grown man. Dawson, with what was to become the Edwardian romancer's taste both for the potential of indirect rule and for the risks attaching to it, most definitely could.

From my point of view, stories like *The White Prophet* and 'The Richard Merlin Document' are of interest because they at once celebrate and profoundly distrust imitation. In both, the protagonist attempts to absorb another culture, and to be absorbed into it, by imitating its costume, manners, and attitudes. In both, disgust alone, a disgust eventually indistinguishable from self-disgust, indicates the point at which the white man or woman has gone too far. As we have already seen, paranoid narrative incorporated from its origins a visceral loathing for the idea of disguise. Caleb Williams and Walter Hartright both disguise themselves, at times, in order to evade their persecutors, or contemplate doing so. Both regard such mimicry with abhorrence. The paranoiac wishes above all, and at any cost, to be recognized for what he uniquely is, and the loss of identity which mimicry entails is fatal to that project. The descriptive theory put forward by Edwardian popular fiction includes a critique of social mimesis. It is that critique, that fundamental revision of the imperial imaginary articulated by Stevenson, Haggard, and Kipling, which should form the basis of any comparison with Modernist writing. What the Edwardian romancers found in extraterriroriality was a further source of enabling persecutions. That is certainly true of the text to which I now turn, a text whose extraterritoriality is generally reckoned to belong at once to literary experiment and to popular romance, Conrad's *Lord Jim*.

CHAPTER 5

CHAPTER 5

One of Whom? *Lord Jim* and 'Ability in the Abstract'

FOR HISTORIANS OF English literary culture, one text above all has brought into focus the issue I addressed in the final section of the previous chapter: the issue of the relation between Modernist experiment and turn-of-the-century popular romance. That text is Joseph Conrad's *Lord Jim* (1900). In what is probably the most influential study of the novel to have been published in the last twenty years or so, Frederic Jameson observes that the novel's method combines an avant-garde 'practice of style' with the 'diversion and distraction' an Edwardian reader would have expected to find in a nautical yarn by R. M. Ballantyne or Frederick Marryat. In Jameson's formula, *Lord Jim* is part Proust, part Robert Louis Stevenson: it combines an austere Modernism with the 'commercialized cultural discourse' characteristic, in his view, of a 'media society'.[1]

There are ample grounds for considering the novel in such terms, schematic though they necessarily remain. Its first twenty chapters proceed by a complex sifting of the testimony which surrounds the scandal of the *Patna*, by austere inquiry into the basis of Jim's 'character'; the remainder chronicle mythologically his splendid rehabilitation and death in exotic Patusan. This 'break' in the narrative could be understood as the displacement of conventions appropriate to domestic realism by conventions appropriate to romance, or perhaps even to tragedy.[2] Jameson regards it as evidence of 'institutional heterogeneity', of the widening gap between élite and mass culture.[3] I shall argue here that the difference between the two parts

---

[1] *The Political Unconscious: Narrative as a Socially Symbolic Act* (London: Routledge, 1981), ch. 5.

[2] For an authoritative account of this displacement, see Ian Watt, *Conrad in the Nineteenth Century* (Berkeley, Calif.: University of California Press, 1979).

[3] *Political Unconscious*, 207.

of the novel is not as absolute as the criticism would have us believe. It seems to me, on the contrary, that the first part of the novel *requires* the second. In the previous chapter, I suggested that one thing élite and mass culture had in common was an interest in charismatic professionalism and its discontents. It is that interest, I believe, which unites the two parts of *Lord Jim*. For there is a paranoiac in this text, and his paranoia is the product of a challenge to his professional identity (or strictly speaking to the charisma with which he would wilfully endow that identity).

During the first day of the inquiry into events aboard the *Patna*, Jim rapidly loses any hope he might once have had that his case would receive sympathetic attention from those assembled in the courtroom. 'They wanted facts. Facts! They demanded facts from him, as if facts could explain anything!' As he scans the crowded room, his eyes settle on a white man sitting apart, who returns his gaze quietly but with unmistakable interest.

Jim answered another question and was tempted to cry out, 'What's the good of this! What's the good!' He tapped with his foot slightly, bit his lip, and looked away over the heads. He met the eyes of the white man. The glance directed at him was not the fascinated stare of the others. It was an act of intelligent volition.[4]

The man is Marlow, of course, Conrad's most celebrated intermediary, and the reasons for the interest he develops at this moment in the chief mate of the *Patna* could be said to remain obstinately at issue not only in the rest of the novel, but in much of what has been written about it. Is the basis of the fellow-feeling which draws Marlow to Jim, and Jim to Marlow, racial, or social, or moral, or even, as some critics have suggested, sexual? The question matters because it is not too much of an exaggeration to say that a great deal of Conrad, a great deal of what his books are still read for, lies in that relationship. And yet the feeling which brings the relationship about through acts of intelligent volition, a feeling unmistakably present in those acts, has rather surprisingly passed without comment. The relationship between Marlow and Jim is a relationship begun, developed, and brought to a close in paranoia. Marlow, in effect, becomes intimate with

---

[4] *Lord Jim*, ed. Cedric Watts and Robert Hampson (Harmondsworth: Penguin Books, 1986), 63, 66. Henceforth *LJ*.

the scope and texture of Jim's overmastering delusion of reference. Intelligent volition: that is exactly what the paranoiac expects in those who observe him.

As Marlow makes his way out of the courtroom at the end of the inquiry's second day, a stranger engages him in conversation. 'We were then just through the door, passing behind Jim's burly back.' His companion stumbles over a yellow dog which has been weaving its way in and out of people's legs. 'The dog leaped away without a sound; the man, raising his voice a little, said with a slow laugh, "Look at that wretched cur", and directly afterwards we became separated by a lot of people pushing in.' Jim, meanwhile, has spun round, and now stands in Marlow's way, confronting him aggressively, but on a basis which remains unclear. 'It was very much like a meeting in a wood, only more uncertain in its issue, since he could possibly want neither my money nor my life— nothing that I could simply give up or defend with a clear conscience.' In paranoid narrative, the clarifying encounter between the protagonist and the enemy whose relentless hostility is the only adequate measure of his achievement takes the form of single combat in a world suddenly emptied of mere contingencies. Jim, it transpires, has overheard the remark about the 'wretched cur', and believes not only that it refers to him, but that he was meant to hear it. In this 'extraordinary delusion', as Marlow terms it, which converts accident into solid proof of conspiracy, lies the beginning of a relationship which before very long neither man can do without.[5] There surely cannot be any closer parallel in literature to Freud's account of the distress felt by the victim of paranoid delusion when strangers, from whom he rashly expects love, laugh to themselves as they go by, or flourish their sticks, or spit on the ground—in all these ways systematically expressing, as he supposes, their hatred for him.[6]

---

[5] *LJ* 94–6. Kraepelin observed that paranoia begins in the attention paid to random events. 'Any doubts as to an evident purpose in all this are sooner or later dispelled by remarks accidentally overheard. In this way false interpretations gradually assume greater prominence, and the resultant *persecutory delusions* are constantly increased and aggravated': *Clinical Psychiatry: A Text-Book for Students and Physicians* (London: Macmillan, 1902), 318.

[6] *The Standard Edition of the Complete Psychological Works*, ed. James Strachey *et al.*, 24 vols. (London: Hogarth Press, 1953–74), xviii. 226.

TRUE LITERATURE'S DISEASE

Conrad, of course, was a man of two distinct professions, or three, if one counts being Polish as a profession.[7] In *A Personal Record*, he broods at some length on the rather exiguous motivation for his first career-move, from Pole to seaman. 'The truth is that what I had in view was not a naval career but the sea.' Conrad had always known that he was meant for this 'mysterious vocation', it seems, while remaining uncertain, even in retrospect, as to its 'somewhat exceptional psychology'. But there can be little doubt that he discovered in the examinations he took in the 1880s in order to qualify successively as second mate, chief mate, and master mariner a fund of symbolic capital: not just a certificate, that is, but a recognition both of his 'Englishness' and, in the shape of an examiner's paternal blessing, his masculinity.[8] Like H. G. Wells, Conrad was brought if not into being, then at least into full self-consciousness, by certification. Unlike Wells, however, he found in his second career-move, from certificated seaman to writer, a radical discontinuity. Wells gave education up, but he remained to a significant (and sometimes wearying) extent an educationalist. Conrad, by contrast, could scarcely sail his novels, though one sometimes feels that he would have liked to. That radical discontinuity was inevitably at issue in the novel he wrote, at a time when he had by no means established himself as a writer, about the failure of a ship's officer's certification to mean anything in the heat of catastrophe.

Conrad finished *Lord Jim* shortly after sunrise on the morning of 14 July 1900. The book had taken the better part of ten months to write, developing in the process from a short story into a novel. At the turn of the century, literature was still a notoriously uncertificated profession, even though writers now knew that they could draw on the commercial and legal expertise of agents and associations if they wished to put their literary expertise to profitable use.

---

[7] Among Conrad's biographers, Frederick Karl is the one who has most explicitly organized his account around this periodization by career-development: *Joseph Conrad: The Three Lives* (London: Faber & Faber, 1979). Geoffery Galt Harpham explores the implications of this apportionment of 'lives' in *One of Us: The Mastery of Joseph Conrad* (Chicago: University of Chicago Press, 1996).

[8] *A Personal Record* (London: J. M. Dent, 1946), 112–21. The best recent account of what the sea might have meant to Conrad is Harpham's, in *One of Us*, 71–97.

It was a lack of confidence in his own credentials which caused Conrad to rebuff, in August 1899, a first approach from the literary agent J. B. Pinker. 'I generally sell a work before it is begun, get paid when it is half done and don't do the other half till the spirit moves me. I must add that I have no control whatever over the spirit—neither has the man who has paid the money.'[9]

'Recognition shall come. Strictly speaking, what people think does not matter,—and yet everything is in that.' That, at any rate, is what Conrad told Mabel Reynolds, John Galsworthy's sister, on 5 September 1900. It was Galsworthy he had in mind, but his next sentence might in retrospect be thought to apply rather more closely to himself than to the man who went on to publish *The Forsyte Saga*. 'I am afraid he can never look forward to other than limited appreciation.'[10] Where expertise is concerned, everything is indeed in what people think; and yet the professional who based his or her conduct wholly on what people think would thereby suffer a loss of self-respect, and thus, perhaps, in the longer run, diminishing returns on expertise. Recognition is essential, and untrustworthy. The letters Conrad wrote at the time he was writing *Lord Jim* reveal a writer in search of the limited appreciation which would secure him at once from public indifference and from certifiability by commercial success alone.

Two examples from the correspondence should make clear the effort Conrad put into the accumulation of symbolic capital. William Blackwood he sought to portray as a patron rather than an employer. In a letter of 11 June 1898 thanking Blackwood for £35 for 'Youth' and £5 on account for the embryonic 'Jim: A Sketch', he explained that the 'manner' of the publisher's letter had meant as much to him as the 'matter' of the cheque it enclosed. 'A word of appreciation,' he maintained, 'a friendly act performed in a friendly manner, these are as rare as nuggets in gold-bearing sand and suddenly enrich the most obscure, the most solitary existence.'[11] The nuggets are a trademark figure in Conrad's early novels, a prod-

[9] *Collected Letters*, ed. Frederick R. Karl and Laurence Davies, 8 vols. projected (Cambridge: CUP, 1983–), ii. 195. Letter of 23 Aug. 1899. By 19 Sept. 1900, he had changed his mind; in response to a further approach, he agreed that Pinker should handle the novel he was then writing with Ford Madox Ford, *Romance*: *Letters*, ii. 294.

[10] Ibid. 290.

[11] Ibid. 67. Karl suggests that it was Meldrum, rather than the altogether more conservative Blackwood, who kept patience with Conrad: *Joseph Conrad*, 485–6.

uct of the 'practice of style' which would continue to distinguish his work from the merely popular. Conrad in effect pays Blackwood back in his own coin, the coin of firm friendship rather than that of a contract between employer and employee. The practice of style which will speak goldenly in Blackwood's magazine is pure gold, a symbolic wealth outshining mere coinage.

In the last letter he ever wrote, on 14 May 1900, Stephen Crane told Sanford Bennett that he was still worried about Conrad. Edward Garnett, an influential figure in literary and publishing circles, had advised him that Conrad's work would never be popular 'outside the ring of men who write'.[12] The ring of men who wrote happened to include, in addition to Crane and Garnett, such as Galsworthy, Wells, Ford Madox Ford, W. E. Henley, Henry James, and R. B. Cunninghame Graham. To have found appreciation among these discerning readers, as Conrad did, was no mean feat. His reliance on them encouraged him to fetishize not only his own practice of style, but the tokens of regard with which they assiduously made a point of favouring him. The fetishization is evident in the pride with which he forwarded to Garnett a letter of praise from Henry James ('Wonderful old man, with his record of wonderful work!'), and in the circumspection with which he solicited its immediate return.[13]

For the margin his accumulation of symbolic capital left him over penury on the one side and mere commercial success on the other was precarious. Indeed, it was in the symbolism that, no doubt with his previous career in mind, he often felt most deficient. What made it worse was that the standard he might be thought to have fallen short of was a standard set by members of the ring of men who wrote. 'It was Henley and his friends', Ford wrote in *Ancient Lights* (1911), 'who introduced into the English writing mind the idea that a man of action was something fine and a man of letters a sort of castrato.'[14] A castrato Conrad was not. But he did feel that his abandonment of the sea had turned him into a man of inaction, and thus perhaps no man at all. It was in

---

[12] R. W. Stallman, *Stephen Crane: A Biography* (New York: George Braziller, 1968), 283–4.

[13] *Letters*, ii. 303.

[14] *Ancient Lights and Certain New Reflections, Being the Memoirs of a Young Man* (London: Chapman & Hall, 1911), 241–2.

1894, the year he completed his first novel, *Almayer's Folly*, that he met Edward Garnett, who was to become a close friend and mentor. In the 'Author's Note' to *An Outcast of the Islands* (1896), Conrad held Garnett responsible for the inception of his second novel, and thus for his choice of career. The note describes the state of 'immobility' and 'indolence' he was in at the time, suspended between careers:[15] a state 'so much at odds with the dominant Victorian ideals of masculinity', as Andrew Roberts puts it, 'and so much a part of their decadent mirror-image'.[16] Immobility, indolence, and worse were to remain a troublesome habit throughout his career as a writer.

No wonder he sometimes thought he was going mad. The letters to Garnett frequently speak of a state of doubt and 'powerlessness' associated with his inability to develop further the expertise upon which he relied for the generation of symbolic capital. 'I seem to have lost all *sense* of style and yet I am haunted, mercilessly haunted by the *necessity* of style.'[17] In a letter of 7 January 1902 to David Meldrum, Conrad recalled that during the composition of *Lord Jim* he had always felt 'on the brink of the grave'. 'Explain it who may. And perhaps true literature (when you "get it") is something like a disease which one feels in one's bones, sinews and joints.'[18] And perhaps in one's mind? In a letter of 12 October 1899 to the schoolmaster E. L. Sanderson, he complained that literature, even true literature, was a fool's business. 'The unreality of it seems to enter one's real life, penetrate into the bones, make the very heart beats pulsate illusions through the arteries.'[19] On 29 December 1899, he told Blackwood that he suffered at times from 'optical delusions' where the coherence of his own work was concerned.[20] By this account, it is madness itself which

---

[15] *An Outcast of the Islands* (Harmondsworth: Penguin Books, 1975).

[16] *Conrad and Masculinity* (Basingstoke: Macmillan, 2000), 45.

[17] *Letters*, ii. 49–50. What overwhelms Conrad, as Harpham points out, is not doubt, which is after all a stable cognitive position, but the unexpectedness of the incertitudes afflicting him. This is a trouble brought on by the outline of a success whose dimensions remain unknown rather than by predictable failure. Both the sea and the 'sea of doubts' stand, as Harpham puts it, 'at the margin between the unreality of Poland and the reality of "images"—the gateway, for Conrad, to literature, and the gateway, for literature, to modernism': *One of Us*, 96–7.

[18] *Letters*, ii. 368.   [19] Ibid. 205.

[20] Ibid. 230.

is the source of and model for narrative structure. Should we say that the two parts of *Lord Jim* are related by 'optical delusion' only?

For it may be that there was a method in the madness, a method worked by substituting a drama of acceptance and rejection within the ring of men who wrote for the chanciness of the market-place.[21] In a letter of 12 November 1900 to Garnett, Conrad managed to find evidence of recognition even (or especially) in damning comment. Garnett had drawn attention to what he regarded as a serious flaw in *Lord Jim*, its division into two parts. His comment implicitly damned the novel by identifying its narrative structure with optical delusion. In reply, Conrad readily made concessions. He acknowledged the novel's 'want of power'. For someone as 'satanically ambitious' as himself, he went on, the disclosure of flaws of that magnitude could not be anything other than a severe 'humiliation'. And yet as he thought about the effect Garnett's comments had had on him, he began to discern in them a remedy for want of power. The humiliation which was the result of those comments had somehow engendered in him a 'pathos' he could not help regarding as a 'triumph': the kind of triumph, in fact, which no mere 'criticism' could possibly touch. Conrad, we might say, had constructed in and through his attitude to what the men who wrote might say about his work a parallel universe. In this parallel universe, the only adequate standard for the degree of grandeur generated by satanic ambition was the degree of satanic hostility—a hostility beyond mere criticism, that is, a pitiless exposure of want of power—with which it had been met. Within the ring of men who wrote, humiliation defined triumph, and triumph humiliation. By a strange coincidence— for the paranoiac, there is no such thing as coincidence—a letter of praise had arrived that morning from none other than Henry James. 'Ah! You rub in the balm till every sore smarts—therefore I exist.'[22]

---

[21] I have in mind, of course, that it was not until *Chance* (1913) that any of Conrad's novels could be said to have earned a wide readership. It did so, as far as one can tell, by riding its promotional luck, rather than by a simplification of literary method.

[22] *Letters*, ii. 303.

THE SOLIDARITY OF THE CRAFT

'I liked his appearance; I knew his appearance; he came from the right place; he was one of us. He stood there for all the parentage of his kind, for men and women by no means clever and amusing, but whose very existence is based upon honest faith, and upon the instinct of courage.'[23] Marlow's assessment of Jim has itself customarily been assessed either as though it were a remark about class and nation (Marlow values Jim because he is both English and genteel),[24] or as though it were a remark about masculinity (Marlow values Jim because he is a man).[25] These interpretations of course reflect the emphasis predominant in recent studies of Conrad: an emphasis on the mutual implication in his writing of an inquiry into the basis of colonialism and an inquiry into the basis of gender difference.[26] My aim here is not to deny the significance of these qualities in the view both Marlow and Conrad might be thought to take of Jim. But I want to suggest that they derive their significance from their function as forms of symbolic capital: forms of symbolic capital which Jim could be said to have

[23] *LJ* 74.

[24] Linda Dryden, *Joseph Conrad and the Imperial Romance* (London: Macmillan, 2000), 140. Dryden argues that Marlow would never have included women as well as men in this assessment if he had meant to claim Jim merely for the merchant marine. But the 'men and women' he refers to constitute the *parentage* of Jim's kind, which must perforce have included both sexes.

[25] According to Scott McCracken, the 'professional body' of seamen 'bonded' by work is the product of a 'gendered libidinal economy' built on an 'exclusive ideology of masculine desire': '"A Hard and Absolute Condition of Existence": Reading Masculinity in *Lord Jim*', in Andrew Roberts (ed.), *Conrad and Gender* (Amsterdam: Rodopi, 1993), 17–38, p. 19. For a more nuanced account of homosocial and homoerotic feeling in Conrad's Eastern tales, see Harpham, *One of Us*, 106–10, 117–23. It is the 'moral ambivalence' of a 'disavowed homosexual attraction' between Marlow and Jim, Harpham says, which drives the narrative on (p. 120).

[26] For a valuable addition to studies of the colonial context, see Robert Hampson, *Cross-Cultural Encounters in Joseph Conrad's Malay Fiction* (Basingstoke: Palgrave, 2000). I have found Padmini Mongia's work of particular value on account of the emphasis it places on Conrad's use of the Gothic: 'Narrative Strategy and Imperialism in Conrad's *Lord Jim*', *Studies in the Novel*, 24 (1992), 173–86; 'Empire, Narrative and the Feminine in *Lord Jim* and *Heart of Darkness*', in Keith Carabine, Owen Knowles, and Wiesław Krajka (eds.), *Contexts for Conrad* (New York: Columbia University Press, 1993), 135–50; '"Ghosts of the Gothic": Spectral Women and Colonized Spaces in *Lord Jim*', in Roberts (ed.), *Conrad and Gender*, 1–16. Equally valuable in this respect is Roberts's *Conrad and Masculinity* (see above, n. 16).

inherited from men and women by no means clever and amusing, and which it was the purpose of his training as a ship's officer to develop. The novel is Conrad's meditation, at a time when he did not yet possess in authorship an equivalent to the certificates which had made him a seaman, on professional identity.[27] It is his version of the 'class war and hatred between Europeans' which Leonard Woolf was to experience in 1904 as a 'curious feature of British imperialism in the East'.[28]

In *Lord Jim*, Andrew Roberts observes, the 'principal male bond' evoked is a 'professional code'. The bond 'implicates' gender and race in that the code applies exclusively to European males. It is 'sanctified' by 'moments of male intimacy which transcend professionalism and reach uneasily for the metaphysical': the medium of transcendence being the 'masculine textual economy' established by various acts of narration.[29] It is not clear to me that the intimacy between Marlow and Jim does transcend professionalism. It begins, as I have already shown, in professionalism's discontents; and it is a moot point whether it ever develops in any terms other than those proposed by professionalism and its discontents. When, at the very end of the novel, Marlow reaffirms that Jim had indeed been 'one of us', he does so with explicit reference to Jim's abandonment of a 'living woman' for a 'shadowy ideal of conduct', an ideal elaborated throughout the novel in terms of expertise.[30] That is what being 'one of us' means. It is Roberts's argument, rather than any act of narration, which 'transcends' professionalism by the explanatory status it attributes to the categories of race and gender.[31] Jim's travails, I shall suggest, begin and

---

[27] The novel's epigraph, from Novalis, might be thought to apply as closely to Conrad's position within the ring of men who write as it does to Jim's position within the ring of men who sail. 'It is certain my Conviction gains infinitely, the moment another soul will believe in it' (*LJ* 41).

[28] For a survey which very usefully takes an important aspect of the professionalization of English (colonial) society into account, see Daniel Bivona, *British Imperial Literature, 1870–1940: Writing and the Administration of Empire* (Cambridge: CUP, 1998).

[29] *Conrad and Masculinity*, 58, 44.   [30] *LJ* 351.

[31] 'Jim's life is the product', Andrews argues, 'of the imperial export of masculinity.' To put it another way, the context for the novel's understanding of colonial identity is a 'crisis of masculinity at home': *Conrad and Masculinity*, 59, 61. Here, the category of gender transcends (by determining) the category of colonialism, and both transcend the category of expertise. Jim is, first, a man in crisis; second, a white man in crisis abroad; third, a ship's officer in white masculine crisis abroad.

end in expertise. They may take place in the Far East, but the text which mediates them is a novel set in the American South whose main preoccupation is with the training of mind and body: Stephen Crane's *The Red Badge of Courage* (1894).

When we first meet Jim in chapter 1, he is in the middle of his second career as a water-clerk. Rather like writing, this is a career which cannot be measured in certificates. 'A water-clerk need not pass an examination in anything under the sun, but he must have Ability in the abstract and demonstrate it practically.' Water-clerk-ing is a profession in the practice of which charm and integrity matter more than a head for figures. To a ship's captain, the water-clerk is 'faithful like a friend and attentive like a son, with the patience of Job, the unselfish devotion of a woman, and the jollity of a boon companion'. Ability in the abstract is thus a surplus within or beyond expertise, a dangerous supplement. The relation it subtends is a relation between professionals masquerading as a rela-tion between non-professionals. Its medium is trust. By exercising ability in the abstract, by engendering trust, Jim is able to recreate himself professionally without having to undergo further certifica-tion. 'Thus in the course of years he was known successively in Bombay, in Calcutta, in Rangoon, in Penang, in Batavia—and in each of these halting-places was just Jim the water-clerk.' He seems to have abstracted himself even from his surname.

Like Caleb Williams, however, Jim the water-clerk is pursued wherever he goes by a 'fact', by certification's aboriginal failure to mean as much as it ought to mean. Eventually, his 'keen perception of the Intolerable' will drive him away for good from sea-ports and white men, 'even into the virgin forest', where the Malays of the jungle village where he has chosen to conceal his 'deplorable faculty' will further supplement his supplementary abstraction of himself from certification by surname. 'They called him Tuan Jim: as one might say—Lord Jim.'[32] There, ability in the abstract, of which Jim has from the outset had rather too much, despite his descent from men and women neither clever nor amusing, will bring him face to face with another supplementary abstraction, in the shape of Gentleman Brown, and he will fail again.

One of the five sons of a Norfolk parson, Jim can scarcely be

[32] *LJ* 9.

said to be of humble birth. But he has none the less his own way to make in the world. Caleb Williams would have understood the scope and intensity of the ambition he develops while training as an officer of the mercantile marine.

> His station was in the fore-top, and often from there he looked down, with the contempt of a man destined to shine in the midst of dangers, at the peaceful multitude of roofs cut in two by the brown tide of the stream, while scattered on the outskirts of the surrounding plain the factory chimneys rose perpendicular against a grimy sky.[33]

Not for him an existence under a peaceful roof. The contempt of a man destined to shine in the midst of dangers: as Conrad strives to define the scope and intensity of Jim's ambition he floods his narrative with a preoccupation central to *The Red Badge of Courage*. Conrad's rendering of Jim, at this moment, exactly reproduces Crane's rendering of Henry Fleming. It is no doubt as a result of its classification as a Far Eastern novel, as Orientalism's artefact, that so little attention has been paid to the presence in *Lord Jim* of another novel about running away, a novel written by a writer Conrad admired greatly.[34] That novel is nowhere more fully present than during the description of the event which defines Jim once and for all: a boat is launched from the training-ship to rescue men from a ship in distress, and Jim hangs back, with the mortifying result that he has to watch while his schoolmates return in triumph.[35] In order to understand the significance of this momentary flooding of one text by another, we must first grasp the extent to which *The Red Badge of Courage*, like *Lord Jim*, is a book about the psychopathies of expertise.

When his regiment is attacked for a second time, Henry Fleming runs away. By the time he resumes contact with it, he has equipped himself with a fully functioning paranoid view of the world. The most banal questions put to him epitomize 'a society that probes pitilessly at secrets until all is apparent'. He interprets a companion's 'chance persistency' as a plot to elicit his guilty secret,

---

[33] *LJ* 47.
[34] For Crane's impact on the 'community' of writers assembled in Kent and East Sussex, see Nicholas Delbanco, *Group Portrait: Joseph Conrad, Stephen Crane, Ford Madox Ford, Henry James, and H. G. Wells* (London: Faber & Faber, 1982), ch. 2.
[35] *LJ* 48–50.

and can think of little but the 'insolent and lingeringly cruel stares'
he imagines his comrades directing at him. In the event, of course,
no persecution ensues. During his wandering away from his regiment he has gained a random blow to the head which at once
endows him with the appearance of heroic suffering. He realizes
that as long as he can conceal the origin of the blow, which was
in fact delivered in blind panic by a fellow deserter, he has nothing to fear. As ever, the aspiring paranoiac must banish accident.
Fleming does not so much conceal the originating event as
disavow it altogether. He permits no 'thoughts of his own' to keep
him from an 'attitude of manfulness'. Fleming believes his
comrades when they believe in him. 'He had performed his
mistakes in the dark, so he was still a man.' His growing conviction that no light will now be thrown on his mistake permits him
to act 'pompous and veteranlike'.[36]

It is at this point that Fleming puts into place the final and fully
symmetrical element in his system of meanings and values by
explicitly identifying an enemy: not in those on his own side who
once persecuted him, and now know him as a man immune to
petty persecution, a man wearing the red badge of courage, but in
those on the other side whose allegiance is still and will for ever
remain a bar to due acknowledgement of his grandeur. The paranoiac finds the persecutor he needs in a person or persons *struc-*
turally disqualified—by membership of an opposing army, say, or
an opposing class—from due acknowledgement. For it is only by
surviving a persecution which *cannot* waver that he proves himself
fully a man. 'And, furthermore, how could they kill him who was
the chosen of gods and doomed to greatness?' The identity of
Henry Fleming's persecutor changes, as the identity of Ernst
Wagner's was to change, from people who may or may not be
whispering about an event they may or may not have witnessed to
people who will until death stubbornly decline to recognize his
'extraordinary virtues'. Like Wagner, he itches to revenge himself
on them, to bring about the death at his own hands which is all
the acknowledgement they are ever going to grant him.
Consumed by destructive mania, like Wagner, like Adam Jeffson

in *The Purple Cloud*, he becomes a 'war devil', a warrior to excess. Only in a heroism which his comrades recognize as excessive does Henry find paranoid symmetry, a proper balance of persecution and grandeur. 'He had been to touch the great death, and found that, after all, it was but the great death'; 'and was for others', the manuscript adds, discerning in his achievement of homeostasis an end-of-the-world fantasy which would have done credit to Schreber himself. 'He was a man.'[37]

Any reader at all familiar with *The Red Badge of Courage*, a literary event not likely to have been forgotten by 1900, would have heard in the contempt Jim expresses from his position in the fore-top the very accent of Henry Fleming. Later, after the rescue which has made a hero of one of his fellow cadets, he consoles himself for his own failure by the thought that the tumult and menace of wind and sea were after all 'contemptible', an 'inefficient menace'. 'Now he knew what to think of it. It seemed to him he cared nothing for the gale. He could affront greater perils. He would do so—better than anybody. Not a particle of fear was left.' Although regretting his unpreparedness, he feels glad that he did not have to waste his energy on the 'lower achievement' appropriate to a minor peril. He consoles himself that by holding back he had 'enlarged his knowledge' to a much greater degree than those who had actually done the work. His chance will come as soon as there are more demanding perils in the wind. 'When all men flinched, then—he felt sure—he alone would know how to deal with the spurious menace of wind and seas.'[38] In much the same terms had Henry Fleming consoled himself for running away while his comrades threw the enemy back. 'The imbecile line had remained and become victors.' The fight must have been a 'perfunctory popping', Fleming decides, rather like the 'inefficient menace' of the storm Jim sits out, a challenge not worth the taking. Fleming, too, imagines himself better suited to genuine crises, 'a blue desperate figure leading lurid charges with one knee forward and a broken blade high'. It was his superior 'powers of perception', he claims, not cowardice, which made him run.[39] These men know that for them expertise in itself will never be enough. So they

37 *RBC* 153–4, 163, 166, 211.   38 *LJ* 49.
39 *RBC* 98, 104, 124, 127.

imagine a demonstration of expertise so vivid in its singularity that it lodges them beyond criticism and indifference alike. They find in enemy fire the 'pathos' Conrad was to find in Garnett's comments, a pathos which *triumphs*. The moment at which they succumb to psychopathy is the moment at which they accept that their only hope of triumph lies in humiliation. After the rescue, Jim can detect no trace of emotion in himself: 'the final effect of a staggering event was that, unnoticed and apart from the noisy crowd of boys, he exulted with fresh certitude in his avidity for adventure, and in a sense of many-sided courage'.[40] The pattern of behaviour is one we have already discerned: for example in Rud Whitlow, in Wells's *The Holy Terror*, whose incapacity for relationship returns as 'a vague, cloudy desire to be appreciated, admired, obeyed—loved by all the world'. There will be other examples.

No surprise, then, that the amply certificated Jim who stands watch on the bridge of the *Patna* still has a mind full of 'imaginary achievements': 'They were the best parts of life, its secret truth, its hidden reality. They had a gorgeous virility, the charm of vagueness.' There is in this aspiration to a gorgeous virility a distant echo, too, of Adam Jeffson's pasha-like self-reinvention, in *The Purple Cloud*. Jim already has one foot in a parallel universe whose allure is sharpened, along the axis not of race or gender, but of expertise, by the sloven-liness and rapacity of those with whom he shares the bridge. The *Patna*'s German captain is the very epitome of a bad professional whose expertise is no more than a means to the end of maximum self-enrichment with minimum effort. He brings Jim's reverie to an abrupt end by making a 'professional remark' which by its very incongruousness provokes a violent disavowal. 'Jim started, and his answer was full of deference; but the odious and fleshy figure, as though seen for the first time in a revealing moment, fixed itself in his memory for ever as the incarnation of everything vile and base that lurks in the world we love.'[41] The Captain is another Uriah Heep, condemned even while technically still innocent by the revul-sion he causes. It is along the boundary drawn by nausea, as we have seen, that the war breaks out between factions *within* a class.

Sensing the pathos in this nausea, Conrad's 'practice of style' retaliates on Jim's behalf, by an assertion of the aesthetic value of

---

[40] *LJ* 49–50.   [41] *LJ* 58.

description. 'The thin gold shaving of the moon floating slowly downwards had lost itself on the darkened surface of the waters . . .' This is Conrad's gorgeous virility, as much as Jim's, the expertise in figuration which William Blackwood could have expected to purchase with his £5 on account. Neither of them can sustain it, any more than Adam Jeffson could. The description of the moon is followed immediately by a description of the Captain's tendency to let loose without warning 'a torrent of foamy, abusive jargon that came like a gush from a sewer'. Among the things abused by such jargon one might count professionalism itself, of whose specialized vocabularies it is a brutal burlesque. The humiliation Jim suffers in keeping low (German) company generates enough pathos to ensure a triumph of a kind. 'Jim went on smiling at the retreating horizon; his heart was full of generous impulses, and his thought was contemplating his own superiority.' Gazing at the wondrous horizon, or at Conrad's wondrous prose, Jim can feel his own difference from the foaming embodiment of sloth and greed.

His gorge rose at the mass of panting flesh from which issued gurgling mutters, a cloudy trickle of filthy expressions; but he was too pleasurably languid to dislike actively this or any other thing. The quality of these men did not matter; he rubbed shoulders with them, but they could not touch him; he shared the air they breathed, but he was different.[42]

Henry Fleming would have been proud of him.

The young man who presents his case to the official inquiry in chapter 4 is a young man who has trained himself in charisma. The court has the power to annul his treasured certificate of seamanship. But for Jim, as for Caleb Williams, true justice transcends the formal categories of jurisprudence; private judgement will always remain superior to the judgements delivered by institutional law. So it is that he puts his parallel universe in place, the universe in which his unique qualities will be recognized, at the very moment when the court is preparing to condemn him. He finds in the crowd a pair of eyes gazing at him with 'intelligent volition'. He makes ready for his henceforth defining delusion of reference, which we learn about at the end of chapter 6, from Marlow's narration.[43]

---

[42] *LJ* 59–61.   [43] *LJ* 66, 94–8.

The narrative time between these two incidents is filled with Marlow's ruminations on the nature of professional conduct. Marlow has fond things to say about the youngsters he has 'turned out' in his time

for the service of the Red Rag, to the craft of the sea, to the craft whose whole secret could be expressed in one short sentence, and yet must be driven afresh every day into young heads till it becomes the component part of every waking thought—till it is present in every dream of their young sleep.

Jim's qualities are the qualities which a sound training might have been expected to convert, to its own further enhancement, into symbolic capital. Marlow worries, however, that the capital is merely symbolic: that the masculinity and the Englishness are not sufficiently grounded in and by the craft of the sea. 'He looked as genuine as a new sovereign, but there was some infernal alloy in his metal.' Marlow, of course, will subsequently try to persuade us of Jim's mettle. On this occasion, his acknowledgement of the parallel universe which the third-person narrator of the first four chapters had begun to construct on Jim's behalf remains implicit. He, too, sees the gleam of gold in and around Jim; he, too, feels sick at the sight of the lard-like German captain.[44] In the parallel universe, triumph and humiliation are each other's measure.

Marlow conducts his ruminations by reference to a ring of men who sail. The interest he takes in Jim's case is taken as a member of 'an obscure body of men held together by a community of inglorious toil and by fidelity to a certain standard of conduct'. This is a community held together by charisma rather than by certification. Brierly, captain of the crack ship of the Blue Star line, and one of Jim's assessors, tells Marlow that the body of men to which they both belong is not 'organised', and that the only thing which holds it together is a name for decency. So offended is Brierly by Jim's indecency that he commits suicide. One might note that the opinion to which Marlow appeals is decidedly international. Those consulted include not only the ultra-English Brierly, but a Frenchman, and an Australian.[45] Qualities like Englishness and masculinity only feature in this anthology of private judgements in so far as they constitute a deployment of expertise.

[44] *LJ* 75–8.   [45] *LJ* 80, 93, 150, 160.

The ring of men who sail might be thought to intimate, in their knowledge of craft secrets, the ring of men who write. What kind of knowledge is it that *Lord Jim* conveys, and to whom? Conrad's friendship with Hugh Clifford is of particular interest in this respect. Clifford began his career as a colonial civil servant in 1883. He first wrote to Conrad in May 1899, after returning home from a tour of duty as British Resident in the State of Pahang, Malaysia. He was later appointed to the governorships of the Gold Coast, Nigeria, Ceylon, and the Straits Settlements. He was the author of several volumes of sketches and stories, and collaborated on a Malay dictionary.

Sent Clifford's *Studies in Brown Humanity* for review, in April 1898, Conrad thought the book unrivalled in its knowledge of its subject, but 'not literature'.[46] Clifford, writing anonymously in the *Singapore Free Press*, in September 1898, observed that Conrad's own studies in 'brown humanity' were certainly literature, but full of mistakes. 'Extremely laudatory,' Conrad reported to Blackwood, 'but in fact telling me I don't know anything about it.' Conrad considered that he *did* know something about it, having researched some 'dull, wise books'.[47] The point, perhaps, was that Clifford did not have to rely on books. Apologizing to Clifford for the review of *Studies*, on 17 May 1899, Conrad admitted that his own assumption of 'malay colouring' in his novels and stories might well exasperate 'those who *know*'. But he found consolation in Clifford's liking for his prose.[48] There is a kind of competition, here, for the status of being in the know, which Clifford won. 'His knowledge is unique,' Conrad told Blackwood on 22 August 1899, adding that if he himself had ever possessed such knowledge he would have been able to move mountains.[49] What gave him the final advantage, he thought, was a different kind of knowledge. Writing to Clifford on 9 October 1899, he produced an incisive critique of the stories collected in Clifford's *In a Corner of Asia*, in which he managed to reserve for himself alone the dilemmas confronting the 'mere craftsman'.[50]

Thereafter, Conrad was happy to congratulate Clifford on the

---

[46] *Letters*, ii. 57. The review appeared in the *Academy* on 23 Apr. 1898, and subsequently in *Notes on Life and Letters* (London: J. M. Dent, 1949), 58–61.

[47] *Letters*, ii. 130.   [48] Ibid. 180.   [49] Ibid. 194.

[50] Ibid. 200.

progress of his diplomatic career. A letter of 13 December 1899 expresses unrestrained delight at his friend's appointment as Governor of Labuan and North Borneo, and comments favourably on the 'simplicity of treatment' in a story about a French missionary in Malaya. The story starts him reminiscing about rum characters met during his own days in the Archipelago. *Lord Jim*, he says, is going to be 'a hash of episodes, little thumbnail sketches of fellows one has rubbed shoulders with'. The novel, in short, will redeploy the symbolic capital amassed during one career in the advancement of another. But for Conrad there was always a dangerous supplement, a form of expertise over and above that acquired by knocking about, as he and Clifford had done, in the Far East. 'Of course,' he adds, 'you are favoured by the subject while I have always to struggle with a moral horror of some sort. It looks like my choice but it may be only my fate.'[51]

Conrad's awareness of what was at issue in the professionalization of European societies extended beyond the expertise one might acquire by knocking about. Writing to Blackwood about *Heart of Darkness*, on 31 December 1898, he felt he had to defend the story's topic, though not its workmanship. 'The criminality of inefficiency and pure selfishness when tackling the civilizing work in Africa is a justifiable idea. The subject is of our time distinctly— though not topically treated.'[52] The justifiable idea is an idea about professional identity and its abuses in empire. Where *Lord Jim* is concerned, the idea might be regarded as a commentary on the conduct of the Boer War. The war produced in Conrad an anxiety which is often hard to distinguish from the anxiety produced by the novel's composition. The war had brought in an 'element of incertitude', he told Cunninghame Graham on 14 October 1899, which mere military success would not in itself eliminate.[53] A letter of 26 October 1899 to Ted Sanderson, an officer in a territorial battalion, begins with battlefield strategy and ends with literary ambition.[54]

Conrad did not worry, as one is now inclined to think that everyone then did, about the degeneracy of the race. He did not worry about 'English' valour and resolution. He worried about the

---

[51] Ibid. 226–7.   [52] Ibid. 139–40.
[53] Ibid. 207.   [54] Ibid. 210, 212.

British army's ability to conduct itself in a professional manner.[55] Thus in a letter to Sanderson of 28 December 1899, he declared that the war was from every conceivable point of view an unsatisfactory business. 'I say from every point of view because the disclosure of our military weakness is not compensated by the manifestation of colonial loyalty.' He was glad that Roberts was going, in addition to Kitchener, who was not, he felt, to be trusted by himself. Kitchener had enjoyed spectacular success in the Sudan; but Roberts was the more professional, an organizer as well as a fighter.[56] Conrad's anxiety about Kitchener is his anxiety about Jim, and about himself. Jim, of course, will go on to enjoy spectacular success, a success in spectacle. But is there some infernal alloy in his metal?

PATUSAN

Jim's relocation to Patusan, courtesy of Stein, is a departure from the novel's basis in fact.[57] It is a departure explicable, I believe, in terms of the narrative structure elaborated by novels like *Caleb Williams* and *The Woman in White*. In these novels, protagonist and antagonist share the conviction that private judgement is superior to the judgements delivered by institutional law. In their shared contempt for institutions, they become utterly transparent to each other, an insufferable mutual transparency which can only be resolved by a duel to the death. Patusan, of course, is a place beyond the reach of Western institutional law, a place where charisma counts for more than certificates. There, a commoner can become a lord. 'He left his earthly failings behind him and what sort of reputation he had, and there was a totally new set of conditions for his imaginative faculty to work upon.'[58]

---

[55] It was Michael Levenson who first suggested to me that the Boer War was worth considering as a context not only for Conrad's general dubiousness, but for his specific preoccupation with professionalism.

[56] *Letters*, ii. 233.

[57] A. P. Williams, the model for Jim, who in Aug. 1880 had organized the abandonment of the steamship *Jeddah* and its 900 passengers, spent the rest of his career as a ship's chandler in Singapore, where his story was well known: Norman Sherry, *Conrad's Eastern World* (Cambridge: CUP, 1966), 66–86.

[58] *LJ* 203–4.

Jim's imaginative faculty does indeed get to work. A delusion of grandeur once again calls forth the delusion of persecution which alone will guarantee its validity. Gentleman Brown, emissary of the way of life he has renounced, pursues him in his retreat.[59] The piratical Gentleman Brown is a perfect match for Jim because he, too, is paranoid. Observing him on his deathbed, Marlow reflects that certain forms of evil are 'akin to madness', arising as they do from an intense egoism 'inflamed by resistance'. Brown has Adam Jeffson's sense of superiority, and his destructive mania. Driven by a 'blind belief in the righteousness of his will against all mankind', he desires above all 'to play havoc with that jungle town which had defied him, to see it strewn over with corpses and enveloped in flames'. His unprovoked attack on the contingent led by Doramin's son, Dain Waris, is the culmination of mania. 'It was then that Brown took his revenge upon the world which, after twenty years of contemptuous and reckless bullying, refused him the tribute of a common robber's success.'[60] Brown is of course no more than a grotesque or 'parodic' version of Jim.[61] Neither man will achieve advancement in any other way than through mutual assured destruction. 'To me the conversation of these two across the creek appears now as the deadliest kind of duel [at] which Fate looked on with her cold-eyed knowledge of the end.' The outcome of the duel, that Jim should pay with his life for Dain Waris's death, is a crowning delusion of grandeur. ' "Nothing can touch me," he said in a last flicker of superb egoism.' This last flicker, which denies the meaning and value of his wife's love for him, confirms him in hypermasculinity. And the landscape promptly turns sublime, as it does during Henry Fleming's more megalomaniac moments. 'She sobbed on his shoulder. The sky over Patusan was blood-red, immense, streaming like an open vein.'[62]

I have argued that the 'break' in *Lord Jim*—the transformation

[59] *LJ* 328. One might compare Heyst's words to Lena, in *Victory* (1915). 'Here they are, the envoys of the outer world. Here they are before you—evil intelligence, instinctive savagery, arm in arm': *Victory* (London: Dent, 1948), 329.

[60] *LJ* 297, 317, 341.

[61] Robert Hampson gives a careful account of their similarities and differences in *Joseph Conrad: Betrayal and Identity* (Basingstoke: Macmillan, 1992), 132–6.

[62] *LJ* 328, 348–9. Ch. 9 of *The Red Badge of Courage* concludes with Henry converting his humiliation on the battlefield into a 'philippic'. 'The red sun was pasted in the sky like a wafer': *RBC* 116.

of a novel into a tragedy or a romance—the displacement, if you prefer, of one cultural institution by another—is entirely consistent with the strategies of paranoid narrative. It is comparable in effect to Rudolf Rassendyll's Ruritanian holiday, or the poisoning of the world's population in *The Purple Cloud*; the difference being, of course, that mass-market fiction brutally truncates the preliminary novelistic investigation of background and temperament. Like Ruritania, or a depopulated globe, Patusan is the place where paranoid symmetry finally comes into its own. Jim transmutes into Lord Jim, and his persecutory delusion finds its object in Gentleman Brown. The proof of this consistency lies in the repetition of the gesture which founds and sustains paranoid narrative. At three crucial junctures in *Lord Jim*, an expression of nausea brings home to us the systematic nature of the fantasy of advancement and recognition to which the protagonist has so exuberantly committed himself.

I have already described the first of these scenes, on the bridge of the *Patna*, when the gorgeous virility of Jim's dreams is punctured by the emergence on deck of his odious captain. 'There was something obscene in the sight of his naked flesh. His bared breast glistened soft and greasy as though he had sweated out his fat in his sleep.' The second takes place when Marlow, on his way to Patusan, encounters the official in charge of a little place on the coast, 'a big, fat, greasy, blinking fellow of mixed descent, with turned-out, shiny lips'. 'I found him lying extended on his back in a cane chair, odiously unbuttoned, with a large green leaf of some sort on the top of his steaming head.' Like the similarly hybrid and unbuttoned captain of the *Patna*, this man curses in German. He, too, has to endure a great deal of obtrusive irony, much of it directed at his ludicrous social aspirations ('I am a Government official') rather than his greasiness. It is from his turned-out, shiny lips that Marlow first hears of the mysterious jewel which a 'white vagabond' has obtained, 'partly by the exercise of his wonderful strength and partly by cunning, from the ruler of a distant country'. The jewel is of course Jewel, Jim's wife, and his acquisition of this priceless asset is the cornerstone of what Marlow calls the 'Jim-myth'. The official is a figure of hybridity or chanciness, a figure which must be summoned so that the narrative may triumph in and through its expulsion. Marlow wonders whether he is drunk, or mad. 'He perspired, puffed, moaning feebly, and scratching himself with such horrid composure that I could not bear the sight long enough to find out.'[63]

Like the German captain, the half-breed official is a figure, a rhetorical exercise, an occasion for Conrad's hallmark ironies. One would expect the fatal blurring of distinctions they represent to find its externalization in Patusan; and it does, in Cornelius, Jim's predecessor as Stein's agent, and Jewel's stepfather. It is the thought of Cornelius in the latter capacity which prompts Marlow's argument, at the beginning of chapter 29, that the Jim-myth has meaning and value, even though it cannot be verified.

But do you notice how, three hundred miles beyond the end of telegraph cables and mail-boat lines, the haggard utilitarian lies of our civilisation wither and die, to be replaced by pure exercises of imagination, that have the futility, often the charm, and sometimes the deep hidden truthfulness, of works of art? Romance had singled Jim for its own—and that was the true part of the story, which otherwise was all wrong. He did not hide his jewel.

Our recognition of the purity of this exercise of imagination depends on our recognition of Cornelius's impurity, about which Marlow leaves us in little doubt. 'He reminded one of everything that is unsavoury. His slow laborious walk resembled the creeping of a repulsive beetle, the legs alone moving with horrid industry while the body glided evenly.'[64] 'Swarming things', as Mary Douglas points out in her analysis of the abominations of Leviticus, 'are neither fish, flesh, nor fowl.' Their characteristic crawling and creeping movement cuts across the 'basic classification', and thus threatens the very capacity of a beleaguered people to make sense of experience.[65] The shadowy Cornelius, Marlow explains, is the 'hateful embodiment' of all the difficulties Jim has found in his path. Unlike the German captain and the half-breed official, he has a decisive function in the story. He it is who, in his hatred of Jim, tells Gentleman Brown how to ambush Dain Waris and his party.[66]

Cornelius is the last in a series of figures of hybridity, of that

---

[63] *LJ* 58, 248–50.   [64] *LJ* 251, 253.
[65] *Purity and Danger: An Analysis of the Concepts of Pollution and Taboo* (London: Routledge & Kegan Paul, 1966), 56.
[66] *LJ* 259, 337–8.

messiness which must be eliminated if paranoid narrative is to constitute and sustain itself. Since he belongs in a romance or a tragedy rather than a novel, the elimination he brings about by his actions is that of the protagonist, in a flicker of superb egoism which for ever seals the Jim-myth. *Lord Jim* is proto-Modernism's best shot at paranoid narrative.

PARANOIA AND THE NEAR-MISS

The low point of Jim's campaign for rehabilitation, or failing that anonymity, and the moment when he becomes convinced that he will never live the *Patna* down, is a bar-room brawl in Bangkok, after which Marlow takes him away on his ship. A seaman, Marlow reports, even if only a passenger, will normally take an interest in the 'sea-life' around him. 'In every sense of the expression he is "on deck"; but my Jim, for the most part, skulked down below as though he had been a stowaway.' Jim's despondency so infects Marlow that he cannot bring himself to discuss professional matters with him or give orders to the ship's officers in his presence. 'For whole days we did not exchange a word.' Paranoia's system-building, its investment of the world with meaning and value, has come to an abrupt halt in muteness and avoidance. Before very long, realizing that Jim has lost 'some of that elasticity which had enabled him to rebound back into his uncompromising position after every over-throw', Marlow decides to consult Stein on his behalf.[67] The episode is comparable in theme and mood to 'The Secret Sharer' (1910), in which the narrator, who has just taken charge of his first command, gives shelter to a stowaway, an officer from another ship who has killed a man in a fit of rage. Like Jim, the stowaway, Leggatt, is the son of a Norfolk parson.[68] In both cases, it could be argued, a secret or semi-secret coexistence, so that the 'stowaway' becomes an intimate possession ('my' Jim, my Leggatt), in some way either constitutes or renews the narrator. Marlow resolves to see Stein; the ship's captain establishes an invincible authority over a sceptical crew. What gets shared secretly, in both cases, is paranoia.

[67] *LJ* 189–90.
[68] *Typhoon and Other Tales*, ed. Cedric Watts (Oxford: OUP, 1986), 253, 255. Henceforth *TOT*.

'The Secret Sharer' is of particular interest here because, ten years on from *Lord Jim*, in the thick of the events usually thought to have given shape to Modernism in Britain, it still owes equal allegiance to both of Jameson's competing 'cultural institutions'. In the early autumn of 1909 Conrad had a visit from Captain Charles Marris, a 'man out of the Malay Seas', who clearly provoked in him powerful memories of his time in the merchant marine. The encounter, Conrad wrote, was 'like the raising of a lot of dead— dead to me, because most of them live out there and even read my books and wonder who [the] devil has been around taking notes'. These readers, he went on, 'shall have more of the stories they like'.[69] If this episode was the catalyst for 'The Secret Sharer', its form, as Conrad first conceived it, had a lot to do with an offer from the literary editor of the *Daily Mail* of £5 per 1,200 words for a series of short sketches. He intended it for the sea captains, and the *Daily Mail*'s million readers. However, tempted as he was by the prospect of 'a guinea a week at least', Conrad could not altogether overcome his anxiety about the compromises an arrangement with the *Mail* would involve. He did not have the heart to 'throw [his story] away'. 'The Secret Sharer' is 'the result', as he put it, 'of that reluctance'. The speed with which the story eventually wrote itself ('12000 words in ten days') seemed like a vindication of the stand he had taken against literary commerce. He reported that he was feeling as well as he had felt in the *Lord Jim* days, 'which were the last good ones'.[70] Indeed, Michael Levenson has seen 'The Secret Sharer' as a 'willed response' to the 'crisis of modernity': to the harsh challenge to 'high' literature confronting Conrad after the failure of Ford Madox Ford's editorship of the *English Review* in 1909, and with it the possibility of a forum for complex and innovative practices of writing.[71] If Conrad was able to combine high and low in 'The Secret Sharer', a story both for the ring of men who sailed and for the ring of men who wrote, this is perhaps because its major preoccupation is with charismatic professionalism.

The kernel story of 'The Secret Sharer' does not differ greatly

---

[69] *Letters*, iv. 277–8. [70] Ibid. 296–8.

[71] 'Secret History in "The Secret Sharer"', in Daniel R. Schwarz (ed.), *Joseph Conrad: The Secret Sharer* (Boston, Mass.: Bedford Books, 1997), 163–74, p. 171.

in its essentials from that of *The Woman in White* or *Lord Jim*: an ambitious young man seeks validation beyond that afforded by the efficient performance of the tasks appropriate to a particular station in life. In this case, the young man, taking charge of his first command, as Conrad himself had done in 1888 when he took charge of the *Otago*, his first and only command, determines to impose his authority on his crew by carrying out a manœuvre whose purpose and scope he alone is aware of; he uses their scepticism, their conviction that he has gone mad and that his unimaginable rashness will destroy the ship, to confer on himself the status of a superman. The ship's officers are men well equipped with qualities. The mate, for example, has a methodical manner, an ample supply of platitude, and a face 'overcharged by a terrible growth of whisker'. 'But what I felt most was my being a stranger to the ship; and if all the truth must be told, I was somewhat of a stranger to myself.' A man without qualities, the captain can allow for an 'adequacy' of masculine habits and abilities in his subordinates, while putting himself to a more rigorous test. 'They had simply to be equal to their tasks; but I wondered how far I should turn out faithful to that ideal conception of one's own personality every man sets up for himself secretly.'[72]

It is this strangeness, this cleaving to an ideal conception, which prompts the captain to take the first watch himself, thus clearing the decks, as it were, for paranoid self-renewal. His encounter with ship and crew had after all begun in brute contingency, in the vagaries of appointment and the mess of imminent departure. 'Fast alongside a wharf, littered like any ship in port with a tangle of unrelated things, invaded by unrelated shore people, I had hardly seen her yet properly.'[73] A ship in port is the very epitome of entanglement in the world. This one will have to be cut free from the tangle of 'unrelated things' which clogs any inauguration, and then subjected to an act of will, before the captain can be said to have taken command of it.

So he peremptorily disturbs the 'established routine of duties' by taking the first watch himself. 'My action might have made me appear eccentric.'[74] This ex-centricity, or departure from routine, opens up a parallel universe within that occupied by his officers

---

[72] *TOT* 245–6.   [73] *TOT* 247.   [74] *TOT* 249.

and crew. A ladder has been left hanging from the side of the ship which would not otherwise have been left hanging, and up it climbs Leggatt, the secret sharer. The need for concealment, for the keeping of the secret, could be said to impose itself in advance of any very clear understanding of Leggatt's character and position; and for reasons which have to do with the captain's strangeness, not Leggatt's.[75] 'I felt that it would take very little to make me a suspect person in the eyes of the ship's company.' The stowaway's presence in his cabin provides a wonderful opportunity for the captain to suppose that his officers have begun to watch him closely, and to whisper among themselves about his eccentricities. The subsequent arrival of Archbold, captain of the *Sephora*, in which Leggatt had served as mate, and a man built to harbour suspicions, confirms the feeling of persecution: 'everything was against us in our secret partnership'. On one occasion, the mate comes suddenly on deck, 'as it were by chance'; but in the parallel universe nothing ever happens by chance, and before long he has begun to steal looks at his commander, 'for signs of lunacy or drunkenness, I suppose'.[76]

Persecution generates a grandeur of which it is the only true measure. Taking risks he would not otherwise have taken, and which his officers implore him not to take, the captain sails his ship close enough to land for the secret sharer to swim ashore. By this manœuvre, whose purpose and scope he alone is aware of, he achieves something he would not otherwise have achieved, 'the perfect communion of a seaman with his first command'.[77] Its success endows him not just with expertise, but with sublimity.[78] In 'The Secret Sharer', as in *The Woman in White* and *Lord Jim*, the secondary plot (of 'actual' conspiracy against a person or place the protagonist holds dear) supervenes on the primary plot, of ambition's madness, in order to validate it.

There is a politics to this paranoia, as Michael Levenson has convincingly established. The 'lure of the psychological' is so

---

[75] One could of course give the strangeness of this secret relationship a paranoid content by calling it 'homoerotic' or 'homosexual', as Bonnie Kime Scott does: 'Intimacies Engendered in Conrad's "The Secret Sharer"', in Schwarz (ed.), *Joseph Conrad*, 197–210, pp. 206–7.

[76] *TOT* 262, 265, 275, 287.   [77] *TOT* 295.

[78] Longinus, after all, repeatedly described the sublime as a *near*-disaster such as a ship narrowly missing a dangerous shoal. *On the Sublime*, ed. and tr. W. Rhys Roberts (Cambridge: CUP, 1899), 73–4.

pronounced in 'The Secret Sharer', Levenson observes, that it strongly discourages any consideration of social and political context. The story's source is a murder committed in 1880 on board the *Cutty Sark*, the legendary tea clipper, which in the age of steam was fast becoming a relic. The violent and despotic mate, Sidney Smith, struck dead a black crewman, John Francis, who had apparently disregarded an order given during a storm of hurricane force. When the captain, J. S. Wallace, subsequently made it possible for Smith to escape, the crew refused to obey his orders. Wallace himself, overcome by guilt and shame, committed suicide. The *Cutty Sark* incident, a story of oppression and revolt, of authority at once weak and excessive, may well have seemed to Conrad a reflection of the destiny of modern Europe: the replacement of savage autocracy by the chaotic pursuit of 'material interests'. Levenson interprets Archbold's determination to bring Leggatt to justice as an 'emblem' of an 'exhausted modernity' which can offer no persuasive self-justification other than obedience to routine. Commonplace through and through, yielding to his second mate, his steward, his wife, this weak captain (this weak man) exemplifies the loss of authentic conviction Conrad so deplored in the moral life of his epoch. 'Within the reign of moral formula and social convention, it becomes nearly impossible to recognize the claims of *difference*.'[79] This is the politics of paranoid narrative, as I have defined it, a militant objection to social mimesis. The captain's embrace of Leggatt can thus be understood as a refusal of the norms which have unmanned Archbold, a critique of 'leveling modernity'. There is the outline, here, in paranoia's assertion of difference at all costs, of a postliberal politics whose substance and tone I shall try to describe in my next chapter, on Conrad's erstwhile friend and collaborator, Ford Madox Ford.

[79] 'Secret History', 166–7.

CHAPTER 6

Ford's Impressionism

ONE DAY IN 1914, Ford Madox Ford, then 40 years old and feeling it, found himself for a while in the custody of the youthful Percy Wyndham Lewis, a writer whose work had appeared in Ford's magazine, the *English Review*, and who was about to launch a magazine of his own, the rather more intemperate *Blast*. Gripping Ford by the elbow, Lewis, who was as usual in incendiary mood, poured scorn on him and his associates. 'You and Mr Conrad and Mr James and all those old fellows are done', he was to be heard insisting. 'Exploded! . . . *Fichus!* . . . *Vieux jeu!* . . . No good! . . . Finished!' Lewis's beef was with literary 'impressionism': with novels which sought intricately to render the movements, at once furtive and immense, of a consciousness enmeshed in and inseparable from worlds not of its own making. 'You fellows try to efface yourselves; to make people think that there isn't any author and that they're living in the affairs you . . . adumbrate, isn't that your word? . . . What balls!' Adumbration had been Flaubert's method, and Turgenev's, and James's, and Conrad's. It was rather ostentatiously the method of Ford's *The Good Soldier*, whose opening chapters were shortly to appear in *Blast*. Lewis thought that people had had enough of all that. They did not want self-effacement. They wanted brilliant fellows like him performing stunts and letting off fireworks. 'What's the good of being an author if you don't get any fun out of it?'[1]

Ford told this story several times in several different ways, each time effacing himself assiduously, the better to adumbrate Lewis's brilliant performance. The version recounted in *Return to Yesterday* situates Ezra Pound at his other elbow, talking incessantly in an incomprehensible accent.[2] Ford, it would seem, could barely set

---

[1] *Mightier than the Sword* (London: Allen & Unwin, 1938), 282–3.
[2] *Return to Yesterday* (Manchester: Carcanet, 1999), 311–12: henceforth *RTY*.

foot outside his front door without importunate persons of one kind or another falling in beside him. When he lived in Holland Park Avenue, he would take his morning walk with Ezra Pound at one elbow, barely visible beneath an immense sombrero, and at the other the leopardskin-clad Mrs Gwendolen Bishop, who danced snake dances and made pottery; Mrs Bishop, although proceeding away from rather than towards her home, carried in one hand a string bag full of onions, which Ford felt it his duty to carry.[3] Ford attracted neediness. Beggars, runaways, lost property, writs, stray opinions, unwelcome confidences, random abuse: all attached themselves to him as though to a magnet. And there can have been few moments in his adult life when there were not at least two women competing for his sexual attention. Scandal, another kind of neediness, proved equally adhesive. He was suspected of more or less anything, from sleeping with his sister-in-law to leaving rashers of bacon between the pages of the books he read at breakfast.

Return to Yesterday, first published in 1931, is a memoir of literary life in England in the late Victorian and Edwardian eras. It begins in 1891, with Ford immersed in Kipling's 'Only a Subaltern', on a train in Sussex; and ends at a countryhouse party in Berwickshire in August 1914, during which someone reads aloud from *A Portrait of the Artist as a Young Man*, then appearing in the *Egoist*, and war is declared.[4] It thus describes two successive changings of the literary guard—from the Great Victorians (here represented by various Pre-Raphaelites, and, distantly, George Meredith) to the Great Moderns (Hardy, James, Conrad, Crane, Kipling, Wells), and from the Great Moderns to really modern Modernism (Pound, Lewis, Eliot, Joyce). There is autobiography in this picture of a 'sort of world and time', and autobiography's function is to interfere in the mere devising of literary history. It preserves the memoir from mere commemoration, from elegy. Ford took literature very seriously indeed, but not for granted. In so far as *Return to Yesterday* is a portrait of the artist as a young man, it is the portrait of a young man who for much of the time would rather be a subaltern, a historian, a pig-farmer, indeed anything at

---

[3] *RTY* 277–8.
[4] *RTY* 9–10, 325. *Thus to Revisit* (London: Chapman & Hall, 1921) also begins with the first stirrings of 'the Writer's conscious literary life', as he read, and then met, Conrad, James, Stephen Crane, and W. H. Hudson.

all, than an artist. It is a book about 'pure letters', and about what the purity of those letters might amount to in a society professionalized from top to bottom. It is indispensable, if we want to understand what it was that Lewis thought he was denouncing in 1914, and, just as significant, why he felt he had to denounce it.

Recollection was a habit Ford acquired at a relatively early age. *Ancient Lights* (1911), a book about the Pre-Raphaelite Brotherhood, is subtitled 'the memoirs of a young man'. *Return to Yesterday*, which cheerfully cannibalizes this and several other volumes of reminiscence, improves upon them, and upon much that has been written about him, by implicitly deriving the consistency of his literary method from psychic and imaginative need. Ford's impressionism—sharply attentive to consequence and inconsequence alike, to consequence framed by inconsequence—was the product of the attribution to him, from childhood onwards, either of consequence or of inconsequence, but rarely of both at the same time.

Ford belonged to the 'governing classes' of the late Victorian literary and artistic worlds: his maternal grandfather was Ford Madox Brown, his uncle William Michael Rossetti.[5] The only possible career for the children of these classes was that of a genius. Ford's Rossetti cousins had written Greek dramas at the ages of 5, 9, and 14 respectively. It became his duty always to aspire to consequence. 'To me life was simply not worth living because of the existence of Carlyle, of Mr Ruskin, of Mr Holman Hunt, of Mr Browning, or of the gentleman who built the Crystal Palace.' Life was not worth living because he knew, and everyone else knew, that he did not have it in him to build the next Crystal Palace. His father, recalling a phrase from a child's primer, referred to him as 'the patient but extremely stupid donkey'. He might not be capable of building the next Crystal Palace, but he still had to behave like someone who just might, at a pinch. Madox Brown's command always to adhere to the 'best standard of conduct' laid the foundation for a durable paranoia: 'it is as well to know beforehand that such a rule of life will expose you to innumerable miseries, to efforts almost superhuman, and to innumerable betrayals—or to transactions in which you will consider yourself to have

[5] *RTY* 16.

been betrayed.'[6] Note that Ford reckons the 'efforts' (the aspirations) as much of an exposure as the 'betrayals'.

Return to Yesterday advances this tale of multiple exposures into the 1890s, and Ford's friendships with the two contemporary writers he admired most, James and Conrad. By this time he had discovered in himself an ability to provoke in other people—and especially in Great Victorians like Samuel Butler and Frederic Harrison—abrupt and inexplicable furies. Here, too, James and Conrad did not let him down. The opening chapter of *Return to Yesterday* describes an invitation to dine with James. Dinner proves something of an ordeal, as James sits sideways to him across the corner of the table and interrogates him mercilessly about his habits and opinions. Ford's answers are received with 'no show at all of either satisfaction or reproof'. Indeed, he might just as well have remained silent, since James, having absorbed all this information, does nothing with it, but instead lets himself go in a 'singularly vivid display of dislike' for the persons rather than the works of his family circle. James's deduction from the fact that Dante Gabriel Rossetti once received him at teatime in what he thought was a dressing-gown is that the eminent artist had been 'disgusting in his habits, never took baths, and was insupportably lecherous'. What was worse, Rossetti habitually devoured 'masses of greasy ham and bleeding eggs' for his breakfast. James goes on to denounce W. M. Rossetti (hopelessly dull) and Swinburne (couldn't swim). It is, in its shamelessness, a magnificent performance. 'I do not think that Mr James had the least idea what I was, and I do not think that, till the end of his days, he regarded me as a serious writer.' Conrad, whom Edward Garnett brought to Ford's cottage at Bonnington in September 1898, was not much of an improvement. Every inch the ship's captain, he thrust his hands firmly into the pockets of his reefer-coat and pointed his 'black torpedo beard' in a vaguely navigational manner at the distant horizon. Ford he mistook for the gardener. Like James, Conrad was capable of rages which were 'sudden, violent, blasting and incomprehensible'.[7]

---

[6] *Ancient Lights* (London: Chapman & Hall, 1911), pp. ix–xii. Ford remembered Madox Brown telling him that he should never refuse to help a lame dog over a stile. 'Never lend money: always give it . . . Beggar yourself rather than refuse assistance to any one whose genius you think shows promise of being greater than your own' (pp. 197–8).   [7] *RTY* 16–18, 45–6, 24.

It shocked Ford that men he held in veneration, men who had taken the trouble to interrogate him extensively about his personal and professional affairs, men who furthermore did not hesitate to ask him for advice and support when it suited them, could still treat him like a criminal or an idiot. There was betrayal in their rage, as well as an oblique acknowledgement of the 'efforts' he continued to make on their behalf, and on literature's. He wanted to know where it came from. The Great Victorians put Ford out by rages which he knew, on reflection, to be arbitrary and generic (though no less mortifying for that). The Great Moderns made him wonder whether there was not something in him which provoked rage. He began to take it personally.

Indeed, he found in his own annoyingness a certain strength, or at least evidence that he was not a person to be easily overlooked. By the time he had acquired protégés of his own, as editor of the *English Review* in 1908 and 1909, and then, from December 1923, of the *Transatlantic Review*, passive or indirect provocation was a way of life. Max Saunders finds in the profit-sharing arrangements Ford made with regard to the *English Review* a 'disconcerting sense that he expects his closest friends to betray him; even that he is contriving their treachery'.[8] Ford *meant* the young writers he promoted to turn on him, to betray him, to insult him behind his back, and they did not let him down. It would no doubt have been a grave disappointment had Wyndham Lewis taken him by the elbow only in order to whisper mellow commendations in his ear.

Lewis was further to oblige with some wonderful descriptions of Ford as a Great Modern. Ford, Lewis wrote, 'was a flabby lemon and pink giant, who hung his mouth open as though he were an animal at the Zoo inviting buns—especially when ladies were present. Over the gaping mouth damply depended the ragged ends of a pale lemon moustache'.[9] The outbursts of bile Ford coaxed from other people form a necessary complement to his reminiscences. In March 1924, for example, Ernest Hemingway, then assistant editor of the *Transatlantic*, favoured Pound with his opinion of the editor. Ford, he admitted, could

---

[8] *Ford Madox Ford: A Dual Life*, 2 vols. (Oxford: OUP, 1996), i. 243.
[9] *Rude Assignment*, ed. Toby Foshay (Santa Barbara, Calif.: Black Sparrow Press, 1984), 131.

'explain stuff'—'but in private life he is so goddam involved in being the dregs of an English country gentleman that you get no good out of him'.[10] *Return to Yesterday* describes the formation of this lemon–and–pink flabbiness from the inside.

Ford's ascent to lemon–and–pink flabbiness in the years before the war coincided with his emergence as a serious novelist, notably in *The Good Soldier*, which he wrote under the joint tutelage of James and Conrad. *The Good Soldier* has often been described as the finest French novel ever written in English, and it might also be thought of as the finest Conrad novel ever written in English. It is a book about betrayal, about the realization that essential moral soundness allied to high tone and high colour is compatible with sexual and emotional ferocity: a lesson Ford had begun to learn a long time before. The narrator, John Dowell, effaces himself to the point of colluding with, or ignoring, or not even noticing, his wife's seduction by his best friend, Edward Ashburnham, the perfect English gentleman. Dowell observes that he has had twelve years of 'playing the trained poodle', twelve years of faithful ministering to the very people who have betrayed him.[11] In August 1914, Wyndham Lewis brought with him to the countryhouse party in Berwickshire the proofs of the novel's opening chapters. My aim here is to describe how it came about.

THE ARTIST AS YOUNG MAN WITHOUT QUALITIES

What was the matter with Ford? The symptom which presented itself most vividly during his 1904 breakdown was agoraphobia. Just getting to the continental sanatoria where the condition could be treated by cold baths and a diet of pork and ice-cream was an achievement in itself. But the German mania for mania at least made him feel at home. 'There's such a lot of nervous breakdown in the land', he reported. 'They've a regular name for lack of walk-ing power here: Platz Angst.'[12] The clinical status of agoraphobia was not at all clear, in 1904. Some regarded it as a form of

---

[10] *Selected Letters*, ed. Carlos Baker (London: Granada, 1981), 113.
[11] *The Good Soldier: A Tale of Passion* (Harmondsworth: Penguin Books, 1972), 114.
[12] Quoted by Saunders, *A Dual Life*, i. 176.

psychosis, others as a hereditary mental disorder.[13] Freud thought of it as an 'anxiety neurosis' or 'anxiety hysteria'.[14] 'Brain Fag' was about the best Ford's doctors could do by way of diagnosis, and they may well have been right.[15]

There was never any shortage of strong opinions as to his state of mind. When Conrad fell out with Ford, in 1909, he did so in part because he did not like being patronized by his protégé. 'He's a megalomaniac who imagines that he is managing the Universe', Conrad told the literary agent J. B. Pinker, 'and that everybody treats him with the blackest ingratitude.' Conrad thought that Ford's mildness concealed a 'fierce and exasperating vanity'. 'Writing to you *in confidence* I do not hesitate to say that there are cases, not quite as bad, under medical treatment.'[16] Conrad's letter demonstrates that at least one person who knew Ford very well discerned in his behaviour the classic symptoms of paranoia. It is not unreasonable to think of him in those terms.[17] What will concern me here is his ability to think of himself in those terms.

Ford certainly knew a psychopathy when he saw one. His book about Madox Brown, published in October 1896, shortly before his twenty-third birthday, discerns in Brown's attitudes and experience the paranoid pattern which was so punishingly to inform his own career; it is at once a sober work of history, and uncannily prescient. Its prescience stems not only from Ford's conviction that he could scarcely do better than to emulate his grandfather, but also from his awareness of the extent to which his grandfather's attitudes and experience were the inevitable outcome of the role allotted to the serious artist in nineteenth-century British society. In England, he was to maintain in his 1914 book on Henry James, 'the author, as such, ranks beneath the governess and the vicar and

[13] G. E. Berrios and C. Link, 'Anxiety Disorders: Clinical Section', in G. Berrios and R. Porter (eds.), *A History of Clinical Psychiatry* (London: Athlone Press, 1995), 545–62, pp. 551–2.

[14] See e.g. the brief mention in the *Introductory Lectures*: *SE* xvi. 400 (full publication details, Ch. 2 n. 4).

[15] Saunders, *A Dual Life*, i. 181.

[16] *Collected Letters*, ed. Frederick R. Karl and Laurence Davies, 8 vols. projected (Cambridge: CUP, 1983–), iv. 265–6.

[17] Saunders e.g. speaks of the 'quickness to feel threatened or offended' which became apparent during Ford's 1904 breakdown: *A Dual Life*, i. 165. There are ten entries under 'paranoia' in the index to vol. i of Saunders's biography.

just above the servants'. Having 'no canons, no costume, no habits as a class and no rank in the State', he or she is literally indescribable.[18] For the rest of his life, Ford continued to associate the writer with those groups whose social indeterminacy has traditionally been thought to breed paranoia. *Return to Yesterday* even withholds the consolation of parity with the vicar. 'Ranking socially with the Governess and the Butler—a little above it if he prospers, a little below if he is poor—he cannot, *qua* writer, be a Gentleman. In consequence he tries to achieve Importance outside his Art.'[19] Achieving importance, inside or outside his art, is here reckoned to be the artist's primary (paranoid) motive. *Ford Madox Brown* is a book about profesional identity and its relation to class, among other things.

For Ford, the English artist was the man without qualities *par excellence*. I say 'man' advisedly, because his writing about literature's social status and function expresses an anxiety about gender. 'It was Henley and his friends', Ford wrote in *Ancient Lights*, 'who introduced into the English writing mind the idea that a man of action was something fine and a man of letters a sort of castrato.' The difficulty for the man of letters was that his lack of an established role might well deprive him of charisma (which Ford astutely understands as a social rather than a personal quality). Because he had no 'position'—no canons of behaviour, no uniform—the man of letters could not expect to compete sexually with the man of action: the Guards officer, say, or the 'returned colonist'. Women, Ford concludes, tended to regard the man of letters (the very epithet is dampening) as 'something less than a man' and the returned colonist as 'something rather more than two supermen rolled into one'.[20] Thus, perhaps, might Collins's Walter Hartright have reflected on a drawing-master's necessary emasculation. Like Ford, Collins wrote his first book about an ancestor who had been a professional artist. Ford's was about his grandfather, Collins's about his father.[21] Collins sent Walter Hartright to South America in order to transform him into a man of action, and a fit husband for Laura. Ford, however, like Collins,

---

[18] *Henry James* (London: Martin Secker, 1914), 146.
[19] *RTY* 64.
[20] *Ancient Lights*, 241–3.
[21] *Memoirs of the Life of William Collins, Esq., R.A.*, 2 vols. (London: Longman, 1848).

knew that sunburn was not enough. His acute and persistent concern with the professional status of the artist or man of letters made it possible for him to understand masculinity as a form of symbolic capital—that is, as a demonstration, an artefact—which if properly invested in marriage would yield a rich return. He knew that charisma was a demonstration and an artefact because he could not stop asking where the artist or the man of letters was to get it from. How, for example, had Henry James come by his virility and masterfulness, qualities not wholly unconnected, it would seem, with the 'cold fury' which sometimes shook him, with things 'spat out' in response to clumsiness or slight?[22]

The biography of Madox Brown answers this question by identifying the self in Brown's selflessness. As we have already seen, the main injunction of the moral code by which Brown unflinchingly lived was always to help a lame dog over a stile. Ford historicized this selflessness by establishing a social and political context for it in the violence of the disdain Brown felt for the modern world: for commerce, for tradespeople, for the philistinism of journalists and Academicians.[23] Understanding selflessness as a relation rather than an absolute value, as an expression of disdain for social mimesis, Ford also understood it as a source of feelings of grandeur. Brown's transformation of himself into a man without qualities had about it, Ford observes, the 'morbidness' of the 'ignored innovator':[24] an attitude which the *Review of Reviews* would have had little difficulty in defining as paranoid. The book shrewdly and lovingly traces the development of this attitude, at once a philosophy, a madness, and a social condition, in Brown's life and art.

From the outset of his career, lack of public recognition made Brown an awkward customer. When, in March 1849, he received a letter full of praise for his work, he thought someone must be having him on. He immediately took the letter round to the address from which it had been sent, in 'rather a dubious frame of mind', and demanded to know its meaning. Thus began the most

---

[22] *RTY* 16, 23. Ford recalls a tea-party given by one of James's most 'gentle and modest' admirers, at which the young man made the mistake of interrupting the master, who thereupon brutally 'indicted his manners, his hospitality, his dwelling, his work, with a cold fury in voice and eyes'.

[23] For Brown's hatred of tradespeople, see also *Ancient Lights*, 162.

[24] *Ford Madox Brown* (London: Longmans, Green, 1896), 51.

'memorable' friendship of his life, with Dante Gabriel Rossetti. In 1853, Brown suffered some kind of nervous breakdown, as his grandson and biographer was to do fifty years later. This 'period of gloom' saw the conception of some of his best-known paintings, including *Work* and *The Last of England*. The doctors told him that he was suffering from a melancholia which had no connection with any of the 'mysterious brain or internal maladies' his imagination had conjured up. The vivid conjuring-up may in itself have been symptomatic, of course. Brown's tendency to an 'exaggerated, almost incomprehensible, suspiciousness' would seem to have been a legacy, Ford observes, from that period in his life.[25]

The suspiciousness shaped Brown's career. 'Brown, although the most courteous and genial of men under ordinary circumstances, repeatedly damaged his prospects by resenting over-hastily and answering unguardedly slights that were frequently imagined.' He made enemies easily, and just as easily held them responsible for the set-backs he was subsequently to suffer. Ford was emphatic about the element of madness in Brown's belligerence. 'His own suspicions led him to discover "plots" where it is certain that none existed.' Thus a parallel universe was created in which the degree of persecution became the only appropriate measure of the degree of achievement. 'To an artist convinced, rightly or wrongly, of his own genius and of his own industry, and who has relied upon those qualities for the making of those "friends at court" who hang pictures in the place of honour and insert laudatory articles in society or literary journals, the existence of a "combination" seems almost self-evident.' Brown had in all conscience enemies enough, Ford sombrely concludes, without imagining them, or going out of his way to create even more by the 'injudicious brusqueness' that occasionally manifested itself in his manner. When he returns in his final pages to the subject of Brown's altruism, he is able to see it as the *product* of suspiciousness, as the catalyst of a recognition more valuable than that yielded by laudatory articles or pictures hung in the place of honour: as symbolic capital. 'With open eyes he would assist people who had again and again imposed upon him, having constantly in his mind the thought that, however unneedful his help before had been, it might now

[25] *Ford Madox Brown*, 52, 94–6.

be really needed.'[26] They hate me because I am special; I am special because they hate me, and because I do not repay their hatred in kind.

Ford's life of Brown is a brilliant reflection not only on a career, but on attitudes and feelings which inform the work of writers like Dickens, Collins, and Mill. Like Brown, he understood suspiciousness as a social or psychosocial affliction whose incidence varied according to occupation and status.[27] Did he observe in himself tendencies he had observed in his grandfather, and which others (Conrad, for example) were to observe in him? *The Benefactor*, a novel published in 1905, but begun in 1901, during the period of his intensive collaboration with Conrad, suggests that he did.

George Moffat, the benefactor, is, like Ford in 1901, primarily a poet, and furthermore, like Ford in 1901, a poet whose writing is 'so very little an essential part of the man' that hardly anyone knows about it.[28] He eventually achieves success, as Ford would very much have liked to do, but did not, with a florid historical romance entitled *Wilderspin*.[29] He is also the author of a biography of his father, an eminent portrait painter who 'had impressed upon him that you must never lose a chance of helping any lame dog over a stile, because you never know what he might not become'.[30] Eyes

---

[26] Ibid. 176, 249, 251, 382, 401. It is at this point that the argument I am developing here touches that developed by Jonah Siegel in *Desire and Excess: The Nineteenth-Century Culture of Art* (Princeton: Princeton University Press, 2000). Siegel, too, wants to demonstrate that the challenge posed to the status (indeed, the very idea) of art by 'self-consciously new movements', Modernist and postmodern, has its source in the 19th-cent. 'culture of art' which gave rise to the figure and institution of the 'modern artist'. By 'culture of art', he means the work dynamically done, in a particular place at a particular time, to establish the significance of art in society. My hope is that attention to the psychopathies of expertise, as felt and reflected on by 19th-cent. writers and artists, will illuminate the dynamism of that work.

[27] Brown saw as clearly as anyone e.g. the 'delusions' Rossetti harboured 'to the purpose that the whole world was in a conspiracy against him': *Ford Madox Brown*, 273.

[28] *The Benefactor: A Tale of a Small Circle* (London: Brown, Langham, 1905), 10. Henceforth *B*.

[29] Ford's florid romance, entitled *Romance* (1903), and written in collaboration with Conrad, did not prove florid enough to attract a large readership. It has since become the focus for a speculative inquiry into the dynamics of collaboration which throws considerable light on the gendering of literature in the early 1900s: Wayne Kostenbaum, *Double Talk: The Erotics of Male Literary Collaboration* (London: Routledge, 1989), 166–73.

[30] *B* 9. The 1st edn. intriguingly has 'style' for 'stile', and Moffat could indeed be said to help his lame dogs over styles, since his aim is to encourage good writing.

wide open, presumably, Moffat dispenses money and advice to all and sundry. 'The pity was that as soon as the men he had helped stood on their own feet they invariably dropped George and generally insulted him.' The pity! Does he not know that the ingratitude is the whole point? Fortunately, there is a young woman, Clara Brede, who sees in his persecution a grandeur otherwise beyond measurement. 'That was it. He spoiled everybody he met. He was too good. People could not appreciate him. They *must* treat him badly. It was inevitable.'[31]

The Benefactor is at its most vivid in its anxiety about both the class and the gender of benefaction. Inevitably, Moffat's rival for Clara Brede is a returned colonist, Carew, who, if not quite two supermen rolled into one, looms large in his fantasies. 'He had an image of the bearded, jaunty colossus, swinging with his horseman's stride down his—George's—own steps and along the clear, quiet streets to Brede's cottage.' Carew, he assumes, is on his way to court Clara. In his own life, there is no beardedness, no horseman's stride. All he has is the satisfaction—the status, the masculinity—to be derived from the loathing his inevitable betrayal by others will allow him to feel, the cold fury it will bring to his voice and eyes. He cannot but be gratified, therefore, when Hailes, one of the lame dogs whom he has helped over a stile (or style), decamps with some valuable books and water-colours. It is not the books and the water-colours Moffat minds, but the spirit in which Hailes took them. 'And he could picture Hailes, with the hidden dislike that servant has to master, going about the house picking up these perquisites.'[32] The loathing Moffat feels for Hailes is the loathing Dickens's David Copperfield had felt for Uriah Heap. In both cases, there is gratification, an insurgence of status and of masculinity, in the loathing.

The Benefactor passes in review, as it were, the difficulties and dangers of the moral code—the technique for accumulating symbolic capital, the madness—Madox Brown had bequeathed to his grandson.[33] Like the life of Brown, like the memoirs, it recapitulates paranoia's refashioning, from the 1840s onwards, as a

---

[31] B 6, 96.   [32] B 236, 47.

[33] Critical opinion is divided as to whether Ford achieved sufficient 'distance' from his protagonist to be able to judge him: Saunders, *A Dual Life*, i. 200–1.

critique of social mimesis. That critique informs the books Ford wrote in the years leading up to the First World War, to which I now turn.

THE POLITICS OF IMPRESSIONISM

Does the charismatic professionalism of the modern artist and writer, assiduously developed in and through paranoia, possess a politics? And, if so, does that politics constitute a form of symbolic capital? I frame these questions awkwardly, or in an unfamiliar way. But they are questions which have been asked often enough about Modernism, albeit from a different point of view.[34] We still want to know why radical literary experiment proved conducive to flirtations with fascism. I shall suggest here, and in subsequent discussions of D. H. Lawrence and Wyndham Lewis, that paranoia did produce a distinctive politics, which I term 'postliberalism'.

The politics of a man or woman without qualities become manifest not in an utterance or an act, but in the pattern of their evolution. 'In his early days he was nearly a Whig; in his later life he was by temperament a good deal of a "Tory of the old school", but his intellect made him a Socialist of an extreme type.'[35] Ford is talking about his grandfather here, but he could also, with the appropriate adjustment of party-political labels, be talking about himself. He, too, began as an 'advanced democrat' and ended as a staunch upholder of the feudal system.[36] For both men, furthermore, political faith was the product not so much of the coherence of any proposition they might advance as of the intensity of the resistance it met. They knew themselves by reflux, by the heat and light playing fiercely on the obverse of the views they advanced. Ford, for example, saw in the cold fury directed at him on one occasion by Ramsay MacDonald, when he put forward a view held by the radical Labour leadership, another version of the cold furies he had so often seen before in the voice and eyes of many a Victorian or Modern patriarch. 'The good journalist', he recalled,

---

[34] To my mind, the most productive formulation of the problem is that offered by Raymond Williams, in the essays collected in *The Politics of Modernism*, ed. Tony Pinkney (London: Verso, 1989).

[35] *Ford Madox Brown*, 401.   [36] *Henry James*, 66.

'became at once the black hater.' It was out of the blackness of this hatred, rather than in the view he was advancing, which he did not share, that Ford created a politics of his own.[37]

There was plenty of liberalism in Ford's politics, and in particular in the views put forward in *England and the English*, first published in America in 1907, which collects into one volume his three books about Englishness: *The Soul of London* (1905), *The Heart of the Country* (1906), and *The Spirit of the People* (1907). England's great achievement, Ford concludes, is to have evolved a rule-of-thumb system by which people may live together in large masses. England has shown 'how great and teeming populations may inhabit a small island with a minimum of discomfort, a minimum of friction, preserving a decent measure of individual independence of thought and character'.[38] *England and the English* is a democratic book, perhaps even a liberal book.[39]

And yet Ford was never a good or consistent liberal in that he could not bring himself to advocate or to enjoy consensus. Consensus, after all, precludes paranoid symmetry: the adjustment of the degree of fantasized grandeur to the degree of fantasized persecution. So Ford cannot wholly have believed his own propaganda about rule-of-thumb systems and muddling through. *England and the English* provides plenty of evidence to suggest that the great and teeming populations have not always inhabited the small island with a minimum of discomfort and friction. For example, Ford can foresee no immediate end to the ancient hostilities between the lower classes and the representatives of the law: 'occasionally, as things are at present constituted, for some obscure reason, having its rise in some too virile tradition, a wave of senseless violence will rise—supra-criminally—from these depths'.[40] In that supra-criminality, that excess of virile tradition, there is a black hatred which utterly disowns liberalism's faith in consensus. To say that Ford is postliberal is to say that he seems fascinated by

---

[37] *RTY* 75.

[38] *England and the English* (New York: McClure, Phillips, 1907), 252.

[39] *The Critical Attitude* (1911), which assembles essays first publ. in the *English Review*, has even been described as the epitome, in its unflustered balancing of views, of Gladstonian liberalism: Ann Barr Snitow, *Ford Madox Ford and the Voice of Uncertainty* (Baton Rouge, La.: Louisiana State University Press, 1984), 136.

[40] *England and the English*, 250.

the obscure reason for the waves of senseless violence which rise and fall without any reference to parliamentary politics. When, exactly, does a tradition become too 'virile', and how? Might there not be something to admire, albeit with a shudder, in that virility?

Furthermore, if England could plausibly be regarded as muddling through, in 1905, or 1907, this was surely not the case five years later. The period between 1910 and 1914 is often thought to have witnessed the 'strange death of liberal England' in a welter of strikes, mutinies, and suffrage stunts.[41] Ford himself endorsed some of the most inflammatory opinions available. He was in favour of Irish Home Rule, and votes for women. I shall suggest that his intimacy with paranoia, and specifically with that cultivation of a distaste for social mimesis which liberalism had fostered, and which was to outlive it, made him one of the most acute witnesses we have, if not to the strange death of liberal England, then at least to the widespread and vivid perception, in the years before the war, that a particular social and political consensus was indeed on its last legs.

The proof lies in some remarkable essays on 'the relations and the differences between the sexes' conceived in January 1911 and written over the next year or so.[42] These essays, eventually published as 'Women and Men' in the *Little Review* in 1918, and then as a book in 1923, were meant to fulfil Ford's long-standing ambition to describe 'ordinary lives'. However, the most memorable among them concern issues such as the social and political impact of Otto Weininger's inflammatory *Sex and Character* (1903), which was published in translation in 1906. The book

---

[41] George Dangerfield's *The Strange Death of Liberal England* (1936) and R. C. K. Ensor's *England 1870–1914* (1936), the interpretative studies which set the tone for historical analysis of the years immediately before the First World War, have by now become topics in their own right. In a valuable concise account of the period, Richard Shannon points out that events which have often been taken to constitute 'a pattern of extremism amounting to a pathological social morbidity' were in fact considerably less disruptive than the riots and assassinations of the 1880s. Both the strikes of 1912–13 and the Irish crisis of 1913–14 involved notable displays of discipline and order. 'The really dangerous manifestations of violence were international rather than domestic or Irish.' Even so, as Shannon freely admits, it was events like the Marconi scandal, the mutiny at the Curragh, or the vandalizing of the Rokeby Venus which caught the public attention: *The Crisis of Imperialism 1865–1915* (London: Paladin, 1976), 447–8.

[42] Letter to Pinker of 31 Jan. 1911: *Letters*, ed. Richard M. Ludwig (Princeton: Princeton University Press, 1965), 46–7.

answered the prayers of those young men of liberal opinion who, although in principle in sympathy with the suffrage movement, none the less felt, as Ford puts it, 'extraordinarily angry with Mrs Pankhurst and her followers'. Weininger's 'nonsensical work' had supposedly proved that women were morally inferior to men. Ford observes that the tones in which liberal young men spoke about it contained 'a mixture of relief, of thanksgiving, of chastened jubilation, of regret and obscenity'. For years they had trained themselves to believe that women should have justice done to them. Now Weininger had proved scientifically that women should not have justice done to them. In doing so, he had reunited the intellectual with the 'ordinary male man'. 'It made them very happy.'[43] What is of interest here is Ford's insight into the black hatred—the obscenity—at the heart of the New Liberalism. Ford discovers in the reflux of this obscenity, its beating back upon a view put forward, a position taken, the stimulus to politics. If these young men hated political women so blackly, then political women must be special, and their cause worth supporting.

Equally striking is Ford's insistence that the analysis of gender difference, in Britain in 1911, required an analysis of attitudes to class. It is class hatred he found in the average middle-class household, a hatred which aligns wife, children, and maid-servants against the paterfamilias. These dependants will have evolved a 'sort of freemasonry', Ford claims, to maximize their exploitation of the head of the household. 'And behind his back they will be perpetually whispering their servants' discontents.'[44] The discontents recall the 'hidden dislike' which Hailes is thought to express, in *The Benefactor*, when he goes about Moffat's house looking for objects to steal.[45] Ford, it should be said, identifies thoroughly with the 'unfortunate camel' who is their focus. The persecuted paterfamilias finds in the intensity of his persecution a grandeur he would not have known through the more orthodox domestic acknowledgements of love and respect.

Ford pursued the autobiographical emphasis of *Ancient Lights* and the concern with class and sex war evident in 'Women and Men' in three unjustly neglected 'satires': *The Simple Life Limited*

43 *Women and Men* (Paris: Three Mountains Press, 1923), 30–2.
44 Ibid. 24–5.   45 B 47.

(1911), *The New Humpty-Dumpty* (1912), and *Mr Fleight* (1913).[46] Satire was the obvious medium for a paranoid postliberal politics: the satirist, after all, can without great difficulty be represented as a man or woman so put upon by the world's all-enveloping imbecility and corruption that he or she has no choice but to fight black hatred with black hatred. Satire carefully adjusts the degree of fantasized grandeur to the degree of fantasized persecution. Hence its significance for Modernism. Anyone unfortunate enough to have frequented London literary circles between 1908 and 1920, Pound was to write, would know how close the 'apparent fantasia' of *The Simple Life Limited* and *Mr Fleight* was to the 'utter imbecilities of [the] milieu they portray'.[47] He could say this (he would say this) because the point of view these books establish on that milieu was the point of view he and his contemporaries had, by 1920, adopted as their own.

The Simple Life Limited is in part Ford's recollection of Limpsfield, in Kent, the centre of a colony of social reformers, where he and his wife had lived for a while in the late 1890s. Gerald Luscombe, a Tory squire and Moffat-like benefactor, agrees to convert some of the cottages on his estate for the use of a group of simple lifers led by Simon Brandson, né Simeon Brandetski, and Horatio Gubb. Brandson is the guru, Gubb the manager. Both are in their ways thoroughly manipulative. Gubb, a solicitor by profession, and physically insignificant, has always had to 'toady' to people who imagine themselves his better. The Simple Life Limited is his great opportunity, and he seizes it with the malevolence fomented by a life of servitude. In one of the book's most explosive scenes, a scene which recalls Micawber's denunciation of Uriah Heep towards the end of *David Copperfield*, Luscombe, who has hitherto suffered Gubb's impositions in silence, exposes him as a charlatan and crook. Luscombe will show, by his grasp of Gubb's scheming, that his is not, for all its amiable passivity, a 'jellified' intelligence. Ford so relishes the discomfiture of the petty-bourgeoisie, as Dickens had done before

---

[46] For a very useful account, from which I derive their classification as 'satires', see Snitow, *Ford Madox Ford and the Voice of Uncertainty*, 126–56.

[47] *Pound/Ford: The Story of a Literary Friendship*, ed. Brita Lindberg-Seyersted (London: Faber & Faber, 1983), 70.

him, that he brings Luscombe's wife in to express the feelings of triumph Luscombe himself is too much of an English gentleman to admit to. Gratifyingly, Gubb behaves like a 'shopkeeper' to the end.[48] The political view Ford advances in this scene is that of John Stuart Mill's (already postliberal) contempt for social mimesis.[49]

Polish, or part-Polish in origin, and author, in a life before the Simple Life, of a novel entitled *Clotted Vapours*, Simon Brandson 'ineluctably calls Conrad to mind'.[50] In fact, though, Brandson's resemblance is perhaps less to Conrad than to one of Conrad's characters. A man of action before he became an author, a navvy, a superintendent of plate-layers in British East Africa, he has gone spectacularly to seed, rather in the fashion of Conrad's dockside loafers, since joining the Simple Lifers. Damp, clammy, obese, and unbuttoned, he 'might have been some strange gelatinous creature existing amongst the weeds and twilight at the bottom of the sea'. On one occasion, he comes 'groaning and lurching' out of his carriage 'like a large mass of jelly'—or like the Captain of the *Patna* in *Lord Jim*. Brandson has been made gelatinous so that he can regenerate himself physically and morally. This he does by cutting his hair and beard firmly short, and then beating up a drunken villager. The violence makes him a man again, and ends his involvement in social reform. Brandson might be regarded as Ford's response to W. E. Henley's call for a remasculinization of literature. His belief that violence is the best way to 'clear things up a bit' puts the professional writer on a level with the returned colonist.[51] Conrad, who had been a man of action before he became a writer, obviously played a part in the framing of this fantasy.[52] But only a part. When we last see him, Brandson has just enjoyed massive success with a play based on his colonial experiences, *The White*

[48] *The Simple Life Limited* (London: John Lane, 1911), 271–3, 280, 369. Henceforth *SLL*. The novel was published under the pseudonym 'Daniel Chaucer'.

[49] The difference being, perhaps, if one was to take the novel as a whole, that Gubb must also be reckoned, in his inveterate discipleship, its most Fordian character: Saunders, *A Dual Life*, i. 321.

[50] Ibid. Conrad and Ford had quarrelled bitterly in the summer of 1909, about Ford's separation from his wife, and his handling of the *English Review*.

[51] *SLL* 53, 96, 227–8, 232.

[52] Conrad's letters, Ford was to say in *Return to Yesterday*, often gave the impression of a 'weak, rather whining personality'. 'But no impression could be more false. Conrad was a man, a He-man if you like, who fought against enormous odds with undying—with almost unfaltering courage' (*RTY* 153).

Man's Burden, and is now contemplating a romantic treatment of the London Stock Exchange.[53]

The Simple Life is a parallel universe gone horribly wrong. Ford associates its failure with psychosis. The Garnett circle at Limpsfield had endured more than its fair share of psychotic episodes. In 1893, Constance Garnett's brother, Arthur Black, killed his wife, his son, and finally himself, with knife, revolver, hammer, and chloroform. In 1901, the Garnetts' hired man, Bill Hedgecock, went mad, and had to be put away. It would seem that in his madness he laid siege to the house to which the family had fled, battering at the door with an axe, and throwing the dogs in the air.[54] In *The Simple Life Limited*, Brandson's cousin Brandetski, a sleazy *agent provocateur*, takes revenge on the people who have unwittingly slighted him by setting fire to their houses, and shooting at them as they emerge: the fate the undeniably paranoid Ernst Wagner was to inflict on the innocent villagers of Mühlhausen-an-der-Enz.[55]

If the colony of Simple Lifers was one way to imagine a parallel universe, then Ruritania, as we have already seen, was another. The protagonist of *The New Humpty-Dumpty*, Count Macdonald, is Moffat, or Luscombe, on a grander scale: his project being the Complex Life Limited, or counter-revolution in the Republic of Galizia. Much of the book's interest lies in its representation of the Gubb-figure, Herbert Pett, leader of the 'scientific reactionary movement', who, with his wife Anne, supplies the political theory upon which counter-revolution is to be based.[56] The Petts are cockneys, products of the Education Act of 1870, and the theory they expound is of a democracy in which imitation will raise everyone to the same level, that of the English lower middle classes. This vision of a cockneyfied England has been fed through

---

[53] *SLL* 374.   [54] Saunders, *A Dual Life*, 1. 320–1.

[55] David Garnett was later to publish a novel based on the Hedgecock episode: *Beany-eye* (London: Chatto & Windus, 1935). Garnett, like Robert Gaupp, in his analysis of Wagner, placed great stress on the way in which the madman had made 'preparations for going insane' (p. 57)—e.g. by assembling weapons. Some effort is made to characterize the resulting insanity. 'Was it due to syphilis, or was it dementia praecox, or nothing more than an acute attack of delirium tremens?' (p. 93).

[56] *The New Humpty-Dumpty* (London: John Lane, 1912), 184. Henceforth *NHD*. Like *The Simple Life Limited*, the novel was published under the pseudonym 'Daniel Chaucer'.

anxieties about the social status of the man of letters. Herbert Pett has something of the Sidney Webb about him, and something of the Herbert George Wells.[57] One scene, in which Macdonald dazzles Pett by display of natural authority, is a transposition of a scene in which Ford himself similarly dazzled Arnold Bennett, another writer from a lower middle-class background.[58] The novel's politics are certainly postliberal, in that it offers Macdonald's counter-revolution a full if despairing endorsement. They are also paranoid. Thus the feelings of persecution which overwhelm Macdonald after Pett has tried to blackmail him are described as a kind of madness. 'The psychological bitternesses of men of a sensitive nature are most often experiences similar—as Macdonald had said—to those which take place in a fever.' These bitternesses 'are shapes horribly vivid for the time; then they go out'.[59] Macdonald is Ford's most ambitious portrayal of the bene-factor as paranoiac. And one might note that Pett is consistently associated with mess, with mere contingency. When we first see him he is in his cyclist's kit, still dusty from the road, and 'wiping his brow with a handkerchief that resembled an oil rag'. When he confronts Macdonald with his demands, he happens to be 'wet all over with sweat, blood, and hoar-frost'. There is even a little 'red foam' between his lips, and his wife adds vulgarity to dirt by step-ping between the antagonists like an 'enraged coster girl' deter-mined to punish her 'bloke'.[60] Macdonald gets to expel him, as Luscombe had Gubb, as Mr Micawber had Uriah Heep.

Ruritania had proven a home-from-home for the benefactor-as-paranoiac. But Ford evidently felt the need to embed his new creation in a recognizable world. The result is *Mr Fleight*, whose main protagonist, Mr Blood, exists, as the paranoid benefactor should, in a state of suspended animation. We see him ensconced at the window of his club, on Derby Day, assessing the proportion of horse-drawn to motorized transport on the Embankment: a spec-tacularly pointless occupation, as almost no one fails to point out. Mr Blood is exactly what his name suggests: gentility embodied.

[57] And just conceivably something of the William Pett Ridge (1857–1930), author of suburban novels such as *Nine to Six-Thirty* (1910).

[58] *NHD* 72; *RTY* 301.

[59] *NHD* 366–7.

[60] *NHD* 2, 324.

The only description which will do justice to this man without qualities is a negative one. 'He was, in fact, just an anachronism, and an inactive one at that. He hunted the fox, but he seldom troubled to try to be in at the death; he was very wealthy, but he made not the least use of his wealth. He did not marry; he did not sit in Parliament.' And so on, through a lengthening list of things Mr Blood does not do. What he is, however, in his inactivity, is 'masculine' to an excessive or even criminal extent: 'that he had a violent character gave him a certain distinctness'. He is said to have strangled a groom at Newport, Rhode Island, 'where, presumably, grooms are cheap'.[61]

Mr Blood creates a parallel universe for himself by using his wealth and position to manipulate a corrupt social and political system. He decides to give a leg up to Aaron Rothwell Fleight, millionaire son of the soap-manufacturer Aaron Rothweil (he is *in* flight, one might say, until Blood arrests his runaway progress, and orders him to resume his patronymic).[62] By the end of the story, Blood has secured for Fleight a seat in the House of Commons and a blonde German-Scottish wife, Augusta. ' "I mean," Mr Blood was saying, "to try an experiment. I've had it in my mind a long time—just the way a man like you *might* climb. I've speculated upon it often—you can't get away from it in these days when the chief characteristic of Society is the multitude of climbers—so that it might amuse me".'[63] Mr Blood's experiment is in effect a satire on social mimesis.

The satirist himself cheerfully acknowledges the megalomania to which his creation of a parallel universe can be attributed.

'What is all this fairy tale?'
'This is your life, Augusta,' Mr Blood said. 'Your life and my fun.'
'You talk like God Almighty,' Augusta commented.
'That is rather my attitude,' Mr Blood answered.

The fairy tale is also, as Augusta points out, a 'nasty dirty business',

[61] *Mr Fleight* (London: Howard Latimer, 1913), 1–2, 8, 1. Henceforth *MF*.

[62] According to Bryan Cheyette, *Mr Fleight* foregrounds a 'double-edged representation of semitic "racial superiority"' from a 'more general conservative and Imperial perspective': *Constructions of 'the Jew' in English Literature and Society: Racial Representations 1875–1945* (Cambridge: CUP, 1993), 60–1. Ford's 'perspective' could never by any stretch of the imagination have been described as 'Imperial'. I have tried to suggest that it does not bear all that much resemblance to conservatism.

[63] *MF* 19–20.

and the cynicism with which Blood manipulates people both expresses and is in some sense justified by a powerful feeling of disgust. 'It's the thing that modern life has become,' he explains, 'the disgusting thing that it has become.'[64] The world in which Blood operates is a world whose complex systems have made corruption at once easy and undetectable. It is the world of the Marconi scandal, which caused such a stir in 1912 and 1913.[65] The obscenity Luscombe had found in Gubb, and Macdonald in Pett, Blood finds in modern life in general. His is accordingly the more political response: to build his own Member of Parliament. But it is still a politics informed through and through by nausea.

Ford redeems Blood from monstrosity, not by putting him through a change of heart, but by attributing to his unfortunate brother, Reginald, a purer form of the psychopathy he himself might be said to exhibit. Reginald Blood has been involved in a sordid divorce case which turns on his discovery in 'a large hamper of dirty clothes at Bristol Goods Station'. This turns out to have been a far worse place in which to be caught than a married woman's bed. For the circumstances of Reginald's discovery have earned him universal derision, and the nickname of 'Falstaff'. Humiliated and discredited, Reginald has become a 'hopelessly morbid monomaniac'. Like Conrad's Lord Jim, he imagines that people are always talking about him behind his back. 'Thus, once, when in Valetta harbour, the steward of a small steamship had exclaimed, "All clear aft", Mr Reginald Blood had screamed out and jumped over the side of the boat, because he imagined that the man had exclaimed "Falstaff".' His one consolation, and the antidote to chance discoveries, is an excessive orderliness. He takes it upon himself constantly to adjust the shutters of the mansion he shares with his brother so as to keep each room at an ideal temperature.[66] His fanaticism recalls the patient described by James

---

[64] MF 189, 193-4.

[65] Three members of the Liberal government (the Attorney-General, Sir Rufus Isaacs; the chief whip, the Master of Elibank; and the Chancellor of the Exchequer, David Lloyd George) speculated in shares of the American Marconi Co., which was associated with the English Marconi Co., which had a contract from the government to provide a system of wireless telegraphic communications. Godfrey Isaacs, Rufus's brother, was managing director of the English company. There was a virulent strain of anti-Semitism in the assaults on Isaacs, and on the Postmaster-General, Herbert Samuel.   [66] MF 117-19.

Cowles Prichard who would steal into other people's bedrooms in order to keep them in perfect order.[67] Reginald plays a relatively small part in the story. What matters about him is his madness, which might so nearly have been Blood's. Or Ford's.[68] Blood is a monster, and a man without qualities, and almost, but not quite, a psychopath. His stunt is Ford's version of a postliberal politics, a politics at once productive in its power of diagnosis and self-consuming, because its agenda has been set by the outburst of black hatred (someone else's black hatred) which brought it into being. The novel's final chapter returns Mr Blood to his seat in the club window.

Perhaps the most fitting memorial to the idea of Mr Blood was Ford's own performance as a man without qualities, at a house-party given by the novelist Mary Borden Turner, in Berwickshire, in August 1914. This was the occasion on which Mrs Turner read from Joyce's *Portrait of the Artist as a Young Man*, which was appearing in the *Egoist*, and Ford himself from the proofs of *The Good Soldier*, at that time entitled 'The Saddest Story', and shortly to appear in the first issue of *Blast*. Appropriately enough, Ford's performance consisted of a diagnosis, and implicit indictment, of liberalism. Wyndham Lewis described it vividly.

Mrs Turner was emphatic; she seemed very sure of her ground. I remember admiring her political sagacity.

'There won't be any war, Ford. Not here. England won't go into a war.'

Ford thrust his mouth out, fish-fashion, as if about to gasp for breath. He goggled his eyes and waggled one eyelid about. He just moved his lips a little and we heard him say, in a breathless sotto voce—

'England will.' He had said that already. He passed his large protruding blue eye impassively over the faces of these children—absorbed in their self-satisfied eras of sheltered peace.

'England will! But Ford,' said Mrs Turner, 'England has a Liberal Government. A Liberal Government cannot declare war.'

'Of course it can't,' I said, frowning at Ford. 'Liberal Governments can't go to war. That would not be liberal. That would be conservative.'

[67] *A Treatise on Insanity and Other Disorders Affecting the Mind* (London: Sherwood, Gilbert & Piper, 1835), 35.

[68] Saunders points out that *Mr Fleight* is 'dense with intimations of Ford's own experiences'. In Feb. 1913, Ford's wife had sued the *Throne* for describing Violet Hunt as 'Mrs Hueffer', and won. Ford felt utterly humiliated by the attention given during the trial to the collapse of his marriage: *A Dual Life*, i. 372–9.

Ford sneered very faintly and inoffensively: he was sneering at the British Government, rather than at us. He was being omniscient, bored, sleepy Ford, sunk in his tank of sloth. From his prolonged sleep he was staring out at us with his fish-blue eyes—kind, wise, but bored. Or some such idea. His mask was only just touched with derision at our childishness.

'Well, Ford,' said Mrs Turner, bantering the wise old elephant. 'You don't agree!'

'I don't agree,' Ford answered, in his faintest voice, with consummate indifference, 'because it has always been the Liberals who have gone to war. It is *because* it is a Liberal Government that it *will* declare war.'[69]

GOOD SOLDIERING

'The Saddest Story' was, whatever Lewis might have thought about its lack of explosions, a literary experiment: an attempt to adapt and further refine the narrative techniques James and Conrad (and before them Flaubert) had used in their comprehensive overhaul of the assumptions built into domestic realism. In this chapter, I have tried to situate Ford as a writer formed professionally and politically by extensive, acute reflection on the 'state of the art', as it was around 1900: on the position of the male artist in a commercialized culture; on the forms of symbolic capital available to him in that culture (Englishness, breeding, masculinity); on the ways in which he might seek to exert influence, politically or otherwise; and on the modes of writing (biography, memoir, satire) by means of which a certain influence and a certain symbolic capital might unobtrusively accumulate, with or without the culture's blessing. I have discerned in his life and in his writing a tendency to create a parallel universe in which the standards of social recognition informing modern society have been suspended. In this parallel universe, neither wealth, nor status, nor nationality, nor gender has any meaning *in itself*. Instead, paranoid symmetry adjusts the degree of fantasized grandeur to the degree of fantasized persecution. The black hatreds which bear down on the man without qualities bring him into being. The benefactor lives to be betrayed. The satirist longs for insult. What remains is to examine the provocation paranoid symmetry constitutes to literary experiment.

[69] *Blasting and Bombardiering* (London: Calder & Boyars, 1967), 58–9.

For Ford, impressionism was a relation between consequence and inconsequence. James's characters will 'talk about rain, about the opera, about the moral aspects of the selling of Old Masters to the New Republic', and these affectless exchanges will somehow convey to the reader that the 'quiet talkers' are 'living in an atmosphere of horror, of bankruptcy, of passion hopeless as the Dies Irae'. Reading James, we vibrate between the 'apparent aspect of things' and the 'essentials of life': the depth of consequence is rendered by a remorseless attention to inconsequence, to rain and opera and the selling of Old Masters.[70] Before James and Conrad, Ford remarked, the novel had always gone 'straight forward' in its apprehension of 'character'; whereas in real life you never go straight forward, but obliquely, or round about. You meet a beefy English gentleman at your golf club.[71] 'You discover, gradually, that he is hopelessly neurasthenic, dishonest in matters of small change, but unexpectedly self-sacrificing, a dreadful liar but a most painfully careful student of lepidoptera and, finally, from the public prints, a bigamist who was once, under another name, hammered on the Stock Exchange.' To describe such a man, it is not enough to begin at the beginning and work straight forward 'chronologically' to the end. 'You must first get him in with a strong impression, and then work backwards and forwards over his past.'[72] In Ford's impressionism, I shall suggest, it is paranoia which breaks chronology, which discerns the pattern of consequence buried deep beneath the ostentatiously inconsequential.

In the preface to *Return to Yesterday*, Ford wrote that he had first

---

[70] *Henry James*, 153.

[71] Golf looms unexpectedly large in Ford's accounts of literary impressionism. He himself had taken the game up in 1897, when an uncle left him some money (*RTY* 131). His subscription to the Hythe Golf Club is dated 30 Oct. 1897. Golf was, Saunders says, a way to 'keep up his old country gentleman style' (*A Dual Life*, i. 97). It was also a way to meet influential people. At Hythe, Ford played with two future Liberal ministers: Macnamara, president of the National Union of Teachers in 1896, an MP in 1900, and Lloyd George's Minister for Education in 1920; and Masterman, an MP from 1906 to 1914, and briefly a member of Asquith's Cabinet. We might say that for him the golf-club represented a museum of the man with qualities: there, a man was *all* quality (a certain beefiness, a handicap, a way with stories, or with brandy and cigars). When the crash came, and the man had to learn to live without qualities, it was all the more spectacular for the ornateness of the display which had preceded it. See *Henry James*, 154–5.

[72] *Joseph Conrad: A Personal Remembrance* (London: Duckworth, 1924), 129–30.

conceived the form of the book when looking up at the 'criss-cross of beams' in a ceiling above his head. Thereafter, the shape taken by his memories as they came back to him had been 'inextricably mingled with those Cubist intricacies'.[73] John Dowell's first-person narrative, which constitutes *The Good Soldier*, is no less Cubist, no less abstract, in its search for formal symmetry. We need to recognize in it, as Max Saunders does, not just abstraction, but the will-to-abstraction. 'Form,' Saunders argues, 'is thus something that Dowell *needs* to secure his sense of his own existence . . . As the novel's form makes us feel the need of form, it becomes expressive of that need.'[74] Like Luscombe, and Macdonald, and Mr Blood, like Madox Brown, Dowell will only ever secure a sense of his own existence through the experiment which is benefaction.[75] He will only ever know himself through betrayal, by becoming the innocent object of black hatreds. The account he renders, of course, is of the Good Soldier, Edward Ashburnham, a man sublimely 'with qualities' (though, strangely, not a golfer). Indeed, it is Ashburnham's very possession of qualities which betrays Dowell, and provokes him into satire.

'We can only speculate,' Saunders says, '*where* Ford's conviction of significance comes from.'[76] I shall argue here that the concept of paranoia offers some insight into the way in which *The Good Soldier* renders or makes manifest that conviction of significance. It is in the third of the novel's four parts, above all, I believe, that paranoia establishes itself as a literary method, as impressionism. The other three parts all conclude with that most definitive of events, a death. Maise Maidan, one of Edward Ashburnham's infatuations, dies untidily of heart failure at the end of part i; Florence Dowell commits tidy suicide at the end of part ii; and Ashburnham, in an act which clinches the sadness of this 'saddest story', blows his brains out at the end of part iv. Part iii, by contrast, attempts to understand destiny by a fictional means other than sudden death. It is an inquiry explicitly into the pattern of Ashburnham's life (the pattern of good soldiering); and implicitly into the pattern of John Dowell's (the pattern of good, that is, of

---

[73] *RTY* 3.   [74] Saunders, *A Dual Life*, i. 431.
[75] Dowell = Do Well. Does he do well? Does he do good?
[76] Saunders, *A Dual Life*, i. 443.

criss-cross, or Cubist, remembrance). In each case, I shall suggest, the pattern manifests itself in the creation of a parallel universe.

Part ii concludes with an unwelcome revelation. In the hotel at Nauheim, a man chatting to Dowell recognizes Florence as the young woman he once saw some years before coming out of the bedroom of a young man called Jimmy at five o'clock in the morning.[77] Dowell had previously supposed that Florence was without a sexual history. Bagshawe, the man in the hotel, whose only appearance this is, serves much the same function as the 'big, fat, greasy, blinking fellow of mixed descent' Marlow encounters in the little place on the coast 230 miles south of Patusan river, who tells him that Jim has got hold of a jewel without price.[78] Like the blinking fellow, Bagshawe occupies the gap between two orders of reality: one in which the 'norms' of (upper-class English) behaviour apply, one in which they do not. Bagshawe's hybridity is social rather than racial, of course: he has a 'pallid complexion' which suggests vices practised in secret and 'an uneasy desire for making acquaintance at whatever cost'.[79] But the nausea he provokes serves the same purpose. It tells us that we have arrived at a break in the narrative. Beyond this point, orthodoxy no longer obtains. Disgust is the only feeling creatures like Bagshawe arouse, and disgust becomes henceforth the source of Dowell's identity (as it had been of Luscombe's, and Macdonald's, and Blood's). Florence, having seen her husband in conversation with Bagshawe, hurries up to her room, where she is later found dead.

Part iii opens with the further revelations that Florence had had an affair with Ashburnham, and that her death was suicide. Dowell gets the news 'full in the face' from Leonora, at a later date, and after yet another funeral, that of Ashburnham. It provokes in him 'no emotion of any sort'. The two of them are sitting at the time in Leonora's study at Branshaw Teleragh, and all Dowell can remember about the moment of revelation is her remark that 'Edward has been dead only ten days and yet there are rabbits on the lawn'.[80] The profound consequences for Dowell of what she

---

[77] *The Good Soldier: A Tale of Passion* (Harmondsworth: Penguin Books, 1972), 96. Henceforth *GS*.

[78] *Lord Jim*, ed. Cedric Watts and Robert Hampson (Harmondsworth: Penguin Books, 1986), 197–8.

[79] *GS* 96.   [80] *GS* 100–1.

has to say find both the medium and the limit of their expression in an entirely inconsequential statement. But there is something odd about this moment of revelation, an oddness induced by the time-shift which juxtaposes it to the moment in the hotel at Nauheim. Unlike the nauseous Bagshawe, Leonora provokes only admiration. And yet the news she brings is scarcely welcome. Indeed, since it relates to Florence's behaviour since her marriage to Dowell, it is potentially a lot more hurtful than anything Bagshawe had to reveal. So, do we believe Dowell's indifference to it, his lack of emotion? Do we believe *impressionism*'s indifference?

The remainder of the first section of part iii pieces together events surrounding Florence's death. She had evidently overheard Ashburnham declaring himself to Nancy Rufford, outside the Casino, and returned in distress to the hotel, only to find her husband in conversation with the odious Bagshawe. Ashburnham's conduct on this occasion prompts an inquiry into his motives. Nancy Rufford was his great passion, and Dowell suggests that the 'sex-instinct' counts for little in a really great passion. 'It can be aroused by such nothings—by an untied shoe-lace, by a glance of the eye in passing—that I think it might be left out of the calculation.' Sexual desire thus seems to Dowell the epitome of inconsequence, of meaningless event. 'It is a thing, with all its accidents, that must be taken for granted, as, in a novel or a biography, you take it for granted that the characters have their meals with some regularity.' The sex-instinct cannot be the source of meaning, value, purpose, of the criss-cross pattern in a life. The 'real fierceness of desire', Dowell maintains, lies in the craving for recognition. 'We are all so afraid, we are all so alone, we all so need from the outside the assurance of our own worthiness to exist.' By this account, what Ashburnham looks for in sexual experience, like any man, is 'the assurance of his own worth'. When he declares himself to Nancy, outside the Casino, he creates *ex nihilo* a parallel universe in which his own worth has been assured. 'Before he spoke, there was nothing; afterwards, it was the integral fact of his life.'[81] Dowell goes further than Ford himself had ever done. For him it is not just masculinity which can be considered a form of symbolic capital, but sexual experience, and indeed love itself.

Having got that far with Ashburnham, Dowell returns to Florence, and to his own marriage. The other side of the desire for recognition at one's best, he claims, is the desire not to be recognized at one's worst. All intimacy is driven, he goes on, by the desire to deceive the person with whom one lives as to some 'weak spot' in one's character or career. 'For it is intolerable to live constantly with one human being who perceives one's small meannesses.' Now it is persecution, rather than grandeur, which provides the criss-cross pattern in a life. The 'secret weakness' in Florence's career is the early escapade with the young man called Jimmy. She is a social climber desperate for the recognition which marriage into the English landed gentry alone will bring. Dowell's wealth (his inadvertent benefaction) is thus simply the means by which she hopes to transfer herself from a 'low fellow' like Jimmy to a high fellow like Edward Ashburnham. If she is to achieve this ascent she must conceal both from Dowell and from Ashburnham that there ever was a Jimmy. 'Do you know what it is to shudder, in later life, for some small, stupid action—usually for some small, quite genuine piece of emotionalism—of your early life? Well, it was that sort of shuddering that came over Florence at the thought that she had surrendered to such a low fellow.'[82] The criss-cross pattern Dowell discerns in Florence's life is the *relation* between the feelings of persecution aroused by intimacy with the low fellow and the feelings of grandeur aroused by intimacy with the high fellow.

Florence's shudder at the memory of Jimmy is Dowell's shudder, first felt during the encounter with Bagshawe, at the memory of her. Listening to Bagshawe, he makes about her the decision Daniel Paul Schreber had once made about those he could not help coming into contact with: to him, she is henceforth no more than a hastily improvised representation of a person. In his 'inner soul', Dowell had already begun to feel that Florence 'represented a real human being with a heart, with feelings, with sympathies and with emotions only as a bank-note represents a certain quantity of gold'. Florence is the pure product of social mimesis. 'I thought suddenly that she wasn't real; she was just a mass of talk out of guide-books, of drawings out of fashion-plates.' Dowell's Schreberian shudder would appear to have momentous consequences. When Florence rushes past, in the hotel at Nauheim, he does not go after her, despite her evident distress. Had he done so, he might have prevented her from killing herself. 'I just couldn't do it; it would have been like chasing a scrap of paper—an occupation ignoble for a grown man.' He does not do it, we deduce, because she has ceased to exist for him. 'Florence didn't matter.' The indifference with which he greets Leonora's revelation of the affair with her husband is the product of familiarity. The shudder of disgust has long since been incorporated into the criss-cross pattern, the principle of form Dowell so desperately needs. It makes grandeur possible. Its product is a new desire, to marry Nancy Rufford. Dowell decides to prepare himself for Nancy, as Walter Hartright had prepared himself for Laura Glyde, by a visit to America: 'what I then had to do was a little fighting with real life, some wrestling with men of business, some travelling amongst larger cities, something harsh, something masculine'.[83] It is as though the shudder has made it possible for the accumulation of symbolic capital to begin in earnest.

The remaining sections of part iii chronicle the marriage of Edward and Leonora Ashburnham, finding within it, as one might by now have come to expect, a criss-cross pattern which relates feelings of grandeur to feelings of persecution. We learn, for example, that Leonora came of a family of small Irish landlords, 'that hostile garrison in a plundered country'. Her father, Colonel Powys, has 'tenants on the brain', having several times been shot at from behind hedges by his own. The father's siege-mentality would appear to have shaped the daughter's resentment of her husband's man-with-qualities largesse, which she regards as 'megalomania'. His subsequent sexual largesse provokes in her the direst of suspicions:

She had at that period what I will call the 'monstrous' theory of Edward. She was always imagining him ogling at every woman that he came across. She did not, that year, go into 'retreat' at Simla because she was afraid that he would corrupt her maid in her absence. She imagined him carrying on intrigues with native women or Eurasians.

[83] *GS* 114, 119, 115.

This, perhaps, is Leonora's 'shudder': the bouts of nausea aroused by the possibility of intimate contact, albeit indirect, with those of a 'lower' class or race. Were the unfortunate Edward actually to intrigue with 'Eurasians', he would bring about the collapse of the distinctions upon which empire depended. Paranoia steps in where a sense of obligation has failed, or is about to fail. Its revulsions make the principle of limit known once again: thus far, and no further. Its delusion of reference (Edward's oglings as an attempt to humiliate her) supplies meaning, value, and purpose. She realizes that she wants Edward back with 'a fierce passion that was like an agony'.[84]

Section iv resumes the inquiry into Edward's motivation for polygamy. He was not, Dowell insists, a 'pathological case'. The outline of his life had been 'an outline perfectly normal of the life of a hard-working, sentimental and efficient professional man'. So why the predatoriness, the compulsive adulteries? Dowell's answer is a digression which finds in his own remasculinizing experiences in America a clue to Edward's behaviour. Arriving in Philadelphia, he says, was like emerging from a museum (the museum of the man with qualities) into a 'riotous fancy-dress ball'. The riotousness in this fancy-dress ball is, precisely, paranoia. Dowell's relatives are very pleasant, but strangely consumed by 'what appeared to me to be the mania that what they called influences were working against them'. 'I never got to know what it was all about; perhaps they thought I knew or perhaps there weren't any movements at all.' Dowell manages not to succumb to this mania, but he cannot but be impressed by the energizing effects of a belief that the world is obscurely against one. Ashburnham, it transpires, had not had the least idea that he could ever be unfaithful to his wife until the fateful day he found himself in court for kissing a nurse-maid in a railway carriage. The court accepts his explanation that he just felt sorry for the young woman, but the 'dirty-mindedness' with which counsel disputes his intentions puts it into his head that he could conceivably have seduced her. 'And, from that moment, that girl appeared desirable to him—and Leonora completely unattractive.' In his womanizing, Edward sees himself as the 'victim of the law'. Leonora's support for him during the

---

[84] GS 136, 133, 138, 164, 170.

case has the paradoxical effect of making her seem 'by so much the more cold in other matters that were near his heart—his responsibilities, his career, his tradition'. The nurse-maid in the railway carriage, whom the law has produced as the stereotypical rake's stereotypical victim, might perhaps have been warm to those responsibilities, to that tradition. Leonora's coldness, by contrast, rivets him to 'the idea that he might find some other woman who would give him the moral support that he needed'. And there are indeed plenty of women ready to assure him of his own worth. Sexual experience is thus constructed as a delusion of grandeur. Squeezed into 'odd moments' in the routine of a normal life, Edward's adulteries are his parallel universe.[85] The Cubism of this marriage is the mutual dependence within it of feelings of grandeur and feelings of persecution. Or is it Dowell's Cubism?

Part v carries Dowell's remasculinizing by paranoia through to a conclusion. 'In my fainter sort of way I seem to perceive myself following the lines of Edward Ashburnham. I suppose that I should really like to be a polygamist.' Edward, Dowell decides, the better to identify with him, was an exceptional man. 'Society does not need individuals with touches of madness about them.' Leonora, on the other hand, no longer suspicious, has reverted to sanity. 'Leonora survives, the perfectly normal type, married to a man who is rather like a rabbit. For Rodney Bayham is rather like a rabbit, and I hear that Leonora is expected to have a baby in three months' time.' Dowell's reduction of Leonora to normality is as savage as his earlier disavowal of Florence. It is achieved by an extraordinary change of tone, as he contemplates the way in which Leonora and Nancy exacted their revenge on Edward:

Those two women pursued that poor devil and flayed the skin off him as if they had done it with whips. I tell you his mind bled almost visibly. I seem to see him stand, naked to the waist, his forearms shielding his eyes, and flesh hanging from him in rags. I tell you that is no exaggeration of what I feel.

Seeing Edward as a victim, as he had seen himself, Dowell is able to identify with him. He can now feel on his own mind and body the impact of the black hatreds directed at his friend and betrayer.

<hr />

[85] GS 140–6.

The black hatreds tell him that he, too, is exceptional. 'But then, I don't like society—much. I am that absurd figure, an American millionaire, who has bought one of the ancient haunts of English peace. I sit here, in Edward's gun-room, all day and all day in a house that is absolutely quiet.'[86] Like Edward, he has in a sense kept the rabbits off the lawn. Edward Ashburnham may or may not have been a 'pathological case'. Dowell probably is. And Dowell's paranoia, his will-to-abstraction, is Ford's experiment.

[86] GS 213–14, 227.

CHAPTER 7

The Will-to-Abstraction:
Hulme, Lewis, Lawrence

PEOPLE NO LONGER wanted the self-effacements of impressionism, Wyndham Lewis told Ford Madox Ford in 1914. And while I have tried to show in my previous two chapters that literary impressionism was less self-effacing than one might suppose, nobody could doubt that the stunts and firework-displays Lewis had in mind were of a different order to the sad stories told by Conrad and Ford. 'What's the good of being an author', Lewis demanded, 'if you don't get any fun out of it?'[1] This chapter is in part an attempt to determine what it was that Lewis got his fun out of. For the purpose of the stunts he performed in the years before the war was to outshine impressionism. Ford (Hueffer, as he then was) had given Lewis his big literary break by publishing some pieces in the *English Review*. He was ripe for outshining.

Lewis had studied intermittently at the Slade School of Art from 9 January 1899 until 10 June 1901, when he finally engineered his own expulsion. He had begun writing verse, and his sonnets won the approval of the scholar and critic T. Sturge Moore. The painters with whom he consorted—Walter Sickert, William Rothenstein, Augustus John—chose to regard him as a poet. 'The Fine Arts they imagined were already in good hands,' he recalled in *Rude Assignment* (1950), his second volume of autobiography, 'namely their own.'[2] But it was as a writer of prose sketches that he first made his mark, when three pieces appeared in the *English Review*, in May, July, and August of 1909. Lewis is said either to

---

[1] Max Saunders, *Ford Madox Ford: A Dual Life*, 2 vols. (Oxford: OUP, 1996), ii. 188–9.
[2] *Rude Assignment*, ed. Toby Foshay (Santa Barbara, Calif.: Black Sparrow Press, 1984), 123.

have thrust his bundle of manuscripts wordlessly into Ford's hands, or to have burst into the bathroom and read them aloud, while the editor sat in his tub, as Lewis's biographer puts it, 'nonchalantly plying his sponge'.[3] These sketches were the product of holidays in Brittany, where Lewis had found, or thought he had found, a culture whose ritualized antagonisms were a physical reflection of his own developing metaphysical commitment to what one might term 'anti-pathos'.[4] By August, it seems, the editor's charm had worn off. 'Hueffer', he explained to Moore, 'is a shit of the most dreary and uninteresting kind.'[5]

'It was like an opening world', Ford remarked of the period before the war. 'For, if you have worried your poor dear old brain for at least a quarter of a century over the hopelessness of finding, in Anglo-Saxondom, any traces of the operation of a conscious art—it was amazing to find these young creatures evolving theories of writing and the plastic arts.'[6] The young creatures in question included, among others, D. H. Lawrence, whose poems Jessie Chambers had submitted to the *English Review* in the autumn of 1909. Ford was soon to find in the opening paragraph of 'Odour of Chrysanthemums' evidence enough of Lawrence's genius. Visits (real or imaginary), parties, readings, and critical exchanges ensued.[7] Lawrence, like Lewis, tended to explode in Ford's direction. 'He makes me jolly mad', he told Violet Hunt on 9 February 1911. 'I think the ironic attitude, consistently adopted, is about as tiresome as the infant's bib which he says I wear for my mewling and puking—in other words, he says it, mind.'[8] Benefaction had as usual done good work in arousing black hatreds.

Lawrence and Lewis are writers not normally associated in histories of Modernism. Yet they both made a name for themselves in the years before and during the war by explosive opposi-

---

[3] Paul O'Keeffe, *Some Sort of Genius: A Life of Wyndham Lewis* (London: Jonathan Cape, 2000), 93.

[4] I develop this concept further in relation to Lewis's work as a whole in Ch. 9. For a preliminary account, see *The Making of the Reader: Language and Subjectivity in Modern American, English and Irish Poetry* (London: Macmillan, 1984), ch. 5.

[5] O'Keeffe, *Some Sort of Genius*, 94.

[6] *Thus to Revisit* (London: Chapman & Hall, 1921), 136.

[7] Saunders reviews the available evidence in *A Dual Life*, i. 248, 283–4, 297–9, 311–12.

[8] *Letters*, ed. James T. Boulton *et al.*, 7 vols. (Cambridge: CUP, 1979–93), i. 226–8.

tion to the 'ironic attitude'. These explosions will bear scrutiny in relation both to each other and to the attitude they were supposed to render obsolete. The texts I have in mind are Lawrence's 'The Prussian Officer' (1913) and Lewis's *Tarr* (1918), which I hope to triangulate by reference to the theory Sigmund Freud had by then expounded, of paranoia as the suppression of homoerotic feeling. Lawrence and Lewis had not read Freud's essay on paranoia. Like Freud, however, they sought to develop in the years before the First World War a psychodynamic 'model' of the mind which had as an important focus a particular kind of behaviour.[9] Before examining their sketches of a psychopathology, I need to establish the terms in which young creatures writing or painting in the years between 1910 and 1914 might have conceived the stunts they meant to pull. This will involve some mention of the poet, philosopher, and art critic T. E. Hulme.

HULME AND LEWIS

In 1910, the year of Roger Fry's first Post-Impressionist Exhibition, Lewis would have been better known, thanks to Ford, as a writer than as an artist. However, the success of that exhibition generated a flurry of experiment in the visual arts, and Lewis took up his brush again, to considerable effect. Before long, his

---

[9] If one wished to identify a common stimulus towards the psychodynamic, or a context which might permit talk of a 'will-to-abstraction', then the obvious candidate is the writings and reputation of 19th-cent. philosophers such as Friedrich Nietzsche and Arthur Schopenhauer. Freud, to his chagrin, found in Nietzsche and Schopenhauer formulations concerning the unconscious and the work of repression which meatily anticipated psychoanalysis: Peter Gay, *Freud: A Life for our Time* (London: J. M. Dent, 1988), 128–9. Lewis first read Nietzsche, along with other modern philosophers, during his student days in Paris. 'The degree to which this intellectual, cultural, and political world remained at the core of Lewis's own work and thought', Paul Edwards observes, 'can be seen in his frequent references to its most prominent figures throughout his life': *Wyndham Lewis: Painter and Writer* (New Haven, Conn.: Yale University Press, 2000), 10. Lawrence first read Schopenhauer in 1906–7, and Nietzsche in 1910, and both made a deep impression on him: John Worthen, *D. H. Lawrence: The Early Years, 1885–1912* (Cambridge: CUP, 1992), 174, 210–12. For Nietzsche's effect on Lawrence's writing, see John Burt Foster, *Heirs to Dionysus: A Nietzschean Current in Literary Modernism* (Princeton: Princeton University Press, 1981), ch. 4, and Colin Milton, *Lawrence and Nietzsche: A Study in Influence* (Aberdeen: Aberdeen University Press, 1987).

work was sustaining comparison with that of major figures in the continental avant-garde. There followed, between 1913 and 1915, the period of his most intense commitment to geometrical abstraction. *Blast* appeared, Vorticism arose. During what he thought of as the '*Blast* days', that heady period of Vorticist carnival brought to an end, in his case, for a while at least, by the combined effects of gonorrhoea and officer training, Lewis trafficked assiduously between media. 'My literary contemporaries', he was to recall in *Rude Assignment*, 'I looked upon as too bookish and not keeping pace with the visual revolution.' *The Enemy of the Stars*, an unperformable play published in the first issue of *Blast*, in July 1914, and *Tarr*, a novel just about as abstract as he could make it, were his most rebarbative attempts to 'show them the way'. This punishing Vorticist programme had, however, one drawback. 'It became evident to me at once, . . . when I started to write a novel, that words and syntax were not susceptible of transformation into abstract terms, to which process the visual arts lent themselves quite readily.'[10]

How should we understand the force, or the animus, behind Lewis's utter determination to show his contemporaries the way? He was not, of course, the only determined Modernist, though he may well have been the *most* determined. There is, for example, ample evidence of a powerful will-to-literature in Eliot's commendation of Joyce's use of Homeric myth. The solution to literature's inadequacy in the face of the futility of the modern world, Eliot seemed to say, was *more* literature: the novel would render itself less 'novel', less abjectly the expression of an abject age, if it began to associate with epic.[11] To Lewis, by contrast, this was mere bookishness. What he had in mind was *less* literature in literature, not more. His aim was to import into literature that other version of the will-to-experiment which had already declared itself in the visual arts as a will-to-abstraction.

Such manœuvres became Lewis's signature. It is not just that he

---

[10] *Rude Assignment*, 139. One might note that Lewis's fervent objections to Lawrence centred on the latter's devotion to the 'romantic abdominal *Within*' rather than the 'sunlit pagan surface of the earth': *Men without Art*, ed. Seamus Cooney (Santa Rosa, Calif.: Black Sparrow Press, 1987), 99.

[11] I develop the idea of a 'will-to-literature' in 'The Modernist Novel', in Michael Levenson (ed.), *The Cambridge Companion to Modernism* (Cambridge: CUP, 1999), 70–99, pp. 74–7.

notoriously trafficked between genres, and between media, as both William Blake and Dante Gabriel Rossetti had done before him, but that he sought to bring about change, and to theorize the necessity of change, by the strategic substitution, as circumstances appeared to demand, of one genre for another, one medium for another. In 'What Art Now?', an essay published in the *English Review* in April 1919, Lewis was to suggest that experiment in art involves 'a stepping aside from artistic production, almost, for the moment, into science'. In this case, he went on, the stepping aside had already taken place, before the war. 'So, because you had a revolution six years ago, you need not expect another next month.'[12] In the full flush of that revolution, Lewis had stepped aside from literature into art, which he was able to regard, for the moment, as a science. It was by the light of such 'science' that literature was to be renewed.

Something needs to be said, at this point, about T. E. Hulme, for a while Lewis's accomplice in the will-to-experiment.[13] 'It was mainly as a theorist in the criticism of the fine arts', Lewis wrote in *Blasting and Bombardiering* (1937), his first volume of autobiography, 'that Hulme would have made his name, had he lived.' He himself, he went on imperturbably, would undoubtedly have played Turner to Hulme's Ruskin. 'In England there was no-one else working in consonance with an "abstract" theory of art to the same extent as myself. Neither Gaudier nor Epstein would in the end have been "abstract" enough to satisfy the requirements of this obstinate abstractionist. He would have had to fall back on me.'[14] It is the *obstinacy* of Hulme's abstractionism, its animus, which seems to me, as it did to Lewis, its characteristic feature.[15] Why did

---

[12] 'What Art Now?', in *Creatures of Habit and Creatures of Change: Essays on Art, Literature and Society 1914–1956*, ed. Paul Edwards (Santa Barbara, Calif.: Black Sparrow Press, 1989), 46–9, p. 49. For Lewis's reflections on Blake and Rossetti as artist-writers, see 'Beginning' (1935), ibid. 262–7.

[13] Hulme has fallen into relative neglect. It may be significant that Peter Nicholls's justly influential 'literary guide' to the period includes no more than a single passing reference to him: *Modernisms: A Literary Guide* (London: Macmillan, 1995), 179.

[14] *Blasting and Bombardiering* (London: Calder & Boyars, 1967), 100.

[15] In this respect, the inquiry I shall attempt here runs in parallel with recent investigations of the fantasies encoded in abstract painting, sculpture, and design. See e.g. Bryony Fer, *On Abstract Art* (New Haven, Conn.: Yale University Press, 1997); and for a more general and rather more haphazard discussion, David Batchelor, *Chromophobia* (London: Reaktion Books, 2000). In *Fashioning Vienna: Adolf Loos's*

Hulme, and Lewis after him, for a while, insist so often and so strongly on abstraction in everything?

In Hulme's career, as in Lewis's, the obstinacy took shape in or as a set of strategic substitutions, of one doctrine for another, and of one job for another. Michael Levenson has described in meticulous and illuminating detail his evolution from a Bergsonian preference for intuition over reason through classicism to an abandonment of the entire world-view implicit in Western philosophy since the Renaissance.[16] Levenson makes instructive use of Hulme's intellectual 'volatility' to demonstrate the degree of divergence between different emphases within Modernist doctrine. Hulme, we can now be sure, did indeed change his mind. But if we want to know *why* he changed it, we must, I believe, consider his doctrinal volatility in its performative dimension. For Hulme, like Wyndham Lewis, liked to step aside every now and then. One of the points Lewis makes in *Rude Assignment* is that the freedom he had enjoyed in the pre-war years to pick and choose among specialisms was underwritten by an allowance from his mother.[17] Hulme was in exactly the same position, except that *his* allowance came from a sympathetic aunt.[18] He, too, could pick and choose among marginally remunerative occupations. His Bergsonian incarnation required the role of poet and philosopher, his classicism that of political commentator, and his anti-humanism that of art critic.

Hulme, furthermore, was as self-conscious as Lewis in his stepping aside. He was fond of Nietzsche's comment that all philosophy is autobiography, and inveterately cast the development of his

---

Cultural Criticism (London: Routledge, 2000), Janet Stewart pays careful attention to the circumstances in which and for which a different set of texts relating to the will-to-abstraction were produced.

[16] *A Genealogy of Modernism: A Study of English Literary Doctrine 1908–1922* (Cambridge: CUP, 1984), chs. 3 and 6.

[17] *Rude Assignment*, 115. The financial demands Lewis placed on his mother, who much to his embarrassment ran a laundry, are a constant theme in the early chapters of O'Keeffe's *Some Sort of Genius*. As late as Sept. 1912, Mrs Lewis was still chiding her son for his lack of professionalism and his shortcomings 'from the business point of view': *Some Kind of Genius*, 117.

[18] Alun R. Jones, *The Life and Opinions of T. E. Hulme* (London: Victor Gollancz, 1960), 22–4.

thinking in the form of 'personal confession'.[19] The man who found in Rousseau's thought the epitome of the world-view he spent much of his career contesting *wrote* like Rousseau, in a mode which, as we have already seen, may under some circumstances lend itself to paranoia. Like Rousseau, Hulme preferred the start and finish of each phase of his career to be as emphatic as possible. Thus he stopped being a poet-philosopher by declaring his profound disappointment in a series of lectures Bergson gave at University College London in October 1911, and by publishing his 'Complete Poetical Works' (all five of them) in the *New Age* in January 1912.

Hulme's subsequent reinvention of himself as an art critic, in 1913, was the product of two factors: a point of view, and a need to occupy himself. His reading of Wilhelm Worringer's *Abstraction and Empathy* (1908) provided him with the first of these. According to Worringer, the two fundamental urges to be found in the history of aesthetic styles, the urge to empathy and the urge to abstraction, correspond to different attitudes to experience, one an expression of confidence, the other an expression of anxiety, or even terror.[20] The second factor in Hulme's self-reinvention was that 1913 was a good year for art critics. The success of the Post-Impressionist Exhibitions had shown that there was now a market, of a kind, for abstract art, and therefore a need for expert assessment.[21]

On the evening of 22 January 1914, Hulme and Lewis shared a lecture platform at Kensington Town Hall. Their topic was modern art. While Hulme was speaking, in a barely intelligible murmur, Lewis informed his neighbour in the body of the hall that you have to hold your head up when you speak in public. He himself spoke next, rapidly, and in a husky voice, addressing himself entirely to the piece of paper in front of him.[22] Hulme's part in this rivalrous professionalization was a lecture entitled

[19] 'A Tory Philosophy', in *Collected Writings*, ed. Karen Csengeri (Oxford: Clarendon Press, 1994), 232–45, p. 233; 'Notes on Bergson', *Collected Writings*, 125–53, p. 126. Henceforth *CW*.

[20] *Abstraction and Empathy: A Contribution to the Psychology of Style*, tr. Michael Bullock (New York: International Universities Press, 1953), 14–15.

[21] In *Desire and Excess: The Nineteenth-Century Culture of Art* (Princeton: Princeton University Press, 2000), Jonah Siegel has much of interest to say about the emergence of the critic as a crucial figure in 19th-cent. propaganda for art.

[22] O'Keeffe, *Some Kind of Genius*, 145.

'Modern Art and its Philosophy'. The lecture put Worringer's distinction between urges to empathy and abstraction to polemical use.[23] Hulme put forward the 're-emergence' of a geometrical art in the work of Epstein, Lewis, and others as vibrant proof of the re-emergence of the corresponding attitude towards the world, and the consequent 'break-up' of Renaissance humanism. Those in the audience who could actually hear the words he spoke would have done well to take them in, because his position, as art critic of the *New Age*, was an influential one. The week before, on 15 January 1914, he had reviewed the Grafton Group show at the Alpine Club, blessing Lewis, Nevinson, and Etchells, and blasting the 'mediocre stuff' shown by Fry and his followers. Eleven days later, Fry was still in shock. The 'Lewis group', he complained bitterly, had somehow 'got hold' of the *New Age* critic.[24]

At the private view for the first exhibition of the London Group at the Goupil Gallery, on 4 March 1914, Lewis, observing Hulme deep in discussion with Kate Lechmere in front of one of his own drawings, suspected the worst. Lechmere was currently his main source of income, as the money behind the Rebel Art Centre, and had been his lover. He now thought that he might be replaced in one capacity by Hulme's man Epstein, and in the other by Hulme himself (he was half right). The item in front of which the discussion took place, which Lewis had told Lechmere to steer Hulme towards, was described in the catalogue as a drawing for sculpture, and it may well have been meant to compete with the small flenite figures by Epstein which Hulme was known to admire.[25]

Worringer described *Abstraction and Empathy* as a contribution to the 'psychology of style', and its crucial insistence is that all art should be assessed in terms of the 'psychic presuppositions' which give rise to it. At some places in his argument, the psychology of style tips over into a psychopathology of style. In 'primitive' cultures, Worringer says, the urge to abstraction derives from an 'immense spiritual dread of space' which can be compared to agoraphobia, a 'pathological condition to which certain people are prone'. In more 'developed' cultures, a different problem makes

[23] 'Modern Art and its Philosophy', in *CW* 268–85, p. 269.
[24] *Letters*, 2 vols., ed. Denys Sutton (London: Chatto & Windus, 1972), ii. 378.
[25] O'Keeffe, *Some Kind of Genius*, 147–8.

itself felt, a dread of space which stands 'above' rather than 'before' cognition. The problem here, among the 'civilized peoples of the East', for example, has to do not with the emptiness of space but with the 'unfathomable entanglement of all the phenomena of life'. The urge it prompts is to rescue the object from its entanglement, from its 'arbitrariness', and thus construct for oneself 'a point of tranquillity and a refuge from appearances'. Abstraction alone will enable the artist to 'wrest' the object from its 'natural context', to 'purify' it of all its 'dependence upon life'. In abstraction, life has finally been 'effaced': 'here is law, here is necessity, while everywhere else the caprice of the organic reigns'.[26] In Worringer's understanding, abstraction, wherever and whenever it occurs, is both violent and compulsive. He stops short of attributing psychosis to the 'civilized peoples of the East', but not by much.

It seems to me that the account Worringer gives of abstraction's effacement of life provides another way to conceive the kind of behaviour which the early psychiatric nosologies and case-histories construed as 'monomaniacal' or 'paranoid'. Of particular interest in the context of Modernism's will-to-abstraction are the analyses developed in turn-of-the-century psychiatry of paranoia's cognitive or epistemological dimension. I am thinking in particular of paranoia's rejection of contingency, something remarked on by Krafft-Ebing, as we have already seen, and by Freud. 'The category of what is accidental and requires no motivation,' Freud observed in *The Psychopathology of Everyday Life* (1901), 'in which the normal person includes a part of his own psychical performances and parapraxes, is thus rejected by the paranoiac as far as the psychical manifestations of other people are concerned. Everything he observes in other people is full of significance, everything can be interpreted.'[27] In paranoia, meaning displaces event. There is no such thing as chance, no such thing as a causal sequence devoid of (malevolent) purpose. Paranoiacs, Freud was to remark in a paper published in 1922, 'cannot regard anything in other people as indifferent'.[28] They construct a parallel universe—a refuge against appearances,

---

[26] *Abstraction and Empathy*, 15–17, 20–1.

[27] *The Standard Edition of the Complete Psychological Works*, ed. James Strachey *et al.*, 24 vols. (London: Hogarth Press, 1953–74), vi. 255. Henceforth *SE*.

[28] 'Some Neurotic Mechanisms in Jealousy, Paranoia, and Homosexuality', *SE*. xviii. 223–32, p. 226.

Worringer might have said—by acts of (over)interpretation. Their rejection of the possibility that other people might remain indifferent, absorbed as they are in projects of their own, or in each other, is a rejection of that infinite entanglement of one phenomenon in another which constitutes the world as most people know it. Paranoia, as Schreber had made plain, cannot abide entanglement.

In 'Modern Art and its Philosophy', Hulme reproduced Worringer's terms, and at the same time his attribution of psychosis to 'primitive' peoples alone. Pure geometrical regularity, he said, gives a 'certain pleasure' to people 'troubled by the obscurity of outside appearance'. 'The geometrical line is something absolutely distinct from the messiness, the confusion, and the accidental details of existing things.' He went on to insist that such a 'condition of fear' is not a necessary prerequisite of the 'tendency to abstraction'; in the Indian and Byzantine cultures, the tendency takes an altogether different form.[29] This seems to me a defensive manœuvre, on Hulme's part, as it is on Lewis's part, in the version of the hypothesis he put forward in the first issue of *Blast*.[30] Neither man was keen, for obvious reasons, to have abstraction associated with psychosis. But abstraction, in Worringer's account, fulfils more or less the same function as paranoia, in Freud's: to

[29] 'Modern Art and its Philosophy', *CW* 268–85, p. 274.

[30] The 'modern town-dweller' for whose benefit the new abstract art will be produced has nothing at all to do, Lewis maintains, with the 'primitive' African who 'cannot allow his personality to venture forth or amplify itself, for it would dissolve in vagueness of space'. The problem for the modern town-dweller is not space-shyness but entanglement. 'Life is really no more secure, or his egotism less acute, but the frontiers interpenetrate, individual demarcations are confused and interests dispersed.' The ego such conditions require will be an *abstract* ego: 'The New Egos', *Blast* 1, facsimile edn. (Santa Barbara, Calif.: Black Sparrow Press, 1992), 141. The first issue of *Blast* also contained Lewis's *Enemy of the Stars*, a work much preoccupied with Max Stirner, the philosopher of absolute egoism. Stirner's *The Ego and his Own* (1844), tr. into English by Steven T. Byington in 1912, conceives the 'I' as the antithesis of communal organizations such as the state which require self-effacement. For Stirner's influence on *Enemy of the Stars*, see Edwards, *Wyndham Lewis*, 156–9; for his influence on Anglo-American Modernism in general, see Levenson, *Genealogy*, 63–8. Stirner had a great deal to say about the prevalence of 'fixed ideas', inside and outside the asylum, and his own conception of egoism combined megalomania ('I secure my freedom with regard to the world in the degree that I make the world my own') with feelings of persecution: 'The State does not let me come to my value, and continues in existence only through my valuelessness: it is for ever intent on *getting benefit* from me, exploiting me, turning me to account, using me up.' *The Ego and his Own*, ed. John Carroll (London: Jonathan Cape, 1971), 59–60, 120, 163.

create a refuge from the unfathomable entanglement of all the phenomena of life, from the caprice of the organic.

Hulme may have felt a little defensive because the abstract art he championed was indeed both violent and compulsive in the fury with which it 'wrested' the object from its 'natural context'. Or, conceivably, because the role he had chosen seemed itself to require a certain violence. In *Blasting and Bombardiering*, Lewis took pains to indicate the peculiar hybridity of that role. Hulme, he observes, was an art critic of a philosophical 'turn'. 'Although he has been called "a philosopher", he was not that, but a man specializing in aesthetic problems.' Lewis cannot quite make up his mind about the validity of the expertise engendered by that specialization. On the one hand, he adamantly maintains that Hulme's work should not be dismissed as the product of some bureaucratic programme for the training of experts in art-theory. 'His mind was sensitive and original, which is a better thing obviously than the routine equipment of the teaching profession.' On the other hand, Hulme's 'equipment' for the task did not seem altogether adequate. Hulme, Lewis points out, was 'a journalist with a flair for philosophy and art, not a philosopher. Of both these subjects he was profoundly ignorant, according to technician-standards.' And there is no mistaking the relish with which Lewis describes Hulme's discomfiture, in a debate about Kant, at the hands of a 'little university professional'. 'Hulme floundered like an ungainly fish, caught in a net of superior academic information.'[31] By Lewis's account, Hulme was both more and less than merely expert.

Jealousy and hatred apart, there is, I think, an important context for the equivocal feelings Lewis expressed about Hulme the art critic: the search, among some members of the Edwardian intelligentsia, for a charismatic professionalism. The *New Age*, the journal for which Hulme wrote, had been founded in disagreement with the policies put forward by those apostles of bureaucratic rationalism, Sidney and Beatrice Webb. However, although 'simple life' in tendency, under the editorship of Alfred Orage, the *New Age* did not by any means abandon the advocacy of what Lewis was to term 'technician-standards'.[32] Its dilemma was

[31] *Blasting and Bombardiering*, 99–100.
[32] For a concise account of the *New Age* at the time of Hulme's association with it,

Bradley Headstone's, and Ernst Wagner's: how to develop 'technician-standards' which would illuminate rather than obscure a 'sensitive and original' mind. This became Modernism's dilemma, too. And it drove Hulme and Lewis, if not to pushing people into canals, as Headstone does, or setting light to villages, then at least to murderous impulse.

My final piece of evidence is Hulme's first contribution as the *New Age*'s art critic, an essay about 'Mr Epstein and the Critics' published on 25 December 1913. The essay makes it clear that Hulme meant to invest the intellectual capital accrued from his conversations with Worringer in equipping himself with the appropriate expertise. The charisma he brought to the role was an insider's knowledge of the imminent 'break-up' of the very foundations of 'all philosophy since the Renaissance'. It was the 'business' of all honest men and women, he announced, with a sternness which would surely have won the Webbs' approval, to clean the world of the 'sloppy dregs' of humanism.[33] And he proposed to get to work in the Augean stable of the magazine for which he himself wrote. For the main target of his vitriol was A. M. Ludovici, a member of the *New Age* staff, and no fan of Epstein's work.[34]

Ludovici had published a book about Nietzsche, which according to Hulme gave 'the impression of a little Cockney intellect which would have been more suitably employed indexing or in a lawyer's office, drawn by a curious kind of vanity into a region the realities of which must for ever remain incomprehensible to him'.[35] The book by Dickens in which this assault on cockney intellect was shaped is not *Our Mutual Friend*, but *David Copperfield*. The thing to remember about Uriah is that he is

---

see Jones, *T. E. Hulme*, 25–9. 'Nominally Fabian,' as Norman and Jeanne Mackenzie put it, 'Orage was out of sympathy with the bureaucratic collectivism of Webb and closer to the Fabian mood of earlier days': *The First Fabians* (London: Weidenfeld & Nicolson, 1977), 344.

[33] 'Mr Epstein and the Critics', *CW* 255–62, pp. 257–8.

[34] Ludovici had written about Epstein in the *New Age* (18 Dec. 1913). The dispute between Hulme and Ludovici rumbled on in the pages of the journal during the early months of 1914. Lyn Pykett has described Ludovici's post-war writings as an advocacy of 'masculine renaissance' comparable to that undertaken during the same period by Lawrence and Lewis: *Engendering Fictions: The English Novel in the Early Twentieth Century* (London: Edward Arnold, 1995), 49–51.

[35] 'Mr Epstein', 259.

nauseating, in David Copperfield's eyes, long before he has done anything wrong. Uriah is a slimy contamination, rather than a person.[36] The reason for the nausea he provokes becomes plain as soon as he identifies himself, which he does with some exuberance, as David's professional and sexual rival. Uriah's crime is mimesis. He seeks to obscure the essential differences between David and himself, and ultimately to *become* David, by mere slavish imitation. He is the first in a line of sickening cockney intellects which culminates in the pimply young man in the draft of *The Waste Land*, his hair thick with grease and scurf, whom Eliot imagines either as a house agent's clerk or as a follower of the arts who hangs out in the Café Royal with the Futurist C. R. W. Nevinson.[37] The hesitation, effaced in the poem's published version, is symptomatic. Pimply young men were disgusting in large part because they aped the writer or artist of genuine talent.[38]

Contempt for cockney intellects, for social mimesis, became a key weapon in Modernism's polemical armoury, and an argument for the reimposition of technician-standards. Thus Hulme expressed his amazement that Ludovici had been able to produce in the book about Nietzsche 'a shoddy imitation which may pass here in England, where there is no organised criticism by experts, but which in other countries, less happily democratic in these matters, would at once have been characterised as a piece of fudge'. It is no surprise, then, that Ludovici should proceed to fail the art-critical 'test' Hulme sets him, by preferring a feeble cartoon by Augustus John to Epstein's *Carvings in Flenite*. The cartoon, Hulme fulminated, 'lacks precisely that quality of virility which Mr Ludovici finds in it, and is admired by precisely those "spinsterly", sloppy and romantic people whom, he imagines, dislike it'.

---

[36] Hulme was to describe Nietzsche as a romantic passing his 'slimy fingers' over the 'classic point of view': *CW* 235.

[37] *The Waste Land: A Facsimile and Transcript of the Original Drafts*, ed. Valerie Eliot (London: Faber & Faber, 1971), 32–3.

[38] In 'What Art Now?' (1919), in a passage strikingly similar in tone and intent to Eliot's, Lewis excoriated the '*café*-haunting microbe' liable to be mistaken for an artist. 'For, as he generally lets the hair at the back of his head grow long, and appears in many ways untidy and unusual, he is just the public's idea of an artist, and every small vulgarity that suggests itself to this shop-assistant allowed to stray is supposed by the unenlightened beholders to be the peculiar mentality that this occupation of picture painting engenders.' The proliferation of such impostors, Lewis argues, is a reason to start training an 'élite' audience for art: *Creatures of Habit*, 48.

What the advocacy of abstraction did for Hulme, and subsequently for Lewis, and indeed for Modernism in general, was to reunite charisma with expertise. One proof of the power it infused into Hulme's art-criticism lies in the generation of further forms of symbolic capital, including a self-conscious and self-assertive masculinity. Indeed, the antidote Hulme recommends to Ludovici and his like carries, in the pleasure it takes in the removal of sloppy dregs, a distant echo of Micawber's hugely gratifying expulsion of the loathsome Uriah Heep from *David Copperfield*. 'The most appropriate means of dealing with him would be a little personal violence'.[39] By such expressions of virility Hulme hoped to accumulate the symbolic capital necessary to the role of art critic.

It was Hulme's campaign against social and aesthetic mimesis which Lewis resumed, on his return from the war, in 1919, as we shall see in Chapter 9. My topic here is the novel Lewis worked on during the bout of gonorrhoea which was for him the beginning of the end of the Vorticist carnival. In it, the will-to-abstraction got wholeheartedly to work.

LEWIS'S *TARR*: MONOMANIA AND SWAGGER SEX

Something needs to be said straight away about the history of the composition of *Tarr*. The novel began in the summer of 1909 as a short story about Otto Kreisler, a failing German artist in Paris, and then grew in Conradian fashion until it had acquired a new hero, Tarr, an English artist whose success or failure still hangs in the balance, and a variety of new characters and episodes. By March 1911 the short story had become a novel, *The Bourgeois-Bohemians*, and now included the dance at the Bonnington Club at which Kreisler finally loses his senses, and Anastasya Vasek, the woman who has driven him to it. The conversations in which the English artist tries to break off his engagement to a German bourgeois-bohemain, Bertha Lunken, date from the summer of 1911, at which point the novel was to be called either *Between Two Interviews* or *Otto Kreisler's Death*. To balance the composition, Lewis added at a later date, certainly after 1913, the episodes in

---

[39] 'Mr Epstein', 259–61.

which Tarr delivers impromptu lectures on the subject of art and life to three English friends, Hobson, Butcher, and Lowndes, and to Anastasya Vasek; their content derives from essays he had written in the summer of 1911, and the views they express are undoubtedly his own.[40] The English artist had by this time sufficiently got the upper hand over the German to commandeer the title. In the preface, Lewis describes Tarr as one of his showmen.[41] Tarr's performance is the firework-display with which Lewis had threatened Ford Madox Ford in 1914. The work published as *Tarr* in 1918 thus incorporates two more or less distinct narratives, one of which, as we shall see, could be said to enfold and comment on the other.

'Otto Kreisler's Death', the novel within the novel, should be regarded as one of English Modernism's most explicit studies of paranoia. Kreisler suffers from usurpation. As the novel commences, his father, who has already put a stop to his sexual development by marrying his fianceé, threatens to cut his income off as well—unless he gives up Art and accepts a post in a solid commercial concern. In despair, Kreisler has followed his patron, Ernst Volker, from Rome to Paris. In Paris, his mood is not improved when a 'Russian-Pole', Louis Soltyk, takes his place as Volker's chief dependant. This, one might think, is a man who has some reason to feel persecuted. It does not take him long to add a little unreason to the already abundant reason. When we first meet him, he is shaving himself, morbidly. 'Life did not each day deposit an untidiness that could be whisked off by a Gillette blade, as Nature did its stubble.' Like all budding paranoiacs, Kreisler wants above all to eliminate mess from his life. And he proceeds to do so by selecting an antagonist in whose systematic persecution of him he can see reflected the system of his own uniqueness. Soltyk, who has usurped him in his patron's favour, becomes his necessary opposite, his 'efficient and more accomplished counterpart, although as empty and unsatisfactory as himself'.[42] In 1910 Lewis told Augustus John that he had just completed an 'analytic' novel about a German student, 'any beauty it may possess depend-

[40] This account of the novel's composition is based on Paul O'Keeffe's meticulous detective work: *Tarr: The 1918 Version*, ed. O'Keeffe (Santa Rosa, Calif.: Black Sparrow Press, 1990), 361–5.

[41] Ibid. 15.   [42] Ibid. 81, 78, 90.

ing on the justness of the psychology—as is the case in the Russian novels'.[43] Soltyk, in short, is Kreisler's Dostoevskyan double.[44]

What transforms mere doubling into paranoid symmetry is Kreisler's belief that Soltyk means to take his place not only in Ernst Volker's affections, but in Anastasya Vasek's. The sight of Soltyk and Anastasya in conversation at the Café Berne inflames his 'persecution mania'. He becomes convinced that Soltyk has set out to blacken his name. 'His stepmother fiancée, other tales, were being retailed. *Everything* that would conceivably prejudice Anastasya, or would not, he accepted as already retailed.' At the Bonnington Club dance, Soltyk's behaviour towards Anastasya does not mark him as a rival. But Kreisler thirsts for 'conventional figures', for paranoid symmetry, for someone to embody his feeling that he has been conspired against. He invents a rivalry. 'Soltyk's analogies with Kreisler worked in the dark to some end of mutual destruction.'[45] When Anastasya laughs at his abruptness, without malice, he feels that she has singled him out for humiliation.

Kreisler is a paranoiac, and he seeks clarification, the mutual transparency of one system to another, by challenging his antagonist to a duel. The success of single combat as the expression of a definitive will-to-abstraction can best be measured by the 'disintegrating mess' it makes of the persecutor. 'All that organism he, Kreisler, would be turning into dung, as though by magic.' Kreisler cleanses his soul, as he had once cleansed his chin, by the production of waste matter. Paranoia's measure is the ability to remain utterly abstract, as Kreisler does. 'A cruel and fierce sensation of mixed origin rose hotly round his heart. He *loved* that man! But because he loved him he wished to plunge a sword into him, to plunge it in and out and up and down! Why had pistols been chosen?'[46] There can surely be no closer parallel in Modernist fiction to Freud's figuring of paranoid delusion as a series of propositions: '*I* (a man) *love him* (a man)', 'I do not *love* him—I *hate*

---

[43] *Letters*, ed. W. K. Rose (London: Methuen, 1956), 65. It is now thought that Rose misdates this letter: Walter Michel, 'On the Date of Writing *Tarr*', *Enemy News*, 28 (1989), 22–3.

[44] For a summary of the parallels noted by critics between *Tarr* and Dostoevsky's *The Double* (1846), see O'Keeffe's commentary, in *Tarr*, 379–82.

[45] Ibid. 121, 150.   [46] Ibid. 270.

him', 'I do not *love* him, I *hate* him, because he persecutes me'.[47]
Otto Kreisler exists in the novel which once bore his name as a
case-study. He has been set aside or set apart in the revision of the
novel as the embodiment of a state of mind which Lewis was
perfectly capable of recognizing in himself, and which could not
be allowed to determine its overall shape and structure.

The addition of Tarr's story to Kreisler's added a philosophical
to a psychological frame of reference. For Tarr has a theory about
Kreisler's behaviour, which could perhaps be understood as a
1914–15 showman's gloss on the 1909–10 Russian narrative. 'I
believe that all the fuss he made was an attempt to get out of Art
back into Life again.'[48] Kreisler's failure, by this account, is a failure to sublimate his sexual drives through creativity; it is sex he
tries to get back into, in his rape of Bertha Lunken, in his pursuit
of Anastasya, in his hatred of Soltyk. It is Nietzsche who is the
crucial influence, here, rather than Dostoevsky, as Alistair Davies
has pointed out. According to Davies, Kreisler is a pathological
specimen, doomed by his weakness to failure, and Tarr an aristocrat of the spirit whose sublimation of his sexual drives through
creativity will enable him to defy and transcend a decadent bourgeois culture. After Kreisler's death, Tarr achieves a 'superhuman
quality': vigorous and vital in a way Kreisler has never been, he
dispels the illusion of his commitment to Bertha Lunken with
appropriate brutality and shapes both his art and Anastasya Vasek
to his iron will. Our response to the novel's ending should be one
of 'metaphysical gaiety'.[49]

Tarr begins with a series of encounters between Lewis's aristocrat of the spirit and a series of men with (some) qualities: Hobson,
Butcher, Lowndes. The first and most remarkable of these,
between Tarr and Hobson, hits the reader at squall-force in the
book's opening chapter. Tarr declares himself enraged by the opti-
mism of a culture which blandly worships strong white supermen,
'great soldiers', 'great artists', ' "civilization" and stuff'. He is a new

[47] *SE* xii. 63.   [48] *Tarr*, 302.

[49] '*Tarr*: A Nietzschean Novel', in Jeffrey Meyers (ed.), *Wyndham Lewis: A
Revaluation* (London: Athlone Press, 1980), 107–19, pp. 108–9, 116–18. Davies argues
that *Tarr* is an expanded version of the Nietzschean novella, a form perfected by
Thomas Mann in *Tonio Kröger* (1903) and *Death in Venice* (1912) and by Rainer Maria
Rilke in *The Notebooks of Malta Laurids Brigge* (1910).

kind of super-superman, a 'Panurgic–Pessimist, drunken with the laughing gas of the Abyss'. Hobson asks of this performance the question one might also ask of the protagonists of paranoid narrative, of Caleb Williams, say, or Walter Hartright, or Rudolf Rassendyll. 'What sort of prizes could he expect to win by his professional talents? Would this notable arriviste be satisfied?' Stripping himself of mere qualities, reinventing himself as an Artist, Tarr sets out to eliminate the messes (the mimesis) which might yet entangle him in contingency: messes such as women, whose presence near the man consumed by ambition's madness is 'like a slop of children and the bawling machinery of the inside of life'. The masculinity Tarr proposes to cultivate is no more and no less than a part of the symbolic capital he will need rapidly to accumulate in order to succeed as an artist. Hobson, too, finds himself denounced as 'systematic slop', a creature of social mimesis, a crowd rather than an individual. Hobson and his like should not be allowed to propagate, Tarr yells, the paranoiac's destructive mania convulsively let rip; and he finishes by knocking Hobson's inappropriately bohemian hat off his head into the road.[50]

And the arriviste does arrive. Tarr acquires as his mistress the undeniably classy Anastasya Vasek.[51] 'He felt immensely pleased with himself as he walked down the Boulevard Clichy with this perfect article rolling and sweeping beside him.' The 'clean and solid' Anastasya contrasts most satisfactorily in his eyes with Bertha Lunken's petty-bourgeois 'mess'. It is to her, significantly, intoxicated by pride of possession, by 'swagger sex', that he delivers another of his lectures on art and life. Here he speaks, in terms which have often been taken to characterize Modernist abstraction, of art's 'deadness', of its 'absence of soul'. Art, he tells Anastasya, is 'ourselves disentangled from death and accident'. Swagger sex is Tarr's symbolic capital.[52]

[50] *Tarr*, 26–7, 29, 33–5.

[51] Establishing himself in a studio in Paris at the end of 1903, Lewis had by Apr. 1904 acquired that most important of bohemian prerequisites, a mistress. Ida Vendel was the daughter of a well-to-do German merchant, and Lewis took to referring to her as 'my German allotment': O'Keeffe, *Some Sort of Genius*, 53–5. There can be little doubt that he thought of her as a career-move.

[52] *Tarr*, 297–301. For a discussion of the representativeness of Tarr's views, see e.g. Nicholls, *Modernisms*, 268–9. It is of course the swagger in the sex, and in the attitude to women the sex enacts, which has led to the recent interest in Tarr, and through

But we surely cannot take him at face value. Davies's claim that Tarr achieves a 'superhuman quality' in his ultimate shaping both of Anastasya and of his art, or at least his theory of art, does not entirely square with what we learn of his romantic career; of his career as an artist we learn, as Davies admits, nothing at all. Bertha Lunken's announcement that she is pregnant strikes one as a resounding defeat for the aristocrat of the spirit. 'This event rose up in opposition to the night he had just spent, his new promises and hopes of swagger sex in the future. = He was beaten.' Thereafter, Tarr's pendulum swings, as Lewis puts it, between women of the Anastasya Vasek type and women of the Bertha Lunken type. Tarr himself describes his enduring susceptibility to petty-bourgeois mess, to accident, as a fondness for 'Kreisleriana'.[53] Kreisler, in Tarr's view, had failed in paranoia. There must be some doubt as to whether Tarr, in Lewis's view, succeeds where Kreisler had failed. His vacillations do not really sound like cause for metaphysical gaiety. And it may be significant that he is initially characterized, in the encounter with Hobson, by his 'repeating habits': that is, by mimesis. 'Tarr had a way of beginning a reply with a parrot-like echo of the words of the other party to the dialogue; also of repeating *sotto voce* one of his own sentences, a mechanical rattle following on without stop.' There is no purpose to these repetitions. 'Tarr only repeated things arbitrarily.' As we have seen, Kraepelin and Bleuler had various terms for this parrot-like echoing, which they considered typical of schizophrenia: echopraxis, echolalia. Tarr, oddly enough, given his tendency to monomania, may in fact be the first schizophrenic in English literature. In the account it gives of 'persecution mania' and of the need to eliminate mess from art, *Tarr* can be considered Modernism's closest approximation, *Women in Love* apart, to paranoid narrative. In the end,

him Lewis, as the exponent of a masculinist Modernism. The consequences of Lewis's distaste for 'messy femininity' have been explored by Bonnie Kime Scott: *Refiguring Modernism*, 2 vols. (Bloomington, Ind.: Indiana University Press, 1995), i. 100, 104–5. See also Lisa Tickner, 'Men's Work? Masculinity and Modernism', in Norman Bryson, Michael Ann Holly, and Keith Moxey (eds.), *Visual Culture: Images and Interpretations* (Hanover: Wesleyan University Press, 1994), 42–82; and David Peters Corbett, 'Landscape, Masculinity and Interior Space between the Wars', in Steven Adams and Anna Gruetzner Robins (eds.), *Gendering Landscape Art* (Manchester: MUP, 2000), 102–15.

[53] *Tarr*, 311, 320, 312.

however, it fails to clear either its protagonist or itself from entanglement in the 'immediate world'.[54]

'GOING IRRITABLY INSANE': LAWRENCE'S PRUSSIAN OFFICER

Lawrence met Wyndham Lewis on 1 July 1914; the result was a 'heated and vivid discussion'.[55] At that time, he was revising intensively a group of short stories he wanted to get into publishable shape before he and Frieda left England for Germany and Italy. On 9 July, he sent the first batch of revised stories to his publisher, Duckworth; by 14 July, the volume was complete, apart from one story, 'Vin Ordinaire', subsequently 'The Thorn in the Flesh', which he thought needed 'writing over again, to pull it together'. That, too, was ready by 17 July.[56] The speed with which the volume finally came together is extraordinary. Lawrence rewrote substantial sections of nearly all the stories in just under three weeks, while also leading a full and appropriately Vorticist social life in London, and, on 13 July, getting married.

The volume, to which Edward Garnett gave the title of *The Prussian Officer and Other Stories*, included work drawn from the whole length of Lawrence's career to date. 'His early novels were slow and painful in their progress into print', as John Worthen puts it. Short stories, which he conceived and wrote with relative rapidity, thus became both the stimulus to and the condition of a career as a writer.[57] The conclusion of his previous career as a teacher, in the autumn of 1911, and his elopement with Frieda Weekley in May 1912, forced the issue. The purpose of the stories Lawrence had typed up in the summer of 1913 was magazine publication; in December 1913, he told Ezra Pound that he would 'make them print me and pay me, yet'.[58] Paying was, of course, by no means the whole point: the capital he meant these stories to accumulate would be in large measure symbolic. In the three months following the completion of the draft of *Sons and Lovers*,

[54] Ibid. 26–7, 29.   [55] *Letters*, ii. 193.   [56] Ibid. 196–8.
[57] Introduction to *Prussian Officer: The Prussian Officer and Other Stories*, ed. J. Worthen (Cambridge: CUP, 1983), p. xxvi. Henceforth *PO*.
[58] *Letters*, ii. 132.

in November 1913, he began to experiment with forms new to him, forms contrary to the charged domestic realism for which he was at that time best known. These new beginnings included a historical novel, a dialect play, a symbolic fable, and a philosophical treatise. And he had a go at first-person narrative.[59] This was to be a charismatic professionalism steeped in experiment.

By 5 March 1913, Lawrence was halfway through a new novel, a 'weird thing', then known as 'The Insurrection of Miss Houghton'.[60] Insurrection was indeed the book's (non-selling) point. Nobody would publish it, he told Edward Garnett six days later, because it was both sexually outspoken and 'a stratum deeper' than any novel had gone before. 'It is all analytical—quite unlike *Sons and Lovers*, not a bit visualised.' So he wanted to get his insurrection done, and then write 'another, shorter, absolutely impeccable—as far as morals go—novel'. If he did not, he and Frieda would have hardly anything to live on.[61] The other, 'impeccable' novel was 'The Sisters', the precursor of *Women in Love* (1920). By June it was done, in its first version. Lawrence celebrated by writing three new stories: 'Honour and Arms' (subsequently 'The Prussian Officer'), 'New Adam and Old Eve', and 'Vin Ordinaire'. The first and third of these would eventually appear in *The Prussian Officer*. All three attempt to go 'a stratum deeper' than any of his stories had previously gone; all three are 'analytic'. 'Honour and Arms', in particular, became by its 'extremity', by the harshness of its attention to violent feeling, a turning-point in Lawrence's 'view of character'.[62] Lawrence found it difficult to dissociate charisma from extremity.

In 'German Books: Thomas Mann', an essay written at that time for the *Blue Review*, Lawrence expressed his dissatisfaction with the Flaubertian craving for form-as-mastery. Mann, he declared, was the latest and possibly the last 'sick sufferer from the complaint of Flaubert'.[63] This dissatisfaction has been used to separate him off not

---

[59] See Mark Kinkead-Weekes, *D. H. Lawrence: Triumph to Exile, 1912–1922* (Cambridge: CUP, 1996), 67.

[60] *Letters*, i. 525. We remember Lewis telling Augustus John about his 'analytic' novel.   [61] Ibid. 526.

[62] Kinkead-Weekes, *Triumph to Exile*, 77.

[63] *Phoenix: The Posthumous Papers*, ed. Edward D. MacDonald (New York: Viking Press, 1936), 312–13. Lawrence regarded Ford Madox Ford as the major English exponent of a Flaubertian sense of form: *Letters*, i. 417.

only from Mann, but from the 'Men of 1914', from Eliot, Joyce, Pound, and Lewis: 'where Modernist emphasis fell on the artist-self as creator,' Kinkead-Weekes argues, 'Lawrence emphasized *transformation* of the self at the hands of the Other—hence the vital importance of sexual relationship'. According to this view, the thorough revision of the *Prussian Officer* stories Lawrence carried out in the days after his meeting with Lewis took his work in a direction contrary to that soon to be taken by Modernisms, including Lewis's, 'which he would have seen as dangerously enclosed'.[64]

However, it does not seem to me wholly inappropriate to speak of the more 'analytical' tendency in Lawrence's writing at this time, a tendency which culminated in *The Rainbow* (1915) and *Women in Love*, in terms of abstraction. He himself did so, of course, when he declared that he had put an end to the 'old stable ego of the character': that is, to mimesis, to the literary conventions which had hitherto made it possible to attribute a coherent meaning and value to a person in a novel. 'There is another ego', Lawrence maintained, 'according to whose action the individual is unrecognisable, and passes through, as it were, allotropic states which it needs a deeper sense than any we've been used to exercise, to discover are states of the same radically-unchanged element.'[65] The new and deeper literary sense *abstracts* the unchanging 'element' hidden beneath the appearances so exhaustively registered by nineteenth-century domestic realism; it draws the man or woman out of and away from the mere qualities which have hitherto been thought to constitute identity. What else did James Joyce do when he invited readers of *Ulysses* to map Leopold Bloom's passage through the Dublin streets on to Odysseus' passage across the Mediterranean? Lawrence's deployment of scientific terminology in a letter to a friend is itself, of course, an abstraction.

We have to recognize the force in Lawrence's life and writing of a certain disentanglement. His abrupt rejection in May 1912 of the meanings and values of community had significant moral, political, and literary consequences for his work.[66] By becoming

---

[64] *Triumph to Exile*, 137.   [65] *Letters*, ii. 182–4.

[66] The critic who has explored those consequences most perceptively is Raymond Williams, who argues that in Lawrence's early writing the language of the writer is 'at one' with the language of his characters, in a way which had not happened before; whereas in the later novels the 'removal' of the characters from an 'actual society' has

a professional writer, he disentangled himself not only from a part of the world, but from the messiness of his own life, from autobiography: getting beyond *Sons and Lovers* meant, among other things, the bitter end of his long friendship with Jessie Chambers.[67] His abrupt rejection at about that time of mimesis has in it the force of a lived disentanglement. By July 1914, marriage had made *Sons and Lovers* seem even more remote. 'In marriage one must become something else', he told Garnett; as a writer, he was no longer able to concern himself with 'manners and circumstances and scenes'.[68] In what remains the most exhaustive study of Lawrence's extensive revision of the *Prussian Officer* stories, Keith Cushman has described the renewal of outlook and method those revisions enact in terms which emphasize the boldness of its commitment to the abstract. The purpose of the renewal, Cushman maintains, was to supply the 'systematic basis' palpably lacking in the 'vision' articulated by *Sons and Lovers*; Lawrence 'came into his own' by founding his work on the 'interplay of art and metaphysic'. The formulation of a metaphysic became in the summer of 1914 the 'explicit purpose' of his career. 'He was now equipped with a style and, increasingly, with a theoretical vocabulary sufficient to his ambition to write about men and women from such a grandiose perspective.'[69] Lawrence's 'theoretical vocabulary' was not Lewis's, of course, or Hulme's. In all three cases, however, there is a connection between the theory's distinctive emphasis and the grandeur of the 'perspective' it luminously encodes.

One of the first reviewers of *The Rainbow* wondered whether the author had not fallen under the 'spell' of 'German psychologists'.[70] The German psychologist under whose spell Lawrence had come closest to falling, albeit in an indirect fashion, was Freud's disciple Otto Gross. When Frieda Weekley travelled to Germany with Lawrence, in May 1912, she took care to pack a bundle of letters from Gross, who had once been her lover, and

as its consequence a new kind of fiction, a 'hardening abstract form': *The English Novel from Dickens to Lawrence* (London: Chatto & Windus, 1970), 172–3, 180–1.

[67] Kinkead-Weekes, *Triumph to Exile*, 54.   [68] *Letters*, ii. 142–3.

[69] *D. H. Lawrence at Work: The Emergence of the* Prussian Officer *Stories* (Hassocks: Harvester Press, 1978), 13, 25, 37.

[70] Cited by Harry T. Moore, *The Priest of Love: A Life of D. H. Lawrence*, rev. edn. (Harmondsworth: Penguin Books, 1976), 312.

whose euphoric vision of her as the Woman of the Future was crucial to her self-image.[71] Gross was fascinating and brilliant, but unreliable, and a drug-addict. Freud had rapidly lost patience with his enthusiasm for sexual and political revolution. One might note that Gross's view of German psychology was not just that of an exponent. On 13 May 1908, Ernest Jones reported to Freud that Gross was now a patient in the Burghölzli, and suffering from severe withdrawal symptoms. Jones himself had been treating his wife, who hated him for his infidelities, but was herself deeply in love with another man. 'Gross gets great delight in getting other men to love her—no doubt a perverse paranoic development of his free love ideas.'[72] By Jones's account, Gross needed the feeling of persecution which his wife's betrayal of him had brought on in order to enjoy to the full the feeling of mastery brought on by his betrayal of her. Paranoid symmetry does not get much more symmetrical than this. That any of it ever came to Lawrence's ears seems unlikely. But he himself was soon to explore perversities of a comparable order in his own writing. I shall argue here, and in the next chapter, that Lawrence abstracted himself from autobiography and mimesis by a *study* of the forms taken by and in abstraction for which parallels can be found in the psychiatric textbooks and case-histories.[73]

In the summer of 1913, when he wrote 'The Prussian Officer', Lawrence had not yet met the English Freudians who were to represent his most sustained encounter with psychoanalytic theory, and there is absolutely no evidence to suggest that he had read or even heard about Freud's discussion of Schreber.[74] Even so, there are intriguing similarities between Freud's description of the 'mechanism of paranoia' and Lawrence's description of the intensity of the

---

[71] The story of the affair is told by Martin Green in *The von Richthofen Sisters: The Triumphant and the Tragic Modes of Love* (New York: Basic Books, 1974), 32–73. The letters are repr. in E. W. Tedlock (ed.), *Frieda Lawrence: The Memoirs and Correspondence* (London: Heinemann, 1961), 94–102.

[72] *Complete Correspondence of Sigmund Freud and Ernest Jones 1908–1939*, ed. Andrew Paskauskas (Cambridge, Mass.: Harvard University Press, 1993), 1.

[73] As Kinkead-Weekes puts it, Lawrence's description of his new work as 'all analytical' implies 'the psychologist's attempt to understand movements of consciousness that the characters themselves cannot': *Triumph to Exile*, 67.

[74] He met Barbara Low, David Eder, and Ernest Jones in summer 1914: Kinkead-Weekes, *Triumph to Exile*, 133.

Captain's feelings for his orderly. It is the freedom and warmth of
the orderly's movements which first makes his master aware of
him. 'And this irritated the Prussian. He did not choose to be
touched into life by his servant.' From the outset, the officer finds
in his servant's 'unconscious presence' an intolerable affront. 'It
was not that the youth was clumsy: it was rather the blind, instinctive sureness of movement of an unhampered young animal that
irritated the officer to such a degree.' Penetrating his 'stiffened
discipline', the young soldier's influence 'perturbed the man in
him'. 'He, however, was a gentleman, with long fine hands and
cultivated movements, and was not going to allow such a thing as
the stirring of his innate self.' The perturbation of the man in him
provokes him to harshness and violence. He seems to be going
'irritably insane'. The discovery that the young orderly has a
sweetheart drives him 'mad with irritation'.[75]

As the Prussian officer goes irritably mad, his madness follows
the course described by Freud in his account of the 'mechanism of
paranoia'. A Freudian analysis would suggest that the love he
cannot admit has turned into hatred: he harasses and assaults the
man he would like to seduce. By this account, hatred then under-
goes a further transformation. The officer locates those feelings he
cannot acknowledge as his own in the world, in someone else.
The proposition 'I hate him' is converted into the proposition '*He
hates* (persecutes) *me*, which will justify me in hating him.'[76] Thus
the Captain justifies the hatred with which he conceals his love for
his orderly by the orderly's persecution of him. 'The officer tried
hard not to admit the passion that had got hold of him. He would
not know that his feeling for his orderly was anything but that of
a man incensed by his stupid, *perverse* servant. So, keeping quite
justified and conventional in his consciousness, he let the other
thing run on.'[77] The emphasis on 'perverse' is Lawrence's, an
underlining in pencil in the manuscript, now restored. It indicates
that the Captain has identified the source of his hatred outside
himself, in someone else's failure to show him the respect he
deserves. The perversity is not his, but the world's. The young
orderly can thus be understood to have brought upon himself the
beatings the Captain feels obliged to inflict. 'Whatever there might

be lay at the door of a stupid, insubordinate servant.'[78] Lawrence's story thus reproduces the terms of Freud's analysis of paranoia: in each case, the paranoiac converts inadmissible love into hatred, and inadmissible hatred into retribution.

The Prussian officer is a 'case-study', I would argue, not just for the literary historian who has read Freud, but also for Lawrence himself, who at this point in his life most probably had not. The cases he had in mind were not strictly speaking psychiatric; but it was undoubtedly the psychosis in them which caught his attention. In November 1912, he had read two recently published books: Edward Garnett's *The Trial of Jeanne d'Arc*, and Edward Browne's *The Reign of Terror at Tabriz*. One concerns the interrogation of Jeanne d'Arc, the other atrocities committed by Russian troops in Persia.[79] In a letter to Garnett, who had sent him the books, Lawrence argued that cruelty is a form of 'perverted sex'.

Priests in their celibacy get their sex lustful, then perverted, then insane— hence Inquisitions—all sexual in origin. And soldiers, being herded together, men without women, never being *satisfied* by a woman, as a man never is from a street affair, get their surplus sex and their frustration and dissatisfaction into the blood, and *love* cruelty. It is sex lust fermented makes atrocity.[80]

Lust, perversion, insanity: such is the Prussian officer's progress. Soldiering, as a profession, demands not just the development of a 'surplus' of masculinity, but its ostentatious display. Not finding in barrack-life the recognition it would ordinarily receive through domestic union, this excess desire converts itself into a bitter hatred of those who are thought to remain indifferent to it, or in some way obstructive; the resulting psychosis makes inquisition and atrocity more or less inevitable. The psychic mechanisms Lawrence studied in his Prussian officer were comparable to those Jones had studied in Gross, and Freud in Schreber. My hypothesis is that the availability of case-studies of one kind or another—of the case-study as a genre, if you like—made it possible for him to

[78] *PO* 9.

[79] Edward Garnett, *The Trial of Jeanne d'Arc* (London: Sidgwick & Jackson, 1912); Edward G. Browne, *The Reign of Terror at Tabriz: England's Responsibility* (Manchester: Taylor, Garnett, Evans, 1912). The photographic evidence Browne supplied is compelling and horrific.

[80] *Letters*, i. 46.

conceive his officer after a certain fashion, with a certain economy of effort; and that this economy of effort in turn made it possible for him to conceive and think through the consequences of inquisition and atrocity, their effect on the victim. Lawrence knew that paranoia routinely performs small miracles of integration; but he also wanted to describe disintegration.

'The Prussian Officer' begins *in medias res*, with the orderly on the march with his regiment, nursing the bruises the Captain had inflicted on him the night before. It then folds back on itself, to describe the Captain's career, and the events which led up to the infliction of the bruises, before catching up once again with the troops on the march. The function of the narrative loop is to supply with the crispness and dispatch of a case-study information which a novel would be able to supply at leisure. The Captain is, we learn, a competent professional man whose abilities and status have never received their due acknowledgement. A Prussian aristocrat, 'haughty and overbearing', with high expectations, he has ruined his 'prospects' in the army by gambling; he will never rise above the rank of captain. His failure to marry is put down to professional and personal reasons. On the one hand, his 'position' will not allow it; on the other, no woman has ever moved him to it. As a result of these cumulative disappointments, he has always 'the look of a man who fights with life'. What sustains him in his fight with life is professionalism. 'Occasionally there had been a duel, an outburst before the soldiers. He knew himself to be always on the point of breaking out. But he kept himself hard to the idea of the Service.'[81]

One might compare the Captain's sudden passion for (and against) his orderly to Ernst Wagner's bestiality. In both cases, the act violates a professional code by letting loose an 'innate', or untrained 'self'. An officer cannot be known to adore his servant, a schoolmaster cannot be seen sexually harassing sheep. Disavowal of this innate self at first takes the form of a vivid reassertion of the principles of soldiering and schoolmastering, of the 'idea of the Service'. The Service, however, has proved something of a disappointment. In both cases, it has (perversely) chosen not to reward the trained self with promotion: the finest horseman in the army languishes as an infantry captain; a first-class mind has been left to

[81] *PO* 2, 4.

rot in Mühlhausen-an-der-Enz. The next step is the conversion of a self-loathing aroused by failure to live up to a code, by moral lapse, into a loathing of others, of all those who simply could not recognize in the fine horseman and the first-class mind the charismatic embodiment of that code, its radiant excess. The houses Wagner set light to were houses belonging not just to people who may or may not have caught sight of him in a field with a sheep, but to people whose indifference to his ability he simply could not forgive. By slapping and kicking his servant, the Captain gets even with a system which has conspired to humiliate him. 'He would not know that his feeling for his orderly was anything but that of a man incensed by his stupid, *perverse* servant.'[82]

Within this narrative loop, our point of view is for the most part that of the Captain, as he struggles to disavow his inadmissible desire. Lawrence's sense of his protagonist as a 'case' enables him to complete that point of view from within, to round it off; and by the same gesture to move beyond it, to abandon the past and re-enter a present which will belong to someone else. The morning after he has in the 'drunkenness of his passion' beaten up the young orderly, the Captain remembers nothing. 'He had not done any such thing—not he himself. Whatever there might be lay at the door of a stupid, insubordinate servant.' He has sealed himself off into psychosis, and the narrative can move beyond him. Thereafter, point of view reverts to the orderly. On two further occasions only do we participate in the officer's thoughts (that is, in his psychosis): once when he sits on his horse, 'feeling proud', pleased by his company's 'subjection' to him; and once when the orderly brings him some beer and bread, and he suddenly yields, as though overwhelmed by the world's malign obtuseness, before 'the solid, stumbling figure with bent head'.[83] Sealed into paranoia, he exists only in the symmetry between fantasized grandeur and fantasized persecution.

Drawn into paranoia's orbit, the orderly experiences for a moment, in the loathing he feels for his persecutor, its miracle of integration. 'Inside had gradually accumulated a core into which all the energy of that young life was compact and concentrated.'[84] Thus concentrated, he finds the strength to fight back. But the

---

[82] *PO* 6.   [83] *PO* 9, 12, 14.   [84] *PO* 13.

story of his resistance does not in itself constitute a case-study. The young soldier would appear to be a conscript. There is little to know about where he came from, or what he thinks he is doing. All the history he has is a scar on his thumb, from an accident with a wood-axe. Contingency, that negation of the pre-disposing factors which go to make up a properly understood psychosis, has inscribed itself on his body. There is of course a social fact in that accident: the only people who cut themselves with axes are people whose work requires them to use axes. Lawrence, however, seems less interested in the social fact than in the condition it gives rise to: the condition of relative immunity to monomania.[85] Unlike the events through which the Captain converts love into cruelty, this injury cannot be disavowed. The scar obtrudes itself like the writing on the wall. The Captain has to use all his 'will-power', all his professionalism, to avoid seeing it. 'He wanted to get hold of it and —. A hot flame ran in his blood.' The contrast between officer and orderly is the contrast not between aristocrat and peasant but between integration and disintegration. The officer comes together, in the systematic renewal of love as cruelty which is his turbulent profession of madness, his profession's madness; the orderly, marked from the outset by accident, and thereafter 'divided among all kinds of separate beings', falls apart.[86] Schizophrenia, it would appear, is the orderly's fate. It is in Kraepelin and Bleuler, one suspects, that a parallel might be found for the delirium described in the story's penultimate section.

I would argue that it was the idea of the case-history which enabled Lawrence to see the excess of coherence deforming his Prussian officer, and thus freed him to explore the incoherence which so vividly informs the life of a young conscript. Psychiatry was his means to abstraction, as it had been Lewis's. In order to pursue this line of inquiry further, I want now to turn to *Women in Love*, a novel which, like 'The Prussian Officer', sets disintegration off against an excess of integration conceived as paranoia. It is

---

[85] The contrast I have in mind is with a moment in *The White Peacock* when the desire aroused in Lettie Beardsall by a deep cut across George Saxton's thumb does seem to be a desire aroused by class-difference: *The White Peacock* (Harmondsworth: Penguin Books, 1982), 74.

[86] *PO* 4, 20.

Women in Love, a novel crucially concerned with professional identity, which in abstract fashion carries forward the study of psychosis undertaken in *Lord Jim*, in *Mr Fleight*, in *The Good Soldier*, and in *Tarr*.

CHAPTER 8

D. H. Lawrence: Women in Love, Men in Madness

OF THE TWO major works in which Lawrence exercised his new metaphysic, *The Rainbow* (1915) and *Women in Love* (1920), it is the latter which could be said to engage most fully with the abstractive Modernisms I have been investigating in this book. *Women in Love* is crammed with self-consciously Modernist arte-facts and aspirations. Gerald Crich is struck by the pictures 'in the Futurist manner' in Halliday's London flat, Rupert Birkin by the reproductions from Picasso Will Brangwen has hanging in his house in Beldover. The Picassos are the idea of his daughter Gudrun, who has lived the bohemian life in Chelsea, and whose ultra-Modernist ambition is to live and study in Rome, Munich, Vienna, St Petersburg, or Moscow. The guests at Breadalby have in a sense already gone to Moscow, as they demonstrate when they attempt a 'little ballet' in the style of Pavlova and Nijinsky. But Lawrence also found plenty of Modernism among his own acquaintance: Mark Gertler's *The Merry-Go-Round* (1916) is the model for the granite frieze Loerke installs in a factory in Cologne.[1] And so on. If there is a 'theoretical vocabulary' at work in *Women in Love*, then, it is one fully informed by a knowledge of the activities of the European avant-garde.

Tony Pinkney has described the 'procedure' of *Women in Love* as a 'systematic cataloguing' of all those brands of Modernism which are ultimately consonant with the 'classicist tradition', either because they intensify that tradition's 'abstract intellectual-ism', or because, in violent reaction, they embrace abstract intel-lectualism's chief fetish and mirror-image: the primitive. One by

---

[1] *Women in Love*, ed. David Farmer, Lindeth Vasey, and John Worthen (Cambridge: CUP, 1987), 74, 255, 423–4. Henceforth *WL*.

one, the novel consigns each florid variety of artistic experiment to
a bonfire of 'bad Modernisms'. However, this procedure is itself, as
Pinkney points out, Modernist through and through.[2] *Women in
Love* transforms itself by catalogue into an encyclopedia to rival *The
Waste Land*, or *Ulysses*, or Pound's *Cantos*. It does so, furthermore,
in the implicitly classicizing spirit of its main protagonist, Rupert
Birkin, whose opinion that 'a dry soul is best' Pinkney compares to
T. E. Hulme's assault on the slush and slither of Romanticism.[3]
Dry, hard, impersonal, clear, cool: Birkin's key words, Pinkney
observes, are straight out of the Hulme thesaurus.[4] It is the Hulme
in Birkin, and in *Women in Love*, which will interest me here; or,
rather, the monomania in the Hulme in Birkin, and in the novel.
Those among the novel's first readers who dismissed it as a book
full of mad people may not have been altogether wide of the mark.[5]

GENDERED PROFESSIONS, PROFESSIONS OF GENDER

When Rupert Birkin says that he feels 'all tangled and messed up'
and that he simply 'can't get straight anyhow', the difficulties he
has in mind have to do with sex, primarily, and perhaps gender.[6]
Critiques of the misogyny and 'phallic language' of canonical
Modernism have of course consistently found in Lawrence a fruitful provocation,[7] while literary and cultural historians have drawn

---

[2] *D. H. Lawrence* (Hemel Hempstead: Harvester Wheatsheaf, 1990), 81–2, 96–7.
[3] *WL* 173.
[4] *D. H. Lawrence*, 86–8.
[5] John Worthen has collected samples of commentary to this effect in *D. H.
Lawrence and the Idea of the Novel* (London: Macmillan, 1979), 89. The *Observer* review
was headed 'A Mad World'. The extremely advanced Rebecca West remarked that
'many of us are cleverer than Mr D. H. Lawrence and nearly all of us save an incar-
cerated few are saner'. *John Bull* thought most of the characters 'obviously mad', while
the *London Mercury* felt that 'one would have to sweep the world before getting
together such a collection of abnormalities'. What these commentators found in the
novel was not neurasthenia, but psychopathy. Middleton Murry described it in less
palpably psychiatric terms as 'five hundred pages of passionate vehemence, wave after
wave of turgid, exasperated writing impelled towards some distant and invisible end':
D. H. Lawrence: The Critical Heritage, ed. R. P. Draper (London: Routledge & Kegan
Paul, 1970), 168–9.
[6] *WL* 125.
[7] e.g. Lawrence looms large in Sandra Gilbert and Susan Gubar's account of Modernism as a battle of the sexes, a 'reaction-formation' against women and femininity:

attention to his eager participation in turn-of-the-century debates about gender and sexuality.[8] Those who have written on *Women in Love* have often seemed to share its protagonist's desire, which may also be its author's desire, to get gender and sexuality straight first, and worry about everything else later. The book's explicit preoccupation with such matters is certainly a challenge to anyone who believes, as I do, that masculinity was for some Modernist writers not so much a posture or a doctrine as a form of symbolic capital. Masculinity could of course have been all three things at once, for those writers, since the symbol in symbolic capital often consists of a belief, or a form of behaviour. My emphasis here will be on the ways in which, in *Women in Love*, gender and sexuality mediate professional concerns.

On 2 May 1913, Lawrence told Edward Garnett that he had completed 180 pages of a new novel with the provisional title of 'The Sisters'. 'I can only write what I feel pretty strongly about,' he insisted: 'and that, at present, is the relations between men and women. After all, it is the problem of today.'[9] The establishment of a new relation between men and women remained for him, as 'The Sisters' became 'The Wedding-Ring' and then eventually *The Rainbow* and *Women in Love*, not only the social problem of today, but its literary solution. On 2 June 1914, writing from Italy to Arthur McLeod, a correspondent eager for the discussion of new ideas, he complained about Futurism's commitment to 'intellectual and scientific purpose'. The only 're-sourcing' or 're-vivifying' of art, he went on, 'is to make it the joint work of man and woman'.[10] In his case, as it turned out, the joint work of man and woman was to be by no means devoid of 'intellectual and scientific purpose'.

Lawrence's belief that struggle is the very condition of sexual relationship, and thus of creativity, found its most vivid expression

No Man's Land: The Place of the Woman Writer in the Twentieth Century, i (New Haven, Conn.: Yale University Press, 1988). More recent accounts have tended, with due qualification, to take his part: e.g. Carol Siegel, *Lawrence among the Women: Wavering Boundaries in Women's Literary Traditions* (Charlottesville, Va.: University of Virginia Press, 1991). The term 'phallic language' is Lynn Pykett's: *Engendering Fictions: The English Novel in the Early Twentieth Century* (London: Edward Arnold, 1995), 12.

[8] Pykett, *Engendering Fictions*, ch. 7. See also Hilary Simpson's *D. H. Lawrence and Feminism* (London: Croom Helm, 1982).

[9] *Letters*, ed. James T. Boulton *et al.*, 7 vols. (Cambridge: CUP, 1979–93), i. 546.
[10] Ibid. ii. 180–1.

in a 'sort of interpretative essay' which he wrote between September and November 1914.[11] The 'Study of Thomas Hardy' is a study of Hardy's people (the original commission), and an expression of his own anger at the 'colossal idiocy' of the war which had broken out in August. It contains all kinds of 'queer stuff'.[12] In it, Lawrence argues that the categories which define gender-difference are 'arbitrary, for the purpose of thought'. Masculinity and femininity exist in struggle within every man and woman, as well as between them. 'So we may speak of Male and Female, of the Will-to-Motion and of the Will-to-Inertia.'[13] It is Lawrence's sense of the arbitrariness of the available categories, his sense of the Will-to-Motion and the Will-to-Inertia as contrary *performances*, which encourages me to suggest that for him, too, masculinity could be conceived as a form of symbolic capital—and a form of madness.

For in *Women in Love*, which Lawrence embarked on in March 1916, that which completes a man is not union with a woman in marriage, but something else, a further union, a supplement to marriage. 'We want something broader.—I believe in the additional perfect relationship between man and man—additional to marriage.' This is Birkin's attempt to persuade a sceptical Gerald Crich that the relationship between man and man can be as 'perfect' as the relationship between man and woman. It is an attempt which the novel itself neither gives up on nor carries through to a resolution. The novel ends with Birkin and Ursula, now husband and wife, still in dispute over his need for the 'perfect union' with a man which would 'complete' his existence.

> 'I don't believe it,' she said. 'It's an obstinacy, a theory, a perversity.'
> 'Well —' he said.
> 'You can't have two kinds of love. Why should you!'
> 'It seems as if I can't,' he said. 'Yet I wanted it.'
> 'You can't have it, because it's false, impossible,' she said.
> 'I don't believe that,' he said.[14]

The story has come to an end, but much remains unspoken, and in a sense over-spoken, too fiercely articulated, in the absolute

---

[11] Ibid. 193.   [12] Ibid. 212.
[13] *Study of Thomas Hardy and Other Essays*, ed. Bruce Steele (Cambridge: CUP, 1985), 60–1.   [14] *WL* 352, 481.

difference between Ursula's explicit 'can't' and implicit 'should-
n't', and Birkin's 'don't'. Supplementarity, the novel seems to say,
that which is left over after it has ended, and has been already left
over long before it ended, is the modern (Western) masculine
condition. In so far as *Women in Love* is a book about relations
between men and women, it is a book about the extent to which
relations between men and women can never be enough, for a
man. In it, masculinity is made to reflect on itself, on the ways in
which it can add to itself in order to become more fully itself,
rather than on its Other. My interest is in what brings this reflection about, what makes it necessary.

It is often forgotten, or reckoned of little significance, that the
relationship between Ursula Brangwen and Rupert Birkin begins
as a relationship between schoolteacher and school inspector.
Ursula, we are told in chapter 1, already wants to know him
better. 'She had spoken with him once or twice, but only in his
official capacity as inspector.' She thinks that he has acknowledged
a 'kinship' between them. It is as an inspector that he next appears
in her life, in chapter 3, when he drops in on her botany class; and
on this occasion he very definitely does not hold back from professional advice, telling her to make a pictorial record of the facts of
sex for her pupils. Hermione Roddice follows him into the room,
and a savage disagreement ensues between them as to the value of
education. What they are really disagreeing about, it might seem,
is the reason for the unsatisfactoriness of their relationship. But we
should not regard the debate about education simply as the
medium through which the topic of relations between men and
women can be addressed. If there is sexual anger, here, as
Hermione imagines Birkin drifting away from her, there is also
anger, on his part, at her obliviousness to the good Ursula might
actually be doing to her pupils.[15]

Birkin, it must be insisted, is not a school inspector by accident
(his problem, perhaps, is that he is nothing by accident). What
happens in chapter 3 is that the novel begins its investigation of
supplementarity; and begins it, furthermore, in the sphere of
professional rather than of gendered identity. It has begun, already,
to reconceive Birkin, to imagine that supplement to school-

inspecting which will complete him professionally, and *therefore* as a man. To be sure, one might think, as Birkin himself comes to think, that he and Ursula will only ever find salvation by giving up their jobs. In the end, though, I believe, Lawrence thought of Birkin not as professionalism's outside, but as its vastly amplified inside. In its unobtrusive way, this chapter shows how. Birkin begins it as a school inspector identifiable by his 'qualities'—expertise, peremptoriness, command of a mildly esoteric terminology—and ends it as a would-be prophet or spiritual leader identifiable through fluctuations of gendered feeling within a specific environment. This second identification—not of Birkin's qualities, but of his qualitylessness—is the novel's own dangerous supplement, its supersession of mere qualities by and in the new 'analytical' manner.

Prophecy, too, is a profession, albeit one without certificates, and thus dependent on the fugitive symbolic capital yielded by charisma.[16] Birkin's passionate advocacy of the 'great dark knowledge you can't have in your head' unites in scepticism the two women who will shortly compete for his love. 'The two women were jeering at him, jeering him into nothingness. The laugh of the shrill, triumphant female sounded from Hermione, jeering him as if he were a neuter.' This, clearly, is a gendered difference. But it is not a difference *about* gender. The absoluteness of the female triumph—gender serving as the effect or symptom of absoluteness, here, rather than its cause—is a foretaste of the persecution which will always greet the prophet wherever he or she goes, and in which he or she will find the guarantee of uniqueness. Lawrence imagines Birkin as a man, as a man neutralized, in order to imagine him as a prophet, that is, as a super-professional. Gender-difference becomes here, and will remain throughout the novel, the material out of which paranoid symmetry can be constructed. Indeed, the chapter ends with Hermione and Ursula flattened by

---

[16] According to Weber, 'prophetic revelation' is charisma's 'specific form'. 'Charismatic belief revolutionizes men "from within" and shapes material and social conditions according to its revolutionary will ... Instead of reverence for customs that are ancient and hence sacred, it enforces the inner subjection to the unprecedented and absolutely unique and therefore Divine': 'Charisma and Its Transformation', *Economy and Society: An Outline of Interpretative Sociology*, 2 vols., ed. Guenther Roth and Claus Wittich (Berkeley, Calif.: University of California Press, 1978), ii. 1111–57, pp. 1114–17.

a final salvo. 'There was silence in the room. Both women were hostile and resentful. He sounded as if he were addressing a meeting.' Prophecy is a profession in which charisma matters above all else; and yet the absoluteness of the acknowledgement charisma so feverishly demands can arouse hostility, a hostility which will somehow have to be understood as a further source of absolute acknowledgement. Hermione loses Birkin by not paying attention to the prophecy in him. Ursula, on the other hand, recognizes the 'sense of richness and liberty' which comes through his pallor 'like another voice, conveying another knowledge of him'.[17] One could not dissociate, in that voice, gender, or sexuality, from expertise (a prophet's expertise, rather than a school inspector's).

The most useful commentary on this episode is an ambitious, powerful, and repetitive essay Lawrence wrote in 1918, 'Education of the People'. The essay is a diatribe against an educational policy which prepares children from disadvantaged backgrounds neither for work nor for selfhood. It begins with the impossible plight of the Ursula Brangwens, the elementary schoolteachers whose job is to put that policy into practice. Insulted from 'below', by parents and children who jeer at and despise his 'wretched idealist sort of authority', and from 'above', by the inspector of schools, a university man with little understanding of or respect for elementary education, the teacher finds himself in a 'vile and false position'. Neither wage-earner nor professional, he has absolutely no 'base' except in his own 'isolate will'; once the 'natural pride' has been ground out of him, he will either give up or cultivate some unpleasant *suffisance* (a self-sufficiency, or conceitedness) which 'makes him objectionable for ever'. Ernst Wagner, elementary schoolteacher in Mühlhausen-an-der-Enz, made himself objectionable, as we have seen, by mass-murder; Lawrence's analysis of the psychological effects of an over-reliance on the isolate will is consistent throughout with Robert Gaupp's analysis of the origins of Wagner's paranoia. Wagner, too, one might say, found himself in a vile and false position, his 'natural pride' destroyed by sneering parents and children (and no doubt by sneering inspectors) long before he took to the fields one night on his way home from the pub. And Lawrence does indeed go on to name the mental illness which has in his view consumed all of those with a stake in elementary education, from the sneering parents to the Olympian policy-makers in Whitehall. 'It has become an *idée fixe*,' he says, 'the idea of earning, or not earning, a living. And we are all mono-maniacs in it.'[18] This, Lawrence concludes, is what has made authority impossible: the fear, not of death, but of life.

Lawrence, then, had thought through the weaknesses inherent in the position of men and women whose authority was of the 'wretched idealist sort'—an authority in effect without access either to certification or to a charisma transcending certification—in terms close to those of the German psychologists. The solution he put forward in the essay, and arguably in *Women in Love* as well, was to train the educators in fearlessness. 'Educators will take a grave responsibility upon themselves. They will be the priests of life, deep in the wisdom of life. They will be the life-priests of the new era. And the leaders, the inspectors, will be men deeply initi-ated into the mysteries of life, adepts in the dark mystery of living . . .' Step forward Rupert Birkin. It is at this point that 'Education of the People' takes an unexpected turn towards the abstractive Modernism of a Hulme or a Lewis, as Lawrence inveighs against social mimesis, and against the 'seeking' or 'sympathetic' centres which encourage a person to model himself or herself upon some-one else. 'A nervous child yearns and frets ceaselessly for complete identification. It wants to merge, to merge back into the mother, with the ceaseless craving of morbid love.' No longer apart and integral, the male child 'crawls helplessly and parasitically from the sympathetic centres, to establish himself in a permanent life-oneness with another being, usually the mother'. Lawrence held mothers to blame for this deplorable state of affairs. 'And the mother too rejoices in this horrible parasitism of her child, she feels exalted, like God, now she is the host of the parasite.' The solu-tion was to remove children from their mothers, and thus force them back into an integral apartness, into dark pride. Like Worringer, Lawrence opposes abstraction to empathy; like Hulme and Lewis, he genders abstraction masculine. 'Let men realise that their life lies ahead, in the dangerous wilds of advance and

---

[18] 'Education of the People', in *Reflections on the Death of a Porcupine and Other Essays*, ed. Michael Herbert (Cambridge: CUP, 1988), 87–166, pp. 91–2.

increase. Let them realise that they must go beyond their women, projected into a region of greater abstraction, more inhuman activity.'[19] That Lawrence should rely so heavily on gender-difference to establish a metaphysic and a politics, both here and elsewhere, is of course highly significant.[20] My point is that in this case the reliance stems from the need to define the training in charisma which will single out the life-priests of the new era. By associating social mimesis with what he regards 'for the purpose of thought' as a woman's fundamental role, with motherhood, he can associate abstraction with what he regards, again for the purpose of thought, as a man's fundamental role. In this projection beyond the very principle of social mimesis, men learn to reflect on themselves, and to supplement a mimetic masculinity by and in that reflection. 'There, in the womanless regions of fight, and pure thought, and abstracted instrumentality, let men have a new attitude to one another.' The model for this pure instrumentality is the figure of charismatic professionalism developed in Edwardian popular romance: the scout, the outrider.[21] Step forward Richard Hannay. The womanless regions of fight, as we have already seen, are paranoia's domain. One of the fascinations of *Women in Love* is that it recognizes as much.

DEMENTIAS

In *Women in Love*, Lawrence develops the narrative pattern Robert Musil was later to define and perfect, of a contrast between a man (or men) with qualities and a man without qualities. Gerald Crich is a man with qualities if ever there was one, and we know a lot about them. An entire chapter, 'The Industrial Magnate', is devoted to an account of his abilities and ambitions. He has a

---

[19] 'Education of the People', 107, 140, 166.

[20] For an account of its significance in this particular context, see Pykett, *Engendering Fictions*, 133–5.

[21] 'Education of the People', 165–6. Like Wells, Lawrence remained an educator even after he gave up educating. 'He could no more give up the hope of changing people', Worthen remarks, 'than he could finally escape from that fundamental belief in progress and advance which had been one of his inheritances from his mother, and from the nineteenth century. And he could not escape from either the desire, or the job, of writing novels to express that belief' (*D. H. Lawrence*, 86).

history. When Catherine Carswell, who had been sent a copy of the 1916 typescript, criticized the placing of this chapter, Lawrence made it clear that the density with which it endows Gerald was crucial to his conception.

About the Gerald-Work part: I want it to come where it does: you meet a man, you get an impression of him, you find out *afterwards* what he has done. If you have, in your arrogance, writ him down a nobody, then there is a slap in the eye for you when you find he has done more than you have done.[22]

What mattered was that the reader should not be left in any doubt as to the magnitude of Gerald's achievements and the density of his social presence. This man is a somebody.

Birkin, by contrast, is not accounted for. Lawrence went to considerable lengths to minimize his curriculum vitae. In the novel's earliest version, the 'Prologue' and 'Wedding' chapters written in April 1916, and subsequently discarded, we do learn a little about Birkin's background and career. We are told that when he first met Hermione Roddice he was already at 21 a Fellow of Magdalen College, Oxford, 'one of the young lights of the place, a coming somebody'.[23] But these few details do not survive into the later versions, where Birkin stands out by his *lack* of density. Lawrence wrote Birkin down a nobody in order to redeem him from a culture crammed with somebodies, a culture whose respect for 'qualities' was, he thought, its undoing. The contrast between the man with qualities and the man without them is insisted upon, lightly, throughout the novel. Thus, Gerald is scrupulous about his appearance, as Lawrence is in describing it. 'He wore silk socks, and studs of fine workmanship, and silk underclothing, and silk braces.' Birkin, on the other hand, has no time for silk underclothing. 'This was another of the differences between them. Birkin was careless and unimaginative about his own appearance.'[24] Birkin's quality, if one can call it that, is to be unimaginative about qualities.

Unlike Musil, Lawrence extended this narrative pattern into a parallel contrast between a woman with qualities and a woman without them. Gudrun Brangwen is a talented artist. The opening of chapter 21, for example, finds her 'away in London, having a

---

[22] *Letters*, iii. 57.   [23] *WL* 491.   [24] *WL* 273.

little show of her work, with a friend, preparing for flight from Beldover'.[25] This is clearly a woman with qualities, or at any rate with stockings, to which Lawrence devotes as detailed an attention as he does to Gerald's silk socks and braces.[26] Her sister Ursula appears by contrast uncertain and amorphous. The history with which *The Rainbow* richly endows Ursula, in her long struggle for independence of mind and body, has been stripped out in *Women in Love*. Lawrence had to write her too down as a nobody, so that she might become Birkin's partner in redemptive qualitylessness. It is rather hard not to agree with Mark Kinkead-Weekes when he observes that Gudrun and Gerald 'may seem the more interesting couple'.[27]

From 'The Sisters' through to *Women in Love*, Lawrence had consistently put women first, in the arrangements of his narrative if not in the arrangements of his thought. *Women in Love* opens with Gudrun and Ursula in debate, about men and marriage, about qualities and the lack of them; no one could doubt the centrality of the relationship between the two sisters. And yet its first draft, of which only the 'Prologue' and 'Wedding' chapters survive, puts the men first, and in doing so establishes with utter directness a rather different preoccupation. I do not only mean the frank portrayal in 'Prologue' of Birkin's homoerotic desire. I mean also the distinction sharply drawn between Birkin and Gerald. 'In the last issue, [Birkin] was callous, and without feeling, confident, just as Gerald Crich in the last issue was wavering and lost.'[28] Here, Lawrence rushes ahead to a 'last issue', a culminating polarity, which it will take the published text 500 pages to arrive at. He does so, I think, because his account of this polarization between

---

[25] *WL* 277.

[26] In *Women in Love*, Philippa Tristram observes, the men have loins, the women stockings: 'Eros and Death: Lawrence, Freud and Women', in Anne Smith (ed.), *Lawrence and Women* (London: Vision, 1978), 136–55, p. 143. This is, I think, to attribute to Lawrence's preoccupation with gender-difference an explanatory function it does not in fact possess. The more interesting difference, in *Women in Love*, may be between those men and women whose clothes merit remark and those whose clothes do not.

[27] *D. H. Lawrence: Triumph to Exile, 1912–1922* (Cambridge: CUP, 1996), 337. Reviewing the novel in the *Dial*, Evelyn Scott remarked that 'the love of Ursula and Rupert is presented to us with a conjectural uncertainty that makes it pale against the vivid, nameless actuality of the instinctive relationship of Gudrun and Gerald Crich': *Critical Heritage*, 163.

[28] *WL* 491.

extreme callousness and extreme wavering is a way to conceive masculinity and its discontents. He vindicates in advance, as it were, Birkin's stubborn refusal to relinquish the prospect of fulfilment beyond marriage, of fulfilment between men. The consequence of his plain talking about last issues is that by the time Gudrun and Ursula appear on the scene, in 'Wedding', the terms of the novel have been well and truly set. The distinction drawn there between the sisters merely repeats that already drawn between Birkin and Gerald. The sisters constitute, as it were, another masculinity. They are the way in which the novel, seeking to understand the masculine as a structure of supplementarity, supplements itself. It is not that they are nothing in themselves.[29] It is, rather, that at those moments when masculinity becomes unequivocally the 'last issue', they stand in, as I shall show, for the men they are in love with. They are at such moments redundant, and it is by their redundancy that we define Lawrence's preoccupation with the masculine. The reordering of the novel's first two chapters after 1916, which puts the sisters first, does no more than dissimulate the priority it gives, in the final analysis, to masculinity's reflection on itself.

In 'Prologue', Birkin's desire for men is characterized as a neurosis. He represses it, only to encounter it everywhere in its negation or displacement. But the chapter, like the short story, also finds another set of terms for his predicament. Birkin, the great educator, believes that humankind has undergone a process of 'decay and decomposition' in which there is no great sustaining 'philosophic idea', and thus nothing to educate people in, or for. Under these circumstances a commitment to education seems to him 'like dementia'. 'It created in him a feeling of nausea and horror. He recoiled from it.' Birkin's recoil does not, however, provoke nihilism. Quite the opposite. His determination to evolve a new 'philosophic idea', and thus restore meaning and value to the world, becomes itself a kind of madness. Hermione, we learn, 'dreaded his way of seeing some particular things vividly and feverishly, and of his acting upon this special sight. For once he

---

[29] Though that was the line Middleton Murry took. 'We should have thought that we should be able to distinguish between male and female, at least. But no! Remove the names, remove the sedulous catalogue of unnecessary clothing—a new element and a significant one, this, in our author's work—and man and woman are indistinguishable as octopods in an aquarium tank': *Critical Heritage*, 170.

decided a thing, it became a reigning universal truth to him, and he was completely inhuman.' What she especially does not want Birkin to see and to become inhuman about, of course, is her own redundancy. 'He had stuck fast over this question of love and of physical fulfilment in love, till it had become like a monomania.'[30] It is in monomania, or from monomania, that he articulates, as a reigning universal truth, his desire for a fulfilment in addition to marriage. The shadow of the German psychologists falls on this chapter, as it had on 'The Prussian Officer'. Lawrence may or may not have regarded homosexuality as a disease. He certainly made use of psychiatric terminology to describe Birkin's search for meaning and value in a world without philosophic ideas, a search which involves the devaluation of marriage.

In *Women in Love*, the separation between the man without qualities and the man with them is along the line of the separation in the early psychiatric literature between paranoia and schizophrenia. The author's implicit preference, like the clinician's, is for the paranoiac, who survives (just about), while the man with qualities goes to his death. The narrative constitutes a double helix of psychoses: a double double helix, one might say, in so far as the women's actions and utterances reproduce the men's. Its fundamental movement is that of a chiasmus, or crossing over. When we first meet him, in the opening chapters, Birkin, like the schizophrenics described by Kraepelin and Bleuler, is an exponent of echopraxis. At the wedding ceremony and the reception afterwards, having no will of his own, he adapts to circumstance, to other people's expectations: 'he subordinated himself to the common idea, travestied himself'. 'He affected to be quite ordinary, perfectly and marvellously commonplace. And he did it so well, taking the tone of his surroundings, adjusting himself quickly to his interlocutor and his circumstance, that he achieved a verisimilitude of ordinary commonplaceness that usually propitiated his onlookers for the moment, disarmed them from attacking his singleness.' It is from here that Birkin crosses over, during the next 500 pages or so, to callous confidence, to paranoia. Gerald, the 'very pivot' of the ceremonies, the man who finds an 'almost religious exaltation' in 'forcing order into the established world',

---

[30] *WL* 504, 495, 496, 499.

crosses over in the opposite direction, to schizophrenia. He wavers, loses himself, his promiscuity an index to his ultimate lack of purpose.[31] Monogamy, Lawrence told Lady Ottoline Morrell in February 1916, should not be required of those 'who can't have full satisfaction in one person, because they themselves are too split, because they act in themselves separately'.[32] Pure as an 'arctic thing', with his 'clear northern flesh' and his fair hair glistening 'like cold sunshine refracted through crystals of ice', Gerald finally camouflages himself to death in snow. For him, echopraxis proves fatal.[33]

Paranoia was reckoned by the German psychologists to involve an adherence to system—an abolition of randomness—of which a philosopher might be proud. In chapter 2 of *Women in Love*, Birkin demonstrates his powers of adaptability in an encounter with the trying Mrs Crich. Arising out of this encounter, by way of casual afterthought, is a meditation on contingency. Mrs Crich returns for a moment to Birkin, to ask him to befriend Gerald. The request prompts Birkin to reflect that Gerald, for all his pivotal density, is something of an outcast; as a young boy, he had killed his brother in a shooting accident. Was the killing accidental? 'Or is this not true, is there no such thing as pure accident? Has *everything* that happens a universal significance?' Was Gerald always meant to kill his brother, whether he wanted to or not, as Cain was always meant to kill Abel? Birkin begins to cross over towards paranoia, towards a belief in universal significance, when he decides that Gerald is indeed cursed, a modern Cain. 'He did not believe that there was any such thing as accident. It all hung together, in the deepest sense.'[34] The beginning of paranoia is the deep sense that it all hangs together.

Lawrence incorporated this difference of attitude, which I have so far described in psychiatric terms, into his novel in various ways. In the first place, he doubled the narrative's double helix. When Ursula and Gudrun discuss Gerald's killing of his brother, a little later, it is Ursula who becomes convinced that there was an 'unconscious will' behind Gerald's action, while Gudrun cannot regard it as anything other than the 'purest form of accident'. Already the two sisters have begun to cross over in the same direction as the men

---

[31] *WL* 20, 23, 227–8, 418, 413.   [32] *Letters*, ii. 539.
[33] *WL* 14.   [34] *WL* 26.

they are falling in love with. Accident punctuates the relationship between Gerald and Gudrun. By the time of the water-party at Shortlands during which their passion for each other becomes apparent he has acquired a mysterious injury to his hand, an incapacity which draws Gudrun into intimacy with him. The episode concludes with an accidental death by drowning; or at least with a death which does not seem all that accidental to the increasingly aloof Birkin.[35] Is Gerald doomed? Or simply more vulnerable to accident than other people?

Lawrence figures these contrary crossings over by a delineation of habit. Gerald's (schizophrenic) habit is to plunge in, to immerse himself in the world. The sisters' next sight of him, after the wedding, is his naked dive into Willey Water. At the water-party, he dives repeatedly into the lake in a desperate attempt to rescue his sister. Gudrun feels that she must 'jump into the water too, to know the horror also'. Birkin's (paranoid) habit, by contrast, is of withdrawal, or suspension. He it is who stops Gerald diving, and later reproaches him for forcing himself into horrors. Ursula, falling in love with him, imitates his aloofness. 'She was perfectly callous about all the talk of the accident, but her estranged air looked like trouble.' The divergence of habit between the two sisters has already become apparent, in chapter 10, when they spend a day sketching by Willey Water. Gudrun stares 'fixedly' at the water-plants which emerge 'thick and cool and fleshy' from the 'soft, oozy, watery mud': 'she could feel their turgid fleshy structure as in a sensuous vision, she *knew* how they rose out of the mud'. Ursula, by contrast, seems more interested in the butterflies. Indeed, she follows their example. She drifts away, 'unconscious like the butterflies'—into the next chapter, where she is to be found still drifting, this time in the punt Birkin has just repaired.[36]

The social and political consequences of a habit of immersion are a theme of the novel's opening chapter. Ursula and Gudrun walk down the main street of Beldover. 'Gudrun, new from her life in Chelsea and Sussex, shrank cruelly from this amorphous ugliness of a small colliery town in the midlands. Yet forward she went, through the whole sordid gamut of pettiness.' She has already gone forward, in a sense, already immersed herself, courtesy of the

[35] *WL* 49, 160, 174, 176, 185.   [36] *WL* 46, 181, 183, 188, 190, 119.

demonstrative 'this', which in English carries associations of intimacy and relatedness. We do not learn much about the main
street; but we know that its 'sordid gamut' has entered into the
woman who has put herself close to it, contaminating her for ever.
Exposed to 'every stare', Gudrun camouflages herself by yet
deeper immersion. 'Why had she wanted to submit herself to it,
did she still want to submit herself to it, the insufferable torture of
these ugly, meaningless people, this defaced countryside?' Living
in Beldover is like 'being mad', she thinks. But the madness
becomes a habit. She works on her camouflage. 'She struggled to
get more and more into accord with the atmosphere of the place,
she craved to get her satisfaction of it.' She and her boyfriend stroll
the streets, 'absolutely adhering to the people, teeming with the
distorted colliers'. Gudrun's ultimate desire is to be kissed in the
darkness under the bridge where the colliers kiss their girlfriends,
by the man who is master of them all, Gerald Crich.[37]

The point about Birkin and Ursula is that they are never
tempted to immersion. They suspend themselves, unconscious like
the butterflies, above the dust in which Gudrun toils, above the
ooze into which Gerald repeatedly plunges. Sitting on the tram-
car, on her way out of town to visit Birkin, Ursula passes into a
'dream world'. 'She watched the sordid streets of the town go by
beneath her, as if she were a spirit disconnected from the material
universe. What had it all got to do with her?' Palpitating and
formless within the flux of this 'ghost life', Ursula has begun to
shed her qualities. 'She could not consider any more, what
anybody would say of her or think about her.' *Could* not: withdrawal has become a habit. Afloat on an adequate private income,
Birkin decides that they ought to give up their jobs. Before very
long they have begun to think furniture beneath them. You
should leave your surroundings 'sketchy' and 'unfinished', Birkin
argues, so that they never define you.[38]

As Gerald Doherty has pointed out in a fine analysis, the novel
discriminates one character from another as much by tropology, by
attitude to metaphor, as by description of habit. Lawrence has organized its rhetoric around the metatrope of the leap. 'He plays off the
lure of the unknown, the as-yet uncoded, against the counter-lure

---

[37] *WL* 11, 116, 118, 330.   [38] *WL* 144, 317, 356.

of the known, the completely coded.' In their desire to encompass and enclose (and, one might add, to be encompassed and enclosed), Gudrun and Gerald avoid the leap; while Ursula and Birkin, in their taste for the unconditional, espouse it, perhaps achieve it. One pair focus on objects, the other on gestures.[39]

The advantage of conceiving the various narrative and tropological crossings over which constitute *Women in Love* in terms drawn from contemporary psychiatry is that it enables us to understand them as the performance of a new 'philosophic idea': that of the life-priest whose charismatic (hypermasculine) professionalism may yet redeem a negligent and corrupt society. Birkin goes mad in order to transform himself from an inspector of schools into a scout or outrider: his leap is a leap at once within and beyond professionalism. Woven into his performance of the new philosophic idea are his trademark end-of-the-world fantasies. Freud, as we have seen, was struck by the prominence of such fantasies in paranoia, where they dramatically enhance the patient's delusions of grandeur by envisaging an ultimate exemption from the criticism and harassment hitherto directed at him or her. Thus, no sooner has Birkin ferried Ursula across to the island in his punt, in chapter 10, enacting a leap of a kind, a suspension, than he favours her with a particularly colourful endorsement of genocide. There would be no absolute loss, he tells her, if humankind were to be swept away. 'The reality would be untouched. Nay, it would be better. The real tree of life would then be rid of the most ghastly heavy crop of Dead Sea Fruit, the intolerable burden of myriad simulacra of people, an infinite weight of mortal lies.' This is a protest, similar to ones we have already explored, and like them close to nausea, against social mimesis. The people who ought to be swept away are simulacra. Relieved of the intolerable burden of mimesis, those who remain will know a grandeur, an absolute singularity. Although Ursula finds Birkin's vision of a 'humanless' world immensely attractive, she also recognizes the paranoia in it, the delusion of grandeur, the 'Salvator Mundi touch'. Indeed, Birkin could be said to have enjoyed his moment of paranoid illumination already, after Hermione's intensifying persecution of him

---

[39] *Theorizing Lawrence: Nine Meditations on Tropological Themes* (New York: Peter Lang, 1999), 88.

finally spills over into assault. Her attack on him convinces him
that he has made a mistake in wanting people at all, in wanting a
woman. Alone in the woods, he dreams away the human race.
'Here was his world, he wanted nobody and nothing but the
lovely, subtle, responsive vegetation, and himself, his own living
self.' He knows that he will have to go back into society, but does
so rejoicing in 'the new-found world of his madness'. For Birkin,
however, as for Ernst Wagner, the grandeur thus induced is a
function of the persecution to which he has been subject. Walking
down the road to the station, he worries lest anyone should have
seen him lying naked in the woods.

What a dread he had of mankind, of other people! It amounted almost
to horror, to a sort of dream terror—his horror of being observed by
some other people. If he were on an island, like Alexander Selkirk, with
only the creatures and the trees, he would be free and glad, there would
be none of this heaviness, this misgiving. He could love the vegetation
and be quite happy and unquestioned, by himself.[40]

CHARISMATIC FORM

For Lawrence, then, the 'new era' required the transformation
rather than the abandonment of expertise. 'It is time to start afresh.
And we need a system.' 'There must be a system; there *must* be
classes of men; there *must* be differentiation: either that, or amorphous nothingness. The true choice is not between system and no-
system. The choice is between system and system, mechanical or
organic.'[41] In *Women in Love*, Birkin first chooses system over non-
system, and then (the 'Salvator Mundi touch'), organic system over
mechanical system. Lawrence explores in Birkin the madness this
second choice entails: the madness entailed by the construction of an
organic system, a system which allows for charisma. Such is the
connection he establishes in his novel between psychosis and the
professionalization of English society. What does the connecting is
the charisma of the novel's form: a literary experiment which supplements, through its excess of organic system, the mechanical system
constituted by the standard narratives of Edwardian domestic realism.

[40] *WL* 128, 107.   [41] 'Education of the People', 111.

Towards the end of 1917, as Lawrence's search for a publisher became increasingly desperate, his agent J. B. Pinker arranged a lunch with John Galsworthy. The two men did not get on. At the same time, he found out that George Moore, another potential convert, had deplored the tendency of his more recent work to abandon human beings in favour of 'vague animal abstractions'.[42] Such minor persecutions can only have strengthened his commitment to organic system.

Raymond Williams has described *Women in Love* as a 'radical *simplification*'. Lawrence, Williams says, developed in it a 'whole and separate form: crystalline certainly, with its own loveliness and intensity of structure'.[43] It is at the level of the chapter that he seems most to have insisted on separateness, on crystalline intensity. Each chapter could be seen as a more or less self-contained enactment of the new philosophic idea, as one of a set of 'linked parables'.[44] In narrative terms, Tony Pinkney argues, *Women in Love*, in sharp contrast to its predecessor, *The Rainbow*, is 'premised utterly upon the event'. 'The characteristic time-span of a chapter is a single, vivid instant: Birkin stoning the image of the moon in the pond, Gerald viciously restraining the Arab mare as the train rattles by, the rabbit Bismarck tearing Gudrun's flesh.' Pinkney finds in this reduction to crystalline event a deep complicity with the classicist Modernism of Katherine Mansfield, a Modernism which turns away in its search for an 'autotelic formal perfection' from the 'messy, unmastered chaos of physical life'.[45] Mansfield's representative in *Women in Love* is the far-from-admirable Gudrun Brangwen, creator of exquisite miniature sculptures, who dreams of reviving the classical ambitions of Goethe and Schiller in Weimar.[46] Gudrun, we learn, prefers mechanical to organic system. But it may be that the novel has been made in her image (in her Imagism).

Lawrence's will-to-abstraction, however, like Hulme's, was sufficiently informed by paranoia not to lapse into schizophrenic minimalism. His chapters, while they have a shape to them, as organic

[42] Kinkead-Weekes, *Triumph to Exile*, 413–14.
[43] *The English Novel from Dickens to Lawrence* (London: Chatto & Windus, 1970), 179.
[44] Frank Kermode, *Lawrence* (London: Fontana, 1973), 73.
[45] *D. H. Lawrence*, 95, 60.
[46] WL 453.

systems should, are not quite as crystalline as has sometimes been made out. In 1917, Lawrence substantially rewrote the 1916 type-script of the novel, introducing in the process new chapter-divisions. The recent publication of the 1916 typescript as *The First 'Women in Love'* has made it possible to assess the significance of the alterations he subsequently made.[47] Lawrence divided some of the lengthy chapters of the 1916 typescript into smaller units; when he did so, he tended to revise the conclusion of the first part heavily, and leave the opening of the second part (the new chap-ter) more or less intact. Thus the first paragraphs of chapters 14 and 27 of *Women in Love* show hardly any changes from the 1916 type-script, while the concluding paragraphs of the episodes from which they were separated, now chapters 13 and 26, are virtually unrecognizable. Lawrence knew very well where he wanted an episode or a scene to start; he was not so sure about where it should end. The episodes begin crystalline, one might say, and conclude when they have arrived at some other shape. On several occasions, Lawrence revised simply in order to say one last thing, and then another last thing, and then another, about the mysteri-ous supplement to marriage which has become Birkin's primary obsession. This is true, for example, of chapters 13, 25, 26, and 32.[48] His method, in short, in conceiving the relationship with a man which Birkin wishes to add to his relationship with a woman, is additive. In this respect, at least, there is no attempt at minimal-ism. An examination of chapter 19 ('Moony'), which was split off from its successor ('Gladiatorial') in the 1917 revision, will reveal the far-from-crystalline structure of supplementarity at work in the novel's construal of organic system.

As 'Moony' opens, Birkin is in France, recuperating from the illness described in a previous chapter, 'Man to Man', where we discover that being laid up has at least given him the chance to work on his paranoia. 'The merging, the clutching, the mingling of love was become madly abhorrent to him.' During these stricken meditations, Birkin's horror of humankind in general finds a focus in the claims women might be considered to make

---

[47] *The First 'Women in Love'*, ed. John Worthen and Lindeth Vasey (Cambridge: CUP, 1998): henceforth *FWL*.

[48] Compare *FWL* 141 with *WL* 154; *FWL* 325 with *WL* 352–3; *FWL* 332–3 with *WL* 362–3; and *FWL* 443 with *WL* 481.

on men. 'Hermione, the humble, the subservient, what was she all the while but the Mater Dolorosa, in her subservience claiming, with horrible, insidious arrogance and female tyranny, her own again, claiming back the man she had borne in suffering.' Birkin fears that Ursula may prove another 'awful, arrogant queen of life'.[49] Structurally, 'Man to Man' supplements—at once goes beyond and repeats—this moment of (supplementary) paranoid illumination by bringing Gerald Crich to see Birkin, man to man.

During Birkin's absence, 'Ursula, left alone, felt as if everything were lapsing out.' This isolation endows her with a new strength. 'She herself was real, and only herself—just like a rock in a wash of flood-water.' We might say that isolation masculinizes her, or at least that it encourages her to think and behave like Birkin. Like Birkin, she expresses contempt for the whole human show, for 'social principle'. Like Birkin, she achieves a certain grandeur through this all-embracing contempt. 'But the strange brightness of her presence, a marvellous radiance of intrinsic vitality, was a luminousness of supreme repudiation, repudiation, nothing but repudiation.' It is thus a thoroughly Birkinized Ursula who finds herself one evening in the vicinity of Willey Water, with the full moon for company. No wonder that she finds in its 'sinister face' something to be afraid of. 'The moon was transcendent over the bare, open space, she suffered from being exposed to it.'[50] This 'cowering' glimpse of the 'white planet' has something of the force of Schreber's vision of sun, not as it usually appears, but 'surrounded by a silver sea of rays'.[51] The Birkin who is shortly to be seen stoning the image of the moon in a pond has thus been doubled in advance, as it were. Birkin regards the moon as the symbol of the Magna Mater, the woman tyrannical in her subservience. Stoning its image, he puts into practice his repudiation of a love which clutches and mingles—and Lawrence's repudiation, in 'Education of the People', of the social mimesis enforced by a mother's irresponsible exercise of sympathy. 'And he was not satisfied. Like a madness, he must go on.'[52] The madness is Birkin's. And yet it has been foreseen—justified in advance—by

---

[49] *WL* 200.   [50] *WL* 244–5.
[51] *Memoirs of my Nervous Illness*, ed. and tr. Ida Macalpine and Richard A. Hunter (London: William Dawson, 1955), 125.
[52] *WL* 247.

Ursula's Schreberian vision. The gender-difference of which Birkin in his hatred of the Magna Mater makes so much is thus the articulation rather than the source of a fantasy of the end of the world. Such supplementarity, mounting one terror upon or within another, constitutes the novel's organic system.

And the chapter has further supplementation to offer. For it is only the reader reading too fast, or the critic not reading fast enough, who remembers it as crystallized out of the event of the stoning. To be sure, something crystallizes, as Birkin considers the implications, for Ursula as well as for himself, of his fantasy's necessary destructiveness. 'And he wanted her to be with him there, in this world of proud indifference.' Her response to him now is the response she had first formulated during his visit to her classroom. '*You—you* are the Sunday school teacher—*you*—you preacher.' The element of truth in the accusation makes him 'stiff and unheeding'. During what remains of the chapter, this truth is pulled into and out of focus by a narrative rhythm at once abstract, in that it performs a recurrent crossing over into paranoia, and organic. A long handwritten addition to the 1916 typescript describes Birkin's discovery of a figure for the 'further sensual experience' he craves in an African carving he had seen in Halliday's London flat, of a woman with a face like a beetle. Birkin associates such immersion in 'purely sensual understanding' with Gerald Crich. For himself, he chooses the world of proud indifference, of suspensiveness, with Ursula in it. He makes his way over to Beldover to propose to her, only to find her indifferent. The calmness of her reception of him prompts the paranoid suspicion that his hopes are to her mere 'accidentals' or 'violations'. After he has departed in a rage, Ursula repeats his lapse into negation, by resuming her intimacy with the relentlessly deprecatory Gudrun; and then she, in her turn, withdraws from negation, and begins to think once again of the life she might make with him.[53] If there is a loveliness and intensity of structure about *Women in Love*, as Williams suggests, it does not have to do with crystal. It has to do with the extent to which the novel is informed, in and from its own expertise as a work of literature, by an understanding of the psychopathies of expertise.

[53] *WL* 250–1, 253–4, 260, 262–5.

THE NEW BOHEMIA

A social group or class Gudrun and Gerald loathe almost as much as Beldover's teeming colliers, and yet cannot stop immersing themselves in, is the London Bohemia which foregathers at the Pompadour, a thinly disguised Café Royal, in chapters 6 and 28. Gerald's first encounter with Bohemia in general, and the Pussum in particular, prompts him, as one might have expected it would, to plunge without delay into 'this silence and this black, electric comprehension in the darkness' (*this* silence, *this* comprehension). Birkin, by contrast, remains immune to Bohemia, even declining a trip to a music-hall. Much later, on their way to Innsbruck via London and Paris, Gerald and Gudrun take in both a music-hall and the Pompadour. Gudrun hates the place, and the people who crowd into it. 'Yet she always called in again, when she was in town. It was as if she *had* to return to this small, slow, central whirlpool of disintegration and dissolution: just give it a look.'[54] We know Gudrun and Gerald by their habit of immersion, and Birkin by his paranoid immunity.

What is most noteworthy about Gerald and Gudrun's visit to the Pompadour in chapter 28 is the depth of the loathing Bohemia inspires in her, even as she cannot tear herself away from it. The loathing was Lawrence's, too. On 1 September 1916, Katherine Mansfield had been in the Café Royal with S. S. Koteliansky and Mark Gertler. A letter of the following day from Gertler to Lady Ottoline Morrell describes how two 'coloured' men and their companion, a redhead, began to talk about 'the new Age' in a 'very advanced manner'. The discussion turned to Lawrence's *Amores*, which had come out in July. Leaning over, Mansfield asked to borrow the book for a moment—and promptly left the room.[55] When told of the incident, Lawrence reacted with horror.[56] The horror is evident enough in Gudrun's contemplation of the scene at the Pompadour. 'And it gave her pleasure to sit there, cheeks flushed, eyes black and sullen, seeing them all objectively, as put away from her, like creatures in some

54 *WL* 73, 80, 380.
55 Gertler's letter is quoted at length in *WL* 571–2.
56 *Letters*, ii. 649–50.

menagerie of apish, degraded souls. God, what a foul crew they were! Her blood beat black and thick in her veins with rage and loathing.' When Julius Halliday begins to read out a letter he has received from Birkin, while the rest of the foul crew make drunken fun of it, Gudrun acts as Katherine Mansfield had done; she seizes the letter, and walks out. The letter denounces the Pompadour set as 'flowers of mud', and at least a part of Gudrun's horror, and Lawrence's, may be a response to *their* denunciation of Birkin as a 'megalomaniac' who thinks he is the 'saviour of man'.[57] We see Birkin's paranoid delusions of grandeur from the outside, as it were, through Gudrun's eyes, just as Lawrence had seen his through Mansfield's. It is Gudrun, here, who becomes Birkin, in her acknowledgement of the persecution to which charismatic expertise has been subjected; but not for very long, since she herself is a flower of mud.

I have tried to draw connections in this book between the paranoia brokered by literary experiment and that brokered by the fantasies informing popular romances of the more sensational kind. I want to suggest now that the intensity of the loathing Gudrun feels for the Pompadour set is not so much an expression as a performance. It *constructs* Bohemia. It is one of many representations in the immediate post-war years of a group or class on whose members the blame for modernity could be laid. A point worth noting about the Café Royal, though it is not one Lawrence makes about the Pompadour, is that it had by this time acquired a certain notoriety as a source for the supply of recreational drugs.[58] To explore that notoriety will take us some way from the events described in *Women in Love*, but not, I think, all that far from the feelings which inform it. Nausea was the making of the new bohemians.

Virginia Berridge has compared the 'construction', in the early years of the twentieth century, of a drug-taking identity and way of life to the construction, during more or less the same period, of a homosexual identity and way of life.[59] Nineteenth-century opium-eaters, from Coleridge and De Quincey to Wilkie Collins,

[57] *WL* 380–6.

[58] It is a notoriety over which the Royal's historians pass lightly: Guy Deghy and Keith Waterhouse, *Café Royal: Ninety Years of Bohemia* (London: Hutchinson, 1955), 143.

[59] 'The Origins of the English Drug "Scene", 1890–1930', *Medical History*, 32 (1988), 51–64.

did not attract the kind of public anxiety and disapproval which would have consolidated their habit and its effects into a way of life, a subculture. Experimentation with opium, hashish, and mescal in turn-of-the-century Decadence was more than a habit, but less than an identity; it was one way among several to be occult, or avant-garde, or more Parisian than the Parisians.[60] It aroused little public anxiety and disapproval, and thus did not provoke the formation of a subculture.

Morphia, which became a recreational drug in bohemian circles in England during the 1890s, seemed more of a threat. Bernard Shaw once scolded the actress Janet Achurch for reverting to her deceitful, 'heavy lidded, morphia injecting self': he advised her to eat stewed fruit and Hovis.[61] Other cures on offer at the time included Turkish baths, hot water enemas, and turtle soup. The novelists were not slow to exploit the possibilities offered by such heavy-liddedness. In Robert Hichens's *Felix* (1903), the rather dim hero falls in love with an older woman, Mrs Ismey, who has an expensive morphia habit to keep up, and exploits his infatuation to that end. The first sign of trouble to come is an unscheduled visit to a chemist in Wigmore Street. While Mrs Ismey rings at the back door, Felix has time to pay nauseous attention to some litter sent 'creeping' across the pavement by a gust of wind, 'like a livid thing that was alive'.[62] The chemist is Mrs Ismey's supplier.[63]

There is in such representations the outline of a drug-taking identity, of a subculture. Mrs Ismey, for example, was introduced

---

[60] Thus, a magazine as respectable as the *Cornhill* was quite happy to publish an (admittedly anonymous) article about hashish. The article describes a somewhat unorthodox breakfast taken in the elegant Paris home of 'the celebrated Dr M —'. Those assembled are merely 'guests', with not a drug-taking identity among them— and the celebrated doctor declares that hashish is, among other things, a 'sovereign remedy for epilepsy': 'Hachisch Eating', *Cornhill Magazine*, NS 22 (1894), 500–5, p. 502.

[61] Berridge, 'Origins', 58.

[62] *Felix: Three Years in a Life* (London: Methuen, 1903), 163. Beatrice Blair, the heroine of Mary Lake's *The Drug Slave*, has read *Felix*, and suspects that her future husband, Raymond Midhurst, is about to go the same way as Mrs Ismey. 'As I stood watching his tall, graceful figure by the table, a queer feeling swept over me, bringing all sorts of ugly, slimy fears in its wake.' Midhurst turns out to be addicted to morphia and cocaine: *The Drug Slave* (London: Cassell, 1913), 2, 4, 28.

[63] According to Alisteir Crowley, Hichens based this obliging chemist on one E. P. Whineray, who owned a shop in Stafford Street and 'knew all the secrets of London': *The Confessions of Alisteir Crowley: An Autohagiography*, ed. John Symonds and Kenneth Grant (London: Routledge & Kegan Paul, 1979), 546.

to the habit by Lady Caroline Hurst, who injects not only herself, but her maid, and even, much to the hero's disgust, her dog. Mrs Ismey describes a visit the two women once made to a 'morphia club' in Paris.[64] George Sims's *The Devil in London* (1908) includes a description of a 'morphia club' for women known as 'The Rosalind', whose members always dressed in male attire: we learn that the club disbanded when the President, a 'woman of quite a serious turn of mind', told members to wear their hair cut short.[65] Hichens and Sims clearly associate drug-taking with a particular social group (upper-class, intellectual) and with a particular style of life. The gendering of these morphia narratives was further reinforced by avid attention to the body of the addict. Morphia was ordinarily injected, and as a result addicts became known as 'needle-dancers'. Mrs Ismey reports that in the Paris club one *morphineuse* had 'torn open all the front of her gown'. Mrs Ismey herself will never be able to wear a low dress again; the hero feels 'physically sick' when he learns that she has become so careless she sometimes forgets to remove the needle.[66] The pitted breast and arms of the *morphineuse* became a key element in the iconography of needle-dancing. Thus the track-marks on the arm of Julie Thibaud, a chemist's daughter, in Rita's *Queer Lady Judas* (1905), are hideously inflamed and discoloured; these stigmata extend yet further the novel's already vivid interest in the permeability of women's bodies, in skin 'clogged with paint and powder and dirt'.[67]

Needle-dancing seems to have remained a discreet upper-class habit.[68] There was little sense that recreational drug-taking constituted a social problem. Neither medicine, in the form of

---

[64] *Felix*, 379, 289–95.

[65] *The Devil in London* (London: Stanley Paul, 1908), 139–40.

[66] *Felix*, 293, 360. A morphia addict in Mary Cholmondeley's 'The Lowest Rung' speaks of the 'infernal machine' necessary to the habit: *The Lowest Rung* (London: John Murray, 1908), 64.

[67] *Queer Lady Judas* (London: Hutchinson, 1905), 166–8, 14.

[68] In Dec. 1915, Lady Diana Manners described to Raymond Asquith, the Prime Minister's son, how she had injected herself and Asquith's wife, Katharine, with morphia. 'O the grave difficulty of the actual injection, the sterilizing in the dark and silence, and the conflict of my hand and wish when it came to piercing our flesh. It was a grand night, and strange to feel so utterly self-sufficient . . .': Philip Ziegler, *Diana Cooper* (London: Hamish Hamilton, 1981), 54–5, quoted by Berridge, 'Origins', 61. Lawrence had met Katharine Asquith the previous July, and liked her, though apparently not to the point of mutual confidences: Kinkead-Weekes, *Triumph to Exile*, 255.

theories of addiction, nor law, in the form of bans and penalties, had as yet declared against it. In Britain, it was the arrival of cocaine during and immediately after the First World War, at a time of mingled unease and exhilaration, which changed attitudes once and for all. Regulation 40B, passed under the Defence of the Realm Act in 1916, severely restricted the availability of opium and cocaine. The 1920 and 1923 Dangerous Drugs Acts introduced more widespread controls. Prosecutions under the 1920 Act reveal that there were three distinct groups of drug-takers: immigrants of Chinese origin, who favoured opium; an older generation of morphine addicts, many of whom had initially been prescribed the drug for medical purposes; and cocaine-users.[69] Cocaine, too, had long been prescribed for medical purposes.[70] But the so-called cocaine epidemic of 1916, when prostitutes were caught selling the drug to soldiers, aroused fears that recreational use would undermine military discipline.[71] In June 1916, the *Evening News* ran a number of pieces about the development of a 'cocaine craze' or 'cocaine curse' in the bohemian *demi-monde*. The writer worried that the habit might render soldiers 'useless to the army', but also found time to contemplate its effect on women.[72] From the

---

[69] For analysis of the figures for prosecutions under the Acts, see H. B. Spear, 'The Growth of Heroin Addiction in the United Kingdom', *British Journal of Addiction*, 64 (1969), 245–55; and Terry Parssinen, *Secret Passions, Secret Remedies* (Manchester: MUP, 1988), 163–8.

[70] The curative properties of the coca leaf, long familiar in the great South American civilizations, began to attract widespread medical interest in Europe and North America in the 1870s. The first (1885) volume of the *British Medical Journal* contained sixty-seven separate pieces on cocaine, the wonder-drug of the *fin de siècle*. The Parisian chemist and entrepreneur Angelo Mariani successfully sold coca extract as Vin Mariani. In the 13 vols. of *Figures contemporaines* drawn from his album, portraits and brief biographies accompany autograph testimonials to 'la gloire de la Coca en bouteille' from over 500 celebrities: *Figures contemporaines tirées de l'album Mariani* (Paris: Ernest Flammarion, 1894–1913). Coca extract was also available in cigarettes, sprays, ointments, lozenges, and, of course, Coca-Cola. Mrs Humphry Ward relied on cocaine for relief from her many ailments; she once said that she had survived a particularly nerve-wracking public lecture only 'thanks to cocaine, egg and port and other amenities': John Sutherland, *Mrs Humphry Ward: Eminent Victorian, Pre-eminent Edwardian* (Oxford: Clarendon Press, 1990), 211–12. For a useful survey, see Lester Grinspoon and James B. Bakalar, *Cocaine: A Drug and its Social Evolution*, rev. edn. (New York: Basic Books, 1985).

[71] Virginia Berridge, 'War Conditions and Narcotics Control: The Passing of the Defence of the Realm Act Regulation 40B', *Journal of Social Policy*, 1 (1978), 285–304.

[72] *Evening News* (13 June 1916), 3; (15 June 1916), 1. In July 1916, the *Umpire*

moment of its arrival, cocaine appears to have required the construction not just of a drug-taking identity, but of a subculture: a *demi-monde* whose susceptibility to it was evidence of degeneracy, and thus a grave threat to society at large.[73]

Cocaine's penetration of Bohemia was given dramatic focus by the death of the young actress Billie Carleton, in the early hours of 28 November 1918, and in the aftermath, ironically, of victory celebrations at the Royal Albert Hall, from a drug overdose of some kind. One of Carleton's associates, Reggie De Veulle, a shady man-about-town, was subsequently accused of conspiring to supply her with cocaine, and of manslaughter; he pleaded guilty to the first charge, and was acquitted of the second.[74] The inquest and trial provoked a moral panic: that is, the perception of particular acts of deviancy as the symptom of a widespread social malaise. The war had been won, but only just; the winning of it had exposed weaknesses in the social order, and drawn attention to a variety of enemies within, from the profiteer to the pacifist. One did not have to look too hard for striking evidence of malaise. The Carleton case encouraged further scrutiny.

Moral panic found its voice in a series of front-page articles in the *Daily Express*. On 29 November 1918, the paper reported Carleton's death from an overdose. Eight days later, it launched a crusade against the new designer drug.

VICTIMS OF THE DRUG HABIT
ALARMING GROWTH MAINLY AMONG WOMEN
DENS OF INIQUITY

Evidence given at the coroner's inquest into the death of Billie Carleton had revealed the 'alarming growth' of the drug habit, particularly among young women in London. Opium, morphia, heroin, hashish, and cocaine were easily available in cafés and on the streets. The context proposed for the alarming growth of the

---

reported that London had taken over from New York, Paris, and Berlin as the mecca for 'needle dancers' (morphia addicts) and 'dope fiends'. Cocaine was readily available from chemists in the Charing Cross area: *The Umpire* (23 July 1916), 3.

[73] For an update on this particular campaign, see Jimmie Reeves and Richard Campbell, *Cracked Coverage: Television News, the Anti-Cocaine Crusade, and the Reagan Legacy* (Durham, NC: Duke University Press, 1994).

[74] For an excellent account of this and other comparable cases, see Marek Kohn's *Dope Girls: The Birth of the British Drug Scene* (London: Lawrence & Wishart, 1992).

drug habit was the war. 'War has increased the nervous tension of the individual to an unheard-of degree. Men and women alike have craved a change from the dead normal to the fantastic and rare.' War is represented as the final turn of modernity's screw. The nervousness and craving for abnormality which are its product have in turn produced a new social group. 'The drug takers and the missionaries of dope are the people of the "border-line". They are not outcasts; they style themselves Bohemian; and the curse of the dope fiend is this—they are ever ready to drag down others with them into the pit.'[75]

In a second article, published two days later, the emphasis again falls on women, and on intermediacy. Female addicts are said to be the 'missionaries' of a crime network which involves drugs, prostitution, and gambling. 'Ten years ago there was a definite hard-and-fast line between the woman of this class and the ordinary bohemian woman artist, actress, or writer. Today it is not easy to distinguish the dividing-line.' Ambiguity, in-betweenness, marginality: it is the absence of definition which defines the cocaine-user. If opium-smokers confined themselves to East End dens, and needle-dancers to Parisian morphia clubs, the female cocaine fiend was to be found throughout fashionable London, in Chelsea, Mayfair, and Maida Vale. 'An obscure traffic is pursued in certain doubtful teashops. The sale of certain beauty specifics is only a mask for the illicit traffic in drugs.' The subculture thus constituted is at once hidden and systematic, or pervasive. 'A young and attractive girl deeply interested in social conditions and political economy made the acquaintance of another woman through a mutual friend. Within three months she had become a confirmed haunter of a certain notorious café. She had lost her looks and health.' The testimony of experts, of solicitors and 'medical men', is invoked to demonstrate the threat drugs pose to respectable middle-class families: to daughters, in particular. 'The queer, bizarre, rather brilliant bachelor girl is a frequent victim to the insidious advances of the female dope fiend.'[76] Cocaine-use could thus be understood as a fallibility of the New Woman, of the woman who had renounced femininity. The 'morphia club' described by George Sims, where women both dope and cross-

[75] *Daily Express* (7 Dec. 1918), 1.   [76] *Daily Express* (9 Dec. 1918), 1.

dress, has undergone a metamorphosis (or metastasis): it now exists as a network of sites and seductions stretching from one end of fashionable society to the other.

The concept of intermediacy made it possible to identify the dope fiend as a new kind of bohemian, socially, sexually, and racially amorphous. In January 1919, an article in the *Empire News* provided a lurid account of a party in what had once been an artist's studio in the 'No Man's Land' of Chelsea. A Spaniard wearing make-up dances with a half-naked woman. Of the seventy or so 'masqueraders', about a dozen are of 'unidentifiable sex'. 'There were men dressed as girls so like that one hesitated to say they were men . . . There were girls dressed as youths.' The writer attributes this blurring of genders to 'woman's war adoption of breeches'.[77] He does not seem to have noticed any doping. The point is, however, that moral panic had by now attributed to the new social class a set of defining features—an essence (intermediacy), a location (Chelsea)—which might or might not include particular activities (doping, homosexuality). Anxiety about one form of transgression fed into anxiety about another.[78] Chelsea is where Gudrun Brangwen had settled when studying at art-school and generally living the 'studio life'.

These defining features took on an even more colourful existence in popular fiction. The heroine of Lady Dorothy Mills's *The Laughter of Fools* (1920), a weak young woman drawn into a bohemian circle known as the 'Binge Club', does visit an opium den in Limehouse; but most of the doping takes place in the Chelsea studio of a Futurist painter.[79] The one novel based directly on the Carleton case, Sax Rohmer's *Dope* (1919), dwells on mixture, on the proliferation of social and racial hybridity. Its heroine, Rita Dresden, an actress, dopes in order to calm her nerves. Dresden graduates from veronal and cocaine to opium, prompted by 'a false vanity which urged her to do everything that was "done" by the ultra-smart and vicious set of which she had

---

[77] *Empire News* (19 Jan. 1919), 2.

[78] Thus, in July 1916, the *Umpire*, the previous incarnation of the *Empire News*, had enthusiastically followed up reports about the 'drug craze' (23 and 30 July, 16 Aug.) with reports about 'unnatural vice' and 'men-women' (20 and 27 Aug.).

[79] *The Laughter of Fools* (London: Duckworth, 1920), 125.

become a member'.[80] Ada Lau Ping, the Scotswoman with a
Chinese husband who supplied Carleton and her friends, reappears
in the novel as Mrs Lola Sin, a 'Cuban-Jewess', the very epitome
of displacement. Rohmer's best inventions are the several resorts
of the set to which Dresden belongs, each one a vortex of hybridity. There is, for example, the Soho night-club where 'women
entitled to wear coronets' dance with 'men entitled to wear the
broad arrow'; or the upper room in a Shaftesbury Avenue restau-
rant run by a 'suave alien', whose occupants are mostly 'unclassi-
fiable', and include 'a masculine-looking lady who had apparently
come straight off a golf course, and who later was proved to be a
well-known advocate of women's rights'.[81]

The novelists found a way to describe cocaine-use in a genre
well adapted to the hybrid and the intermediate, the vampire-tale.
David Garnett's *Dope Darling: A Story of Cocaine* (1919), set during
the First World War, concerns the seduction of a young medical
student and war-hero, Roy Gordon, by a beautiful bohemian,
Claire Plowman; he is eventually redeemed by the love of a fellow
student, Beatrice Chase. The novel's most memorable moments
are those in which Claire begs Roy for cocaine. 'Her face was
convulsed with rage, distorted beyond recognition. She gnashed
her teeth like an animal in a trap, and rolled her eyes wildly.' A
sniff transforms her. 'Claire had never before looked so lovely, so
wonderful, so adorable. "Come here," he said. She came to him
with an almost passionate reasonableness.'[82] Whew! Garnett
admired this effect so much that he had Beatrice, too, provoke the
vampire in Claire by denying her. 'Her lips were bluish, her eyes
positively blazed in the dark street. There was something tigerish
in her movements and in her anger.' Cocaine to Claire, evidently,
is like blood to Count Dracula. Lawrence had first met Garnett in
the summer of 1912, in Germany, and became very fond of him.
Garnett's bisexuality led to an estrangement, and their final
encounter was at an Armistice party on 11 November 1918,
during which Lawrence declared that the hatred men still held in

---

[80] *Dope: A Story of Chinatown and the Drug Traffic* (London: Cassell, 1919), 86–7. In
1919 there was a spate of West End plays based on the case: Philip Hoare, *Noel
Coward: A Biography* (London: Sinclair-Stevenson, 1995), 75–6.
[81] Ibid. 182, 186.
[82] *Dope Darling: A Story of Cocaine* (London: T. Werner Laurie, 1919), 119.

their hearts would soon break out again, in forms far worse than open warfare.[83] Garnett's novel has something of that jeremiad in it, in the horror it expresses at the damage done to society by the vampirism of doping.

These novels construct the new Bohemia in and through expressions of disgust. Disgust maps the threat posed by social, sexual, and racial intermediacy onto manifestations of physical intermediacy: dirt, disfigurement, animality. The 'editor' of the diaries which form the basis of G. P. Robinson's *Testament* (1922) claims that they reveal their author to have been, 'as he always claimed, an abnormal personality'. The diarist, Gordon Sumner, describes how he was introduced to morphia by a handsome but 'unclean' Jew, in 1913, at a self-consciously bohemian party in Chelsea. Wartime adventures and the love of a good woman fail to break the habit. His subsequent decline is etched in physicality, in pollution. The chemist who supplies him with morphia is 'a fat surreptitious man with damp hands which left splodges of moisture on the glass cases of the counter'. Damp hands are the least of the problems which afflict Gordon's brother, Humphrey, a cocaine fiend and homosexual. Arriving at Humphrey's flat, Gordon finds the tapestries in the hall 'torn and stained', and a fine Persian rug burnt and strewn with cigarette butts. The bedroom, where his brother lies dying, proves even worse, a foretaste of his own miserable end. 'The floor was littered with dirty clothing and dyed with a large blood-stain as of a recent haemorrhage. There were also other details too loathsome to set down.'[84] The new (drug-taking, homosexual) bohemian is thus produced rhetorically as an object not of pity or contempt, but of nausea.

In Alisteir Crowley's *The Diary of a Drug Fiend* (1922), yet another war-hero, Peter Pendragon, a flying ace, falls in with bohemians, and the seductive Lou Laleham. At a party in Chelsea (inevitably), a sinister German woman introduces him to cocaine (in revenge, he suspects, for the German airmen he killed during the war). Peter and Lou enjoy an ecstatic 'cocaine honeymoon' in Paris. Like Claire Plowman, in *Dope Darling*, Lou Laleham on

---

[83] Kinkead-Weekes, *Triumph to Exile*, 29–30, 481.
[84] *Testament: The Confessions of a Drug-Taker* (London: Duckworth, 1922), 67, 257, 109.

coke is utterly radiant. 'She represented the siren, the vampire . . .' For the Pendragons, cocaine is, as it had been for Crowley himself, a way to overcome inhibition, a way to suppress disgust at the body. 'Until you've got your mouth full of cocaine, you don't know what kissing is. One kiss goes on from phase to phase like one of those novels by Balzac and Zola and Romain Rolland and D. H. Lawrence and those chaps. And you never get tired!'[85]

Serial novels by those chaps, including *Women in Love*, tended to go on 'from phase to phase' in a uniformly downward direction. The Pendragons' cocaine honeymoon duly comes to an end when they discover heroin. With heroin, mess returns. 'I had a sudden nauseating sense', Pendragon observes, 'of the bestiality of marriage.' The toxic effects of morphia and heroin destroy the body. Foul sweats break out, and 'there is a smell and a taste which cannot be called unpleasant even, it can only be called abominable in the proper sense of that word: that which is repugnant to man'.[86] Pendragon invokes the false etymology of abomination, which derives it not from *ab omine* (ill-omened), but from *ab homine* (repugnant to humankind). His etymology, false or not, ensures that the body's stains (its permeable surfaces, its stench) will once again express a vivid anxiety about the proliferation of hybridity. Peter and Lou are saved, in the end, by a magus who exhorts them to discipline themselves, and to enter into a spiritual marriage.

Towards the end of *Testament*, Gordon Sumner, who has been recovering from his wounds in the country, returns to London to score some drugs. His first port of call is the Café Robespierre— that is, of course, the Café Royal—whose 'conscientiously ragged' clientele looks as though it might include a dealer or two.[87] It is here that Peter Pendragon, in *Diary of a Drug Fiend*, meets Lou Laleham. Crowley's description of the clientele, which includes a number of easily recognizable figures, is notable for its violence. A character based on Lord Alfred Douglas resembles 'some filthy creature of the darkness'. 'At his heels lumbered his jackal, a huge, bloated, verminous creature like a cockroach, in shabby black clothes, ill-fitting, unbrushed and stained, his linen dirty . . .' There is the usual cast of aliens. 'One of the men was a fat German

[85] *The Diary of a Drug Fiend* (London: W. Collins, 1922), 47, 50, 55.
[86] Ibid. 61, 249.   [87] *Testament*, 232.

Jew, who looked at first sight like a piece of canned pork that has got mislaid too long in the summer.' The women are even worse. One of them, like the woman who had so repelled Katherine Mansfield, is a redhead. She reminds the easily nauseated Pendragon of a 'white maggot'. 'She exuded corruption.'[88] None of these people plays an important part in the story. But their dirt, dishevelment, and bestiality identify them as members of a Bohemia whose hidden depravities may yet do more damage to English society than open warfare. The closeness of Gudrun Brangwen's fear and loathing in the Pompadour to Peter Pendragon's in the Robespierre might tempt one to speculate about the part played by moral panic in the radical literary experiment whose purpose was to establish Lawrence as a charismatic professional. The paranoid critique of social mimesis which by 1920 had become one of the ways in which English culture reflected upon itself informs that experiment through and through.

[88] *Diary of a Drug Fiend*, 8, 13–14.

CHAPTER 9

Wyndham Lewis's Professions

FOR BETTER OR for worse this book has by now developed a certain momentum, and it is tempting to press on at once to the obvious conclusion: that Wyndham Lewis's work of the 1920s is the outcome and fulfilment of the habits of mind analysed in previous chapters, in short, of 'paranoid Modernism'. It would, indeed, be rather odd if a book about paranoia, of all things, were wilfully to reverse or dissipate its own delusion of reference, its burgeoning belief that the evidence has a single story to tell. So I shall press on.

Lewis himself did much to endow such a belief with plausibility. During the 1920s, he conducted flamboyant campaigns both against Bloomsbury amateurism and against what he thought of as the bogus or pointless expertise of erstwhile allies like Pound and Joyce. The purpose of the antagonistic or 'Enemy' stance thus exasperatedly taken was no more and no less than to define and assert a charismatic professional identity.[1] Furthermore, the polemics which absorbed so much of his time and energy resume the critique of social mimesis put forward by writers like Dickens and Mill, broadening it to encompass consumer capitalism's newest and most penetrative strategies (advertisement, fashion). Lewis thought, as Dickens and Mill had as yet no reason to, that the paranoid symmetry which so bristlingly informed the 'Enemy' stance was the only alternative to social mimesis, and thus the only instrument available for the definition of a valid (non-soviet, non-fascist) postliberal politics. Much of the fiction he published during the 1920s is in some sense 'about' paranoia; and it develops, uniquely and to compelling effect, a paranoid Modernist style.

Before pressing on, however, I want to consider more fully

---

[1] For an account of these manœuvres, see Sue Ellen Campbell, *The Enemy Opposite: The Outlaw Criticism of Wyndham Lewis* (Athens, Ohio: Ohio University Press, 1988).

what is at stake in any such precipitation. My argument will be that Lewis's paranoid Modernist style was both productive and diagnostic, and that it remains the source of whatever value we might continue to find in his literary writings. It would be foolish to make these claims without first establishing the terms in which the question of value has been put in recent criticism. That the question has been put, and that it will stay put, is the achievement of Paul Edwards's massive *Wyndham Lewis: Painter and Writer*.[2] That it cannot now be answered without reference to Lewis's life, as well as to his art, is the achievement of Paul O'Keeffe's biography, of which I have already made use.[3]

TOE-JAM

The day he first met Wyndham Lewis, shortly after the end of the First World War, Ernest Hemingway was teaching Ezra Pound how to box. The encounter took place in Paris, where Pound had a studio, and Lewis, impassive beneath his trademark wide black hat, seemed content to watch in silence. 'Ezra had not been boxing very long and I was embarrassed at having him work in front of anyone he knew, and I tried to make him look as good as possible.' So wide was the margin between master and pupil, both in musculature and in technique, that Hemingway could without difficulty refrain from doing his opponent any damage. Lewis, he felt sure, wanted to see Pound hurt. He was careful not to oblige. 'I never countered but kept Ezra moving after me sticking out his left hand and throwing a few right hands and then said we were through and washed down with a pitcher of water and toweled off and put on my sweatshirt.'[4]

What is startling about Hemingway's recollection of the event is the way in which it uses all this washing down and toweling off

---

[2] *Wyndham Lewis: Painter and Writer* (New Haven, Conn.: Yale University Press, 2000). For reasons of space, I have had to confine myself in this book to Lewis's writing. Edwards's study is the first analysis of Lewis's career as a whole to give equal weight to the writing and the painting, and it thereby sets a standard. A case could be made, I think, for a painterly paranoia; but it is a case whose terms would require careful elaboration and testing.

[3] *Some Sort of Genius: A Life of Wyndham Lewis* (London: Jonathan Cape, 2000).

[4] *A Moveable Feast* (New York: Touchstone, 1996), 109.

as the basis for an assault on Lewis's character. Hemingway remembers himself as *clean*, above all; and clean, furthermore, after his carefully controlled exertions, in a thoroughly modern way. Lewis, on the other hand, wearing the kind of bohemian 'uniform' favoured by the 'prewar artist', remains somehow archaic and unsalubrious. 'Walking home I tried to think what he reminded me of and there were various things. They were all medical except toe-jam.' Lewis is dirt, then, or perhaps an abortion. 'Under the black hat, when I had first seen them, the eyes had been those of an unsuccessful rapist.'[5] There might presumably have been some hope for Lewis had his eyes merely been those of a *successful* rapist.

In *Blasting and Bombardiering*, Lewis describes a visit to Pound's Paris studio. No one answered his knock, but the door was open, so he went in.

A splendidly built young man, stripped to the waist, and with a torso of dazzling white, was standing not far from me. He was tall, handsome, and serene, and was repelling with his boxing gloves a hectic assault of Ezra's. After a final swing at the dazzling solar plexus Pound fell back upon his settee. The young man was Hemingway. Pound got on like a house on fire with this particular statue.[6]

By comparison with Hemingway's, Lewis's description of the event is coolness itself. It does subtle damage to Hemingway by not discerning in him the agency or control over events his undeniable physical superiority might be thought to have generated. By this account, it is Pound, rather than Hemingway, who brings the bout to a conclusion; and he does so by falling back on a settee— a fixture not ordinarily available in the average gymnasium for the use of wobbly punters. Statuesque or prone, neither protagonist is left with much of a leg to stand on.

And yet there is in the description's coolness a certain residual heat. The stance Lewis favoured was not in fact one of detachment. He liked to get up close, in the world's face. Immediacy mattered to him. A vivid trace often survives in his writing of the impulse which gave rise to it. Here, for example, he makes no effort to avoid the cliché of the house on fire. The cliché is his first thought about Pound's fondness for Hemingway, we are allowed

⁵ *A Moveable Feast*, 109.
⁶ *Blasting and Bombardiering* (London: Calder & Boyars, 1967), 277.

to think, and the first thought will do. It will do, however, not just because it fills space, but because its familiarity in general terms is also its diagnostic value in this particular context: Pound merits a cliché because he has *become* a cliché, a walking susceptibility. Such fusions of impulse and diagnosis are the hallmark of Lewis's writing at its best. They also got him into a lot of trouble.

Paul O'Keeffe's life of Lewis does not hold back on the toe-jam. *Some Sort of Genius* is among other things a compendium of the many reasons people found to dislike its subject. Lewis became, sometimes by circumstance, sometimes by design, the sponsor of a wide range of opportunities for fear and loathing. Women were especially favoured in this respect. O'Keeffe observes that in all his relationships with women Lewis sought to present the image of a man with no attachments or encumbrances. The 'models' available to him included his father, a swashbuckling veteran of the American Civil War who made a habit of infidelity, and eventually left his wife for good in 1901, when Lewis was 18; and Augustus John, his celebrated predecessor at the Slade, whom he sought assiduously to emulate, and whose ever-varying seraglio became an object of fascination. But Lewis's presentation of himself, to women, and to the men with whom he conferred about women, had a polemical edge to it, a toxicity entirely lacking, as far as one can tell, in John's sexual munificence. From an early age, Lewis cultivated what one might term anti-pathos: a strategic, rather than a merely tactical or opportunist, avoidance of sentiment. This strategy was to manifest itself in his art as a preference for the abstract, in his writing as a preference for satire and invective, and in his politics as a tough-mindedness shading almost imperceptibly into advocacy of tough action.

One of the few testimonials which survive from Lewis's relationship with Iris Barry, with whom he lived from 1918 to 1921, is a telegram handed in to the Leicester Square Post Office at 3.35 p.m. on 2 June 1920: PLEASE PREPARE CHOP EIGHT—LEWIS. Barry used its reverse as a shopping-list. As she cooked Lewis's steak and onions, that night, she was also preparing the second of their two children. The pregnancy had been his idea, or so she claimed. She had been made to feel that a second child (the paternity of the first was in some doubt) would be irrefutable proof of her commitment to him. By early August, at any rate, Barry had installed herself in the Nursing Institute at Mitcham, in South London. Lewis, however, was nowhere to be seen. 'The distance is very great', he complained, 'and you are awkward to get at.' After all, he had a studio to find, and a patron for a new journal. Lonely, a little scared, and at a loss what to do about the imminent arrival, Barry pleaded with him at least to let her know where he was. He had already left London for a fortnight's holiday in France with T. S. Eliot.[7]

This holiday has since become a part of Modernist folklore. It was the occasion upon which, at Pound's behest, Eliot delivered a parcel containing a pair of old brown shoes to a distinctly unappreciative James Joyce. The shoes apart, Eliot was having a good time. He considered Lewis the most profitable person he had had to talk to for a long time. In Saumur, Lewis fell off his bicycle, and was soon looking for someone to sue. When, appeased by a row with the proprietor of the cycle shop, he got back to Paris—Eliot was meanwhile on a tour of Gothic churches—he found Barry's letter awaiting him. Replying on 28 August, he said that he wasn't yet sure about his movements. He seems to have been in no great hurry to proceed to Mitcham. 'I don't suppose you will void your foetus for several weeks yet', he cajoled; he would make arrangements about the child on his return. The harshness is clearly a demonstration, a performance, albeit one in which it is hard to tell the dancer from the dance. A telegram dispatched the same day was more encouraging. Lewis told Barry not to worry, and sent his love. Maisie Wyndham was born on 1 September. Neither parent was to have much to do with her upbringing.[8]

The rehearsal of anti-pathos is not, of course, all there was to Lewis, even if his behaviour as a young man left room for little else. O'Keeffe is able to demonstrate what love meant to him, and friendship.[9] But the information he has amassed provides ample evidence of the deliberate cultivation in the life of the attitudes which shape the art and the writing. Anti-pathos was not just the condition of Lewis's work as a writer and artist, the source of its

---

[7] *Some Sort of Genius*, 218–21.   [8] Ibid. 222–6.

[9] Lewis was capable of spontaneous acts of generosity, such as the unstinting support he offered Denis Williams, a 26-year-old Guyanese painter, in 1949. 'Rarely', O'Keeffe observes, 'did Lewis act in anybody's exclusive interest but his own.' In this case, he did. He wrote admiringly about Williams's work, and found him a job at the Central School of Arts and Crafts, in Southampton Row: *Some Sort of Genius*, 547–8.

nourishment, but one of its dominant qualities. The work is inconceivable apart from an understanding of the antagonisms which in its making fused impulse to diagnosis.

The medium in which the attitudes which shape the art and the writing were themselves shaped was that not just of a life, but of a career. It is there that the diagnoses were most impulsively made, and impulse became diagnostic. For in his Modernist phase, in particular, from around 1908 to around 1930, Lewis continually changed direction, sometimes in accordance with his understanding of the market, but more often prompted by an obstinate will-to-experiment. He sought to reinvent himself, to make himself new, by mutations of mode and emphasis. He switched from genre to genre and medium to medium, supplying the lack of a will-to-experiment in one from its over-abundance in another. In his Modernist phase, Lewis effectively became, for the purposes of literary and artistic revolution, a serial careerist.

Before and during the war, avant-gardes had made quite a splash, even in England. After the war, however, Lewis's expectations that he might be able to emulate in England the critical and commercial success Picasso had achieved in France soon faded. He had always attributed his own relative lack of success to the deficiencies of the culture in which he found himself operating, and in 1924 he set art and literature aside in order to concentrate on a systematic analysis of those deficiencies. The neglect endured by genius in the modern world is a constant theme in books like *The Art of Being Ruled* (1926) and *Time and Western Man* (1927). The former attributes post-war revolutions in attitude and lifestyle to monopoly capitalism's insatiable appetite for markets; the latter examines the deepening connections between the emergence of a consumer society and developments in modern literature and philosophy.

When Edwards claims that Lewis's polemical writings constitute 'a permanent insight into the nature of modernity', I am very nearly ready to believe him.[10] The reservation has to do with the trace in the arguments they mount of an impulse which might be regarded as mildly psychotic. Lewis meant *The Art of Being Ruled* as a survival guide, an antidote to Machiavelli. So intent was he on

[10] *Wyndham Lewis*, 316.

tough-mindedness, however, on a thoroughgoing decontamination of liberal pieties, that he came to regard the imminence of fascist rule with an equanimity which could easily be mistaken (and was mistaken) for endorsement.[11] Equally disturbing, in its way, is the first of two chapters about the work of Ezra Pound in *Time and Western Man*.[12] Lewis begins by recalling the generosity and grace Pound had unfailingly shown towards him whenever he was in need of help. He then declares that for the purposes of his 'new enterprise' he must henceforth dissociate himself altogether from his erstwhile ally and benefactor, now exposed as a 'revolutionary simpleton' and a parasite on genuine talent. The critique, although by no means unperceptive, has an edge to it which derives from the satisfaction Lewis so obviously took in not being grateful.

In 1921, Lewis had embarked on another ambitious project, a Rabelaisian fictional anatomy of post-war Britain. Two hefty portions, held back by his skirmishes with consumer capitalism, finally achieved publication at the end of the decade: *The Childermass* (1928), a work of theological science fiction set in an encampment of the dead on the banks of the River Styx; and *The Apes of God* (1930), a satire on amateurism in general, and Bloomsbury in particular. Lewis also renewed his Vorticist creed by revising *Tarr*, in 1928, and by collecting his early Breton sketches and essays, in much-altered form, as *The Wild Body* (1927).

Anti-pathos finds a name in these works: satire, laughter, the absurd. Laughter, Lewis explained in 'Inferior Religions', *The Wild Body*'s scintillating manifesto, is the 'brain-body's snort of exultation'. Laughter at once acknowledges and expresses, or performs, since it is 'all that remains physical in the flash of thought', the idea that the absurdity of the human condition is not relative—the product, sometimes comic, sometimes tragic, of social and cultural difference—but absolute. For Lewis, laughter is what being might look like from the point of view of non-being;

---

[11] 'In ten years a state will have been built in which at last no trace of european "liberalism" or its accompanying democratic "liberty" exists. This will have been the creation of a tyrant or dictator, with virtual powers of life and death: for with his highly disciplined, implicitly obedient, fascist bands, no person anywhere will be able to escape assassination if he causes trouble to the central government, or holds, too loudly, opinions that displease it': *The Art of Being Ruled*, ed. Reed Way Dasenbrock (Santa Rosa, Calif.: Black Sparrow Press, 1989), 322.

[12] *Time and Western Man* (London: Chatto & Windus, 1927), ch. 9.

and antagonism, which puts being at risk, is the primary cause of laughter. 'The opposing armies in the early days in Flanders stuck up dummy-men on poles for their enemies to pot at, in a spirit of ferocious banter.' The fiction of the 1920s indefatigably keeps non-being's point of view in mind by means of a kind of prose impasto: a poultice or compress of descriptive detail applied to human existence in order to draw out its fundamental absurdity, its basis in antagonism. The main casualty of these convulsive literary mantraps is the idea of 'character' as a steadily deepening awareness of self and world. One might find a precedent for them in Rabelais, perhaps, or in that noted Vorticist firebrand, Charles Dickens. But Lewis's concoctions have a pungency all their own. The account in 'Bestre', one of the *Wild Body* stories, of a woman whose 'nodular pink veil' is an 'apoplectic gristle' round her stormy brow has stayed in my mind ever since I first read it thirty years ago.[13]

On 16 November 1930, Lewis travelled to Berlin to find a German publisher for *The Apes of God*. Two months before, the German people had elected 107 National Socialists to the Reichstag. The National Socialist German Workers' Party could now claim 17.5 per cent of the total vote, second only to the Social Democrats' 21.9 per cent. Lewis watched from a balcony in the Berlin Sportpalast as Goebbels and Göring held forth to a crowd of 20,000. In the world's face, as ever, he also took in the lavish decadence of late Weimar democracy, checking for himself the stubble on the chins of the transvestites. On his return to London, unable to resist such an opportunity for diagnosis on a world-historical scale, he wrote the first study in any language of Adolf Hitler and the rise of National Socialism. His motive was to create tolerance in Britain for this latest continental manifestation of authoritarian doctrine, and he therefore argued that Nazi anti-Semitism was a mere sideshow, a 'racial red-herring'. The book brought him a visit from Dr Hans-Wilhelm Thost, English correspondent for the *Völkischer Beobachter* and *Der Angriff*, and a spy, who thought it 'not at all bad for an Englishman', but rather misleading where the *Judenfrage* was concerned.[14] Its argument

---

[13] *The Complete Wild Body*, ed. Bernard Lafourcade (Santa Barbara, Calif.: Black Sparrow Press, 1982), 152–3, 77: henceforth *CWB*.

[14] O'Keeffe, *Some Sort of Genius*, 296–303.

slung together pretty much at random, its jacket cheerfully festooned with swastikas, the book still haunts Lewis's reputation.[15] There is some kind of culmination, here, of paranoid Modernism's postliberal politics, which I shall explore further in Chapter 10 with reference to *Snooty Baronet*, the remarkable novel he published in 1932.

Edwards discerns a 'new humanity and concern for ordinary people' in Lewis's fiction and painting from 1935 onwards. The head-banging had to stop sometime, and it may have stopped during the series of operations Lewis underwent between 1932 and 1937, as an old gonorrhoeal scar in his bladder became infected (O'Keeffe has the details). Edwards sees in the return to portraiture after 1937, in novels like *The Revenge for Love* (1937) and *Self Condemned* (1954), sometimes regarded as Lewis's best, and in *Monstre Gai* and *Malign Fiesta* (1955), which resume *The Childermass*, a 'recognition of the experience of the other'. 'The dualism that had kept an absolute distinction between mind and body during Lewis's most extreme phase has broken down', he argues, with *Self Condemned* in mind, 'and is replaced by a humanistic recognition that the mind is actually nourished by affection, sexual relationships, even, perhaps, parenthood.' In the mid-1930s, in short, Lewis began to acknowledge 'that there might be something pathological in a rejection of such things'. According to Edwards, the later work constitutes a Kierkegaardian advance from aesthetics through ethics to theology.[16] No doubt the imminence of mere death, as opposed to the vital deadness advertised by the Vorticist mantraps, had something to do with it.

Edwards examines in great detail the process of self-examination and the commitment to theological inquiry which give the later work a new and formidable gravity. The problem with this work, as he acknowledges, is that its agenda required it either to reject or to transform the principle of creative antagonism. Under taxing scrutiny, in *Self Condemned* or *Malign Fiesta*, the psychopathy eventually dissolves, and with it a great deal else. 'Just as Lewis's drawing lost a certain kind of intensity when he began to

[15] It is, for example, the prime exhibit in John Carey's withering indictment of his life and work in *The Intellectuals and the Masses* (London: Faber, 1992).

[16] *Wyndham Lewis*, 457–61, 522. For the medical details, see O'Keeffe, *Some Sort of Genius*, 360.

recognize the inner reality of others,' Edwards observes, 'so did his writing.'[17] In the writing, at least, the loss is absolute. The opening pages of *Self Condemned* would have been a rank embarrassment to the author of 'Inferior Religions'. Edwards proves a subtle and informative guide to Lewis's deepening moral and spiritual preoccupations, and many readers will find his defence of the later work entirely persuasive. By investigating further the psychopathy Lewis may or may not have outgrown by the mid-1930s, I hope to reassert, in clarified terms, the alternative to a humanist reading of his literary work. Wild bodies, I think, rather than remorseful minds, are what Lewis did best. It's the apoplectic gristle, stupid.

In 'Inferior Religions', Lewis spoke of beauty as an 'icy douche' of 'ease and happiness' provoked by whatever suggests the perfect conditions for an organism. For Leonardo, he said, beauty was a 'red rain on the side of shadowed heads'; for Uccello, it was a 'cold architecture of distinct colour'; and for Kōrin the 'symmetrical gushing' of water. 'Cézanne liked cumbrous, democratic slabs of life, slightly leaning, transfixed in vegetable intensity.'[18] Of these, Lewis's own idea of beauty was closest to Cézanne's. Unlike Cézanne, however, he did the transfixing by anti-pathos.

What certainly did not happen after the First World War, Edwards rightly points out, though it is often thought to have happened, was an abandonment of 'Modernist effort'. Indeed, he is able to demonstrate, in a highly instructive chapter, the lengths to which Lewis went to keep abstraction going after the war. The paintings and drawings of the immediate post-war period offer one a glimpse of what a critical English Modernism in dialogue with the European avant-garde might conceivably have looked like. The essays Lewis wrote at the time stand to visual Modernism in the same relation as Eliot's essays do to literary Modernism.[19] The climax of his attempt to relaunch an English avant-garde was a pamphlet entitled *The Caliph's Design: Architects! Where is Your Vortex?* (1919), which memorably renews *Blast*'s campaign against amateurism in all its forms.

T. E. Hulme's 'Modern Art and its Philosophy' had included a call for the artist to take a 'more active part' in relation to the

[17] *Wyndham Lewis*, 522–4.   [18] *CWB* 153–4.
[19] *Wyndham Lewis*, ch. 7, esp. p. 219.

machinery by means of which and out of which the engineer had built the streets of London.[20] In *The Caliph's Design*, Lewis defined that more active part as the embedding of Vorticist principles in architecture. He had not researched his subject in any depth, and he did not, in fact, have a great deal to say about architecture as such. But his attempt to envisage contemporary art from the point of view of its usefulness to the architect provided plenty of scope for mordant reflection on its deficiencies. Unsurprisingly, the movements found to be most deficient of all were those which in one way or another threatened to eclipse the London vortex: Synthetic Cubism, in France, and Bloomsbury, in England.

The practice of collage—'these assemblings of bits of newspaper, cloth, paint, buttons, tin, and other débris, stuck on a plank'—enabled Lewis to characterize the most recent work of Braque and Picasso as the dead-end of nineteenth-century naturalism: an ultimate passivity before that part of the world which happened to be in front of the painter's eyes at a particular moment in time. This immersion in the unfathomable entanglement of all phenomena of life, this susceptibility to the caprice of the organic, he cunningly associated with the 'English variety of art man' and his (or presumably her) pursuit of ' "jolly" little objects like stuffed birds, apples, or plates, areas of decayed wall-paper': a tendency responsible, he added, for the 'distinguished amateurish gallantry and refinement' of Roger Fry's Omega workshops. 'Under a series of promptings from Picasso, then, painting in Paris has been engineered into a certain position, that appears to me to bear far too striking a family likeness, in its spirit, to the sensibility of the English amateur to give one much hope for it.' This penetrating critique of contemporary art deliberately conflates the two main objects of Lewis's polemical aversion: mimesis, to which he opposed geometry; and amateurism, to which he opposed the technician-standards of the charismatic professional.[21] Being against those things, which he regarded as *one* thing, was the basis of the

---

[20] *Collected Writings*, ed. Karen Csengeri (Oxford: Clarendon Press, 1994), 283.

[21] *The Caliph's Design: Architects! Where is your Vortex?*, ed. Paul Edwards (Santa Rosa, Calif.: Black Sparrow Press, 1986), 124–5, 127. Kasia Boddy has pointed out to me that the account in *Blasting and Bombardiering* of Hemingway's imitation of a professional boxer follows immediately upon a discussion of literary professionalism and its relative neglect in English culture.

fiction and the polemics he wrote during the 1920s. It *is* his Modernism: the will-to-abstraction incarnate.

And there is about it, in *The Caliph's Design*, just a whiff of paranoia. Like the paranoiac, as described in early twentieth-century psychiatry, Lewis built himself, in the purity of the design he would substitute for the unfathomable entanglement of London, a refuge from appearance. 'I do not need to have a house built with significant forms, lines, masses, and details of ornament, and planted squarely before my eyes', he informed his readers, 'to know that such significance exists, or to have my belief in its reality stimulated. But *you* require that.' The freedom he thus claimed is one which depends on expertise. 'Theoretically, even,' he went on, 'a creative painter or designer should be able to exist quite satisfactorily without paper, stone or paints, without lifting a finger to translate into forms and colours his specialised creative impulse.'[22] In so far as it cuts its exponent off from paper, stone, and paints, and from those of us who can envisage nothing without them, the urge to abstraction might be understood as a psychopathy of expertise. Such it was to become, to brilliant but also inhibiting effect, in Lewis's writing of the 1920s.

MEN OF THE WORLD

It was in the 'Man of the World' project that the doctrines of abstraction Hulme and Lewis had developed before the war—the 'ideology of ear and eye', as Vincent Sherry calls it—became a politics, a wide-ranging analysis of the 'condition' of Western cultures and societies.[23] Lewis's pre-war art and fiction had constituted an inquiry, at once impulsive in its eagerness to get up close to its object and unsparingly diagnostic, into the social and cultural significance of creaturely habit.[24] It grounds attitude in behaviour,

[22] Ibid. 37.

[23] *Ezra Pound, Wyndham Lewis, and Radical Modernism* (Oxford: OUP, 1993), 98.

[24] 'Creatures of Habit and Creatures of Change' was the title of an essay Lewis published in *The Calendar of Modern Letters* in 1926. The essay had originally been conceived as part of the 'Man of the World' project. It has since been regarded as sufficiently indicative of a major direction in Lewis's thinking to serve as the title for a collection of his essays: *Creatures of Habit and Creatures of Change*, ed. Paul Edwards (Santa Rosa, Calif.: Black Sparrow Press, 1989).

and behaviour in physiology: no ideas, it declares, but in bodily mechanism and faculty. Sherry has very usefully connected this approach with the kind of inquiry into attitude and behaviour undertaken a hundred years before, in the aftermath of the French Revolution, by liberal intellectuals like Marie Jean Condorcet, Emmanuel Sieyès, and Antoine Destutt de Tracy. Convinced that the Revolution had failed to transform French society through and through, these thinkers sought to establish a firmer basis for egalitarian ideals in the 'fabric of sentient and perceptual life'.[25] The science which would accomplish this renewal was *idéologie*: the study of the *eidos*, or image. The only true politics was a politics of bodily mechanism and faculty.

During the course of the nineteenth century, *idéologie* became dissociated, in the work of Henri Saint-Simon and Auguste Comte, from its original progressive agenda. By the early years of the twentieth century, sociologists like Gustave Le Bon and Georges Sorel and aestheticians like Julien Benda and Remy de Gourmont were using its identification of the superiority of eye to ear as the basis for a scathing assault on parliamentary democracy. Attentive to the political significance of aesthetic experience, Benda and Gourmont discerned in musical sensation—in the aural empathy which binds listener to sound—the basis and principle of collectivism. Their view was that music reaches the 'vitalist core' of each member of the audience, as Sherry puts it, uniting them in a spurious but formidable unity; mob rule is the product of the fellow feeling thus induced. Benda and Gourmont sought to relocate political authority in a new sensory register. If the populist ear merges, the aristocratic eye divides. Separating subject from object, the eye also makes the distinctions within the object upon which conceptual intelligence relies. It is thus both emblem and instrument of a ruling élite.[26] The influence of these advocates of an optical intelligence on Anglo-American Modernism has long been recognized.[27] The 'Man of the World' project might be seen as Lewis's attempt to establish himself professionally in the form of an ideologue (in the form, one might almost say, as he himself

---

[25] *Radical Modernism*, 9–11.   [26] Ibid. 4–5.
[27] Sherry gives a detailed account of the work of these ideologues and its effect on Anglo-American culture: ibid., ch. 1.

would certainly not have said, of a Lawrentian scout, or outrider). His own politics of the eye had failed; he now sought the reasons for that failure in an analysis of the corruption engendered in post-war Western culture and society by a politics of the ear.

The politics of the eye put forward in *The Art of Being Ruled* and *Time and Western Man* broadens the objection to empathy Hulme and Lewis had formulated before the war into an all-out assault on social mimesis. It has, however, no 'content'. The position put forward is just that, a position: a stance brought into being by and only accountable to the forces aligned against it. In both books, the fantasmal manœuvrings of paranoid symmetry gradually align the degree of fantasized grandeur to the degree of fantasized perse-cution. My contention is that these manœuvrings can best be traced at the level of their language.

The Art of Being Ruled conceives the revolutionary impulse prevalent in post-war Western culture as a fashion accessory, a consequence of the increasing commodification of all areas of modern life. 'It is because our lives are so attached to and involved with the evolution of our machines that we have grown to see and feel everything in revolutionary terms.'[28] The link Lewis discerns between commodification and the revolutionary impulse which has infiltrated the way people see (or hear) and feel is, in effect, social mimesis. Capitalism has to make people the same person so that they will consume the same things, which can therefore be produced *en masse*; and it has to overhaul this person periodically so that he or she will consume even more of the same things, or the same things done up after a different fashion. The revolution-ary impulse does capitalism's work for it, because it encourages people to overhaul *themselves* periodically.

The Art of Being Ruled amounts to a catalogue of the acts of social mimesis by which and through which the citizens of the modern Western world have periodically revolutionized them-selves at capitalism's behest. Undoubtedly the most significant of them, in Lewis's mind, is what he calls the 'child-cult'. 'Some approximation to the super-young or the naïf, he declares, 'is a universal fashionable expedient today.' The child-cult had been responsible for what he regarded as the widespread feminization of

[28] *The Art of Being Ruled*, 23.

post-war Western culture: the 'imitative machinery' built into adult life had been reinforced by a physical transformation, so that people were 'becoming *in reality* more childlike'. It is at this point that gender enters the equation. 'In the levelling, standardization, and pooling of the crowd-mind, as the result of a closer organization from above and greatly increased pressure on any irregularities of surface or temperamental erection, it is the masculine mind that tends to approximate to the feminine rather than the other way round.' Because masculinity has never been the 'natural human state', but rather a 'carefully nurtured secondary development above the normal and womanly', a man must become a woman in order to become a child. Losing his temperamental erection, the man sets his machinery to imitate the woman, who has always retained more of the 'child-like' in her 'mature life'. According to Lewis, the most lethal and the most pervasive of these imitations was homosexuality, which he regarded as a bourgeois revolution, a 'sex fashion' (the 'homo' as the child of the suffragette). All bourgeois revolutions, he concluded, whether they take the form of class war, or age war, or sex war, are an 'attack on *man* and on masculinity'.[29]

In so far as he associates femininity with the 'normal', with the state of nature, Lewis cannot be said to have challenged conventional thinking about gender. Like most other people at the time, he thought that homosexuals were men trying to be women, or vice versa. But his recognition of the supplementarity of masculine attitudes and behaviour is imaginative. It is a recognition made possible, I would argue, by paranoia. Hypermasculinity as such can only be conceived by someone for whom the norms no longer obtain, someone for whom there is no such thing as accident. Lewis has ushered us into the luxurious gymnasium of behaviours where gender is privately put together for public consumption. The male, Lewis reveals, is not naturally 'a man'. 'He has to be propped up into that position with some ingenuity, and is always likely to collapse.' This bloated and sinewy appearance is the result of thousands of years of 'ACTING THE MAN'. A man's hardihood and muscular frame are illusions, 'like everything else about him, provisionally and precariously realized, but no more stable than the muscular development produced by some intensive course of physical exercise'. Manliness, Lewis concludes, is a 'mania'. And we might add that it takes one to know one. Lewis would like to be a man, since he does not want to be a woman, or an imitation woman. But the only way in which a man becoming a man can know that he *is* a man is through the hostility aroused in male and female non-men by the 'unnatural *erectness*' he has had to adopt in becoming a man.[30] In this remarkable passage, paranoid symmetry takes the place of gender-difference.

For Lewis, masculinity, his own masculinity, is a form of symbolic capital. Investment in unnatural erectness strikes a blow against imitation. One works out in the gymnasium of behaviours in order to establish one's difference, one's unique muscular development. For the freedom denied by the revolutionary impulse, at capitalism's behest, is freedom from the 'type-life'. 'The ideally "free man" would be the man *least* specialized, the *least* stereotyped,' Lewis argues, 'the man approximating to the *fewest* classes, the *least* clamped into a system—in a word, the most individual.' What emerges here as an ideal, in opposition to persecutory clampings into type, is Musil's man without qualities. The ideal is not overtly a political ideal in that it endorses fascism and Bolshevism even-handedly, finding in both an admirable willingness to unmask 'parliamentary humbug'.[31] One might perhaps regard Lewis's politics of the eye as a postliberalism, rather than an inclination to the extreme left or the extreme right, because it confronts John Stuart Mill's anxiety about the loss of 'variety of situations' in the modern world without putting much faith in the remedies Mill had proposed.[32] Lewis's aim is to 'dissociate from the pure revolutionary impulse of creative thought all those corrupt imitations which confuse so much the issue, in their overnight utilitarian travesties'. In practical terms, this would seem to involve membership not of a political party, but of an association of professional men (of those whose expertise requires an investment in unnatural erectness). 'All these *odd men out* stand at present glaring at each other as usual, remarking perhaps to themselves that adversity brings them strange

---

[30] Ibid. 247–51.   [31] Ibid. 151, 75.

[32] Contrast Edwards, who finds in *The Art of Being Ruled* evidence of Lewis's 'remoteness from the Anglo-Saxon tradition of political thought' (*Wyndham Lewis*, 299). It is a matter, I think, of how one defines that tradition.

bedfellows. But the time must arrive when *they*, too, in spite of themselves, form a sort of syndic.'[33]

In the preface to the first part of *Time and Western Man*, Lewis claims that his objective is to anger and offend the exponents of social mimesis, and so to 'awaken thought'. What will anger and offend such people, it would appear, is the expression through satire and polemic, through the politics of the eye, of a definite and stable individuality. 'For our only terra firma in a boiling and shifting world is, after all, our "self". That must cohere for us to be capable at all of behaving in any way but as mirror-images of alien realities, or as the most helpless and lowest organisms, as worms or as sponges.' Mirroring figures the social mimesis endemic in mass-culture, while modern science and philosophy invite us to behave as the lowest organisms do; merged into a world which boils and shifts, we each become a 'phalanstery of selves' (a phalanstery is the social unit of Fourier's utopia, a group holding property in common). According to Lewis, the philosophy of modern science is that of 'the nature-sentiment of Rousseau, and the politics of the French Revolution'. He thought that the only way to resist this naturalization of the phalanstery was to single out and adhere to an 'essential' self. Lewis derived his own essential self programmatically from his capacities as an artist: the eye is I. 'So my philosophic position could almost be called an occupational one, except that my occupation is not one that I have received by accident or mechanically inherited, but is one that I chose as responding to an exceptional instinct or bias.'[34] To found an identity on expertise is to protect oneself both from contingency and from imitation.

Having come out as the member of a syndic, Lewis proceeds to follow the analysis of post-war society he had developed in *The Art of Being Ruled* through into an analysis of post-war culture. *Time and Western Man* is an assault on those cultural middlemen and middlewomen, themselves wholly mimetic, who peddle social mimesis in the arts. Written in defence of the 'wave of formal enthusiasm' which swept through the arts in the years before the war, it envisages a deep antipathy between the 'intellectual standards and ideals' of the 'flux-philosopher' and those of the plastic

[33] *The Art of Being Ruled*, 359, 364.
[34] *Time and Western Man*, 5, 175, 186, 7, 186.

or graphic artist. ' "Modern" or "modernity" ', Lewis indicates grimly, 'are words that have come literally to stink.' Stinks of any kind penetrate the boundary the eye has established between subject and object, self and other. Further pollution occurs in the eye itself, as Lewis contemplates the way in which the material world has acquired from flux-philosophy a 'fluid, or flabby, texture and appearance'.[35] Fluidity is troubling, perhaps, but clean; flabbiness provokes nausea.

Paranoia is operative throughout *Time and Western Man* at the level of language. The intellectual standards and ideals of the spokesman for the syndic of odd men out can be identified in the antipathy he again and again expresses towards flabbiness, dirt, and rubbish. In what follows, I shall simply note some instances of the way in which system makes its presence felt against a horizon constituted by messes of one kind or another. Pound, for example, is said to be a creature of social mimesis. By himself, he has neither convictions nor 'eyes in his head'. 'Yet when he can get into the skin of somebody else, of power and renown, a Propertius or an Arnaut Daniel, he becomes a lion or a lynx on the spot. This sort of parasitism is with him phenomenal.' Phenomenal, but not unique. For the nostalgia Lewis finds in Pound is the nostalgia he had already found in Cubist still-lifes. 'But his field is purely that of *the dead*. As the *nature mortist*, or painter essentially of still-life, deals for preference with life-that-is-still, that has not much life, so Ezra for preference consorts with the dead.'[36] The dead with whom Pound consorts, like the random bits and pieces represented in a still-life or bound into a collage, are so much stuff.

Even Lewis would have found it difficult to ignore altogether Pound's claims to membership of the syndic of odd men out. It is significant that when he returned to his critique of Pound in a later chapter of *Time and Western Man*, he should do so by attempting to characterize his ally from the '*Blast* days' not as an amateur, but as the wrong kind of professional. He thus describes the tone of Pound's journalism as terseness of 'a conventional, professional type', and compares it to the tone of two doctors discussing whether or not a patient had fractured his collar-bone. By employing expressions such as 'bunk' and 'tosh', Pound, like the

[35] Ibid. 150, 156.   [36] Ibid. 85–7.

doctors, invests in masculinity: 'he remains convinced that such over-specifically *manly* epithets are universally effective, in spite of all proof to the contrary'. This, clearly, is an uncharismatic professionalism. Lewis thought that Pound had carried the habit over into his poems, where an 'abrupt clipping and stopping' ostentatiously imitates 'the laconicism of the strong silent man'.[37] The comment, if unfair, is by no means without point.

The chapter on James Joyce, the last (and longest) in book i of *Time and Western Man*, again concentrates on identifying the wrong kind of professionalism. Joyce, Lewis decides, is a craftsman pure and simple, and as such susceptible both to social and political doctrine, which he haplessly transmits, and to literary influences. He has neither the will nor the ability to conceive of literature as anything other than imitation. The result, in *Ulysses*, is an immense *nature morte*, a 'suffocating, moeotic expanse of objects, all of them lifeless, the sewage of a Past twenty years old'. The method of *Ulysses* imposes a 'flabbinesss and vagueness' everywhere through its 'bergsonian fluidity'.[38]

Lewis's own method, in his analysis of *Ulysses*, extends beyond nausea to connect with the liberal and postliberal critique of social mimesis. Joyce, Lewis maintains, has always been 'steeped in the sadness and the shabbiness of the pathetic gentility of the upper shopkeeping class'. Lewis almost becomes Mill, for a moment, as he describes the progressive loss of diversity in the modern world, a process accelerated since Mill's day by scientific and technological change, and by the dominance of fashion. 'Everywhere the peoples become more and more alike. Local colours, which have endured in many places for two thousand years, fade so quickly that already one uniform grey tint has supervened.' *Ulysses*, Lewis concludes, is an unironic study of the imitations which are rapidly reducing the modern world to greyness. '*The hero is trying to be a gentleman!* That is the secret—nothing less, nothing more.'[39] If *The*

---

[37] *Time and Western Man*, 88.

[38] Ibid. 107, 120. Gertrude Stein's 'prose-song' is another obvious target for a politics of the eye, and it encourages in Lewis a disgusted insistence on its crimes against clearness of outline. Like Picasso's gigantic human dolls, Stein's protagonists, with their 'fixed imbecility of expression' and 'bloated, eunuchoid limbs', suggest to him 'the mental clinic'. 'They are all opaque fat, without nerve or muscle.' This opaque fat, made known by the nausea which expels it, is system's obverse: ibid. 77–80.

[39] Ibid. 93, 96–8, 115.

Art of Being Ruled gathers up all the odd men out into a professional syndic, *Time and Western Man* establishes Lewis himself as the only one among them with any claim to charisma.

PARANOID MODERNIST STYLE

In 1921 or 1922, Lewis embarked on a project of immense scope and ambition, then known as 'Joint'. 'Lewis's intention was satirical and Rabelaisian', Edwards comments, 'and the complete work would evidently have comprised a fictional anatomy of post-war civilization as comprehensive as the theoretical analysis provided in "The Man of the World".'[40] Joint, a schoolmaster, is married to Plateglass, and the typescript devotes considerable attention to their 'copulative trances'; intellectual intercourse he reserves for his friend Bully, whose eager and affectionate parasitism allows him to appreciate himself as he would like to be. 'Joint' would have been Rabelaisian both in its emphasis on the grotesque body and in its learnedness. From it, Lewis derived his two most innovative fictions of the 1920s, *The Childermass* (1928) and *The Apes of God* (1930). By the time he began to divide up and reassemble 'Joint', probably in 1926, he had brought the 'Man of the World' project close to some kind of conclusion, and the critique of social mimesis and its attendant amateurisms elaborated in *The Art of Being Ruled* and *Time and Western Man* thoroughly informs the satires he conceived in their turbulent aftermath.

In October 1927, Lewis made a selection from pieces which had appeared in a variety of magazines between 1909 and 1917, hastily revised them, added a new essay and two other stories, and published the collection as *The Wild Body* in November. He may have made short work of the revisions, but the material he was revising had either inaugurated or carried forward his career as a writer, and the preoccupations to which it gave shape were of critical and abiding significance to him. 'What I started to do in Brittany', Lewis observed in *Rude Assignment*, 'I have been developing

---

[40] *Wyndham Lewis*, 318; and 318–22 for commentary on what can be inferred about the project as Lewis conceived it at this early stage. The surviving typescript fragments are at Cornell.

ever since.'[41] As Sherry puts it, 'Lewis's mature sensibility returns us to its origins to understand its core, its depth'.[42] As so often with Lewis, it is the haste in the composition (or recomposition) which allows one a glimpse of the core, the diagnostic *point d'appui*. The 1927 *Wild Body* is, I shall suggest, the epitome of paranoid Modernist style.

Comparison of two versions of one story—written as 'Le Père François' in 1909, heavily revised as 'Franciscan Adventures' in 1927—enables Sherry to demonstrate and account for Lewis's derivation of political principle from physiological analysis. The story's protagonist is a tramp the narrator encounters while travelling in Brittany whose voice is his main asset. 'Music was his theme', as the 1909 version has it. The spirit of song, which has its 'darkest and most lugubrious sources' somewhere in the depths of his body, defines him.[43] Here, as Sherry puts it, is a human creature which sounds its credulity again and again through the 'circuit of aural and oral compulsion' mapped by Gourmont and Benda.[44] The 1927 revisions shift these observations on the mechanism of sensory life into a more abstract and more openly political register. 'What emotions had this automaton experienced before he accepted outcast life? In the rounded personality, known as Father Francis, the answer was neatly engraved. *The emotions provoked by the bad, late, topical sentimental songs of Republican France.*'[45] According to Gourmont and Benda, Sherry points out, music binds the members of a democratic society into an 'acoustic amalgam' and thus generates collective feeling as a function of its own sensory effect.[46] Francis's absorption into the fantasies sponsored by sentimental song incapacitates him. 'So he would lose touch more and more with unlyricized reality, which would in due course vomit him into the outcast void.' The narrator regards his aural and oral compulsion as the symptom of the psychopathology of social mimesis. 'Standing in the middle of the road, the moonlight converting him into a sickly figure of early republican romance, he sang to me as I walked away.'[47] To the romance

[41] *Rude Assignment*, ed. Toby Foshay (Santa Barbara, Calif.: Black Sparrow Press, 1984), 121–2.
[42] *Radical Modernism*, 92.
[44] *Radical Modernism*, 92.
[46] *Radical Modernism*, 93.
[43] *CWB* 277–8.
[45] *CWB* 121.
[47] *CWB* 121, 129.

topos of 1909, Lewis has added only the reference to republican-ism. Social mimesis, which soon found in popular patriotic song its most effective medium, a medium at once physical and politi-cal, began with, or within, revolution.

Sherry's account of the evolution of a politics of the eye in Lewis's writing in the 1920s seems to me compelling. But I want to argue, as I have done throughout this book, that the preoc-cupations which so insistently furrow the writing also invite a more broadly sociological inquiry; and one brought more narrowly to bear, where *The Wild Body* is concerned, on the figure of the narrator. For what is at issue, even more pressingly in 1927 than it had been in 1909, is professional identity; to be precise, the *narrator's* professional identity. The fate of someone like Father Francis, the pure product of social mimesis, is to lose touch with unlyricized reality, which will eventually cast him out into the void. The narrator's job is to keep him there. He is, as it were, the embodiment of unlyricized reality. He seeks out characters like Father Francis not in order to succour or reclaim them, not in order to abuse them, or police them, but in order to represent to them, by his pointed lack of lyricism, the reality with which they have catastrophically lost touch. When Francis complains, in a passage added in 1927, that he has been robbed in the pub where the two men have been drink-ing, the narrator is instantly on hand to observe that such claims are the 'immemorial tactic of the outcast'. Also added in 1927 were the passages which demonstrate the narrator's knowledge of disciplines as various as behavioural psychology and the study of Breton folklore, and thus underwrite his professional author-ity. The narrator is the professional embodiment, and thus perhaps the justification, of the anti–pathos Lewis had for so long cultivated both in his life and in his art. He even manages to associate himself, in his attitude to beggary, with no less a figure than Gustave Flaubert. Another of Francis's claims is that he once spent the night in the Château de Chambord, whose state of neglect, in the mid nineteenth-century, had aroused Flaubert's indignation. 'Could Flaubert have observed le père François installed beneath his sumptuous blanket in the entrance court of kings, or addressing himself to his toilet, I feel certain that that impetuous man would have passionately descended the staircase and driven him out.'[48] As this reflection makes abundantly clear, anti-pathos should never be confused with absence of feeling.

In 'Franciscan Adventures', anti-pathos finds its *point d'appui* in a not un-Flaubertian exercise of style in and on the description of physical appearance. I am thinking of the old tramp Emma Bovary sometimes encounters on the journey back from Rouen, after her assignations with Leon. We 'see' him, and the colour of the pus his sores exude, before we find out what Emma will make of it all; in the event, she responds to the melancholy of his voice, rather than to his obliterated face. For Emma, there is pathos in the sound; for Flaubert, perhaps, anti-pathos in the sight.[49] Lewis's exercise of antipathetic style can best be grasped by considering the revisions he made to the narrator's initial apprehension of Father Francis:

With his hat stuck over his eyes, his lips in a drunken and insolent pout, his nose red, and an ironical scowl on his countenance, as he appeared in passing me, I got a very unfavourable view of him.

He passed, his hat struck down over his eyes, a drunken pout of watchful defiance lying like a burst plum in a nest of green bristle and mildewed down, his nose reddening at its fine extremity.[50]

In the 1909 version, Francis's physical attributes seem to belong neither to the body which sustains them, since they are to all intents and purposes generic, nor to the observing consciousness, since their diagnostic value is minimal. To put it another way, the description lacks both order and point. The 1927 version enables anti-pathos to do its work by establishing Francis as the subject of the sentence, and thus apprehending him as a force, a militant agency (his hat now struck down over, rather than merely stuck over, his eyes): force can only be met by force, as Flaubert would have known had the opportunity ever arisen to kick a tramp out of a decaying castle; as Flaubert knew when he described the green crusts surrounding the empty eye-sockets of the beggar who appeals to Emma Bovary. Here, the force of Francis's watchful defiance is met by the force implicit in what Sherry calls Lewis's 'art of extreme metaphor' (or, in this case, extreme simile).[51] The

---

[48] *CWB* 129, 127.

[49] *Madame Bovary*, tr. Geoffrey Wall (Harmondsworth: Penguin Books, 1992), 216–17.

[50] *CWB* 277, 119.   [51] *Radical Modernism*, 106.

simile's violence lies in its painterly reduction of a pout which may
or may not have been meant as a gesture of defiance to the fleshi-
ness of a burst plum. For the comparison brought from afar is
further testimony to the narrator's charismatic professionalism—or
to Lewis's. Since Sherry goes on to suggest that an art of extreme
metaphor and simile runs the risk of randomness, it is worth pointing out that Lewis's revision of his original sentence has ordered as
well as reanimated it. The far-fetched comparison of a pout to a
burst plum now itself bursts apart an otherwise studiedly naturalis-
tic description.

The charisma activated by this comparison—the grandeur of
someone who impulsively recovers from its otherwise unthinkable
distance a simile of immediate diagnostic 'fit'—is too good to
waste. The cigarette Francis accepts from the narrator is promptly
inserted into the 'split plum', 'its dull-red hemispheres revolving a
little, outward and then inward, to make way'. These revolutions
feature on a later occasion as proof of contentment. 'The lips of the
voluptuary were everted again, moving like gorged red worms in
the hairs of his moustache and beard.'[52] Lewis here names his own
technique: eversion. For what the simile brought from afar does is
to turn its object inside out: mind everted is body, the spirit of song
everted a likeness apparent to the eye alone. The fundamental eversion achieved by this stylistic manœuvre is to transform the object's
truth for itself into its truth for other people; or, rather, for an identifiable observer, an observer whose identity rests on that transformation. The narrator's job is not to understand Francis, but to turn
him antipathetically inside out, a task for which his far-fetched
similes provide the instrument. In more general terms, this was the
task Lewis had set himself, as a commentator on modernity.
Eversion was his antidote to inversion, to that turning of outsides
in which he saw everywhere in contemporary culture, and which
prompted him in *Time and Western Man* to characterize the sexual
'invert' as a distraction from art.[53]

We need also to consider the narrative function of these similes.
They come from afar, in a story like 'Franciscan Adventures', whenever there is nothing very much going on, at times of minimal
significance: they punctuate the beggar's performances, offering us a

[52] *CWB* 121, 125.   [53] *Time and Western Man*, 35.

glimpse behind the scenes of beggardom. To get 'behind the scenes', to witness the actors out of their parts, Lewis remarks in 'The Cornac and His Wife', is to be privy to the 'workings and "dessous"' not merely of the theatre, but of life itself.[54] His far-fetched similes make us privy by the laughter they provoke to the workings of life itself, and thus to its essential absurdity. But they do so in a particular way. They do so by converting (e-verting) an object's minimal significance for itself, at a moment when it is not *performing*, into its maximal significance for a specific observer; which is exactly what paranoia was generally thought to do. Paranoiacs, Freud had observed, 'attach the greatest significance to the minor details of other people's behaviour which we ordinarily neglect, interpret them and make them the basis of far-reaching conclusions'. People flourish their walking-sticks, or make a certain hand-movement, or leave a room, or spit in the street, without ulterior motive, without attaching any particular significance to their actions; to the paranoiac, for whom there is no such thing as accident, these are all gestures of hostility. Lewis's similes make a glance in passing, or a puff on a cigarette, the basis of far-reaching (and far-reached) conclusions. In so far as those similes, and the conclusions drawn from them, constitute the narrator's charismatic professionalism, we are in the presence of a psychopathology of expertise.

Or at least we would be, if we could be sure that the narrator of the *Wild Body* stories understood the truths implicit in these moments of non-peformance as meant for him alone. The paranoiac's delusions, after all, are delusions of reference: he or she is the sole object of the hostility manifested by the flourish of a walking-stick. In this respect, one would have to say that the narrator of the *Wild Body* stories, named Ker-Orr in 1927, grows into the role. In 'Bestre', for example, Ker-Orr finds himself caught in the crossfire between the eponymous innkeeper and an artist's wife, both of whom, to adapt the figure proposed by 'Inferior Religions', stick up dummy-men on poles for their enemy to pot at. Bestre's contempt for Madame Rivière strikes him in the chest like a 'hard meaty gust', but he realizes that its 'central gyroduct' has passed by a few feet clear of him; turning, he receives a 'parting volley' from

[54] *CWB* 97.

its intended target, Madame Rivière. In a sense, the 'gyroduct' could be said to pass straight through him, since it in effect reproduces his violently antipathetic description of Madame Rivière, her 'nodular pink veil' an 'apoplectic gristle' round her stormy brow. Eversion rules, in the veil's reappearance as gristle. But he does not know it. Thinking that his role is as witness to a performance, he takes a room in Bestre's inn, 'the stage-box in fact, just above the kitchen'.[55]

Performances, however, are not the point, because performances are for everyone equally. When Ker-Orr last sees him, Francis is singing a love song for some peasants, and wholly reabsorbed into performance. His lips, accordingly, have ceased to be a split plum, or gorged worms. They are back in character. 'There was no recognition in his face while he sang: his lips protruded eloquently in keeping with the sentiment.' Anti-pathos, which disrupts performance by going behind the scenes, requires participation rather than spectatorship. At the time of his encounter with Bestre, Ker-Orr says, he did not realize that he was 'patting and prodding' a narrative 'subject'. He had no intention, then, of taking human specimens for study. 'Later, at the time of my spanish adventure (which was separated by two years from Bestre), I had grown more professional.'[56]

The first story in *The Wild Body*, 'The Soldier of Humour', establishes his credentials in the profession of anti-pathos by describing his Spanish adventure. Ker-Orr characterizes himself as a 'laughing machine' shaped by experience in the trenches. 'As I have remarked, when I laugh I gnash my teeth, which is another brutal survival and a thing laughter has taken over from the war. Everywhere where formerly I would fly at throats, I now howl with laughter. That is me.' This expertise in laughter has taken a psychotic turn, creating a parallel universe centred on and by his delusion of reference. 'I admit that I am too disposed to forget that people are real—that they are, that is, not subjective patterns belonging specifically to me, in the course of this joke life, which indeed has for its very principle a denial of the accepted actual.'[57]

In order to assess his professional identity as a soldier of humour, Ker-Orr must cease to be a bystander. He must put

[55] CWD 153, 77–9.   [56] CWD 130, 80.   [57] CWB 17.

himself in a position to receive the hard meaty gust of Bestre's contempt full in the chest, and to return it with interest, severely, meatily. Indeed, he must do more than that. A soldier of humour—they are for the most part men in Lewis's account, although, admirer that he was of apoplectic gristle, he did not rule women out—always gets his retaliation in first (while sometimes pretending to be, or believing himself to be, the injured party). Anti-mimesis is his weapon of choice: an active denial of the 'accepted actual' which constitutes the victim's self-image or inferior religion. The paranoid symmetry which anti-mimesis has generated between protagonist and antagonist, as each becomes a pattern belonging to the other, is the narrative enactment of the technique of eversion: hard meaty gusts of dialogically hostile laughter.

The 'adventure' which professionalizes Ker-Orr involves a clash of nationalisms. Professional rivalries, as I have argued throughout this book, often turn on competition over the ownership of symbolic capital. Bestre's primary asset as an innkeeper is his physical presence, his surplus masculinity:

> Every variety of bottom-tapping resounded from his dumb bulk. His tongue stuck out, his lips eructated with the incredible indecorum that appears to be the monopoly of liquids, his brown arms were for the moment genitals, snakes in one massive twist beneath his mamillary slabs, riding on a pancreatic swell, each hair on his oil-bearing skin contributing its message of porcine affront.

It is in accordance with this specific investment in hypermasculinity that Bestre should achieve final victory over the gristly Madame Rivière by exposing himself. Ker-Orr, by contrast, has invested his symbolic capital in Englishness. His paranoid belief that 'a *quarrel of humour* divides men for ever' is, he says, an 'english creed'. The antagonist he chooses or is chosen by during his 'spanish adventure' is M. de Valmore, a Frenchman whose excessive self-assurance derives from his adoption of American citizenship and an American accent. The 'illusion of superiority' common to those who think of themselves as 'English' or 'American' ensures that these two will fall out irrevocably during their first encounter, in a hotel in Bayonne.[58] Ker-Orr's tactic thereafter is always to deny the 'accepted actual' of de Valmore's Americanness.

What we need to note here is the part paranoia plays, quite explicitly, in converting that tactic into a strategy. Immediately after their first encounter, Ker-Orr sees de Valmore deep in conversation with the proprietress of the hotel in Bayonne, and automatically assumes that he is the object of the latter's 'discourse'. 'What effectively could be said about me on so short an acquaintance? He would, though, certainly affirm that I was a designing ruffian of some sort; such a person as no respectable hotel would consent to harbour, or if it did, would do so at its peril.' Crossing the border into Spain, Ker-Orr finds that his enemy is ahead of him: he is given the worst room in the hotel he stays at, and before long the patrons of the café where he takes his meals turn against him. His counter-conspiracy involves putting his enemy to the test of social recognition. He persuades some American friends to entertain de Valmore, and then himself puts in an appearance, to be recognized immediately as a long-lost friend, and thus the more authentic 'American'. This moment of paranoid illumination, in full public view, seals his professional identity as a (triumphant) soldier of humour. Ker-Orr's manner throughout is that of the 'fastidious expert'. Adopting the 'figure of the physician', he approaches de Valmore, seated at a table in the café in the company of the Americans, with 'impassive professional rapidity', his eye fixed on him antipathetically, already making its diagnosis.[59]

What is enacted in Ker-Orr's rapid approach to his victim is an anti-pathos which is at once impulsive and diagnostic. As the 'central gyroduct' of his contempt for bogus professionalism—for the faking of symbolic capital—strikes his antagonist full in the chest, he himself can finally be recognized for what he is. This 'spanish adventure', one might note, has by no means exhausted the paranoia of which it is a product. Ker-Orr knows that his effectiveness in subsequent quarrels of humour will depend on the generative force of anti-mimesis. His mood on returning to Bayonne incorporates a residue of 'premonition'. 'It was nothing of course but the usual mechanical working of inference within the fancy.'[60] So all is still well, because all is still paranoid.

---

[59] *CWB* 30, 44.   [60] *CWB* 45.

APES

The Apes of God (1930) is the most programmatic statement, by Lewis or any other writer, of what I have been calling 'paranoid Modernism'. I shall give reasons for thinking that it is not as ori-ginal an achievement as *The Wild Body*; but its adherence to a programme will enable me to test the explanatory value of the cultural history I have been sketching in these pages: the cultural history of expertise and its discontents. In Lewis's case, the programme centres on the critique of social mimesis and its attendant amateurisms articulated in *The Art of Being Ruled* and *Time and Western Man*. His apes of god are those members of the moneyed bourgeoisie who, rather than merely adopting a bohemian lifestyle, produce 'art' in direct competition with the artists whom they might once have supported. Their activ-ities deny both patronage and studio space to the needy among authentic practitioners. Furthermore, Lewis maintains, their amateurism has blurred the boundary between art and life, thus destroying art's anti-mimetic capacities, its unique access to disinter-estedness, and to the transcendent. In *The Apes of God*, these views find utterance in the 'Encyclical' which Pierpoint, a painter turned philosopher, addresses to his disciple Horace Zagreus, whom he has initiated into the London art world. Zagreus, in turn, seeks to initi-ate Dan Boleyn, a beautiful but bemused 19-year-old Dubliner, whom we accompany on a picaresque tour of studios and mansions. That Dan's Gulliver-like obtuseness is no improvement on the inani-ties which everywhere confront and terrify him merely demonstrates the all-encompassing force of Pierpoint's diagnosis.

As Edwards observes, *The Apes of God* is in part the expression of resentments which had accumulated ever since Lewis's break with Bloomsbury in 1913. The Encyclical's reference to genuine painters who, lacking a proper studio, have to paint in 'chilly ill-lit shacks just holding together, that sprawl against each other in some damp court-yard', is a reference to a shack of his own, mounted on concrete blocks and clad in corrugated iron, in Adam and Eve Mews, from which he did a moonlit flit, carrying an unfinished portrait of Edith Sitwell, in October 1923.[61] In April 1924, the section of *The Apes of*

---

[61] *The Apes of God* (London: The Arthur Press, 1930); *The Apes of God*, with an

God containing the Encyclical appeared in T. S. Eliot's journal, *The Criterion*. *The Apes of God* was not just a book. It was a campaign; and Lewis duly discerned in the reception the book met from Bloomsbury and its agents a strategy of 'embargo', 'boycott', and worse. In order to capitalize on such controversy as the book had caused, he put out a follow-up pamphlet, *Satire and Fiction*. This includes letters of commendation from the great and good, some favourable press notices, an expository essay, and the text of a review by Roy Campbell which had been suppressed by Bloomsbury injunction. Lewis's life had apparently been threatened by an 'airman', while anonymous letters of the 'most violent sort' were flowing in at the letter box. He proposed to retaliate by exposing the 'scandal' of Bloomsbury's attempt to 'sabotage' a 'great work of art'.[62]

The Encyclical which inaugurated Lewis's campaign against the apes of god is unmistakably paranoid in tone. It finds a certain inevitability in the behaviour of the apes, who, training on the genuine artist 'all the artillery of the female, or bi-sexual tongue, will abuse the object of their envy one day, and imitate him the next: will attempt to identify themselves with him in people's minds, but in the same breath attempt to belittle him'. The Encyclical's awareness that those who belittle also imitate meticulously adjusts its delusion of grandeur (the genuine artist is worth imitating) to its delusion of persecution (belittlement is the only way to overcome those who are worth imitating). Pierpoint's paranoia is also political. For he manages to associate the apes of god, despite their ostentatious wealth, with republicanism: they form, he says, a 'phalanstery', an obscene swarm; and their republicanism, in turn, associates them with lack of system, with mess. Dressing the part of the penniless 'genius', the apes present 'the curious spectacle of a lot of men and women, possessed of handsome bank balances, drifting and moping about in the untidiest fashion'.[63]

Afterword by Paul Edwards (Santa Barbara, Calif.: Black Sparrow Press, 1981), 120. Henceforth *AG*. The pagination is the same in the 1930 and 1981 edns., and my references are therefore in effect to both. For a note on the autobiographical allusion, see Edwards, *Wyndham Lewis*, 343; for the studio in Adam and Eve Mews, and Lewis's departure from it, see O'Keeffe, *Some Kind of Genius*, 235–6, 249–50.

[62] *Satire and Fiction* (London: The Arthur Press, 1930), 7.
[63] *AG* 123.

Seen through the lens of a paranoia which is their antithesis, drift and untidiness become symptoms of profound disorder. It would take Lewis the rest of a long book to acknowledge that the will to order the apes consistently violate by amateurism and social mimesis exists only in the lens itself, rather than in the world on which the lens has been trained as though it were a bomb-sight or an artillery-piece.

The book itself is a campaign. For a start, there is an awful lot of book to it, in its first edition, almost an *excess* of book: 625 pages, to be precise, weighing in at three pounds and three ounces. This monumentality has often been ignored in the criticism. According to Scott Klein, for example, the novel imagines the physical page, the 'carrier' of the writing which constitutes it, both as an 'evasive cover' for the real and as reality's ultimate victim. 'It is that which must be broken through from within, "like a fist through a sheet of paper," so that the power it occludes can reveal itself.'[64] No one who has hefted the first edition could suppose that Lewis saw his 625 pages as a victim, or as in any way evasive. Try putting your fist through that.

The novel's monumentality is of course symbolic as well as physical. Klein conceives the mutual antipathy of Lewis and Joyce, evident enough in texts like *The Apes of God* and *Finnegans Wake*, as an emblematic opposition between Modernisms. But if we take the book's publication history into account, we must conclude that Joyce was a writer Lewis sought in this instance to emulate rather than to oppose. What ensured the success of *Ulysses*, as Lawrence Rainey has amply shown, was its status as luxury object: a book bought not to be read, but as a collector's item, or an investment.[65] *The Apes of God*, published by the Arthur Press in an edition of 750 signed and numbered copies 'for subscription only', aspires to that status.[66] Like *Ulysses*, it declares its significance both by its monumentality and by its status as luxury object.

[64] *The Fictions of James Joyce and Wyndham Lewis: Monsters of Nature and Design* (Cambridge: CUP, 1994), 144. The quotation is from *AG* 418: the fist breaking through a sheet of paper is the force of an apocalyptic dream or vision Dan Boleyn has, of a landscape of violent insurrection, which he cannot altogether suppress.

[65] *Institutions of Modernism: Literary Elites and Public Culture* (New Haven, Conn.: Yale University Press, 1999), ch. 2.

[66] The Arthur Press was funded by Lewis's most reliable patrons, Sir Nicholas and Lady Waterhouse.

By no means the least significant facet of the monument is the dust-wrapper. For the dust-wrapper makes it clear that the novel is an integral part of a systematic critique of post-war English society. From it, we learn that the dramatis personae are shown in a 'condition of violent restlessness' imposed upon them by the 'instability of the time'. Immersed in the make-believe of the 'adult nursery' previously described in *The Art of Being Ruled*, they have all 'become "irresponsible baby-boys and baby-girls"', in the same way that the French Court, in the days before the Revolution, dressed themselves as shepherds and shepherdesses in their fêtes champêtres'. Now the apes are not so much a phalanstery as an irresponsible ruling élite. Either way, they can be associated with the inauguration of bourgeois democracy, and the social mimesis it entails. The theme of *The Apes of God* is England after the war, and the confusions of intellect and emotion endemic in a society 'beneath the shadow of a revolutionary situation'. The dust-wrapper also proposes a significant connection between *The Apes of God* and the recently reissued *Tarr*, with its 'unforgettable picture' of the 'art-world of Paris'. *Tarr*'s Paris had in fact been a Paris notably without Parisians; but it was a part of Lewis's campaign, as we have seen, to associate Bloomsbury amateurism with whatever Picasso happened to be doing at the time. Lewis missed few chances to underline the systematic nature of his critique of social mimesis.

The method of descriptive eversion plays as important a part in Lewis's reckoning with the ape-like inhabitants of 'Bloomsbury' and 'Chelso-Bloomsbury' as it had in his stories of Breton peasant life. Dan Boleyn's inability to make sense of the Encyclical is demonstrated conclusively, and with wonderful verve, by the description of his efforts to stow the envelope which contains it about his person. 'Dan took it and compelled the powerful envelope to enter his jacket-pocket, bent in an elastic arc. It made a hollow in his clothes, on the side of him. An empty goitre of a pocket it was, as if implemented with whalebone to puff out the hip.'[67] There is in this passage a Dickensian, or more than Dickensian, sense of the wilfulness of inanimate objects: the envelope's power is at once a function of its tensile form and of its encyclical content. Dan's inability to accommodate its form about

[67] *AG* 113.

his person prefigures his inability to comprehend the message it contains. Lewis goes beyond even Dickens in the far-fetchedness of the metaphor which transforms a bulging pocket into a goitre. The metaphor's eversive force, which turns a cultural event inside out to reveal it as a fact of nature, a disease, marks the intrusion of laughter, of the satirist's point of view. Its truth is a truth only for the power of the eye which has produced it.

So far, so paranoid. Satire, Lewis claimed in *Satire and Fiction*, is a form of realism: it is that point of view from which a truth ignored or misunderstood by most people becomes self-evident (that is, evidence of the authenticity of the self for which it is a truth). According to him, *The Apes of God* is a narrative 'of a most objective nature, cast in a mould very near to the everyday aspect of things'. It would only appear 'grotesque' or 'distorted', he went on, 'to those accustomed to regard the things of everyday, and everyday persons, through spectacles couleur-de-rose'.[68] The conspiracy abroad is thus a conspiracy to fail to see the bulging pocket of a Dan Boleyn as a goitre—and to persecute anyone who does.

Lewis confirms the authenticity of the realism implicit in his description of the protuberant pocket by arranging for its fulfilment in and through narrative. The hip puffed out into the shape of a whalebone corset by the introduction of letter into pocket prefigures Dan's subsequent appearance at Lord Osmund Finnian Shaw's Lenten Party dressed in period costume as a woman, and boasting a 'pelvic portentousness' he feels able neither to enjoy nor wholly to disown. It may be significant that the scene in which Dan's costume is applied to him by the Dickensian Mrs Bosun includes an element of meta-commentary. The application of the dress to the young man prompts the thought that human beings can only be justified as '*objects* pure and simple' for the 'laughter', the 'bold stylistic pen', of a Thomas Rowlandson—or a Wyndham Lewis.[69] The laugher the dress provokes has everted its wearer, laid bare his femininity.

The narrative fulfilment of Vorticism's eversive technique—the technique which turns Dan inside out as he inconsequentially pockets a letter—enables us to grasp the insight thus obtained into

[68] *Satire and Fiction*, 48.   [69] *AG* 467, 440.

the absurdity of human existence as in some measure systematic. The insight applies universally, it would seem, at least within the milieu inhabited by Chelso-Bloomsbury's apes of god. To describe that milieu realistically is to find everything everywhere turned inside out. Lewis renders his 'realism' that much more methodical than mere realism by a periodic meta-commentary which identifies the most forceful and manipulative among the apes with the satirist. 'But you were made for *me*, not for yourself', Zagreus tells Julius Ratner. 'I supply the *interest* Julius.'[70] Later, Ratner will accuse Zagreus, as Maxim Libidnikov had accused Rupert Birkin, in *Women in Love*, of 'religious mania'. That the satirist is a human being who claims a god's power to judge is a view to which, as Edwards points out, Lewis himself may well have subscribed.[71] The origin of the book's title, as the dust-wrapper explains, is the early Christian belief that the world swarmed with small devils impersonating the Deity; in so far as he assumes a god-like power of judgement, the satirist could be said to subscribe to it. His representative on earth, in *The Apes of God*, is the inaccessible and authoritative Pierpoint, author of an Encyclical which is a key document in Lewis's campaign against amateurism. It is Pierpoint, Ratner explains, who is responsible for the alteration in Zagreus. 'Pierpoint had altered Horace, all Horace had been changed inside-out.' Pierpoint is in theory the ultimate source of the interest supplied to each member of the gang of nonentities, and Pierpoint is mad. 'Absolutely mad—as a march-hare my dear Julius', Zagreus reports. 'But with such *method*!'[72]

What the meta-commentary freely admits, of course, is that there is nothing at all *to* the apes. Their interest is supplied from elsewhere, by Zagreus, perhaps, by Pierpoint, by Lewis himself. Of course, the more noteworthy the interest supplied by descriptive eversion, the more likely such virtuosity is to strike us as a clip-on exercise in Vorticist style. Thus the wonderful account of Dan pocketing the letter constitutes a separate paragraph which almost begs to be lifted out of its narrative context and set aside for further contemplation (which is what I have done here). The problem is that Dan, as Lewis imagines him, would under no

[70] *AG* 331.   [71] *Wyndham Lewis*, 348, 564 n. 12.
[72] *AG* 414–15, 337.

circumstances be capable of resisting the stylistic and other outrages inflicted upon him. The same could not be said, I think, of the various 'bodies' encountered by Ker-Orr on his travels in Brittany and Spain, who possess a wiliness to match their wildness. To recognize this objection to the method of *The Apes of God*, as Lewis does both by meta-commentary within the text and in the essay which concludes *Satire and Fiction*, is not necessarily to meet it. The problem with the apes is not that they are 'little people': an objection Lewis meets by pointing out that there have been good portraits of peasants and 'idiots' and bad portraits of emperors.[73] The problem is that they are imitations: the all-too-familiar dramatis personae of an assault on the upper bourgeosie and its bohemian tendencies which had been under way for the best part of a hundred years and which had achieved a new breadth and intensity in the immediate post-war years. To grasp their familiarity, we need to see where they came from.

Scott Klein has very usefully drawn attention to the anxieties about the basis of social and political authority in a world recovering from war which pervade Lewis's novel. *The Apes of God* is a book about bohemian high society at empire's metropolitan 'centre'; and yet it envisages Englishness itself as a hybrid construction inseparable from the forces it would exclude. Horace Zagreus, for example, Pierpoint's disciple-in-chief, and tireless Encyclical salesman, is an 'english exile', a returned colonist whose cultural allegiance is no longer to 'England'. He has spent many years in the Orient, and is an initiate of Afghan magic. The exotic costume he dons for Lord Osmund's Lenten Party, where he is to supply the conjuring, incorporates as many Eastern as Western emblems.[74] Klein sees in Lewis's depiction of Zagreus the 'paranoia' of a political centre threatened from without by a superior vitality.[75] He cites Matthew Plunkett's response to the sexual athlete Zulu Blades, a character based on the South African poet Roy Campbell: 'Dirty colonial—they're all the same! Orestylians, Africanders, Kanucks—what an empire!'[76]

If empire strikes back from beyond, in the shape of Africanders and Afghan magicians, then the oppressed classes strike up and through from below. Klein concentrates, as we have seen, on the

---

[73] *Satire and Fiction*, 43–5.   [74] *AG* 295, 377.
[75] *Fictions*, 138–45.   [76] *AG* 79.

fist striking through a sheet of paper: Dan Boleyn's 'vision' of a world 'that ran through things, like pictures in water or in glassy surfaces, where a mob of persons was engaged in hunting to kill other men'. According to Klein, this vision is a vision of a reality which the dominant social order has the power neither to represent nor to control. Dan had first suffered his vision when he was still a schoolboy in Ireland, the night before his father's arrest during the Easter Rising; it now finds its objective correlative in the General Strike which erupts as the novel draws to a close. Class war, in short, is the fist striking through a sheet of paper. By Klein's account, the politics of *The Apes of God* thus lies in its frank acknowledgement of an *hors-texte*, a violence past words. 'The General Strike is a final welling up of chaos, in a world otherwise concerned with representation as a mechanism of order.'[77] I want to propose here that the novel's politics are on the contrary textual through and through: a recirculation of formulae, including formulae for untamed energy and violence past words.

I have already suggested that Ford Madox Ford's pre-war novels, to which Pound drew attention in 1920, but which have subsequently disappeared from view, could be seen as a precedent for *The Apes of God*. Even without the stimulus of post-war confusion, Ford was able to present the fraudulence of bourgeois-bohemian life in terms Lewis would not have disowned. In *The Benefactor* (1905), for example, George Moffat, the epitome of high culture and high moral purpose, finds himself engaged in unsettling sexual rivalry with a returned colonist, Carew. 'He had an image of the bearded, jaunty colossus, swinging with his horseman's stride down his—George's—own steps and along the clear, quiet streets to Brede's cottage. To pay his court to Clara Brede!'[78] George Moffat's anxiety is exactly Matthew Plunkett's. That Ford should have given a particular shape to a particular social anxiety in 1905 does not mean that Lewis was wrong to give the same anxiety the same shape in 1930. But it does mean that the resulting figure must be understood as a literary convention rather than as a challenge to convention in general.

To put it another way, the satires of Ford and Lewis can only

---

[77] *Fictions*, 145.
[78] *The Benefactor: A Tale of a Small Circle* (London: Brown, Langham, 1905), 236.

be understood in relation to the long-standing critique of social mimesis articulated within English liberal tradition. It was John Stuart Mill, after all, who patented the lament at the loss of 'variety of situations' and the consequent pervasiveness of 'ape-like imitation'. Where Lewis is concerned, we need also to bear in mind the example of the nineteenth-century English writer who had most to say about the infection of the aristocracy and the upper bourgeoisie by social mimesis, Charles Dickens. 'Inferior Religions' had included a grudging recognition of Dickens's status as an 'essential artist', an analyst of 'the great play-shapes blown up or given off by the tragic corpse of life underneath the world of the camera'.[79] Dickens is a powerful presence in Lewis's writing of the 1920s, on account both of his descriptive method and of his preoccupation with social mimesis.

The prelude to *The Apes of God* describes the sumptuously decrepit Lady Fredigonde Follett, whose money the Chelso-Bloomsburies are after, at her toilette; her death, after disposing of her husband so that she can marry Horace Zagreus, brings it to a close. Klein regards Fredigonde as an 'explicit parody' of Joyce's Molly Bloom.[80] It may be more useful to regard her as an imitation of some of Dickens's female ancients. I am thinking of the Honourable Mrs Skewton, in *Dombey and Son* (1848), sister to the late Lord Feenix, and aunt to the present Lord, who lives upon 'the reputation of some diamonds, and her family connexions'.[81] Both women are more artefact than person: they have to be taken apart at night by their maids, and reassembled in the morning. Both are trapped within their own decrepitude, and yet both affect a girlishness which would be ridiculous in women a fraction of their age. Dickens and Lewis describe the decrepitude from outside, while allowing the girlishness to betray its imbecility by conversation, in one case, and by internal monologue, in the other.

How is it that Lewis ends up reproducing in his most programmatically Vorticist fiction a figure created by Dickens? The answer to this question lies less in *Dombey and Son* than in *Bleak House*. The accusation levelled there against the aristocracy and the upper

[79] *CWB* 152.   [80] *Fictions*, 116.
[81] *Dombey and Son*, ed. Peter Fairclough (Harmondsworth: Penguin Books, 1985), 362.

bourgeoisie is not that they are monstrous, but that they are negligent. Their inability or unwillingness to exercise an authority based on independence of thought and moral judgement has made it possible for imitation to gain ground everywhere; while they mope and prevaricate, or fall helplessly back upon tradition, the Smallweed clan imitates its way into wealth and power. Lewis, too, discerned social and political negligence in this susceptibility to youth-cult: those who pretend to be something they no longer are thereby lose the ability to resist those who would pretend to be the something they still are. Edwards makes a useful connection between the portrayal of Fredigonde and a passage in *The Art of Being Ruled* which finds an instance of the 'super-freedom' to which the 'revolutionary rich' aspire in 'the case of an old, rich, and pampered invalid lady who succeeds in attracting to herself, by means of her riches, all the advantages of childhood'.[82] 'She in this way may arrive at being carried about, waited on, fed, bathed, flattered, put to bed, and in the morning washed and dressed, and so steeped continually in an atmosphere of self-importance.'[83] At the very end of *The Apes of God*, as Fredigonde expires in Zagreus's arms, the East End chancer and imitation-man Archie Margolin paces the great reception room below. The strong implication is that this golden-haired Uriah Heep, this Smallweed redivivus, will soon inherit the kingdom of the apes: 'with elf-like nigger-bottom-wagging, he traversed the oppressive spaces of this monster apartment—built for victorian 'giants' in their first flower—smiling at himself as he advanced (with his St Vitus puppet-shiver) in the mighty victorian looking-glasses'.[84]

Lewis's description of the imminent supersession of Victorian giants itself depends on the supersessions envisaged in gigantic Victorian novels. If there is a certain amount of Dickens in Lady Fredigonde Follett, then there is a certain amount of Thackeray in Willie Service, Zagreus's insolent, bullying man-servant. In *The History of Pendennis* (1848), during a violent confrontation after a particularly villainous dinner at his club, Major Pendennis learns that his man-servant James Morgan has, while serving his master obsequiously for many years, amassed a fortune by fraud and blackmail; indeed, the obsequious servant now owns the house in

---

[82] *Wyndham Lewis*, 347.   [83] *Art of Being Ruled*, 135.   [84] *AG* 625.

which the master lodges.[85] Service, a great fan of Edgar Wallace, renders himself serviceable by the imitation of service. Like Morgan, however, his aim is to turn the tables on those it has been his duty to serve.

> 'Back! It's no use! You must stop here!' Willie Service's two eyes were in chilly ambush beneath his shining cap-peak of a sham-chaffeur: he stood-easy, chewing an imaginary piece of gum, in imitation of the american film-sleuth.
> 'Why?' asked Dan faintly.
> 'Because I say so. That's good enough for you!'
> The little bully squared his jaw, Dan fell back a step.

For Lewis, as for Thackeray and Dickens, imitation was not just a habit. It was an instrument of class war. As Zagreus puts it, apparently quoting Pierpoint, there is always turbulence of this kind between master and servant before a revolution.[86]

No surprise, then, that Lewis, departing from the historical evidence, should describe the effects of the General Strike in terms appropriate to the kind of modified end-of-the-world fantasy familiar from turn-of-the-century invasion-scare stories and science fiction. When the strike begins, we are told, the whole 'townland' of London is at once 'up in arms' and 'silent as the grave'. Rumours of riot and insurrection spread, while in the rich neighbourhoods a 'grand and breathless calm' reigns.[87] The next thing we know, a Bolshevik army has landed on the Essex coast. Lewis does not quite go that far. But he certainly exploits, as M. P. Shiel had done in *The Purple Cloud*, the sensation of survival in an otherwise deserted, or almost deserted, world. Into this near-void advances Dan Boleyn, Zagreus's now ex-disciple, and in some respects his alter ego. If Zagreus is the Adam Jeffson who dresses himself as an Eastern potentate, then Dan is the Adam Jeffson who had found in the fact that the hands of all the clocks in London were stuck at ten past three something 'hideously solemn, yet mock-solemn, personal, and as it were addressed to *me*'.[88] Dan has learnt paranoia. Scouring the empty streets, he tries desperately not

---

[85] *The History of Pendennis*, ed. J. I. M. Stewart (Harmondsworth: Penguin Books, 1972), 708–10.
[86] *AG* 398–9, 439, 428.   [87] *AG* 618.
[88] *The Purple Cloud* (London: Chatto & Windus, 1901), 216–17.

to catch the eye of the policemen who stare fixedly at him. Equally threatening are the kind-hearted citizens who offer him a ride. 'If he remained in the big streets Dan was always accosted by gentlemen who were riding up and down.'[89] Like the amateur agent in a novel by E. Phillips Oppenheim, he has entered a parallel universe in which there is no such thing as accident. This, however, is the last we see of him. His only ambition is to escape from a predicament which might once—before the war, under different circumstances, in a different kind of novel—have been the making of him.

The Apes of God could be said to recapitulate a distinct phase in the history of the paranoid imagination: the turn-of-the century rewriting of mid-Victorian hostility to social mimesis as apocalypse. It also offers a perceptive if sporadic commentary on the next phase in that history: paranoia's commodification. Zagreus, it turns out, has purchased his entire investigative and expository repertoire—the stratagems, the speeches, the costumes, the party-tricks —from Pierpoint.[90] This is designer paranoia. The problem, once again, is that in describing Zagreus's practice Lewis was in effect describing his own. For some items in *his* investigative and expository repertoire were bought, as it were, off the rack. We remember Gudrun Brangwen's response to the Pompadour set. 'And it gave her pleasure to sit there, cheeks flushed, eyes black and sullen, seeing them all objectively, as put away from her, like creatures in some menagerie of apish, degraded souls. God, what a foul crew they were!'[91] Lewis's denunciations of Chelso-Bloomsbury apishness, like Lawrence's, bore a distinct resemblance to the scare-mongering engendered in popular fiction and the popular press by moral panic.

In the late spring or early summer of 1929, Lewis was introduced to Marjorie Firminger, a 30-year-old actress and fashion correspondent. She had a small maisonette in Glebe Place, Chelsea, where his friend Elliot Seabrooke had a studio. They got on well together, and before long Firminger was feeding him all the gossip she had about the 'bright young people' and the lesbians. The latter

---

[89] *AG* 616–17. [90] *AG* 418–21, 481.
[91] *Women in Love*, ed. David Farmer, Lindeth Vasey, and John Worthen (Cambridge: CUP, 1987), 380.

fascinated Lewis. He insisted that Firminger bring one to meet him. She asked him to look at the typescript of a novel she had written, *Jam To-day*, which had been rejected by a number of London publishers because its subject was lesbianism.[92] He told her—perhaps by way of a down-payment on gossip about Chelso-Bloomsbury lesbians—that he would send the typescript to his American publisher.[93] For Lewis's interest undoubtedly had something to do with a chapter in the novel he was then completing in which the gormless young protagonist is sent to inspect a 'lesbian-ape' in her Chelsea studio, with predictably disastrous consequences.[94] The critique of lesbian-apishness is of course also a fantasy about lesbianism, retailed as much for its sensational effect as for any insight it might offer into the art world. It is comparable to the fantasies about the bohemian underworld to be found, as I have shown, in the journalism and fiction of the early 1920s. In Dorothy Mills's *The Laughter of Fools* (1920), for example, the susceptible young protagonist establishes herself in Chelsea, while most of the doping enjoyed by members of the 'Binge Club' takes place in the studio of a 'futurist' painter.[95] No wonder Dan Boleyn runs into an ape or two straight out of the Binge Club. 'Michael, the Russian *drug-pimp* had Zagreus not said—*cocaine*—was smoking a cigarette at the gate.'[96]

At its worst, *The Apes of God*, intended as a devastating critique of social mimesis, is imitative through and through. The lesbian-apes are 'little people', too little to merit satire, not to the extent that they lack ambition, but to the extent that they are commodities, items to be bought and sold in the literary market-place. That Lewis knew this is almost certainly the case. *The Apes of God*, as I have already suggested, is among other things a reflection on his own satirical or 'Enemy' persona, his own paranoia. At one point, Zagreus and Ratner discuss the increasing fashionableness of pulp fiction. Zagreus maintains that E. Phillips Oppenheim had only

---

[92] *Jam To-day: A Novel* (Paris, 1931): no publisher's name given. *Jam To-day* is an epistolary exchange, of 18th-cent. stateliness in form, but almost pornographic in content, between Kitty, a would-be novelist, who writes from Cheyne Walk, in Chelsea, and her married friend Laura, who writes from Vanly Hall, Leics. Kitty's sexual adventures take in various bohemian men and, in some detail, a bohemian woman. She eventually marries a rising artist with something of the young Lewis about him.

[93] O'Keeffe, *Some Kind of Genius*, 282–9.   [94] *AG* 221–33.

[95] *The Laughter of Fools* (London: Duckworth, 1920), 125.   [96] *AG* 115.

ever been read by a small section of the educated class (politicians, bishops, generals, stockbrokers), and that reading his books had therefore been widely regarded as a sign of stupidity; whereas Edgar Wallace is everywhere the fashion, his popularity symptomatic of 'high-brow capitulation' in the face of 'universal pressure'. Lewis would seem to agree that times have changed: Dan Boleyn is an Oppenheim character, and thus redundant, while Willie Service reads Wallace, and will probably rule the world. Ratner proposes the Parisian avant-garde as a model for resistance to universal levelling. Zagreus remains sceptical. 'And our solitary high-brow pur-sang Lewis?' Ratner enquires. There is no response. What, indeed, of Lewis? *The Wild Body* had been 'pur-sang' all right. But *The Apes of God*?

CHAPTER 10

Beyond Modernism, Beyond Paranoia

MY ARGUMENT CONCERNING 'paranoid Modernism' has reached a point where any further elaboration would be significantly reiterative. It must stand or fall by what it has enabled me to say about works by Conrad, Ford, Lawrence, and Lewis, and about the embeddedness of those works in early twentieth-century English culture and society: their reckoning with professional status and with the psychopathies of expertise, their grasp of masculinity as a form of cultural capital, their postliberalism, their susceptibility to moral panic. To develop the argument further would require the construction of a different frame of reference. I have drawn attention in previous chapters to a major shift of emphasis which took place during the second half of the nineteenth century, at the same time as the establishment in manifestos, magazines, novels, textbooks, case-histories, and 'institutions' of one kind or another of new psychiatric and literary methods. Paranoia ceased to provide a terminology for aspiration, and became instead the focus of a critique of social mimesis. That is the shift of emphasis out of which both literary Modernism and the new psychiatry in some measure arose. What has happened since then (Lewis, for one, could see it happening) is the commodification of paranoia. Postmodern paranoia may look like the product of ideology, of wars variously warm and cold. But it is, above all, a commodity. It is something we possess rather than something we inhabit. No longer a strategy for the acquisition of symbolic capital, it has become a *form* of symbolic capital: proof of a liberal conscience, in Hollywood in the 1970s; proof of literary sophistication, in the novels of Thomas Pynchon, and in the many books and articles written about them. Commodification is the frame of reference which postmodern paranoia requires.

In this final chapter, I have chosen neither to reiterate nor to develop historically my hypotheses concerning paranoid

Modernism. Reiteration would be tedious, and historical development would require another book. What I propose to do instead is to review briefly the ways in which Ford, Lawrence, and Lewis each came to literary terms with his own, or his work's, 'paranoia'. Paranoia was for them an imaginative resource, and a method. They were never locked into it.

LAWRENCE'S WAR: PARANOIA AS NIGHTMARE

It is well known that *Kangaroo* (1923) incorporates a thinly disguised memoir of Lawrence's own experience during the First World War: harassment by the authorities, physical and moral humiliation, a sense of hatred and despair at the wanton destruction of 'old England'. The chapter which constitutes the memoir has since lent its title—'Nightmare'—to books or parts of books whose aim is to define that experience as a turning-point in his life and career.[1] The experience had as its core, I would suggest, an elaboration of paranoid symmetry.

In *Kangaroo*, Lawrence identified England's 'nightmare' with liberalism's eclipse. 'From 1916 to 1919 a wave of criminal lust rose and possessed England, there was a reign of terror, under a set of indecent bullies like Bottomley of *John Bull* and other bottom-dog members of the House of Commons.' The French Revolution, paranoia's most durable political context and content, frames the Lloyd George administration as a reign of terror. Under that administration, Richard Lovat Somers, the novel's essay-writing protagonist, 'had known what it was to live in a perpetual state of semi-fear: the fear of the criminal public and the criminal government'. The fear had been a fear of enforced social mimesis. 'The torture was steadily applied, during those years after Asquith fell, to break the independent soul in any man who would not hunt with the criminal mob.'[2]

The scene of persecution's epiphany is the Cornish coast, where Somers and his wife Harriet live in a remote cottage, as Lawrence

[1] Paul Delany, *D. H. Lawrence's Nightmare: The Writer and his Circle in the Years of the Great War* (Hassocks: Harvester Press, 1979); Mark Kinkead-Weekes, *D. H. Lawrence: Triumph to Exile, 1912–1922* (Cambridge: CUP, 1996), 399–403.
[2] *Kangaroo* (Harmondsworth: Penguin Books, 1950), 235. Henceforth *K*.

and Frieda had done. Submarine warfare had turned Cornwall into an area of considerable military significance. It is perhaps not surprising that the Lawrences—she a German citizen, he a vocal opponent of the war—should have been suspected of espionage. On the morning of 12 October 1917, a young army officer arrived at their cottage, with a police sergeant and two plain-clothes men. He presented a search-warrant, and read out a formal expulsion order which gave them until the 15th to pack up and leave. They would not be allowed to enter any area of military significance, and were required to report to the local police wherever they went, within twenty-four hours of arrival. At the centre of Lawrence's 'nightmare', Kinkead-Weekes remarks, as expressed in *Kangaroo*, 'was the feeling that he must have been surrounded by a miasma of malevolent suspicion and *personal* hatred, his privacy constantly violated by prying eyes, while he lived in blithe ignorance of any such thing'.[3]

Lawrence's more general response to the reign of terror, and to the distortions it had induced even in those who had taken a stand against it, was nausea. The nausea vividly expressed in his letters of the period found its object, as the Douglas–Kristeva hypothesis would anticipate, in creatures thought abominable, during this period of social and political 'semi-terror', not so much in themselves as in their confounding of the classificatory scheme which orders the natural world.

Lawrence's encounter with the homosexual members of the Bloomsbury group, in 1915, provoked a crisis. He dreamt about a beetle that bit like a scorpion. 'It is this horror of little swarming selves', he reported, 'that I can't stand: Birrells, D. Grants, and Keynses . . .' What appalled him about the Birrells and Keyneses, of course, was their blurring of the necessary distinctions between the male and the female of the species. The sight of Keynes wearing pyjamas in the middle of the day provoked in him 'the most dreadful sense of repulsiveness—something like carrion'. Sartorial hybridity made for a sexual hybridity which was not so much morally wrong as physically corrupt. Lawrence concluded that the unfortunate Birrell had 'something nasty about him, like black-beetles'.[4] The black-beetle might be regarded as doubly hybrid,

---

[3] *Triumph to Exile*, 401–2.
[4] *Letters*, ed. James T. Boulton *et al.*, 7 vols. (Cambridge: CUP, 1979–93), ii. 319–21.

since it is strictly speaking not a beetle at all, but a cockroach, an orthopterous insect characterized by incomplete metamorphosis.

As Mary Douglas reminds us, cultures which feel themselves under threat tend to regard any violation of the physical body as a violation of the body politic. Lawrence certainly did.[5] In April 1915, the mechanical sensuality of soldiers on the beach at Worthing reminded him of lice or bugs. 'They will murder their officers one day. They are teeming insects.' Hell, he concluded, must be 'slow and creeping and viscous, and insect-teeming: as is this Europe now—this England'. Intermediate movement (creeping, teeming) was soon to be joined in the lexicon of disgust by an intermediate condition: viscosity. The 'foul world of mud' was rising all about him, he wrote in January 1917; he thought of himself as a winged creature caught a 'vinegary fly-trap'. In April 1917, the introduction of a new Military Service Act prompted a wholesale rejection of the 'wretched conglomerate messing' that experience had become for him.[6] Only in nausea could this England be fully apprehended. In February 1917 he had written some essays on 'The Reality of Peace'. These essays make it plain that in his view the real 'enemy' and 'abomination' was the 'multiplied nullity' of the masses who neither create nor destroy, but merely imitate.[7] War had brought about the universalization of social mimesis.

In a recent account of *Kangaroo* which rightly insists on the novel's signficance for Lawrence's career, and for English literature in the 1920s, David Ayers observes that its theme is the crisis afflicting an individual's perception of the status and scope afforded him or her by a mass society. The novel transposes to Australia the struggle between fascism and communism Lawrence had witnessed in Italy between 1920 and 1922. The political commentary it offers is to the effect that conflict within nations has superseded conflict between nations. As Ayers points out, each kind of conflict is 'a form of collective struggle between masses which demand the allegiance of individuals only in order to extinguish them as individuals'.

<hr>

[5] *Purity and Danger: An Analysis of the Concepts of Pollution and Taboo* (London: Routledge, 1966), 124, 121.

[6] *Letters*, ii. 330–1, iii. 89, 83, 110.

[7] *Reflections on the Death of a Porcupine and Other Essays*, ed. Michael Herbert (Cambridge: CUP, 1988), 41–4.

Richard Somers has to decide whether to align himself with the Australian version of fascism, or the Australian version of communism, or neither. The decision he arrives at, with a little help from Nietzsche, perhaps, is that he must at all costs preserve his 'absolute' and 'isolate' individuality against the 'mass' or 'herd', the 'criminal mob'. *Kangaroo* is a novel about social and political crisis, in the post-war period, and about the crisis which might have been thought to afflict the novel as a genre. Ostentatiously plotless and argumentative, it will not commit itself to literary convention, to mimesis. Ayers rightly remarks on Lawrence's evident determination that it should 'open out on to history' rather than 'attempt to ward off historical crisis through its own aesthetic closure'.[8] One of the histories it opens out onto is the history of paranoia as a critique of social mimesis.

Like Lawrence himself, Richard Somers had learnt about the needs and obligations of the 'independent soul' during his wartime nightmare. The knowledge which enables him to resist seduction by mass political movement is a knowledge forged in the very heat of persecution, during the time he and Harriet spend in their Cornish cottage. 'Somers and Harriet lived now with that suspense about them in the very air they breathed. They were suspects.' When they are kicked out of Cornwall, and return to London, Somers becomes a Caleb Williams, a Walter Hartright. When they move to Oxfordshire, suspicion trails them. 'But still he knew he was being watched all the time. Strange men questioning the cottage woman next door, as to all his doings. He began to *feel* a criminal.' Now he is Richard Hannay, but a Hannay nauseously surrounded by swarming and viscosity. 'The foul, dense, carrion-eating mob were trying to set their teeth in him.'[9]

For Somers, the turning-point or moment of paranoid illumination comes when he realizes that he is being persecuted for what he is rather than for what he has done, or not done. The carrion-eating mob hate him because he is not one of them, because he is special. 'But then his soul revived.' In his case, as in Daniel Paul Schreber's, as in Rupert Birkin's, revival takes the form of a desire

[8] *English Literature of the 1920s* (Edinburgh: Edinburgh University Press, 1999), 129–33.
[9] K 241, 276–7.

to eliminate: 'I despise them. They are *canaille*, carrion-eating, filthy-mouthed *canaille*, like dead-man-devouring jackals. I wish to God I could kill them. I wish I had power to blight them, to slay them with a blight, slay them in thousands and thousands. I wish to God I could kill them off, the masses of *canaille*.' The sheer intermediacy of the masses, their inability to be definitively one thing or the other, justifies their extermination. Through this insurgence of megalomania, paranoid symmetry adjusts the degree of fantasized grandeur to the degree of fantasized persecution. 'Let me watch them', Somers muses, 'to keep them at bay. But let me never admit for one single moment that *they* may be *my* judges.' They hate me because I am special; I am special because they hate me. 'So he discovered the great secret: to stand alone as his own judge of himself, absolutely.' It is this discovery, first made during the wartime nightmare, and recalled in his Australian crisis, which enables Somers to preserve his independent soul from mass culture. Seeing himself in Somers, or the Somers in himself, Lawrence owned up to paranoia. He found in it, as Rupert Birkin may or may not have been able to do, the psychopathy of his own expertise: the sickness, at once maddening and necessary, of his own professional status as 'a preacher and a blatherer'.[10] The admission is by no means the least notable of his literary experiments.

FORD MADOX FORD AND THE QUALITY OF ENTANGLEMENTS

Feelings of individual and collective persecution inform much of the fiction Ford Madox Ford wrote during and after the First World War. He had not previously been a stranger to paranoia, as we have seen. But the feelings of persecution certainly intensified after his arrival in France in the summer of 1916: he rapidly became aware that his commanding officer had little confidence in him, and the first-hand experience he soon gained of the conduct and effects of the war did not inspire confidence in commanding officers of any kind. On 22 October 1917, he met Stella Bowen, and realized that he must finally break off his difficult but durable relationship

[10]   *K* 277–8, 287, 300.

with Violet Hunt. His private life became the object of unfounded rumour and speculation, as did his patriotism. Unlike Lawrence, Ford did not live in a perpetual state of semi-fear; but he did feel suspect.

In 'True Love and a G.C.M.', a fragment of a novel written between September 1918 and March 1919, at a time when he was still anxious about the damage the war might have done to his mind, Lieutenant Gabriel Morton endures sustained persecution ('strafing') from men who are his military superiors but moral inferiors. He is falsely accused of cowardice, and the General Court Martial towards which the story moves would have given both Morton and his creator the chance to refute some of the charges brought against them. This is, or would have been, in the strictest sense a paranoid narrative: a narrative whose function is to produce feelings of grandeur in and through feelings of persecution. Feelings of persecution also feature in another wartime story, 'The Colonel's Shoes'. One of the main protagonists is a Captain Gotch, a man at once attractive and in some way marked, about whom there is 'a good deal of gossip'. Like Conrad's Lord Jim, Gotch imagines that contemptuous words spoken in his hearing about a third party referred to him. Both 'True Love and a G.C.M.' and 'The Colonel's Shoes' concern those whom the war has driven to the very edge of 'unreason', or beyond.[11]

For Christopher Tietjens, the protagonist of *Parade's End* (1924–8), as for Gabriel Morton, there is simply no end to the strafing.[12] Max Saunders has drawn attention to the close resemblance between the 'sense of persecution and disgrace' which haunts Tietjens and the anxieties Ford himself expressed in a letter

---

[11] 'True Love and a G.C.M.' and 'The Colonel's Shoes' have been reprinted in *War Prose*, ed. Max Saunders (Manchester: Carcanet, 1999). The quotations from the latter are on pp. 160–1. A passage omitted from the published version of the story reveals that the gossip about Gotch 'ranged from nasty—very nasty things about him and women and the Colonel of his Reserve Battalion, to the allegation that a firm, in which he had been a junior partner before the war, had been fined heavily for trading with the enemy' (p. 161). As I have mentioned, one of Ford's sensitivities concerned his supposed sympathy for Germany.

[12] The 4 vols. which constitute *Parade's End* are *Some Do Not . . .* (London: Duckworth, 1924), *No More Parades* (London: Duckworth, 1925), *A Man could Stand Up—* (London: Duckworth, 1926), and *Last Post* (London: Duckworth, 1928). I have used the omnibus edn. of *Parade's End* (Harmondsworth: Penguin Books, 1982). Henceforth *PE*.

he wrote to his mother during the long-drawn-out separation from Violet Hunt. But Saunders argues, quite rightly, I think, that *Parade's End*, unlike 'True Love and a G.C.M.', should be considered a 'study of paranoia', rather than its expression.[13] Taken out of context, Tietjens's belief that the war is a huge conspiracy—'All these men given into the hands of the most cynically care-free intriguers in long corridors who made plots that harrowed the hearts of the world'—looks like paranoia. But its context is a bombardment, a literal 'strafe'.[14] The passage is about the way war drives men mad rather than terrified (or as well as terrified). War has reduced Tietjens to feelings of persecution and disgrace which Ford is able to recognize as in some measure delusory. *Parade's End* is a counter-paranoid novel about paranoia, a novel made possible by the failure of 'True Love and a G.C.M.' What interests me about it is the muddle Tietjens forever finds himself in: paranoiacs, by contrast, find themselves by eliminating muddle. In *Parade's End*, Ford celebrated muddle.

Tietjens is a civil servant, and a mathematician of genius; and on those occasions when he is reduced to paranoia by wars military and sexual he sometimes discerns pattern where there is none. But his ultimate strength is that he does not expect the world to conform either to his equations or to his fantasies. The novel's chief exegete and fantasist is his wife, Sylvia, whose unforgiving harassment of her husband drives the story through four volumes to its far-from-bitter end. Sylvia certainly makes messes, but their deliberation shines through the scatter of effects, its malevolence transcending chance. Her first action, after she has been reconciled temporarily with Christopher, in *Some Do Not . . .*, is an inaugural (or reinaugural) mess-making. She throws a plate containing two cold cutlets in aspic and some salad at her husband's head. 'Tietjens had moved slightly as she had thrown. The cutlets and most of the salad leaves had gone over his shoulder. But one, couched, very

---

[13] *Ford Madox Ford: A Dual Life*, 2 vols. (Oxford: OUP, 1996), ii. 74, 235. Paranoia is a persistent theme in Saunders's account of Ford's life. Saunders's critical astuteness is vitiated, in historical terms, by an over-reliance on Freud's definition of the nature and aetiology of paranoia. There were, and are, other things to be said about delusions of grandeur and persecution. John Batchelor points out that other novels by Ford, such as *A Call* and *The Simple Life Limited*, also concern paranoia: *The Edwardian Novelists* (London: Duckworth, 1982), 93, 115. For a discussion of the latter, see Ch. 6 above.

[14] PE 296.

green leaf was on his shoulder-strap, and the oil and vinegar from the plate . . . had splashed from the revers of his tunic to his green staff-badges.' Tietjens is Modernism's great mess-receiver. He tolerates a level of confusion in the world which could be said to match the level of confusion in his own view of the world, and vice versa. The man who before returning to the Front commits himself fully to Valentine Wannop, with whom he has fallen in love, is, among other things, but perhaps above all else, a man wearing his second-best tunic. In *A Man could Stand Up —*, Valentine, reflecting on the misconceptions about Tietjens and herself created by a whole series of chance encounters, identifies him with muddle. 'That', she concludes, 'was the *quality* of his entanglements, their very essence. He got into appalling messes, unending and unravellable—no, she meant un-unravellable!—messes and other people suffered for him whilst he mooned on—into more messes!'[15]

This implicit advocacy of entanglement is not what one would have expected from Ford, whose decisive career as an editor and critic was one long campaign against carelessness of expression. It was Ford, after all, who in a review of Ezra Pound's *How to Read* described the best modern writing as a form of *pointillisme*. 'You put point beside point, each point crepitating against all that surrounds it. That is what Ezra means by "charged" words. They are such as find electricity by f[r]iction with their neighbours.' *Pointillisme*, Ford went on, was Flaubert's solution to the problem that 'words following slumberously—obviously—the one the other let the reader's attention wander'.[16] Thanks to Ford, this drilling of attention is part of what we now mean by Modernism. And *Parade's End* does indeed make full use of literary shock tactics: time-shifts, alterations of point of view, polyphony. To my mind, however, its great achievement is its *slumberousness*, its refusal to make a Modernist row about the reader's attention wandering. A book can be modern without crepitating, or at least without crepitating all the way through.

Slumberousness, or apparent slumberousness, is one of Tietjens's chief characteristics. It is a feature of his physical presence, above all,

---

[15] *PE* 279, 523.
[16] 'Pound and How to Read', *New Review*, 2 (Apr. 1932), 39–45; repr. in Brita Lindberg-Seyersted (ed.), *Pound/Ford: The Story of a Literary Friendship* (London: Faber & Faber, 1983), 105–6.

and of the way in which that presence is represented. Tietjens is
decidedly stout, and his lack of shape is a continued affront to
identities founded, as identities so often are in realist fiction, on
social difference. When he and his older brother Mark stand facing
each other, Mark suggests carved wood, Christopher wheat-sacks.
It is Mark, the man of 'rigid outline', who cracks up, while, to
Sylvia's despair, the 'lumpish' Christopher survives more or less
intact. 'How, she said to herself, could she ever move, put
emotion into, this lump! It was like trying to move an immense
mattress filled with feathers. You pulled at one end, but the whole
mass sagged down and remained immobile until you seemed to
have no strength at all.' Sylvia is by no means alone in her perception of Tietjens's essential shapelessness. When Valentine Wannop
encounters him for the second time, in *Some Do Not*, at a breakfast hosted by Ethel Duchemin, she concludes that he has more in
common with the meat-pies on the sideboard than with the delicate Turners on the wall. Tietjens bulks and looms: he expands, he
overflows; he fills space, and minds. He is to be found 'lumping
opposite' a maddened fellow-officer, Captain McKechnic, or
'splurging heavily down' on a camp-bed, or 'ballooning slowly'
from a doorway.[17] His pneumatic physical presence is a slumberous consistency in a narrative articulated by time-shifts and alterations of point of view: the one thing about which everyone
agrees. It is paranoia's messy antidote, its antidote in mess.

That presence acquires during the course of the tetralogy a
specific narrative idiom, of lumping and splurging. Such moments,
usually seen from the point of view of an omniscient narrator,
though sometimes coloured by the emotions which other protagonists bring to them, are among the book's most traditional. The
language in which they are described is not at all *pointilliste*. Indeed,
it rather ostentatiously lacks Poundian crepitation. Why, for example, should Tietjens be seen to gaze with 'large, fishish eyes' at his
breakfast, when he himself, at a later moment, rather more intelli-
gibly seeks out the 'fish-like eyes' of a military bureaucrat?[18] The
epithet 'fishish', though hard to get one's tongue around, does not
crepitate: it does not find electricity by friction with its neighbours.
It manages to be idiosyncratic without being disruptive. Since we

---

[17] *PE* 199, 217, 15, 406, 86, 294, 342, 342, 261.   [18] *PE* 92, 223.

have a pretty good idea what the writer means, we read slumberously on, as we do when we encounter the idiosyncratic yet nondisruptive 'lumping' and 'splurging'. To settle for 'fishish' seems mere laziness on the writer's part. It *is*, I think, laziness; but not *mere* laziness. Through such laziness, Ford declared his new antipathy to system. *Parade's End* is something of an anti-experiment.

In *Parade's End*, events fulfil, in so far as they relate to Tietjens, some mysterious principle of inadvertency. Sylvia, with her plateful of cutlets, and the Germans, with their high-explosive shells, get close enough to him to do him some damage, but not quite the damage they had intended. From their partial success, strange consequences flow, including serious damage to people other than Tietjens. Sylvia's malicious gossip, which was meant to 'smash' Tietjens, smashes his father instead.[19] The destructive effect of artillery fire is almost entirely collateral, as *A Man could Stand Up* demonstrates at some length. Tietjens's enemies conspire furiously against him, but are saved from their own worst instincts by muddle, rather than by conscience, or by any measure he has taken to protect himself.

One scene, above all, establishes the moral and aesthetic value of muddle. In *Some Do Not*, Tietjens and Valentine Wannop get to know each other, during a moonlit drive in a horse-drawn cart, by correcting each other's misclassifications, misquotations, and mispronunciations. But Tietjens realizes that what Valentine means to him is in part a holiday from his own impossibly high standards, from the duty he has imposed upon himself to correct other people's mistakes: a holiday, that is, from 'clear observation' and 'exact thought'. This in a man who, when we first meet him, has for the past few months employed himself in 'tabulating from memory the errors in the *Encyclopaedia Britannica*, of which a new edition had lately appeared'. The recognition occurs pneumatically, in that wheat-sack body whose slumberous centrality I have insisted on. 'He felt his limbs lengthen, as if they too had relaxed.' And it, too, finds its correlative in an event, in yet another near-miss from which unforeseen consequences flow, as General Campion's motor-car scrapes along the side of the cart, injuring the horse, but not Valentine, or Tietjens.[20]

[19] *PE* 422.   [20] *PE* 130–1, 10, 129, 139–41.

In not quite getting the right word, in getting instead a word which is neither the obvious one nor a miniature vortex, the omniscient narrator, too, fulfils that principle of inadvertency. There is in this respect a kind of mutual infection between the writer and his protagonists, of which events are a symptom. *Parade's End*'s omniscience is modern, paradoxically, because it ignores Ford's own Modernist principles: the commitment to clear observation and exact thought. Thus, the word 'crepitate', when used in *The Last Post* to describe a sound made by Tietjens, rather evidently does not crepitate.[21] It is, in fact, what I have termed a near-miss: the epitome of that slumberousness or obesity which constitutes the tetralogy's great literary achievement. For the narration is at this point coloured by the thoughts and feelings of Mark Tietjens's French wife, Marie Léonie, who has lived in England for most of her life, but not acquired the language. *Crépiter* is a lot more common in French than 'crepitate' is in English: its use here is a French speaker's stab at what an English speaker would probably designate a croak. If Lawrence consciously took on paranoia's shape, after the war, Ford renounced it.

WYNDHAM LEWIS'S POSTLIBERALISM

Neither owning up nor renunciation was ever very much to Lewis's taste. For him, there had to be a better way to understand, and perhaps even to resolve, the paranoid symmetry informing his attitude to literary experiment. In autobiographically owning up to paranoia, Lawrence admitted that his confession did not amount to a novel; in renouncing it, Ford took up once again with the novel's haphazardness, its fidelity to the world as it is. Lewis, by contrast, stubbornly renewed in book after book his attempts to vorticize the novel, to transform it from within. And yet there are parallels in his fiction and criticism of the late 1920s and early 1930s both to Lawrence's owning up and to Ford's renunciation.

The Apes of God was by no means the last shot fired in Lewis's campaign against social mimesis and its attendant amateurisms. The essay which concludes *Satire and Fiction* was reworked and

---

[21] PE 703.

incorporated into *Men without Art* (1934), a series of reflections on individual writers (Hemingway, Faulkner, Eliot, James, Woolf, Flaubert) which finds in their work a sinister if for the most part wholly inadvertent politics of culture. By its author's account, this was yet another book written neither for pleasure nor for gain, but because circumstances demanded it, as an obligation to his own charismatic professionalism. In the years since the First World War, Lewis felt, 'obstacles' to and 'interferences' with the 'free exercise of the artistic faculty' had so proliferated that he really had no alternative but to try to clear them out of the way.[22]

On 30 March 1934, Ernest Hemingway and his wife called at Sylvia Beach's bookshop at 12 rue de l'Odéon. While the two women chatted, Hemingway sat down to read the latest issue of *Life and Letters*.[23] Before long, his face began to flush. Hurling the magazine to the floor, he took a swing at the vase of tulips which stood on a table nearby. The vase crashed to the floor. The item which had so upset him was an essay on his work by Wyndham Lewis. The essay, imperturbably entitled 'The Dumb Ox', subsequently became the first chapter in *Men without Art*, whose title parodies that of Hemingway's collection of stories about soldiers, matadors, and pugilists, *Men without Women*.

According to Lewis, the world of Hemingway's fiction was a world emptied of will. 'His puppets are leaves, *very violently* blown hither and thither . . .' What in all likelihood did for the vase of tulips was the further suggestion that, in sedulously aping the style of Gertrude Stein, Hemingway had *become* a puppet, a literary phantom. 'This infantile, dull-witted, dreamy stutter compels whoever uses it to conform to the infantile, dull-witted type. He passes over into the category of *those to whom things are done*, from that of those who execute.' According to Lewis, Hemingway's work blurs the necessary distinction between art and life, and thus in a dumb-ox manner reproduces the social mimesis which everywhere in the modern world has diminished the ancient 'variety of situations'. It fatally lacks the will-to-abstraction. Lewis regarded writing of this kind as 'one of the first fruits of the *proletarianization*

---

[22] *Men without Art*, ed. Seamus Cooney (Santa Rosa, Calif.: Black Sparrow Press, 1987), 231, 234.

[23] Paul O'Keeffe, *Some Sort of Genius: A Life of Wyndham Lewis* (London: Jonathan Cape, 2000), 342–3.

which, as a result of the amazing revolutions in the technique of industry, we are all undergoing, whether we like it or not'.[24]

In formulating his critique of the decadent 'naturalism' pervasive in contemporary fiction, Lewis turned once again, as he had not done in *Satire and Fiction*, to that most obstinate of abstractionists, T. E. Hulme. It is as though he wished to revive the revolutionary spirit of the pre-war years.

The *naturalist* stream started flowing in Hellas, and it has gone on flowing in the centre of the European consciousness ever since. Only now, at last, has it begun to dry up. I should direct you to Egypt, to China or Japan, to select the monumental counterblast to this last vulgar decadence of the original Hellenic mistake.[25]

Lewis's words, in 1934, could perfectly well have been Hulme's, in 1914. The difference lies in the extent to which the mimeticism to which abstraction opposed itself was now the product of *political* doctrine. Nausea is Lewis's diagnostic tool, as it had been Hulme's, but the amateurism which provokes it has taken on a political guise. What is repulsive about communism's spokesmen is not the political doctrine they put forward, but their desire at once to emulate and to belittle those who, unlike them, are capable of independent thinking. Themselves 'artists *manqués*', they cannot stand the sight of those they wish to replace. The only way to guarantee the livelihood and status of the genuine artist, Lewis goes on, would be a cull of all such politicized apes of god.[26] The argument is postliberal in its conversion of a horizontal class war between bourgeoisie and proletariat into a vertical class war between aspirants to professional status and prestige. In developing it, Lewis draws as if by instinct on the paranoia in Hulme's obstinate abstractionism.

The early 1930s was the period of Lewis's most intense engagement with fascism. The inquiry into the politics of post-war British culture launched in *Men without Art* owes allegiance neither to left nor to right (it is, precisely, postliberal). The few fellow outcasts Lewis was ready to acknowledge *did*, however, in some cases, owe

[24] *Men without Art*, 22–3, 26, 27–8, 33.
[25] Ibid. 96. Hulme provides the explicit focus for a later chapter in *Men without Art* on 'The Terms "Classical" and "Romantic"'.
[26] Ibid. 226.

an allegiance: and not to Karl Marx. 'And now, as I am finishing these notes for my book,' he wrote in the introduction to its final and most overtly political part, 'we are reading of the landing of cargoes of machine-guns for the I.R.A., of the establishment by de Valera of an "Ogpu" (the happy possessor of "a hooded terror") and of preparations for the outlawry of "the Blue Shirts", their antagonists.'[27] In *The Apes of God*, Zagreus had used the 'war-jargon of german peace-politics'—*Entlastungsoffensiven*, *Teiloperationen*—to characterize for Ratner the resistance to mass-culture mounted both by the Parisian avant-garde and by the 'solitary high-brow pur-sang Lewis'.[28] The introduction to *Men without Art* subscribes to this war-jargon to the extent of characterizing the polemical forays which follow as *Entlastungsoffensiven*: offensives designed to relieve pressure.[29] It was during 1934 that Lewis's association with Sir Oswald Mosley became, as O'Keeffe puts it, 'an excuse for cloak-and-dagger theatricals'. The leader of the British Union of Fascists recalled that Lewis would come to see him at dead of night, in the most 'conspiratorial' fashion. 'He suggested that he was in fear of assassination, but the unkind said he was avoiding his creditors.'[30]

Vincent Sherry is surely right to see in Lewis's fellow-travelling the expression of a durable 'inward bent'; and he describes convincingly the 'aesthetic form' that expression took.[31] As I have already shown, there is some reason to think that paranoid symmetry gave shape to Lewis's inward bent, and to the defence of Nazi Germany which was its most elaborate political expression. According to Paul Edwards, Lewis's 'sympathetic exposition' of Nazism in 1931 stemmed, first, from his anxiety (or terror) that

[27] Ibid. 204. Lewis's survey of the 'inconvenient and insanitary bog' of post-war British culture to some extent echoes the language of 'mire' and 'morass' to be found in descriptions of post-war German culture by protofascist *Freikorps* officers. Ibid. 141–2; and Klaus Theweleit, *Male Fantasies*, 2 vols., tr. Erica Carter, Stephen Conway, and Chris Turner (Cambridge: Polity Press, 1987–9), i. 387–92.

[28] *The Apes of God* (London: Arthur Press, 1930), 401–2; *The Apes of God*, with an Afterword by Paul Edwards (Santa Barbara, Calif.: Black Sparrow Press, 1981), 401–2.

[29] *Men without Art*, 14.

[30] *Some Kind of Genius*, 346. The quotation is from Mosley's *My Life* (London: Nelson, 1968), 225. When Naomi Mitchison told Lewis about the manhandling of women protesters at a BUF rally at Olympia, he responded by 'badgering her with counter-evidence of Communist brutality': *Some Kind of Genius*, 344–5.

[31] *Ezra Pound, Wyndham Lewis, and Radical Modernism* (Oxford: OUP, 1993), 118–27.

worsening economic conditions would lead to world war; and secondly from his belief that Nazi policies corresponded to the diagnoses of post-war culture he himself had put forward in books like *The Art of Being Ruled*. As Edwards points out, the economic analyses which occupy part vi of Lewis's book about Hitler are based on the premise that those 'in control' of the world's financial systems have been conspiring with communism to overthrow civilization. It is a fantasy worthy of a thriller by John Buchan, or an essay by Ezra Pound. 'Lewis's paranoia,' Edwards concludes, 'his fear of occult forces working through the financial system and through "agitators" in order to bring about war and enslave the West . . . virtually *is* Nazism (and vice versa) at this stage of the movement's history, before it came to power.'[32]

Hitler was in Lewis's mind another *Entlastungsoffensive*, as its treatment of Nazi theories of racial purity makes abundantly clear. Lewis knew perfectly well that these theories were worthless, but still felt obliged to make use of them.

Really the point is, I think, that we 'Aryans', or whatever we are, are faced with extinction. We cannot afford just now to be philosophers, nor yet humanitarians. No one will be philosophical, nor yet humanitarian, with *us*. Yes, the above argument of Hitler's is an argument for *an emergency*. Everything now almost, since the War, seems a matter of life and death. It is not an argument for the scientific mind, but for the political mind.

Lewis represents himself as the only Englishman (he had not yet met Mosley) fully aware of the extent of the crisis facing 'we "Aryans"'. Once himself a stolid citizen, he has been transformed by his inadvertent possession of the truth about conspiracy into an amateur agent: an outsider, with every man's hand against him, who may yet come back inside again as a charismatic professional, if only someone will acknowledge his charisma. He is Richard Hannay. In Lewis's case, however, it was the Western Front which delivered the moment of paranoid illumination. 'The war, as you are aware, went on and on, and these questions in the end *asked themselves* as it were, with a more obstinate urgency every day. Nothing had warned me, prior to that, to expect such [a] number of shells, bullets, and bombs to rain suddenly out of nothingness, all

---

[32] *Wyndham Lewis: Painter and Writer* (New Haven, Conn.: Yale University Press, 2000), 385–7.

aimed essentially at *my* head.' The connection between Lewis's own predicament and these political questions which ask themselves is the delusion of reference built into mechanized warfare: the thought that all the shells, bullets, and bombs are aimed exclusively at *you* (whereas in fact the ones aimed at you are just as likely to hit someone else, and vice versa, as Christopher Tietjens discovers). 'Unlike, I daresay, most of my companions, I realized that something in this "storm of steel" required explaining . . .'.[33] Lewis persuaded himself that the political questions, like the bombs and bullets, were aimed exclusively at him. He set his creative work aside in order to tackle finance capital's riddle of the sands.

For Frederic Jameson, that decision illuminates the seductiveness of 'protofascism'. Jameson argues that Lewis's politics took the protofascist form of an implacable hostility at once to Marxism and to the middle-class ideologies represented in the parliamentary system. According to him, Lewis's obsession with the formal problem of the 'social and narrative place' to be assigned to the 'essentially placeless observer/satirist' was the product of a ' "petty-bourgeois" stance'.[34] One problem with this view, as Sherry points out, is that Lewis's 'political identity' was formed by resistance to such reductive binary models of political allegiance: fascism as no more than Marxism's antithesis.[35] I would want to argue that it was also shaped by a postliberal obsession with vertical rather than horizontal class conflict. Lewis's *Entlastungsoffensiven* were the culmination of a long-standing antipathy to social mimesis in English society and culture, an antipathy which cannot be associated exclusively with a ' "petty-bourgeois" stance', since that stance is one of its prime targets. Willie Service, in *The Apes of God*, is hateful for the same reason as Uriah Heep in *David Copperfield*: both threaten to usurp the genuine professional, the genuine writer, by imitation.

Fascism's appeal was to Lewis's expertise: in part because its

---

[33] *Hitler* (London: Chatto & Windus, 1931), 127–9.

[34] *Fables of Aggression: Wyndham Lewis, the Modernist as Fascist* (Berkeley, Calif.: University of California Press, 1979), 14–19. Jameson characterizes protofascism as 'a shifting strategy of class alliances whereby an initially strong populist and anticapitalist impulse is gradually readapted to the ideological habits of a petty bourgeoisie, which can itself be displaced when, with the consolidation of the fascist state, effective power passes back into the hands of big business'.

[35] *Radical Modernism*, 102.

policies seemed to confirm his diagnoses of the 1920s, in part because those policies constituted at once an opportunity for and an instrument of further and more ambitious diagnosis. We might recall, once again, Ernst Wagner. In the asylum, Wagner professed literature, and found in Nazism's racial theories a reason to despise the man who had failed to acknowledge his literary pre-eminence, the Jewish poet Franz Werfel. During the 1920s and early 1930s, the figure of the 'Jew' had the 'potential', as Edwards puts it, to become the focus of Lewis's 'paranoid fantasies', and on occasion did so.[36] The political trajectory established in both cases seems to me postliberal rather than protofascist. In constituting himself as a postliberal prompted to ask certain questions by the 'storm of steel', Lewis owns up, as Lawrence had done, to paranoia.

LEWIS GUNS

Lewis, however, knew as well as anyone that the kind of campaign he had mounted before the war on behalf of a charismatic professionalism would only work if the conditions were favourable. In the late 1920s and early 1930s, the conditions were not favourable. The knowledge that they were not favourable can certainly be said to have informed the fiction Lewis wrote at the time.

The Vorticists had thought of themselves as the men best equipped to describe modernity to their fellow citizens. And it did matter, as we have seen, and as many commentators have emphasized, that they were men. They were, as David Peters Corbett has put it, 'exaggeratedly "brutal" in their display of a culturally gendered masculinity'. The point about that brutality was that it worked, in the pre-war years. It yielded symbolic capital. The war, however, put a different complexion on brutality. There was no future, the critic John Cournos announced in 1919, for Vorticism and its 'masculomaniac spokesmen'. Corbett observes that the

---

[36] *Wyndham Lewis*, 391. The most extensive account of the use of anti-Semitic caricature for ideological purposes in Lewis's fiction is David Ayers, *Wyndham Lewis and Western Man* (Basingstoke: Macmillan, 1992). Ayers quite rightly points to a lengthy addition to the 1928 edn. of *Tarr* which describes the part played by Soltyk's second, a 'rat-like' Jew called Pochinsky, in the duel between Soltyk and Kreisler: Pochinsky not only fails to mend the quarrel, but appears to exult in its violent outcome (pp. 139–43).

'confident linkage' of masculinity, creative force, and the public expression of modern experience which had been Vorticism's making proved impossible to sustain in the 1920s. It is no coincidence, he continues, that the protagonists of Lewis's *The Childermass* (1928) are sexually ambiguous and ineffective both in action and in desire: 'the ideological opposites, in short, of the image of the active, heterosexual, male artist which supported the ambitions of Vorticism in the years before the war'.[37] Lewis, like Ford, whom he had once exercised his brutality on, was losing faith in masculomania. The loss of faith is evident enough in *The Art of Being Ruled*. I want now to explore its consequences for the fiction.

The Childermass was the first part of *The Human Age*, a trilogy completed by the publication of *Monstre Gai* and *Malign Fiesta* in 1955.[38] The two protagonists, Pullman, a writer bearing a distinct physical resemblance to James Joyce, and Satterthwaite, who had been his fag at Rugby, and appears to have met his end during the First World War, bump into each other in the afterworld, in a huge encampment on the banks of the River Styx where those awaiting admission to heaven morosely congregate. Promenading in a landscape defined as much by time as by space, they eventually reach an amphitheatre where a bureaucrat-demagogue known as the Bailiff considers applications to enter the city across the river, while the followers of his arch-enemy Hyperides hotly contest his right to do so.

Alectryon, the Hyperideans' chief spokesman, carries cheerfully

---

[37] 'Landscape, Masculinity, and Interior Space between the Wars', in Steven Adams and Anna Gruetzner Robins (eds.), *Gendering Landscape Art* (Manchester: MUP, 2000), 102–15, pp. 103–4. Cournos is quoted on p. 108, from an article on 'The Death of Futurism' in *The Egoist*. Corbett also mentions the passive and powerless protagonist of *Death of a Hero* (1929), by Richard Aldington, a signatory of the *Blast* manifesto.

[38] *The Childermass* (London: John Calder, 1965), henceforth *C*; *Monstre Gai* (London: John Calder, 1965); *Malign Fiesta* (London: Calder & Boyars, 1966). On 3 Feb. 1928, Lewis contracted with Chatto & Windus to produce vols. ii and iii of the trilogy; on 8 Nov. 1932, by which time it had become clear that he was not going to deliver, Chatto & Windus entered a formal claim for damages against him: Omar S. Pound and Philip Grover, *Wyndham Lewis: A Descriptive Bibliography* (Folkestone: Archon-Dawson, 1978), 19. In view of the time it then took him to resume and complete the trilogy, it seems reasonable to discuss the first volume in the terms it proposes for itself, rather than as part of a whole. Alan Munton has already done so to good effect in 'A Reading of *The Childermass*', in Jeffrey Meyers (ed.), *Wyndham Lewis: A Revaluation* (London: Athlone Press, 1980), 120–32. David Ayers offers a critique of Munton's reading in *Wyndham Lewis and Western Man*, ch. 6.

on where *The Art of Being Ruled* had left off. He claims that the 'class-conscious orthodoxy' of the modern world has reduced those possessing 'conspicuous undemocratic abilities' to pariah status. The afterworld imagined in *The Childermass* is exclusively male, and it is no surprise, therefore, that Alectryon, again in accordance with *The Art of Being Ruled*, should develop his paranoid defence of the man of conspicuous undemocratic abilities by means of a critique of the cult of homosexuality, which he regards simply as a fashion promoted by consumer capitalism. 'The "male"', Alectryon says, 'has today been thrust into the defensive and watchful role.' These are, transparently, Lewis's views. Alectryon's speech, like the 'Nightmare' chapter of *Kangaroo*, has a confessional status. Lewis establishes a certain distance from his own views when he allows the Bailiff to damn Alectryon by association with right-wing cadres, with students of the '*French-Action*' or '*Steel-helmet*' type.[39] But the Bailiff is scarcely a disinterested observer. The vigour of Alectryon's argument, and the attention given it as the narrative moves towards its climax, suggest that Lewis was not yet through, in 1928, with paranoia.

As Alectryon prepares to state his case, the Bailiff looks over at Pullman: 'his trusty and well-beloved Anglo-Saxon admirer gazes back at him through his glasses in steadfast silence while the sucker-like fore-paw of Satters wakes into activity and massages the muscles of his patron's arm in secret'. It does not look as though either protagonist will give much thought to what Alectryon has to say. Both have been thrust entirely into a defensive and watchful role. Both are creatures of class-conscious orthodoxy. Pullman exists by ideological mimicry alone, Satterthwaite by physical mimicry alone. In *Time and Western Man*, Lewis had characterized Joyce, Pullman's model, as a craftsman pure and simple, and thus endlessly susceptible both to social and political doctrine and to literary influences. Joyce, Lewis concluded, had neither the will nor the ability to conceive of literature as anything other than imitation. Little hope for Pullman, then. Satterthwaite is the child-man produced by consumer capitalism. His talk is baby-talk, or Stein-talk, his actions pure reflex. These men are the very antithesis of the will-to-abstraction Lewis had championed so

---

[39] *C* 302, 312, 295.

ferociously for so long. And yet they are the novel's achievement. To imagine them, Lewis had subtly to revise his paranoid Modernism.

At one point, Satterthwaite experiences a hallucination. He imagines that Pullman has held up a mirror for him to inspect himself in. Hallucinations are not characteristic of paranoia, which is a delusional disorder, a pathology based on false beliefs. Ernst Wagner was severely deluded in his belief that people were laughing at him behind his back, but he did not imagine that they had put soap in his noodles or grease in his coffee; schizophrenic patients, by contrast, frequently do imagine such things, as the literature makes plain, since theirs is also a disorder of perception. Pullman consoles Satterthwaite by telling him that the inhabitants of the afterworld often find themselves under attack from the appearance of their own image, as though in a mirror; the 'atmosphere' makes for hallucination.[40] The reason why Alectryon will never make much headway in the afterworld is that he has got the wrong disease.

Lewis's main target in *Time and Western Man* is the 'time-cult' or 'time-philosophy' whose revaluation of time at the expense of space serves an ultimate political end: the reduction of identity to a fashion-statement whose constant upgrading provides capitalism with new and ever larger markets, as even the most intimate dimensions of human experience undergo commodification. Lewis argues that time-philosophers like Bergson, Whitehead, Alexander, and Russell have commodified time; their insistence on succession and flux makes it impossible to conceive self and society as in any way stable or unchanging. To this insistence, Lewis opposes his own 'common-sense' view of the physical world as a picture created by perception out of knowledge. In modern time-philosophy, he claims, the 'static mnemo-sensational contemplation of the "object"' has given way to a visual reality constituted by 'flat' images of the type seen in a mirror.[41] Satterthwaite's hallucination is an experience of the world as seen through the lens of time-philosophy. To put it another way, time-philosophy produces schizophrenia.

Lewis did not put it like that. But there can be no question that

[40] *C* 300, 57–71. For hallucinations in dementia praecox, see Eugen Bleuler, *Dementia Praecox, or the Group of Schizophrenias*, tr. Joseph Zinkin (New York: International Universities Press, 1950), 105.

[41] *Time and Western Man* (London: Chatto & Windus, 1927), 408–10.

he regarded his critique of the time-cult as an exercise in psychopathology. In *Time and Western Man*, he claimed that the time-philosophers had sought to establish their 'physics of "events" ' on the basis of an understanding of 'data peculiar to the demented'. To reduce the perceptual object to the status of a mirror-image, Lewis maintained, was in effect to reduce common sense to the status of dementia: time-philosophy confounds the 'physically delusive' with the 'psychologically deluded'.[42] It is hard to know what he meant by 'dementia'. Since Lewis's reference was invariably to Freud, among those who have dwelt upon the 'curiosities of the clinic', we should not be surprised to find Pullman characterizing Satterthwaite's brief encounter with time-philosophy as a hysterical episode.[43] But the one mental illness Satterthwaite is never likely to contract is Alectryon's illness, paranoia.

It seems to me that in imagining this other illness, this other psychosis, Lewis relented somewhat from obstinate abstractionism. The artist, Tarr announces, in a statement which has received a great deal less attention than his declarations in favour of monumentality and armature, should swim in the 'daily ooze', bury his face in the dung-heap. ' "I laugh hoarsely through its thickness, choking and spitting; coughing, sneezing, blowing".'[44] It is worth considering the extent to which Lewis buries his face in the ooze and dung which is the child-man Satterthwaite.

At one point during the promenade, Satterthwaite, feeling himself an impostor from head to foot, removes all his clothes. Pullman observes this performance with contempt.

Pullman plants himself, miniature, erect, jaw set in its impeccable small-scale resolution, and awaits the hurrying naked giant. A formidable elongated bladder of meat, Satters cloppers up his arms flapping fin-like as he runs, useless paddles of dough beating the air up into invisible suds. The red trunk is dark with hair marking its symmetric duality. Pullman's cold steady face receives him.[45]

The narrative appears to 'see' Satterthwaite, coldly and steadily, from Pullman's planted point of view, as an idiot-child. This, we

[42] Ibid. 410.   [43] C 70.
[44] *Tarr: The 1918 Version*, ed. Paul O'Keeffe (Santa Rosa, Calif.: Black Sparrow Press, 1990), 27.
[45] C 111.

might think, is the technique of eversion perfected in *The Wild Body* and *The Apes of God*. And yet the imaginative investment in what Satters does with his arms when he runs would appear to be over and above anything called for by Pullman's disapproval of such antics— that is, by satire. Lewis can surely be said to bury his face in this elongated bladder of meat, as Tarr recommends, and to laugh hoarsely through its thickness. He knowingly chokes on matter. The description is nothing if not mimetic, its aim to remain faithful to, to represent, the world as it is; or in this case the afterworld as it is.

Lewis, moreover, like Ford, is knowingly careless in representation. As Ford had spoken of 'fishish' eyes, so Lewis takes a very rough stab at whatever it is that Satters does with his arms through the neologism 'clopper', or 'clopper up'. There are familiar words in the vicinity of this neologism. Satterthwaite, always liable to clobber someone, is presumably engaged in 'running like the clappers' towards the inscrutable Pullman. Lewis expects us to grasp what he means without stopping to worry about the precise details. Writer and reader collaborate amiably. They agree to agree that the world (the afterworld) needs representing, and that the language they share will have to be pulled about a bit in order to accomplish this task. We are a long way, here, from crepitation, from enemy manœuvres.

'Clopper' might conceivably be a word Satterthwaite himself would use, a man-child's lunge at meaning. If so, it is a schizophrenic word. Bleuler regarded neologism as an 'accessory' symptom of schizophrenia. The schizophrenic feels obliged to invent words for concepts which seem important to him or her, but which the language does not recognize. Hallucinations, in particular, so real and yet so unreal, demand neologism. 'A patient spits "cage-weather juice"; that is, she must expectorate so much because she is full of cage-weather, i.e., she is locked up.' One of Jung's patients, Bleuler reports, thought of her neologisms as 'power-words'.[46] 'Clopper', though, is Lewis's power-word, rather than Satterthwaite's, Lewis's lunge at meaning. A couple of pages later, he uses it to describe Pullman dragging his friend's unconscious body into a hut.[47] 'Clopper' is Lewis's near-miss, the word he needs for something he cannot quite say.

---

[46] *Dementia Praecox*, 151–2.   [47] C 118.

If one were to attach a psychosis to these descriptions, it would be schizophrenia, rather than paranoia. For they significantly reconfigure the nausea which in paranoid Modernism had purified system from within, etching its outline into contingency. Pullman's most powerful response to Satterthwaite is nausea;[48] nausea, indeed, is big business in the afterworld. Eructation and emesis are activities the attendant souls undertake more often and more vigorously than any other. And the nausea is Lewis's, as, Tarr-like, he laughs hoarsely through the thickness of the time-philosophy, spitting, coughing, sneezing, blowing. In *The Childermass*, there is no Tarr, no Ker-Orr. Nausea does not produce paranoid symmetry. How could it, in a place where everyone is forever sneezing and blowing? It performs mimesis: mimesis of a world which has not yet come into being. What Lewis spits out or coughs up through his eversive technique is a literary hallucination.

The psychoanalyst W. R. Bion describes the care with which a schizophrenic patient, at the beginning of each session, would adjust his movements to those of the analyst. On one occasion, the patient paused for a second, gazing into a corner of the room; the pause came to an end with a slight, rapid shudder. Bion's interpretation of the gaze and the shudder was that the patient had taken something in from him, before he sat down, and then expelled it again through his eyes, so that it lay in a corner of the room where he could keep it under observation. The shudder meant that the expulsion had been completed. 'Then, and only then, was the hallucination in being.' If a schizophrenic says he sees an object, Bion concludes, 'it may mean that an external object has been perceived by him or it may mean that he is ejecting an object through his eyes'.[49] The afterworld Lewis represented in *The Childermass* was the product

---

[48] C 39.

[49] 'On Hallucination', in *Second Thoughts* (London: Karnac, 1984), 66–7. In a recent essay which uses W. R. Bion's phenomenology of the consulting-room to illuminate the writing of Butts and Bowen, Jacqueline Rose suggests that the 'turn' to psycho-analysis in relation to Modernism has if anything been a little tame, and that the Freudian economy of repression is inadequate to the qualities of perception their work evokes: 'Bizarre Objects: Mary Butts and Elizabeth Bowen', *Critical Quarterly*, 42 (2000), 75–85. I agree entirely with this, although I believe that the turn to *psycho-analysis* should also be a turn to *psychiatry*. Such a turn would both draw upon and amplify Lyndsey Stonebridge's admirable *The Destructive Element: British Psychoanalysis and Modernism* (Basingstoke: Macmillan, 1998).

of an emesis or eructation through the eye. The abstract nature of the debate which draws it to a conclusion was his attempt to redeem it from schizophrenia—to restore a measure of paranoid Modernism.

These last few paragraphs have been rather more speculative than the methods I have proposed in this book allow for. I do not in fact believe that one ought to ascribe a condition like 'schizophrenia' to specific literary procedures without knowing how it was used by psychiatrists and social commentators at the time. This it should not prove impossible to establish. Bion's thinking, for example, was as decisively shaped by the First World War as Lewis's.[50] But I want to return one last time to a term whose uses during the Modernist period I have expounded at some length. Lewis, unlike Ernst Wagner, understood the nature and implications of paranoid delusion. In *Snooty Baronet* (1932), one of his most inventive if least read novels, he produced a compelling critique of the compulsions which had given shape to all his *Entlastungs-offensiven* from *The Art of Being Ruled* through to *Hitler*.[51]

Sir Michael Kell-Imrie, the Snooty Baronet of the title, was badly injured in the war, and has an artificial leg and a silver plate in his head. After the war, he becomes a big-game hunter, then a deep-sea fisherman, and finally the author of a popular treatise, *People Behaving*, in which human beings are compared unfavourably to animals. Snooty's literary agent, Captain Humphrey Cooper Carter (Humph), arranges an expedition to Persia. Snooty and his girlfriend, Mrs Valerie Ritter (Val), ostensibly researching a book about the survival of Mithraism, are to be kidnapped by arrangement, thus generating a great deal of welcome publicity. At the climax of the bogus ambush, Snooty 'automatically' raises his rifle and shoots Humph twice, through the back of the neck and in the buttocks, deriving immense aesthetic satisfaction from the second shot in particular. His 'instinctive' act is the perfect illustration of the behaviorism he practises. Returning home, he writes

[50] He served as a tank-commander. See *The Long Weekend 1897–1919: Part of a Life*, ed. Francesca Bion (Abingdon: Fleetwood, 1982).

[51] For stimulating discussions of the novel, see Edwards, *Wyndham Lewis*, 434–40; Timothy Materer, *Wyndham Lewis the Novelist* (Detroit: Wayne State University Press, 1976), ch. 5; and John Constable, ' "Meaningless Energies": Hemingway and *Snooty Baronet*', *Enemy News*, 30 (1990), 14–20.

an account of the adventure—*Snooty Baronet* itself, a guaranteed bestseller—while Val attempts to discredit his story by claiming that Humph was in fact killed by a stray shot. Throughout, Kell-Imrie has behaved with wilful and callous indifference towards everyone he encounters. One might think of him as Lewis's version of Ford's Mr Blood. Both are monsters. But their monstrosity is richly diagnostic of the world they inhabit. To put it another way, if *The Childermass* shares the odd procedure with *Parade's End*, *Snooty Baronet* and *The Apes of God* are a continuation by rather more violent means of Ford's pre-war satires.

As Edwards points out, the novel is a satire on the behaviorist theory of J. B. Watson, which Lewis had attacked in *The Art of Being Ruled* and *Time and Western Man* (the narrative employs the American spelling of *behavior* and its variants throughout).[52] But we need also to acknowledge a certain equivalence between the doctrines of behaviorism and Lewis's eversive technique, which often treats human beings as though they were animals, or machines. *Snooty Baronet* is in some respects a variant on *The Wild Body*, Lewis's only previous extensive use of first-person narrative in fiction.[53] In 'Franciscan Adventures', Francis's change of mood when Ker-Orr gets his cigarette case out is described as an abrupt switch into 'delight "Behavior"'.[54] To be able to think of behaviour in behaviorist terms is in fact an advantage to an observer like Ker-Orr, whose interest is in wild bodies rather than sober minds. The difference in *Snooty Baronet* is that Lewis has supplied his protagonist with a motive for behaviorism: the war. Damaged irreparably by the storm of steel, Kell-Imrie takes his revenge through campaigns of indifference, and worse. 'What I suppose I was doing was to hatch a plot against Mankind . . . I would mark down and pursue, selected for the purpose, members of those ape-like congeries—gangs, sets, ant-armies, forces of Lilliput, number-brave coteries, militant sheep-clans—fraternities, rotaries, and crews.'[55] Bernard Lafourcade has pointed out that there is plenty

---

[52] *Wyndham Lewis*, 435.

[53] The turbulently self-aware first-person narrator of Lewis's travel-book, *Filibusters in Barbary* (1932), may also be a model for Kell-Imrie.

[54] *The Complete Wild Body*, ed. Bernard Lafourcade (Santa Barbara, Calif.: Black Sparrow Press, 1982), 121.

[55] *Snooty Baronet*, ed. Bernard Lafourcade (Santa Barbara, Calif.: Black Sparrow Press, 1984), 63. Henceforth *SB*.

of 'buccal horror' in *Snooty Baronet*.[56] Nausea prevails, as it had in *The Childermass*. And yet the bad breath, the permanent yawns, and the retching never cloud our view of the satirist in action. The narrative is not a hallucination. It is the product of paranoid symmetry. They (the crews, the number-brave coteries) hate me because I'm special. I'm special because they hate me.

Kell–Imrie's 'plot' sounds very much like Lewis's own campaigns, over the previous eight or nine years, against social mimesis and the 'ape-like congeries' whose proliferation it had encouraged. The people he marks down and pursues are people who cannot feel. 'They can only mimic feeling, or control feeling.' Aiming at the unfortunate Humph, Kell–Imrie hits the mimetic itself, understood as a social and political principle, an ideology. Like Caleb Williams, he believes that private judgement is superior to the judgements delivered by institutional law. 'The rehabilitation that I seek is not that of a court-of-honour, finally, but such as could be conferred by a tribunal of my peers alone . . . It is a demonstration for the Learned or the expert.' Charismatic professionalism has finally found its champion. Through Kell–Imrie, Lewis inspected his own (paranoid Modernist) commitment to expertise.

On the way to Persia, Kell–Imrie and Val drop in on Rob McPhail, a Hemingway-esque poet who lives in the south of France; during their visit, McPhail is killed in a bullfighting accident. Attending his first bullfight, Snooty declares an immediate preference for the animal over the men, Gulliver over the Lilliputians, the doomed One over the self-important but ineffectual Many. Had he to dispose of a bull himself, he explains, he would do so *expertly*: with a Lewis-gun rather than with lance and sword. 'The former gives better the measure of the genius of man—the Lewis-gun. (Of man the individual—I mean Lewis of course).'[57] The Lewis-gun is satire itself, the eversive method of *The Wild Body* and *The Apes of God*, a superior (postliberal) violence.

Lewis, of course, had witnessed at first hand the havoc wrought

---

[56] 'Afterword', *SB* 255–70, p. 264.

[57] *SB* 184, 102–3, 171–2. Kell–Imrie's interest in Mithraism and all things bullish enables Lewis to fabricate a rather unconvincing parody of D. H. Lawrence. Bulls, in fact, were not really in Lawrence's line.

by such weapons. He now exposes, in Kell-Imrie's insouciance, the complicity of his own method with traumatizing violence and with that exultation in violence which is fascism's signature. The episode of McPhail's death demonstrates that Kell-Imrie, who behaves like a Lewis-gun or a genius throughout, has become, as Edwards observes, a psychopath.[58] After it, the motiveless murder of Humph seems almost predictable. Like Ernst Wagner, Kell-Imrie has decided to mark down and pursue those whom he regards as his persecutors. Like Wagner, he gets his unsuspecting man. The episode is Lewis's commentary—not quite an owning up, not quite a renunciation—on paranoid Modernism.

[58] *Wyndham Lewis*, 436. Although brief, and incidental to the main action, the episode was apparently the germ from which the novel grew: Lafourcade, 'Afterword', 285.

Index

Abraham, Karl 32, 57, 66–7
Adler, Alfred 55, 57, 60, 62–3, 65
Asquith, Katharine 275

Barry, Iris 287–8
Benjamin, Walter 146
Bennett, Arnold 135, 137, 206
Bion, W. R. 349–50
Blackwood, William 163, 165, 174, 176
Bleuler, Eugen 31–4, 39–40, 43, 46, 57,
    61–3, 67, 238, 248, 262, 346, 348
Braddon, M. E.:
    Lady Audley's Secret 121–2, 150
Brown, Ford Madox 189–90, 195–8, 212
Buchan, John 341
    The Half-Hearted 142, 145
    The Thirty-Nine Steps 144–5, 258, 330

Caine, Hall:
    The White Prophet 153–4, 158
Carleton, Billie 277–80
Carpenter, W. B. 35
Cézanne, Paul 293
Childers, Erskine:
    The Riddle of the Sands 144, 150,
    342
Cholmondeley, Mary:
    'The Lowest Rung' 275
Churchill, Winston 128
    Savrola 137, 140
Clifford, Hugh 176–7
Clouston, T. S. 29–30
Collins, Wilkie 48, 197, 273
    The Woman in White 85, 118–26,
    132–3, 138, 141–2, 158, 178,
    184–5, 194, 237, 330
Conrad, Joseph 48, 84, 96, 187, 190,
    192–3, 197, 220, 233, 326
    Heart of Darkness 177
    Lord Jim 12, 98, 158–85, 204, 208,
    213, 249, 332
    An Outcast of the Islands 165
    'The Secret Sharer' 182–6

Crane, Stephen 164, 188
    The Red Badge of Courage 169–72,
    174, 179
Crowley, Alister 274
    Diary of a Drug Fiend 281–3

Dawson, A. J.:
    'The Richard Merlin Document'
    155–8
Diagnostic and Statistical Manual (DSM IV)
    15–16, 20, 66, 69, 75
Dickens, Charles 123, 197, 284, 291,
    315–16, 322
    Bleak House 320–1
    David Copperfield 85, 108–15, 173,
    203, 206, 231–3, 321, 342
    Dombey and Son 320
    Great Expectations 121
    Our Mutual Friend 113–16, 132, 230–1
Dilthey, Wilhelm 85–6

Eliot, George 2, 117–18
Eliot, T. S. 2–3, 188, 223, 241, 288, 313,
    338
    The Waste Land 2–3, 232, 251
Epstein, Jacob 227, 232
Esquirol, J. E. D. 16, 19–24, 26, 30, 43,
    51, 66, 83

Ferenczi, Sándor 51, 55–6, 61, 64
Firminger, Marjorie 323
    Jam To-day 324
Flaubert, Gustave 118, 187, 240, 305–6,
    334, 338
    Madame Bovary 306
Fliess, Wilhelm 51, 54–5, 60
Ford, Ford Madox 5, 48, 84, 118, 128,
    164, 183, 209–10, 220, 234, 240,
    326–7, 331–2, 344
    Ancient Lights 164, 189, 194, 202
    The Benefactor 197–9, 202–3, 205, 319
    The Critical Attitude 200
    England and the English 200

Ford, Ford Madox (*cont.*):
  Ford Madox Brown 193–9
  The Good Soldier 5, 186, 192, 209–19,
    249
  Henry James 193–4, 211
  Joseph Conrad 211
  Mr Fleight 203, 206–9, 212, 249,
    351
  The New Humpty-Dumpty 203, 205–6,
    208, 212–13
  Parade's End 331–7, 342, 351
  Return to Yesterday 187–92, 194,
    199–200, 204, 211–12
  Romance 197
  The Simple Life Limited 202–5, 208,
    212–13, 333
  'True Love and a G.C.M.' 332
  Women and Men 201–2
Freud, Sigmund 11, 32, 44, 47, 49–66,
    73, 78, 85, 92, 94, 98–9, 102, 161,
    193, 243, 308, 333, 347
  Introductory Lectures 51–2, 58, 82
  'Psychoanalytical Notes on an
    Auto-biographical Account of a
    Case of Paranoia (Dementia
    Paranoides)' 11, 51, 54–61, 79,
    104, 133–4, 222, 235–6, 243–5,
    266
  The Psychopathology of Everyday Life
    58–9, 228–9
Friedländer, Adolf Albrecht 63–5, 73
Fry, Roger 222, 227, 294

Galsworthy, John 135, 137, 163–4, 268
  The Man of Property 130
Garnett, David 280–1
  Beany-eye 205
  Dope Darling 280–1
Garnett, Edward 164–6, 173, 190,
    239–40
  The Trial of Jeanne d'Arc 245
Gaupp, Robert 41–7, 50–1, 55, 57, 79,
    119, 205, 256
Gertler, Mark 250, 272
Gissing, George:
  New Grub Street 135–6
Godwin, William 48
  Caleb Williams 85, 92–100, 104–10,
    113, 115, 118, 120–2, 124–6,
    132–3, 141–2, 158, 169–70, 174,
    178, 237, 330, 352

  Enquiry Concerning Political Justice 93,
    97, 100–3, 115
Gross, Otto 242–3, 245

Haggard, Rider 137, 147, 154, 158
Hardy, Thomas 118, 253
  Jude the Obscure 116
Haslam, John 104
  Illustrations of Madness 68–9, 105–7
Hazlitt, William 91–2
Hemingway, Ernest 148, 191–2, 285–8,
    294, 338, 352
Henley, W. E. 164, 194, 204
Hichens, Robert:
  Felix 274–5
Hitler, Adolf 291, 341
Hope, Anthony 48
  The Prisoner of Zenda 137–41, 150–2,
    180, 237
  Sophy of Kravonia 139–40
Hudson, W. H. 188
Hulme, T. E. 3, 5, 222, 224–33, 242,
    251, 257, 293–5, 297, 339
Hume, David 87

James, Henry 118, 164, 166, 187–8, 190,
    192, 195, 338
Jaspers, Karl 31, 34–5, 46
John, Augustus 220, 232, 234, 287
Jones, Ernest 34, 61, 63–4, 243, 245
Joyce, James 188, 223, 241, 284, 288,
    344–5
  Finnegans Wake 313
  A Portrait of the Artist as a Young Man
    209
  Ulysses 130, 241, 251, 302, 313
Jung, Carl 32, 39, 51, 55, 57, 62–5, 348

Kahlbaum, Karl 19
Keynes, John Maynard 328
Kipling, Rudyard 154, 188
  'Beyond the Pale' 155–8
  Kim 156
Kraepelin, Emil 13, 18, 31–40, 43, 45–6,
    49–51, 61, 66, 75, 238, 248, 262
Krafft-Ebing, Richard von 4–5, 18, 25–9,
    50, 58–9, 70–1, 138, 228
Kretschmer, Ernst 41, 45–8, 55, 57, 67

Lacan, Jacques 60
Lake, Mary:

The Drug Slave 274
Lawrence, D. H. 2, 48, 50, 84, 118, 148,
      199, 221, 223, 231, 275, 280, 282,
      297, 326, 332, 337, 343
   Amores 272
   'Education of the People' 256–7, 267,
      270
   Kangaroo 327–31, 345
   'The Prussian Officer' 222, 240–9,
      262
   The Rainbow 241–2, 250, 252, 260,
      268
   Sons and Lovers 240, 242
   'Study of Thomas Hardy' 253
   The White Peacock 248
   Women in Love 5, 130, 133, 238, 240,
      248–73, 279, 282–3, 317, 323,
      330–1
Lawrence, T. E. 154
Lewis, Wyndham 3, 5, 40, 48, 50, 84,
      118, 187–9, 191–2, 199–233,
      241–2, 248, 257, 284–96, 337–43
   The Apes of God 116, 290–1, 303,
      312–25, 337, 342, 348, 351–2
   The Art of Being Ruled 8, 289–90,
      297–300, 344–5, 351
   Blasting and Bombardiering 3, 209–10,
      224, 230, 286, 294
   The Caliph's Design 293–5
   The Childermass 290, 292, 303,
      344–51
   Hitler 341, 350
   Men without Art 338–40
   Rude Assignment 220, 223, 225, 303–4
   Satire and Fiction 313, 316, 318, 337,
      339
   Self Condemned 292–3
   Snooty Baronet 292, 350–3
   Tarr 10, 222–3, 233–9, 249, 290, 315,
      343, 347–9
   Time and Western Man 130, 289–90,
      297, 300–3, 307, 312, 345–7, 351
   The Wild Body 290–1, 293, 303–12,
      318, 325, 348–9, 351–2
Ludovici, A. M. 231–2

Mansfield, Katherine 268, 272–3, 283
Matthews, James Tilly 68–9, 104
Mill, John Stuart 8, 40, 126, 197, 204,
      284, 299, 302, 320
Mills, Dorothy:

The Laughter of Fools 279, 324
Mosley, Oswald 340–1
Musil, Robert 13–14, 40, 47–8, 258–9,
      299
   The Man without Qualities 13–14

Nietzsche, Friedrich 222, 225, 231–2,
      236, 330
Nijinsky, Vaslav 33, 250

Oppenheim, E. Phillips 323–5
   A Maker of History 143–4

Picasso, Pablo 250, 289, 294, 302, 315
Pound, Ezra 187–8, 191, 203, 239, 241,
      284–6, 288, 290, 301–2, 334–5, 341
   Cantos 251
Prichard, James Cowles 19, 23–6, 30, 38,
      45, 66–7, 208–9
Proust, Marcel 159
Pynchon, Thomas 326

Renner, Helene 46–7, 55
Ridge, William Pett 206
Rita:
   Queer Lady Judas 275
Robespierre, Maximilien de 23, 30, 76,
      83, 93, 98, 282–3
Robinson, G. P.:
   Testament 281–2
Rohmer, Sax:
   Dope 279–80
Rossetti, Dante Gabriel 190, 196–7,
      224
Rousseau, Jean-Jacques 80, 97, 120, 141,
      226, 300
   Confessions 85–92

Sartre, Jean-Paul 73
Schopenhauer, Arthur 222
Schreber, Daniel Paul 11, 19, 44, 47, 49,
      51–66, 79, 94, 98–9, 104, 107,
      134, 172, 215, 229, 243, 245, 330
   Memoirs of My Nervous Illness 4, 51–4,
      58, 65, 69–70, 73–4, 145, 270
Shaw, Bernard 274
Shiel, M. P.:
   The Purple Cloud 74–9, 104, 133–4,
      171, 173, 179–80, 322
Sims, George:
   The Devil in London 275, 278

Sinclair, May 50
Stein, Gertrude 302, 338, 345
Stekel, Wilhelm 55, 57, 60
Stevenson, Robert Louis 10–11, 137,
    147, 154, 158–9
Stirner, Max 229
Stoker, Bram:
    Dracula 131
    The Snake's Pass 148
    The Jewel of Seven Stars 149–53

Tasso, Torquato 89, 120
Tausk, Victor 32, 67–8
Thackeray, William Makepeace:
    The History of Pendennis 321–2

Wagner, Ernst 19, 41–8, 51, 55, 66, 115,
    133, 135–6, 171, 205, 230–1,
    246–7, 256, 267, 342, 346, 350,
    353

Wallace, Edgar 322, 325
Wallas, Graham 129–30
Weber, Max 131–2, 146, 255
Weininger, Otto:
    Sex and Character 201–2
Wells, H. G. 75, 128, 133–4, 137, 162,
    206, 258
    The Holy Terror 133, 173
    A Modern Utopia 129, 131–2,
        135
    The New Machiavelli 132–3, 144
    Tono-Bungay 130, 135
    The War in the Air 134
    The War of the Worlds 134
Williams, David 106
Wodehouse, P. G. 143
Woolf, Leonard 129–30, 168
Worringer, Wilhelm 257
    Abstraction and Empathy 226–9,
        231